MW00465616

Essence of
Vajrayana

Also by Geshe Kelsang Gyatso

Meaningful to Behold
Clear Light of Bliss
Buddhism in the Tibetan Tradition
Heart of Wisdom
Universal Compassion
The Meditation Handbook
Joyful Path of Good Fortune
Guide to Dakini Land
The Bodhisattva Vow
Heart Jewel
Great Treasury of Merit
Introduction to Buddhism
Understanding the Mind
Tantric Grounds and Paths
Ocean of Nectar
Living Meaningfully, Dying Joyfully
Eight Steps to Happiness
Transform Your Life

Profits received from the sale of
this book will be donated to the
NKT-International Temples Project
A Buddhist Charity Building for World Peace
UK email: kadampa@dircon.co.uk
US email: info@kadampacenter.org

The Mandala of Buddha Heruka in the Kadampa Buddhist Temple
at Manjushri Mahayana Buddhist Centre, England.

GESHE KELSANG GYATSO

Essence of
Vajrayana

THE HIGHEST YOGA
TANTRA PRACTICE OF
HERUKA BODY MANDALA

THARPA PUBLICATIONS
Ulverston, England
Glen Spey, New York

First published in 1997
Reprinted 2003

The right of Geshe Kelsang Gyatso
to be identified as author of this work
has been asserted by him in accordance with
the Copyright, Designs, and Patents Act 1988.

All rights reserved.
No part of this book may be reproduced
in any form or by any means except for the quotation
of brief passages for the purpose of private
study, research, or review.

Tharpa Publications
Conishead Priory
Ulverston
Cumbria LA12 9QQ, England

Tharpa Publications
47 Sweeney Road
P.O. Box 430
Glen Spey, NY 12737, USA

© Geshe Kelsang Gyatso and New Kadampa Tradition 1997

Cover painting of Solitary Vajrasattva by
the Tibetan artist Chating Jamyang Lama.
Cover photo of Geshe Kelsang Gyatso by Kathia Rabelo.
Colour plates of Heruka body mandala and the celestial
mansion reproduced with kind permission.
Line illustrations by Gen Kelsang Wangchen.
Line illustration of Vajrayogini by Suzanne Downs.

British Library Cataloguing in Publication Data
A catalogue record for this book is
available from the British Library.

ISBN 0 948006 47 1 – papercase
ISBN 0 948006 48 X – paperback

Set in Palatino by Tharpa Publications.
Printed on acid-free 250-year longlife paper and bound
by Cromwell Press, Trowbridge, Wiltshire, England.

Contents

Illustrations

Acknowledgements

This book, *Essence of Vajrayana*, is a complete and authoritative explanation of the Highest Yoga Tantra practice of Heruka body mandala, a powerful method for accomplishing full enlightenment in this lifetime.

The author, Venerable Geshe Kelsang Gyatso Rinpoche, worked tirelessly for several years to prepare this profound text, bringing to it the inestimable benefit of his own vast scholarship and meditational experience. From the depths of our hearts we thank him for his inconceivable patience and kindness in giving us this precious commentary, which for the first time unlocks the secrets of this sublime practice for the Western practitioner.

We also thank all the dedicated, senior Dharma students who assisted the author with the rendering of the English and who prepared the final manuscript for publication.

Roy Tyson,
Administrative Director,
Manjushri Mahayana
Buddhist Centre,
June 1997.

Preface

The main subject of this book, *Essence of Vajrayana*, is training in the stages of the path of Highest Yoga Tantra. Gaining authentic realizations of the uncommon paths of Buddhist Tantra depends upon training in the common paths of Buddha's Sutra teachings, such as the twenty-one meditations of the stages of the path. These are explained in *Joyful Path of Good Fortune* and *The New Meditation Handbook*.

To begin with we need to understand what meditation is and how important meditation is for the attainment of both the temporary happiness of this and future lives, and the ultimate happiness of liberation and full enlightenment. Meditation is a mental awareness that concentrates on a virtuous object. It is necessarily mental awareness and not sense awareness. The sense awarenesses of a Buddha are virtuous whereas the sense awarenesses of sentient beings are always neutral. For example, although our bodily actions can be virtuous or non-virtuous depending upon our motivation, our body awareness itself is always neutral. In the same way, the actions of our eye awareness can be virtuous or non-virtuous but our eye awareness itself is always neutral. Therefore, as meditation is necessarily a virtuous mind whereas our sense awarenesses are necessarily neutral, it follows that we cannot meditate with our sense awarenesses.

Another reason why we cannot meditate with our sense awarenesses is that for us the direct object of meditation is the generic image of an object, and our sense awarenesses cannot perceive generic images. Moreover, although eye, ear, nose, tongue, and body awarenesses can focus on forms, sounds, smells, tastes, and tactile objects respectively, they cannot remember them. Since meditation involves remembering, or holding with mindfulness, the object for an extended period of time, the only type of awareness that we can meditate with is mental awareness.

Meditation is a mental action, or mental karma, that causes us to experience mental peace. At the beginning it does not matter if our meditation is successful or not, because simply by generating a good motivation and trying to meditate we are creating the cause for future mental peace. As humans, we need certain basic conditions such as food, clothing, accommodation, and money; but whether or not these things bring us happiness depends upon our peace of mind. If our mind is not at peace we shall not be happy, even in the best external conditions.

Meditation is the source of all mental peace and happiness. It is true that people who do not meditate, and even animals, occasionally experience peace of mind, but this is only as a result of the virtuous mental karma they created through meditation in previous lives. By training in meditation we can attain a permanent cessation of delusions and thereby experience the permanent inner peace of liberation, or nirvana. We need to attain liberation because for as long as we are trapped in samsara, the vicious cycle of uncontrolled death and rebirth, we shall never find real peace and happiness.

We can attain the ultimate peace of enlightenment by training in the meditations explained in this book. We need to attain enlightenment so that we can benefit all living beings. At present our mind is obscured by the inner darkness of ignorance, which prevents us from seeing the true nature of all phenomena; but by training in wisdom and compassion we can completely remove this inner darkness. Once we have done this, our very subtle body, speech, and mind become inner light, the nature of omniscient wisdom. This is enlightenment, or Buddhahood. Having dispelled all darkness from our mind, we become a Buddha and can see all phenomena of the past, present, and future directly and simultaneously. We are then in a position to benefit all living beings without exception by bestowing blessings, emanating whatever they need, and guiding them along spiritual paths.

To encourage ourself to train in the stages of the path to enlightenment, we should continually recall the three special characteristics of our human life: its freedom and endowment, its rarity, and its great meaning. Due to the limitations of their body and mind, those who have taken rebirth as animals, for example, have no opportunity to understand or practise the path to liberation. Only humans are free from such hindrances and have all the necessary conditions, known as 'endowments', to engage in spiritual paths, which alone lead to everlasting happiness. This freedom and endowment is the first special characteristic that makes our human life so precious.

The second special characteristic of our human life is its rarity. Although there are many humans in this world, each one of us has only one life. One person may own many cars and houses, but even the richest person in the world cannot possess more than one life, and, when that is drawing to an end, he or she cannot buy, borrow, or manufacture another. When we lose this life, it will be very difficult to find another similarly qualified life in the future. Our human life is therefore very rare.

The third special characteristic of our human life is its great meaning. If we use our human life to accomplish spiritual realizations, our life is immensely meaningful. By using it in this way, we actualize our full potential and progress from the state of an ordinary, deluded being to that of a fully enlightened being, the highest of all beings; and when we have done this we shall have the power to benefit all living beings without exception. Thus, by using our human life for spiritual development we can solve all our human problems and fulfil all our own and others' wishes. What could be more meaningful than this?

Through contemplating these three characteristics we arrive at the determination:

I will not waste my human life because it is so precious, so rare, and so meaningful. Instead, I will use it in the most beneficial way.

We hold this determination as our object of meditation without forgetting it, and meditate on it single-pointedly for as long as possible. Having developed this deep desire to make our life meaningful, we then ask ourself, 'What is the essential meaning of a human life?' Finding good external conditions cannot be its essential meaning, for even animals can do this. Many animals are very skilled at finding food, protecting their families, destroying their enemies, and so forth; these abilities are not exclusively human. However, it is only humans who have the opportunity to attain enlightenment for the benefit of all living beings. This is the real meaning of our human life. With this understanding, we can extract the full meaning of our human life by receiving the empowerment and commentary to Heruka body mandala and then putting the instructions into practice.

In general, Vajrayana is the actual quick path to enlightenment, but whether or not we attain enlightenment quickly through Vajrayana practice depends upon our faith, motivation, and understanding. In particular, gaining the realizations of Heruka body mandala – the very essence of Vajrayana – depends upon our having strong faith in the instructions and a clear understanding of their meaning. Then, with a pure motivation, free from selfish intention, we should practise these instructions sincerely and continually until we attain our final goal.

Geshe Kelsang Gyatso,
Dallas, Texas,
March 1997.

PART ONE

Generation Stage

Heruka Father and Mother

Preliminary Explanation

The commentary to the Highest Yoga Tantra practice of Heruka body mandala is presented under three main headings:

1 The preliminary explanation
2 The explanation of the practice
3 Dedication

THE PRELIMINARY EXPLANATION

This has five parts:

1 The pre-eminent qualities of Heruka
2 The origin of these instructions
3 The benefits of practising these instructions
4 Examples of previous practitioners who accomplished attainments through these instructions
5 The qualifications of a sincere Heruka practitioner

THE PRE-EMINENT QUALITIES OF HERUKA

The Sanskrit term 'Heruka' is composed of the three syllables, 'He', 'ru', and 'ka'. 'He' teaches the emptiness of phenomena in general, and 'ru' the emptiness of persons in particular; together they reveal the emptiness of all phenomena. 'Ka' refers to the union of Heruka's mind of great bliss and the emptiness of all phenomena. This union is Heruka's Truth Body. An I, or self, imputed on this Truth Body is definitive Heruka, the real nature of Buddha Heruka. This can only be seen by Buddhas.

Another term for Heruka is 'Chakrasambara'. 'Chakra' means 'wheel', and in this context refers to the 'wheel' of all phenomena. 'Sambara' means the supreme bliss, which is called 'spontaneous great bliss'. Together 'Chakra' and 'sambara' reveal that by practising Heruka Tantra we gain a profound realization that experiences all phenomena as one nature with our mind of great bliss. This realization directly removes subtle dualistic appearances from our mind, and due to this we quickly become definitive Heruka.

To lead fortunate disciples to the state of Buddha Heruka within one life, Buddha Vajradhara manifested his compassion in the form of interpretative Heruka, who has a blue-coloured body, four faces, and twelve arms, and embraces his consort, Vajravarahi. Attaining the state of Buddha Heruka depends upon abandoning the twelve dependent-related links of samsara by gaining the realizations of the four doors of liberation; and in particular it depends upon realizing the union of great bliss and emptiness. These are symbolized respectively by Heruka's twelve arms, his four faces, and his embracing Vajravarahi.

It is possible that those who do not understand the deep meaning of Buddha's Vajrayana teachings may feel uncomfortable with Heruka's wrathful aspect. Such practitioners need to understand that all phenomena are equal in lacking inherent existence. In ultimate truth, emptiness, there are no wrathful or peaceful aspects because all phenomena are of one nature. Therefore, those who possess deep knowledge of ultimate truth have no basis for developing unpleasant feelings upon perceiving unattractive objects because they realize that ultimately there are no truly existent unattractive or attractive objects.

For example, although Heruka's long necklace of human heads may seem to be real, in fact it is a manifestation of Heruka's omniscient wisdom. All the various features of Heruka's body are merely manifestations of his omniscient wisdom and do not exist outside of his mind. However, for faithful practitioners, visualizing the wrathful aspect of Heruka is a powerful method for swiftly receiving his blessings and protection. It is for this reason, as well as to display in a visible manner how to progress along the entire path of Sutra and Tantra, that Buddha Vajradhara emanated the wrathful Deity Heruka.

Buddha Vajradhara, Buddha Shakyamuni, and Buddha Heruka are the same person, differing only in aspect. When Buddha turned the Wheel of Dharma of Sutra he appeared in the form of an ordained person, when he turned the Wheel of Dharma of Tantra in general he appeared in the form of Vajradhara, and when he turned the Wheel of Dharma of *Heruka Tantra* in particular he appeared in the form of Heruka. Heruka is Buddha's mind of compassion manifested as form. Only Buddhas have the ability to display their minds as form. We sentient beings are unable to do this because our mind and body are different natures, but a Buddha's mind and body are the same nature and so wherever their mind goes their body goes too. We always perceive a gap between our mind and its object. This is a mistaken perception, or mistaken appearance. Having completely abandoned this mistaken perception, Buddhas have the ability to display their mind as form, such as the forms of living beings and inanimate objects. For this reason it is said that Buddhas' emanations pervade the whole universe.

Buddha's mind of omniscient wisdom has thirty-seven parts, known as his 'thirty-seven realizations conducive to enlightenment'. These thirty-seven realizations appear in the form of the thirty-seven Deities of Heruka's mandala. We normally say that there are sixty-two Deities in Heruka's mandala, but if we count each union of Father and Mother as one Deity there are thirty-seven Deities. The thirty-seven realizations conducive to enlightenment of Bodhisattvas are causal paths and the thirty-seven realizations of Buddhas are resultant paths. A general explanation of these thirty-seven realizations can be found in *Ocean of Nectar*.

THE ORIGIN OF THESE INSTRUCTIONS

These instructions were originally taught by Buddha at the request of Vajrapani and Vajravarahi. Buddha taught three root and five explanatory Tantras of Heruka. The three root Tantras are: the *Extensive Root Tantra*, which has three hundred thousand stanzas; the *Middling Root Tantra*, which has one hundred thousand stanzas; and the *Condensed Root Tantra*, which has fifty-one chapters. Of these, only the last was translated from Sanskrit into Tibetan. The five explanatory Tantras, which are commentaries to the *Condensed Root Tantra*, are: *Vajradaka Tantra, Abhicharya Tantra, Mukha Tantra, Sarwacharya Tantra,* and *Little Sambara Tantra.* Later, great Indian Buddhist Masters such as Luyipa, Ghantapa, and Krishnapada wrote commentaries to these root and explanatory Tantras, as did many subsequent Tibetan Masters. In particular, Je Tsongkhapa wrote a very blessed and renowned commentary to the root Tantra of Heruka, entitled *Clear Illumination of All Hidden Meanings,* and a commentary to the Heruka sadhana, entitled *Dö jo,* which means 'Wishfulfilling'. Later, other Lamas including Je Phabongkhapa also wrote special commentaries, based on the previous Indian and Tibetan commentaries. This commentary, *Essence of Vajrayana,* written especially for contemporary practitioners, is based on the instructions of Je Tsongkhapa and my kind root Guru, Trijang Dorjechang.

Traditionally there are three systems for practising the instructions of Heruka Tantra: the system according to Luyipa, the system according to Krishnapada, and the system according to Ghantapa. Ghantapa's system has two instructions: the instruction on the outer mandala of the five Deities of Heruka, and the instruction on the inner mandala of the sixty-two Deities of Heruka body mandala. This commentary, *Essence of Vajrayana,* is based on the latter. The lineage of these instructions is completely unbroken.

THE BENEFITS OF PRACTISING THESE INSTRUCTIONS

The *Condensed Root Tantra* praises the special qualities of Heruka practitioners. It says that all the Heroes and Heroines residing in the twenty-four places such as Puliramalaya and Dzalandhara enter into the bodies of sincere practitioners, blessing their channels, drops, and winds, and causing them to gain realizations of spontaneous great bliss, the actual quick path to enlightenment. Because these Heroes and Heroines are emanations of Heruka and Vajravarahi, their bodies are the same nature as their minds and can go wherever their minds go, unobstructed by physical objects. Thus, countless Heroes and Heroines can actually enter into the body of sincere practitioners and bless their channels, drops, and winds. Indeed, Heruka himself always remains at the heart of sincere practitioners, bestowing upon them great powers of body, speech, and mind.

In the *Condensed Root Tantra* it is said that just by seeing a sincere Heruka practitioner we purify our negativities and attain liberation; just by hearing or being touched by such a practitioner we receive blessings and are cured of sickness; and just by being in the presence of such a practitioner our unhappiness, mental disturbances, delusions, and other obstacles are dispelled. Why is this? It is because the actual Deities of Heruka abide within the body of the practitioner and therefore seeing the practitioner is not so different from seeing Heruka himself. In Tibet, there are many sayings to the effect that merely seeing a special Lama or wearing a blessing cord received from such a Lama causes liberation. Je Phabong-khapa said, 'I do not know whether or not these sayings are true, but seeing or touching a Heruka practitioner is a real cause of liberation.'

As times become spiritually more degenerate, it is harder to receive the blessings of other Tantric Deities such as Yamantaka or Guhyasamaja; and, as the number of Gurus in the lineage increases, it takes longer to receive attainments. However, the opposite is the case with Heruka. Kyabje Trijang Rinpoche says in his ritual prayer of Heruka:

As times become ever more impure,
Your power and blessings ever increase,
And you care for us quickly, as swift as thought;
O Chakrasambara Father and Mother, to you
I prostrate.

As times become more impure, Heruka's blessings become more powerful and we receive them more easily; and the greater the number of Gurus in the lineage, the more swiftly we receive attainments. Why is this? When Buddha revealed

7

other Tantras, such as the *Guhyasamaja* or *Yamantaka Tantras*, he emanated the Deities and their mandalas and then reabsorbed them after the discourse; but when he taught *Heruka Tantra* he did not reabsorb the mandalas. There are twenty-four places in particular, such as Puliramalaya and Dzalandhara, where the mandalas of Heruka still remain. Practitioners with pure karma are able to see these mandalas and Deities. The people of this world therefore have a very close connection with Heruka, and if we practise the instructions purely we can easily and swiftly receive great results.

Heruka practitioners can attain the Pure Land of Keajra, Pure Dakini Land, without abandoning their present body. Even if they are very old, the moment they reach this Pure Land their body transforms into that of a sixteen-year-old. In Keajra they can receive empowerments and teachings directly from Heruka and Vajrayogini and, while living with Heroes and Heroines and enjoying the five objects of desire, they can easily attain Buddhahood. If out of compassion they wish to visit ordinary worlds, they can do so at any time through the power of emanation.

In other Pure Lands it is not possible to practise Highest Yoga Tantra and so it is not possible to attain Buddhahood quickly. In general, to practise Highest Yoga Tantra we need six elements: flesh, skin, and blood from the mother, and bone, marrow, and sperm from the father. Bodhisattvas in other Pure Lands such as Sukhavati do not possess these elements, and so they pray to be reborn as humans so that they can practise Highest Yoga Tantra. In Heruka's Pure Land, however, practitioners can possess these six elements. Many practitioners have attained the Pure Land of Heruka, Keajra, without abandoning their human bodies, and so they have a great opportunity to continue with their Highest Yoga Tantra practice.

From a practical point of view all the essential practices of Guhyasamaja and Yamantaka are included within this instruction of Heruka body mandala, and so we do not need to practise Guhyasamaja and Yamantaka separately from Heruka practice. We should integrate the practices of all other Deities within the practice of Heruka Father and Mother, and in this way we shall progress in our practice of Highest Yoga Tantra. We should remember Atisha's advice to the Tibetan translator, Rinchen Sangpo, which is explained in *Guide to Dakini Land*.

If we contemplate these benefits, we shall feel extremely fortunate to have met these precious instructions of Heruka and we shall develop a genuine wish to practise them purely.

EXAMPLES OF PREVIOUS PRACTITIONERS WHO ACCOMPLISHED ATTAINMENTS THROUGH THESE INSTRUCTIONS

By contemplating these examples of previous practitioners, our faith in the Heruka instructions will be greatly increased. If we study the biographies of the eighty-four Mahasiddhas of ancient India, we shall see that most of them attained enlightenment by relying upon Heruka as their personal Deity. There now follow brief life stories of some Heruka practitioners who accomplished attainments by relying upon these instructions.

SARAHA

Saraha was one of the first Mahasiddhas, and was greatly admired by later Mahasiddhas. By relying upon Heruka and practising the stages of Heruka's path, he attained the Pure Land of Keajra without abandoning his human body.

NAGARJUNA

Nagarjuna was one of Saraha's disciples, who attained enlightenment in one life by relying upon Heruka. Four hundred years after Buddha passed away, a son was born to a prosperous Brahmin family living in an area of Southern India known as Bedarwa, or the 'Land of the Palms'. A Brahmin seer predicted that the child would live for only seven days, but that his life span could be extended by a further seven days if gifts were bestowed upon a hundred ordinary people, by seven months if offerings were made to a hundred brahmins, or by seven years if offerings were made to a hundred ordained Sangha. However, the seer knew of no method to extend his life beyond that. Accordingly, his parents made offerings to a hundred ordained Sangha and as a result were able to live happily with their son for seven years.

As the child's eighth birthday drew near, however, they sent him on a pilgrimage with several of their servants, for they could not bear to witness his death. Guided by a manifestation of Avalokiteshvara, the party made its way to Nalanda Monastery where they met the great Teacher Saraha. They explained the boy's plight to Saraha, and he told them that the child could avert an untimely death by staying at Nalanda and ordaining as a monk. He gave the child an empowerment into the long-life practice of Buddha Amitayus and encouraged him to practise this yoga extensively. On the eve of his eighth birthday the child recited the mantra of Amitayus without interruption and, as a result, averted an untimely death. The following day he ordained as a monk and was given the name 'Shrimanta'. He remained at Nalanda where, under the protection of Manjushri, he was able to study all the Sutras and Tantras. He soon became a fully accomplished scholar and Teacher, and his reputation spread widely. Eventually he was appointed Abbot of Nalanda.

Nagarjuna's life comprised three great periods of auspicious deeds that correspond to Buddha's three turnings of the Wheel of Dharma, which is why he is often referred to as 'the Second Buddha'. The first period was during his tenure as Abbot of Nalanda. Unfortunately the moral discipline of the monks had degenerated since the time Buddha first gave the vows, and Nagarjuna was very active in restoring the purity of the discipline. He clarified many points of moral discipline and composed a number of works on pure conduct. These writings, known as the *Collection of Advice*, include such works as *Precious Garland*, *Friendly Letter*, *Tree of Wisdom*, *A Hundred Wisdoms*, and *Drops for Healing Beings*. These activities are likened to Buddha's first turning of the Wheel of Dharma.

Nagarjuna is best remembered, however, for the works of the second period. Not long after Buddha passed away, the *Perfection of Wisdom Sutras*, the principal Mahayana teachings, disappeared from this world. It is said that this is because some nagas who had received these teachings from Buddha took the *Perfection of Wisdom* scriptures to their own world for safekeeping. There remained only a few practitioners who could understand these teachings, and most of them kept their practice secret. The only teachings of Buddha to remain widespread were the Hinayana teachings, and as a result many people assumed that these were the only teachings that Buddha had given. Some time later, the nagas invited Nagarjuna to visit them and returned the *Perfection of Wisdom* scriptures to him. Nagarjuna brought the scriptures to the human world and propagated them widely. Because of his special relationship with the nagas, and because he cured many nagas of sickness by means of special ritual prayers, Nagarjuna was given the name 'Protector of the nagas'. 'Arjuna' was added to his name because he spread the Mahayana teachings with great speed and accuracy, just as the legendary archer, Arjuna, had delivered arrows from his bow. Hence he finally became known as 'Protector Nagarjuna'.

Because he had a very lucid mind and great wisdom, Nagarjuna was able perfectly to understand the *Perfection of Wisdom Sutras* and explain them to others. Through his extensive teachings, he instigated a great revival of the Mahayana doctrine in this world. He presented a system of reasoning which, because it steers a flawless course between the two extremes of existence and non-existence, became known as the 'Philosophy of the Middle Way', or 'Madhyamaka'. Nagarjuna composed many commentaries to the *Perfection of Wisdom Sutras* that elucidate the Madhyamaka view. These treatises, known as the *Collection of Reasonings*, include the famous *Fundamental Wisdom of the Middle Way*, and its four limbs – *Sixty Reasonings*, *Seventy Emptinesses*, *Finely Woven*, and *Refutation of Objections*. He also wrote *Compendium of Sutras*, *Five Stages of the Completion Stage of Guhyasamaja*, and many other commentaries to the Sutras and Tantras. These activities are likened to Buddha's second turning of the Wheel of Dharma.

Nagarjuna's third period of auspicious deeds took place towards the end of his life. Acting on advice from Tara, he returned to Southern India and dwelt at a place called Mount

Splendour, where he gave further extensive teachings on both the Sutras and Tantras, and composed many more texts. These writings, known as the *Collection of Praises*, include such works as *Praise of the Dharmadhatu*, *Praise of the Supramundane*, *Praise of the Inconceivable*, and *Praise of the Ultimate*. These activities are likened to Buddha's third turning of the Wheel of Dharma.

It is not possible in such a brief account even to begin to do justice to Nagarjuna's life and works. Throughout his life he devoted himself entirely to reviving the Mahayana Dharma and to sustaining the Mahayana Sangha. To this end he gave prolific teachings, composed many books, and performed countless other virtuous deeds. In all, Nagarjuna lived for over six hundred years.

SHAWARI

Shawari was a disciple of Nagarjuna. From the point of view of common appearance he was a hunter, but he received empowerment and teachings on Heruka from Nagarjuna and practised them sincerely at Mount Splendour, where he attained enlightenment. It is said that even to this day those with pure karma can see Shawari there.

LUYIPA

Prince Luyipa was Shawari's main disciple. On the tenth day of every month he used to go to a charnel ground to meditate. One day when he arrived there, he saw a group of men and women having a picnic. One of the women gave him a piece of meat and, when he ate it, his mind was blessed and instantly purified of ordinary appearance. He received a vision of Heruka and Vajrayogini and realized that the men and women were in reality Heroes and Heroines. While in the charnel ground, he received teachings directly from Heruka. Because Luyipa was a Heruka practitioner he came under the care of the Heroes and Heroines, and accomplished great results simply from tasting the piece of meat given to him by an emanation of Vajrayogini.

DARIKAPA

King Darikapa received empowerment and teachings on Heruka from Luyipa, who predicted that if Darikapa were to abandon his kingdom and apply great effort in the practice of Heruka and Vajrayogini he would swiftly attain enlightenment. Darikapa immediately left his palace and wandered from place to place as a beggar, practising meditation at every opportunity. In a city in South India he met a wealthy courtesan who was an emanation of Vajrayogini. This woman owned a large mansion in which he worked as her servant for twelve years. During the day he performed menial tasks in and around the house, and at night he practised Luyipa's instructions. After twelve years he attained the fifth stage of completion stage, the union that needs learning. It is said that Darikapa and the courtesan's entire entourage of fourteen thousand all attained the Pure Land of Keajra. This is because Darikapa was a pure Heruka practitioner and so everyone who saw or touched him created the cause to be reborn in Heruka's Pure Land.

DINGKIWA

One of King Darikapa's ministers, Dingkiwa, also received empowerment and teachings on Heruka from Luyipa, who predicted that he would meet a woman wine-seller who was an emanation of Vajrayogini. When he met her, Dingkiwa lived with her and served her for ten years, and as a result of her blessings attained enlightenment in that life. It is said that even the insects living in the place where he attained enlightenment were reborn in Heruka's Pure Land.

GHANTAPA

Ghantapa was another great Mahasiddha. Born as a prince, the son of the king of Nalanda, he later ordained as a monk. He became extremely skilled in practising the stages of Sutra and Tantra and would frequently defeat non-Buddhists in debate. Towards the end of his life he met King Darikapa, from whom he received empowerments and teachings on Heruka, and who advised him to go to a mountain in Bengal to practise meditation. One day while he was meditating there, he heard a voice in space telling him to go to Odiyana where he would meet a female swineherd. Delighted to hear this, he immediately set off for Odiyana, and there, as predicted, he met the female swineherd, whom he immediately recognized as an emanation of Vajrayogini. He received empowerments and teachings on Heruka from this emanation and then went deep into the forest of Odivisha (present-day Orissa), in India, where he engaged in intensive meditation on Heruka and Vajrayogini.

Since he was living in such an isolated place his diet was poor and his body became emaciated. One day the king of Odivisha was out hunting in the forest when he came across Ghantapa. Seeing how thin and weak he was, the king asked Ghantapa why he lived in the forest on such a poor diet, and encouraged him to return to the city where he would give him food and shelter. Ghantapa replied that just as a great elephant could not be led from the forest by a fine thread, so he could not be tempted to leave the forest by the riches of a king. Angered by Ghantapa's refusal, the king returned to his palace threatening revenge.

Such was the king's anger that he summoned a number of women from the city and told them about the arrogant monk in the forest. He offered great wealth to any one of them who could seduce him and force him to break his vows of celibacy. One woman, a wine-seller, boasted that she could do this and she set out for the forest to look for Ghantapa. When eventually she found him, she asked if she could become his servant. Ghantapa had no need of a servant but he realized that they had a strong relationship from previous lives and so he allowed her to stay. He gave her spiritual instructions and empowerments, and they engaged sincerely in meditation. After twelve years they both attained the Union of No More Learning, full enlightenment.

One day Ghantapa and the former wine-seller decided to encourage the people of the city to develop a greater interest in Dharma. Accordingly the woman returned to the king and reported that she had seduced the monk. At first the king doubted the truth of her story, but, when she explained that she and Ghantapa now had two children, a son and a daughter, the king was delighted with this news and told her to bring Ghantapa to the city on a particular day. He then issued a proclamation disparaging Ghantapa, and ordered his subjects to assemble on the appointed day to insult and humiliate the monk.

When the day came, Ghantapa and the woman left the forest with their children, the son on Ghantapa's right and the daughter on his left. As they entered the city Ghantapa was walking as if he were drunk, holding a bowl into which the woman poured wine. All the people who had gathered laughed and jeered, hurling abuse and insults at him. 'Long ago', they taunted him, 'our king invited you to the city but you arrogantly refused his invitation. Now you come drunk and with a wine-seller. What a bad example of a Buddhist and a monk!' When they had finished, Ghantapa appeared to become angry and threw his bowl to the ground. The bowl sank into the earth, splitting the ground and causing a spring of water to appear. Ghantapa immediately transformed into Heruka and the woman into Vajrayogini. The boy transformed into a vajra which Ghantapa held in his right hand, and the girl into a bell which he held in his left hand. Ghantapa and his consort then embraced and flew into the sky.

The people were astonished and immediately developed deep regret for their disrespect. They prostrated to Ghantapa, begging him and the emanation of Vajrayogini to return. Ghantapa and his consort refused, but told the people that if their regret was sincere they should make confession to Avalokiteshvara, the embodiment of Buddha's great compassion. Through the deep remorse of the people of Odivisha, and the force of their prayers, a statue of Avalokiteshvara arose from the spring water. The people of Odivisha became very devoted Dharma practitioners and many of them gained realizations. The statue of Avalokiteshvara can still be seen today.

Because of Ghantapa's pure practice of Heruka and Vajrayogini in the forest, Vajrayogini saw that it was the right time

15

for him to receive her blessings and so she manifested as the wine-seller. Through living with her, Ghantapa attained the Pure Land of Heruka.

KRISHNAPADA

Krishnapada received empowerment and teachings on Heruka from Mahasiddha Dzalandarapa. He attained enlightenment in the intermediate state after attaining ultimate example clear light during the clear light of death. Before he passed away he attained extraordinary miracle powers by relying upon the generation stage of Heruka. He could cause wild animals or attackers to freeze just by staring at them, and could tame wild animals with a glance. He could cause fruit to fall from trees just by looking at it, and could walk without touching the ground. When he wanted to cross a river he would simply take off his upper garment and float across on it while sitting in the vajra posture.

All the lineage Gurus of these instructions, from Ghantapa up to my root Guru, Kyabje Trijang Dorjechang Losang Yeshe Rinpoche, are actual examples of practitioners who have attained the union of Buddha Heruka through the practice of Heruka body mandala. The instructions in this book are the instructions given to Ghantapa by the emanation of Vajrayogini at Odiyana. If we practise them sincerely, we can accomplish all the attainments and become a pure holy being just like Mahasiddha Ghantapa.

THE QUALIFICATIONS OF A SINCERE HERUKA PRACTITIONER

By practising the generation and completion stages of Heruka we can attain enlightenment in one life. However, for this to happen we must be a sincere practitioner with the following five qualifications:

(1) We have experience of renunciation, bodhichitta, and the correct view of emptiness.
(2) We have received the empowerment of Heruka.
(3) We are keeping our vows and commitments purely.

(4) We have a clear and unmistaken understanding
of how to practise both generation stage and
completion stage of Heruka.

(5) We have indestructible faith in the Deity Heruka,
and in the Spiritual Guide from whom we received
the empowerment and commentary to the practice.

Anyone possessing these five qualifications who meditates
continually on the generation stage and completion stage of
Heruka will definitely attain enlightenment in one life. If we
do not yet possess these qualifications, we should strive gradually to attain them.

Once we have received the empowerment, we have a commitment to meditate on the two stages and, if we fail to do
so, we shall lose the blessing of the empowerment. Furthermore, our progress will be hampered if we do not also put
effort into attaining the other four qualities. Most import-
antly, we need to develop deep and unchanging faith in
Heruka and our Spiritual Guide. We should try to overcome
ordinary appearance of our Spiritual Guide and develop faith
in him or her. In this way we shall accomplish great results.
Even if we give our Spiritual Guide an expensive present, if
we lack faith in him or her it will have no meaning. On the
other hand, if we develop pure faith in our Spiritual Guide
we shall be making a great offering to him even if we never
give him presents. Without faith we are like a burnt seed;
just as a burnt seed cannot produce any fruit, so a Tantric
practitioner without faith cannot accomplish any results.

Tantric realizations depend upon faith and imagination.
No matter how much we investigate, it is difficult to prove
that our Spiritual Guide is a Buddha, so, rather than developing doubts, we should use our powers of imagination to
regard our Spiritual Guide as a Buddha and cultivate a pure
mind of faith in him or her. Gradually our mind will become
purer and purer until eventually we shall directly see our
Spiritual Guide as a Buddha.

Vajrayogini

Training in the Basic Practices

These instructions are explained under two headings:

1 Generation stage
2 Completion stage

GENERATION STAGE

The explanation of the generation stage of Heruka body mandala is based on the sadhana *Essence of Vajrayana*, which can be found in Appendix II. This explanation has two parts:

1 How to practise during the meditation session
2 How to practise during the meditation break

HOW TO PRACTISE DURING THE MEDITATION SESSION

This has three parts:

1 The preliminary practices
2 The actual practice of generation stage
3 The concluding practices

THE PRELIMINARY PRACTICES

Before engaging in the meditation session, we prepare offerings in front of our shrine, which should contain statues or pictures of Buddha Shakyamuni, Je Tsongkhapa, Heruka, our root Guru, and Dharmapala Dorje Shugdän. Buddha Shakyamuni is the founder of Mahayana Buddhism. Je Tsongkhapa and Dorje Shugdän are manifestations of the wisdom of all the Buddhas, and Heruka is the manifestation of the compassion of all the Buddhas. Maintaining faith in these holy beings causes us to increase our wisdom and compassion, which are the most important practices of Mahayana Buddhism. Faith in our Spiritual Guide is the root of all spiritual realizations.

We set out three tormas, which can either be made in the traditional way according to the illustration on page 488, or can consist simply of any clean, fresh food such as honey or cakes. The shapes of the traditional tormas symbolize the development of spiritual realizations. The central torma is for the principal Deities, Heruka Father and Mother and the four Yoginis, who together are known as the 'Deities of the great bliss wheel'. The torma to its left is for the supramundane retinues of Heruka, and the torma to its right is for the mundane retinues of Heruka.

In front of the tormas, we set out three rows of offerings. The first row, nearest the shrine, is for the supramundane in-front-generated Deities, and the second row is for the mundane Dakas and Dakinis. Both these rows start from the left side of the shrine, our right, and include water for drinking, water for bathing, flowers, incense, lights, perfume, and food. Nothing is set out for the music offering because music is not a visual object. The third row, which is for the self-generated Deities, starts from the right side of the shrine, our left, and includes water for drinking, water for bathing, water for the mouth, flowers, incense, lights, perfume, and food. On a small table in front of our meditation seat we arrange from left to right our inner offering, vajra, bell, damaru, and mala. In front of these we place our sadhana text. Then, with a pure motivation and a happy mind, we engage in the preliminary practices.

The preliminary practices are now explained under six headings:

1 Going for refuge and generating bodhichitta
2 Receiving blessings
3 Purifying our own mind, body, and speech
4 Purifying other beings, the environment, and enjoyments
5 Purifying non-virtues, downfalls, and obstacles
6 Guru yoga

GOING FOR REFUGE AND GENERATING BODHICHITTA

This has four parts:

1 The causes of going for refuge
2 Visualizing the objects of refuge
3 The way of going for refuge
4 Generating aspiring and engaging bodhichitta

THE CAUSES OF GOING FOR REFUGE

Our final goal is to attain enlightenment, the ultimate refuge, in order to benefit countless mother beings. Right now, however, we need to accomplish a refuge that prevents us from falling into lower rebirths. Without this inner protection, if we simply engage in the meditations of Highest Yoga Tantra expecting to attain enlightenment quickly, we are like someone who attempts to climb a high and dangerous mountain without safety equipment.

The time of our death is very uncertain. Perhaps we shall die today, perhaps tomorrow – we have no idea when we shall die. If we die without refuge, we shall lose all the spiritual progress we have made. At death we shall forget everything we have learned in our life and lose everything we have built up. After death, without any choice, we shall experience another samsaric rebirth with all its associated sufferings. Remembering nothing from our previous life, we shall be unable to maintain the continuum of our spiritual practice. By some miracle we have managed to obtain a precious human life with all the conditions necessary for spiritual practice; but unless we accomplish the inner protection of basic refuge we shall not find another similarly endowed rebirth, and this wonderful opportunity for spiritual development will be lost forever.

To protect ourself from the danger of a lower rebirth, and to create the special opportunity to maintain the continuum of our spiritual practice in life after life, we need to go for refuge to the Three Jewels, avoid non-virtuous actions, and practise giving, moral discipline, patience, effort, concentration, and wisdom. If we practise Highest Yoga Tantra on the firm foundation of this basic inner protection, then, even if we do not gain higher realizations in this life, we can at least carry our practice through death and the intermediate state into our future life. We shall die happily, with confidence. For us death will be like going on holiday.

How do we prepare for our future lives? By practising moral discipline we create the cause for higher rebirth; by giving we create the cause for future wealth; by practising patience we create the cause for beauty; by applying effort to our Dharma practice we create the cause to gain spiritual realizations with ease; by practising concentration or meditation we create the cause to experience mental peace; and by increasing our wisdom we create the cause to attain permanent liberation from suffering. We should integrate these basic practices into our daily life.

Although it is obviously essential that we protect ourself from lower rebirth, as Mahayana practitioners, and especially as Highest Yoga Tantra practitioners, our main motivation for going for refuge should be compassion. To generate compassion we can begin by considering the possibility that we may die this very day, and concentrate on the feeling it evokes. After death, wherever we are reborn in samsara we shall have to experience untold suffering. Contemplating and meditating in this way, we cultivate a strong fear of taking rebirth in samsara in general and in the lower realms in particular. If we then switch the focus of our contemplation from ourself to others, we shall find it difficult to bear their suffering, and compassion will arise naturally. Fear of samsaric rebirth and compassion for all those trapped in samsara are the first two causes of Mahayana refuge. When we develop a mind that cannot bear the sufferings of samsaric rebirth, both for ourself and for all mother sentient beings, we shall naturally seek a dependable source of refuge.

The Dharma Jewel, the realizations of the stages of the vast path and the profound path, is our actual refuge; the Buddha Jewel is the source of our refuge; and the Sangha Jewel, the assembly of Superior beings, are those who have already accomplished refuge. Through building the Dharma Jewel within our mind, we become a Sangha Jewel and finally a Buddha Jewel. We are then in a position to protect not only ourself but all living beings from rebirth in the lower realms in particular and from samsara in general. When we understand clearly that only the Three Jewels are perfect, infallible objects of refuge, deep faith and conviction in their power to protect living beings from suffering will arise. This is the third cause of Mahayana refuge.

To summarize, the causes of Mahayana refuge are fear of taking samsaric rebirth, compassion for all living beings, and faith in the Three Jewels. Cultivating these three causes within our mind encourages us to go for refuge to the Three Jewels and to avoid non-virtuous actions.

VISUALIZING THE OBJECTS OF REFUGE

We visualize the objects of refuge – the Buddha Jewel, the Dharma Jewel, and the Sangha Jewel – as follows. We imagine with strong conviction that in the space before us is the Blessed One Buddha Shakyamuni appearing in the form of glorious Heruka Father and Mother, surrounded by the assembly of Gurus, Yidams, Buddhas, Bodhisattvas, Heroes, Dakinis, and Dharma Protectors. At the beginning we should be satisfied with just a vague image; the most important thing is to believe that the holy beings are actually present before us. Imagining that the principal object of refuge, Guru Heruka, is surrounded by all the other holy beings like the moon surrounded by stars, we recognize the Gurus, Yidams, and Buddhas as the Buddha Jewel; the Bodhisattvas, Heroes, Dakinis, and Dharma Protectors as the Sangha Jewel; and the inner realizations of the stages of the vast and profound paths of all these holy beings as the Dharma Jewel. Reflecting that only the Three Jewels have the power to protect all living beings from the dangers of lower rebirth, samsaric rebirth, and all suffering, we generate deep faith in the Three Jewels.

THE WAY OF GOING FOR REFUGE

First we recall the feeling of fear of taking rebirth in samsara in general and in the lower realms in particular, and then, by realizing that countless mother sentient beings are in exactly the same situation as ourself, we generate compassion. Then we develop deep conviction that only the Three Jewels have the power to protect us from these dangers. With these three causes of refuge – fear, compassion, and faith – from the depths of our heart we make a strong determination:

I will always rely upon Buddha, Dharma, and Sangha, and will accomplish them as my ultimate refuge.

While concentrating on this determination, we recite the refuge prayer from the sadhana:

Eternally I shall go for refuge
To Buddha, Dharma, and Sangha.

These two lines and the two lines on bodhichitta that follow are very blessed and are extracted from Buddha Vajradhara's Tantric scriptures.

GENERATING ASPIRING AND ENGAGING BODHICHITTA

Bodhichitta is a primary mind that spontaneously wishes to attain enlightenment, motivated by compassion and love for all living beings. The way of generating bodhichitta according to Highest Yoga Tantra is superior to the way of generating it according to Sutra. In the practice of *Heruka Tantra*, for example, bodhichitta is a primary mind, motivated by great compassion, that spontaneously wishes to become Buddha Heruka. This bodhichitta can only be generated by Highest Yoga Tantra practitioners who clearly understand how they can become Buddha Heruka through the practice of the generation and completion stages of *Heruka Tantra*. When we develop this bodhichitta we enter the path of Highest Yoga Tantra of Heruka.

We should know the difference between entering the gateway of Highest Yoga Tantra and entering the path of Highest

Yoga Tantra. We enter the gateway of Highest Yoga Tantra by receiving empowerment, but to enter the path of Highest Yoga Tantra we need to develop the uncommon bodhichitta of Highest Yoga Tantra. Initially we generate fabricated uncommon bodhichitta, and later, through continuous training, this transforms into spontaneous uncommon bodhichitta. When we received the empowerment of Heruka body mandala, we entered the gateway of Highest Yoga Tantra of Heruka body mandala. Only through receiving this empowerment do we have the opportunity to study and practise these instructions.

There are two types of bodhichitta: aspiring bodhichitta and engaging bodhichitta. In the practice of Heruka, aspiring bodhichitta is a bodhichitta that simply aspires to become Buddha Heruka. We can generate this bodhichitta by contemplating the meaning of the following words:

For the sake of all living beings
I shall become Heruka.

Engaging bodhichitta is more than the mere aspiration to become Buddha Heruka; it is the sincere determination to engage in the actual path that leads to the state of Buddha Heruka. We can generate this bodhichitta by contemplating the meaning of the following words:

To lead all mother living beings to the state of
**   ultimate happiness,**
I shall attain as quickly as possible, in this very life,
The state of the Union of Buddha Heruka.
For this purpose I shall practise the stages of
**   Heruka's path.**

RECEIVING BLESSINGS

The practices explained above include generating the three causes of refuge, visualizing the refuge assembly, going for refuge to the Three Jewels, and generating uncommon bodhichitta – the determination to engage in the actual path that leads to the state of the Union of Buddha Heruka, the union of his Truth Body and Form Body. These practices are powerful methods for delighting all the holy beings. We are now ready to receive their profound blessings.

We imagine that all the other holy beings melt into light and dissolve into the principal object of refuge, Guru Buddha Heruka. Out of delight he comes to the crown of our head, diminishes to the size of a thumb, enters through our crown chakra, and dissolves into our mind at the centre of our heart chakra. We feel that our mind has become one with Heruka, the synthesis of all objects of refuge, and that we have received his profound blessings.

PURIFYING OUR OWN MIND, BODY, AND SPEECH

Uncommon bodhichitta has two intentions: the intention to lead all mother beings to the state of Buddha Heruka, and the intention to attain the state of the Union of Buddha Heruka ourself. The first intention is the cause of bodhichitta, and the second is the assistant of bodhichitta. Fulfilling these two intentions depends upon purifying our own mind, body, and speech and transforming them into Heruka's mind, body, and speech by relying upon the practice known as the 'yoga of the three purifications'.

The practice of the generation stage and completion stage of Heruka body mandala, the main body of the practices explained in this book, is an extensive practice of the three purifications. We need to integrate the entire practice of generation stage and completion stage into the practice of the three purifications, and to indicate this we practise a brief yoga of the three purifications at this point. This practice also reminds us that our motivation for studying and practising Heruka body mandala should always be uncommon bodhichitta. With this motivation all our study and practice will become powerful methods for fulfilling the two intentions of uncommon bodhichitta.

Purifying our own mind, body, and speech has three parts:

1 Purifying our own mind
2 Purifying our own body
3 Purifying our own speech

PURIFYING OUR OWN MIND

Buddha Heruka, the principal object of refuge, is a manifestation of the great bliss of all the Buddhas. Because he dissolved into our mind and our mind became one with him, we should now develop the conviction that our mind is the nature of great bliss. We imagine that we are experiencing spontaneous great bliss and briefly meditate on this feeling. We then recall that nothing exists from its own side, that everything is the nature of emptiness, and briefly meditate on this understanding. We feel that our mind of great bliss mixes with emptiness like water mixing with water, and firmly believe that our mind has become the union of the great bliss and emptiness of Heruka. We meditate on this union for a short while. This meditation is called the 'yoga of the vajra mind'. It acts as a cause to purify our mind and transform it into Heruka's vajra mind, the inseparable union of great bliss and emptiness.

PURIFYING OUR OWN BODY

While we are meditating on the union of great bliss and emptiness, our mind of great bliss perceives nothing other than emptiness. Then we think:

From the state of bliss and emptiness, like a cloud arising from an empty sky, I instantly appear as Buddha Heruka, with a blue-coloured body, one face, and two hands, holding vajra and bell, and embracing Vajravarahi. I stand with my right leg outstretched. I am Buddha Heruka.

We meditate on this self-generated Deity for a short time. This meditation is called the 'yoga of the vajra body'. It acts as a cause to purify our body and transform it into Heruka's vajra body.

PURIFYING OUR OWN SPEECH

While maintaining the strong divine pride that thinks 'I am Buddha Heruka', we recite the essence mantra of Heruka:
OM SHRI VAJRA HE HE RU RU KAM HUM HUM PHAT DAKINI

DZALA SHAMBARAM SÖHA. We think that our speech is purified and has transformed into Heruka's mantra, which has the
power to fulfil the wishes of all living beings, and we meditate on this special recognition for a while. This meditation
is called the 'yoga of the vajra speech'. It acts as a cause to
purify our speech and transform it into Heruka's vajra speech.

The practice of the yoga of the three purifications indicates
that we should perform all our daily actions with the three
recognitions: (1) that our own mind is Heruka's mind of the
Dharmakaya, (2) that our own body is Heruka's divine body,
and (3) that our own speech is Heruka's mantra. By practising in this way, we purify our ordinary appearances and
conceptions.

As we fall asleep at night we should try to maintain the
first recognition, regarding our mind as Heruka's mind of
the Dharmakaya experiencing the union of great bliss and
emptiness. As we wake up in the morning we imagine that
we arise from the state of great bliss and emptiness as Heruka, we recite the essence mantra, and we then engage in the
yoga of experiencing nectar and so forth. The yoga of experiencing nectar is explained in *Guide to Dakini Land*. Apart from
the times when we are training in common paths, such as
going for refuge and purifying negativities, we should try to
maintain the three recognitions throughout the day and night.

PURIFYING OTHER BEINGS, THE ENVIRONMENT, AND ENJOYMENTS

This practice is a powerful method to fulfil our main intention to lead all living beings to enlightenment as quickly as
possible. To show that we need to maintain this intention
throughout our practice, and to fulfil it as quickly as possible,
we now bring the resultant deeds of a Buddha into the path.
In this way we create a powerful cause to accomplish our
final aim of leading all mother beings to the ultimate happiness of enlightenment.

We imagine that from the letter HUM at the heart of ourself
generated as Heruka, infinite rays of wisdom light emanate

throughout all directions, purifying all worlds and the beings within them. The worlds become Heruka's Pure Land and all beings become Heroes and Heroines. Everything becomes immaculately pure, completely filled with a vast array of offerings, the nature of exalted wisdom and bestowing uncontaminated bliss. We firmly believe that we have fulfilled the two intentions of our bodhichitta, and develop a feeling of joy. We meditate on this feeling for a short while. This meditation acts as a powerful cause to awaken our Buddha nature. Gradually our Buddha nature will transform into actual enlightenment, and we shall then be truly able to lead all living beings to the happiness of enlightenment.

PURIFYING NON-VIRTUES, DOWNFALLS, AND OBSTACLES

This has two parts:

1 Why we need to purify non-virtuous actions and downfalls
2 The actual practice of purification

WHY WE NEED TO PURIFY NON-VIRTUOUS ACTIONS AND DOWNFALLS

In the *Vinaya Sutras* Buddha says:

Abandoning non-virtuous actions,
Practising virtuous actions,
And controlling the mind;
This is Buddhadharma.

Here 'Buddhadharma' refers to the actual refuge that directly protects living beings from suffering. We accomplish this protection by abandoning non-virtuous actions, practising virtuous actions, and controlling our mind.

First we need to develop the inner realizations that directly protect us from lower rebirth. As mentioned before, without this basic protection we are like someone attempting to climb a treacherous mountain without safety equipment. The main cause of all suffering, including lower rebirth, is non-virtue, or negative actions. Once we understand this we can gradually stop creating the causes of future suffering.

However, we have already accumulated infinite non-virtuous actions earlier in this life and in our countless previous lives, and if we do not purify these they will definitely throw us into a lower rebirth where it will be impossible for us to continue with our Dharma practice. Even now, these non-virtuous actions and downfalls are seriously obstructing the fulfilment of our wishes and progress in our Dharma practice. It is vital that we purify them without delay. This ability to purify our non-virtuous actions is one of the main advantages of a human rebirth. Animals have very little capacity to engage in virtuous actions, and naturally perform many negative actions such as killing; but human beings have the freedom not only to refrain from non-virtue but also to purify the potentialities of all their previously accumulated negative karma.

THE ACTUAL PRACTICE OF PURIFICATION

This has four parts:

1 The power of regret
2 The power of reliance
3 The power of the opponent force
4 The power of promise

These are known as the 'four opponent powers' because they have the power to purify completely all the non-virtue we have accumulated since beginningless time. Every non-virtuous action gives rise to four different effects: the ripened effect, the effect that is an experience similar to the cause, the effect that is a tendency similar to the cause, and the environmental effect. The action of killing, for example, has as its ripened effect rebirth in any of the three lower realms – the animal realm, the hungry spirit realm, or the hell realm. The experience similar to the cause of killing is that in subsequent rebirths we suffer from physical pain, poor health, and a short life. The tendency similar to the cause of killing is that in life after life we have a strong propensity to kill living beings. This is the worst effect because it traps us in a vicious circle of killing. Finally, the environmental effect of killing is that the place where we live is impure, making it hard to find uncontaminated food, air, water, and so forth, which in turn causes us to suffer from ill health.

The power of regret purifies the potential for the effect that is an experience similar to the cause; the power of reliance purifies the potential for the environmental effect; the power of the opponent force purifies the potential for the ripened effect; and the power of promise purifies the potential for the effect that is a tendency similar to the cause. By engaging in sincere purification using the four opponent powers, we can destroy the potentialities for the four effects of all non-virtuous actions, thereby attaining permanent freedom from mental and physical suffering, and especially from rebirth in the three lower realms. In this way we can take the real essence of our precious human life. How wonderful!

THE POWER OF REGRET

If we swallowed even the tiniest drop of poison, we would be terrified of its imminent effect, but our terror of the effects of our past negative actions should be far greater. External poison may cause us to become sick or even to die, but it can harm us only in this life. The internal poison of previous negative karma, on the other hand, harms us in all our lives, causing endless physical and mental pain and preventing us from attaining higher rebirth and spiritual realizations. Since this poison is already within our mental continuum, we must develop strong regret and make a determination, to purify the potentials of our negative actions as quickly as possible. Having meditated on this determination, we then put it into practice.

THE POWER OF RELIANCE

Through sincerely relying upon the Three Jewels we can completely purify all our non-virtuous actions and accomplish the ultimate refuge of Buddhahood. Therefore, at this point we need to go for refuge by sincerely relying upon Buddha, Dharma, and Sangha. This is the meaning of the power of reliance.

We first visualize the objects of refuge. Above our crown on a lotus and moon seat sits Vajrasattva, who is inseparable from Guru Heruka. He has a white-coloured body, one face, and two hands, holds a vajra and bell, and embraces his consort. His body is the synthesis of all Sangha Jewels, his speech the synthesis of all Dharma Jewels, and his mind the synthesis of all Buddha Jewels. We firmly believe that the living Buddha Heruka is actually present above our crown in the form of Vajrasattva, and with strong faith in the Three Jewels we contemplate:

> Through relying upon Buddha, Dharma, and Sangha, I will purify all my non-virtuous actions and accomplish the Buddha Jewel so that I can benefit all living beings without exception.

We meditate on this intention for a short while.

THE POWER OF THE OPPONENT FORCE

Whereas the other three opponent powers are like limbs supporting a body, the power of the opponent force is like the body itself because it is the direct opponent to all the negative effects of our non-virtuous actions.

To practise the power of the opponent force according to the sadhana, we visualize as follows. At the heart of Vajrasattva above our crown, in the centre of a moon seat, is a white letter HUM, which is the nature of the principal Deity Heruka. Standing in a circle counter-clockwise around the HUM is the white hundred-letter mantra, which is the nature of the one hundred Deities emanated by Heruka to pacify the non-virtues, downfalls, and obstacles of practitioners. At our heart we visualize the potentials of all our negative actions in the form of a dark mass, and with a mind of strong regret we request Vajrasattva:

O Guru Vajrasattva please listen to me.
There is great danger that I may die before I purify
   my negativities.
So with the water of your compassion
Please purify all my non-virtues and downfalls.

While concentrating on the meaning of this request, we recite the hundred-letter mantra of Heruka Vajrasattva as many times as possible. We think:

> As a result of making these requests, wisdom lights and nectars flow down from the HUM and mantra rosary at Vajrasattva's heart. These enter my body through my crown, reach my heart, and completely destroy the mass of darkness, the potentials of all my negative karma, just as the light of the sun destroys the darkness of night.

We repeat this recitation and visualization many times in each session.

THE POWER OF PROMISE

The definition of non-virtuous action is any action of body, speech, or mind that is the main cause of suffering. Since we wish to avoid suffering, we must stop creating its causes. With this thought we first develop and maintain the intention to refrain from all non-virtuous actions of body, speech, and mind, until eventually we are ready to make a promise to refrain from them completely.

The power of promise depends upon the strength of our determination to refrain from negative actions. If our determination is strong and unchangeable, we are ready to make this promise, but if it is weak we cannot yet do so. Therefore we first practise the power of promise by developing the intention not to commit any more non-virtuous actions. We then need to train in this intention until it becomes stable, at which point we shall have accomplished the actual power of promise.

To generate the power of promise, we contemplate how every non-virtuous action gives rise to the four types of effect.

In this way, we shall develop deep regret for all the negative actions we have committed in the past, and a strong determination to refrain from committing them in the future will arise naturally. If with this virtuous determination we then refrain from engaging in non-virtuous actions, this is the practice of moral discipline, which directly protects us from future suffering. Without making and keeping a promise to refrain from further negative actions, it is impossible to purify completely the negative actions we have committed in the past.

In summary, to purify our non-virtues we first develop strong regret for having created them by remembering that they are the main cause of all our present and future sufferings, problems, and unfulfilled wishes. Then we think:

Since only Buddha, Dharma, and Sangha have the power to protect living beings from suffering and its causes, I must rely upon them from the depths of my heart and, through receiving their blessings, completely purify all my non-virtues.

Having generated this motivation we practise the power of the opponent force, and at the end of each session we develop the strong determination, or at the very least the intention, to refrain from all non-virtuous actions of body, speech, and mind in the future.

The Yoga of the Guru

Guru yoga is presented under two main headings:

1 A general explanation
2 The actual practice of Guru yoga

A GENERAL EXPLANATION

Guru yoga is a special way of relying upon our Spiritual Guide. 'Guru' refers to any Spiritual Guide who gives us unmistaken instructions on how to begin, progress on, and complete the spiritual path, and who sets a good example for us to follow. Here the term 'yoga' reveals a special way of relying upon our Spiritual Guide that is a powerful method for accumulating merit and receiving the blessings of all the Buddhas.

At the moment, because our mind is impure – obstructed by ignorance and negative karma – we cannot directly perceive pure beings such as Buddhas. We see only impure beings who, like ourself, experience problems such as sickness, ageing, and death. However, by practising Guru yoga we can communicate with all the enlightened beings through our Spiritual Guide; through him or her they accept our offerings, respect, and devotion, and grant us their powerful blessings, protection, and care. In the Lamrim teachings it says:

Whenever a disciple relies upon his Spiritual Guide,
Without invitation all the enlightened beings
Enter and abide within the Spiritual Guide's body,
Accepting offerings and bestowing blessings.

Mahasiddha Ghantapa, for example, accomplished the state of the Union of Buddha Heruka by receiving the blessings of all the Buddhas through his Spiritual Guide, a woman who

Saraha

was an emanation of Vajrayogini. All the lineage Gurus of the instructions of Heruka body mandala, from Ghantapa up to Kyabje Trijang Dorjechang Losang Yeshe, attained enlightenment by receiving the blessings of all the Buddhas through their Spiritual Guide.

In these impure times it is only through receiving the blessings of the enlightened beings that we can maintain the mental peace that is the root of our daily happiness. For this reason alone, we can clearly see that the practice of relying upon the Spiritual Guide is supremely important.

During the meditation session, Heruka body mandala practitioners visualize their root Guru in the aspect of Heruka and invite all the Buddhas in the aspect of Heruka to dissolve into his body. With the strong recognition that their Guru is the synthesis of all the Buddhas, they make prostrations, offerings, and requests, and receive his or her blessings. They then integrate this special way of relying upon the Spiritual Guide into their daily life by remembering that he is a manifestation of Buddha Heruka and engaging in actions to delight him such as prostrations, offerings, requesting blessings, and, in particular, sincerely practising his teachings on Lamrim and Highest Yoga Tantra.

For such practitioners, Guru yoga is the actual quick path to enlightenment because, whenever they engage in any actions to delight their Spiritual Guide, the merit they create is multiplied by the number of enlightened beings. Since there are infinite enlightened beings, the virtue of any action done to please their Spiritual Guide is also infinite. For this reason, one moment of Guru yoga can accumulate as much merit as is accumulated over many aeons through other practices. Furthermore, the attainment of Buddhahood, which takes aeons to accomplish through other practices, can be accomplished in one life through the practice of Guru yoga. This was demonstrated by Dromtönpa, the heart disciple of Atisha, and by Khädrubje, the heart disciple of Je Tsongkhapa.

Geshe Potowa says:

Whether or not our Spiritual Guide is precious
Depends upon us and not upon our Spiritual Guide.

If we view our Spiritual Guide as a Buddha we shall receive the blessings of a Buddha, if we view him or her as a Bodhisattva we shall receive the blessings of a Bodhisattva, and if we view him or her as an ordinary being we shall receive nothing. Knowing this is very helpful because for as long as our mind remains impure it is impossible directly to perceive anyone, including our Spiritual Guide, as a real Buddha. Our task at the moment, therefore, is to use our imagination and the many valid reasons explained in *Joyful Path of Good Fortune* to train in the recognition that our Spiritual Guide is a living Buddha. Through continually training in this recognition, our faith will increase and our mind will become purer and purer until eventually we shall directly perceive our Spiritual Guide as a real Buddha. Ghantapa saw his Spiritual Guide as Buddha Vajrayogini; Dromtönpa saw his Spiritual Guide, Atisha, as Buddha Amitabha; and Khädrubje saw his Spiritual Guide, Je Tsongkhapa, as the Wisdom Buddha Manjushri.

THE ACTUAL PRACTICE OF GURU YOGA

This has six parts:

1 Visualizing the commitment beings of the Field of Merit, and inviting and absorbing the wisdom beings
2 Offering the practice of the seven limbs
3 Offering the mandala
4 Receiving the blessings of the four empowerments
5 Requesting the lineage Gurus
6 Accomplishing spontaneous great bliss by dissolving the Guru into ourself

VISUALIZING THE COMMITMENT BEINGS OF THE FIELD OF MERIT, AND INVITING AND ABSORBING THE WISDOM BEINGS

This has two parts:

1 Visualizing the commitment beings of the Field of Merit
2 Inviting and absorbing the wisdom beings

VISUALIZING THE COMMITMENT BEINGS OF
THE FIELD OF MERIT

This has three parts:

1 Visualizing basis Guru Heruka
2 Visualizing Guru Heruka of the body mandala
3 Visualizing the other holy beings

VISUALIZING BASIS GURU HERUKA

In the space in front of us, level with our eyebrows, and at a distance from us of about one arm's length, is a high, vast, and precious jewelled throne. It is square in shape, and adorned with jewels such as diamonds, emeralds, and lapis lazuli. Upon it are five smaller thrones, one in the centre raised higher than the others, and one in each of the four cardinal directions. The thrones are supported by two snow lions at each corner.

On the central throne on a lotus and sun, treading on Bhairawa and Kalarati, is our root Guru, Heruka. He has a dark-blue-coloured body like a lapis mountain. He has four faces, which counter-clockwise are dark blue, green, red, and yellow. He has twelve arms. His two principal hands embrace Vajravarahi and hold a vajra and bell. He has two hands holding an elephant skin, two hands holding a damaru and a khatanga, two hands holding an axe and a skullcup of blood, two hands holding a curved knife and a vajra noose, and two hands holding a three-pointed spear and a four-faced head of Brahma.

He displays the nine moods of a Hero and wears six bone mudra-ornaments. His crown is adorned with a half-moon and a crossed vajra. He wears a long necklace of fifty human heads, the nature of wisdom, and a lower garment of a tiger skin. He stands with his right leg outstretched, in the centre of a mass of blazing fire. Vajravarahi is red in colour and adorned with five mudra-ornaments. She holds a curved knife and a skullcup, and is entwined in embrace with Heruka. This visualization of Guru Heruka is called 'basis Guru Heruka' because the gross and subtle parts of his body are the basis for accomplishing the supporting and supported body mandala of Guru Heruka.

VISUALIZING GURU HERUKA OF THE BODY MANDALA

This has two parts:

1 Visualizing the Principal
2 Visualizing the retinues

VISUALIZING THE PRINCIPAL

The gross parts of basis Guru Heruka's body symbolize the various parts of Heruka's mandala. His two legs forming the shape of a bow symbolize the wind mandala; the triangle at his secret place symbolizes the fire mandala; his round belly symbolizes the water mandala; his square-shaped chest symbolizes the earth mandala; his spine symbolizes Mount Meru; the thirty-two channels at his crown symbolize the lotus; and the trunk of his body, the upper and lower parts of which are equal in size, symbolizes the celestial mansion.

In the centre of basis Guru Heruka's body, inside his heart chakra, his actual white and red indestructible drop appears as Heruka and Vajravarahi. Both Father Heruka and Mother Vajravarahi have the same aspect as basis Guru Heruka Father and Mother.

VISUALIZING THE RETINUES

This has three parts:

1 Visualizing the four Yoginis of the essence
2 Visualizing the Heroes and Heroines of the twenty-four places
3 Visualizing the eight Heroines of the doorways

VISUALIZING THE FOUR YOGINIS OF THE ESSENCE

We visualize as follows. The four channel petals in basis Guru Heruka's heart, which are the paths for the winds of the four elements, appear as the four Yoginis. In the east is Vajradakini, who is a manifestation of Mamaki, the consort of Buddha Vairochana; in the north is Vajralama, who is a manifestation of Tara, the consort of Buddha Amoghasiddhi;

in the west is Khandarohi, who is a manifestation of Benza-rahi, the consort of Buddha Amitabha; and in the south is Vajrarupini, who is a manifestation of Lochana, the consort of Buddha Ratnasambhava.

VISUALIZING THE HEROES AND HEROINES OF
THE TWENTY-FOUR PLACES

The twenty-four places of basis Guru Heruka's body are: (1) the hairline, (2) the crown, (3) the right ear, (4) the back of the neck, (5) the left ear, (6) the point between the eyebrows, (7) the two eyes, (8) the two shoulders, (9) the two armpits, (10) the two breasts, (11) the navel, (12) the tip of the nose, (13) the mouth, (14) the throat, (15) the heart (the point midway between the two breasts), (16) the two testicles, (17) the tip of the sex organ, (18) the anus, (19) the two thighs, (20) the two calves, (21) the eight fingers and eight toes, (22) the tops of the feet, (23) the two thumbs and two big toes, and (24) the two knees. These are the nature of the twenty-four places of Heruka.

The channels of the twenty-four places appear as the twenty-four Heroines, and the drops inside these channels appear as the twenty-four Heroes. Thus, at the place of his hairline, Puliramalaya, are Hero Khandakapala, who is the same person as Bodhisattva Samantabhadra, with Heroine Partzandi as his consort. At the place of his crown, Dzalandhara, are Hero Mahakankala, who is the same person as Bodhisattva Manjushri, and his consort Heroine Tzändriakiya. At the place of his right ear, Odiyana, are Hero Kankala, who is the same person as Bodhisattva Avalokiteshvara, and his consort Heroine Parbhawatiya. At the place of the back of his neck, Arbuta, are Hero Vikatadamshtri, who is the same person as Bodhisattva Ksitigarbha, and his consort Heroine Mahanasa. At the place of his left ear, Godawari, are Hero Suraberi, who is the same person as Bodhisattva Vajrapani, and his consort Heroine Biramatiya. At the place of the point between his eyebrows, Rameshöri, are Hero Amitabha, who is the same person as Bodhisattva Maitreya, and his consort Heroine Karwariya. At the place of his two eyes, Dewikoti, are Hero

Vajraprabha, who is the same person as Bodhisattva Akasha-garbha, and his consort Heroine Lamkeshöriya. At the place of his two shoulders, Malawa, are Hero Vajradeha, who is the same person as Bodhisattva Akashakosha (Space Treasure), and his consort Heroine Drumatzaya. These sixteen Deities of the heart wheel are called the 'Heroes and Heroines of the vajra mind family' because they are a manifestation of all Buddhas' mind.

At the place of his armpits, Kamarupa, are Hero Anku-raka, who is the same person as Bodhisattva Sarvanivarana-viskambini, and his consort Heroine Airawatiya. At the place of his two breasts, Ote, are Hero Vajrajatila, who is the same person as Bodhisattva Gadze Dhupe (Elephant Incense), and his consort Heroine Mahabhairawi. At the place of his navel, Trishakune, are Hero Mahavira, who is the same person as Bodhisattva Lodrö Mitsepa (Inexhaustible Wisdom), and his consort Heroine Bayubega. At the place of the tip of his nose, Kosala, are Hero Vajrahumkara, who is the same person as Bodhisattva Yeshe Tog (Highest Exalted Wisdom), and his consort Heroine Surabhakiya. At the place of his mouth, Kalinga, are Hero Subhadra, who is the same person as Bodhisattva Monpa Kunjom (Dispelling all Darkness), and his consort Heroine Shamadewi. At the place of his throat, Lampaka, are Hero Vajrabhadra, who is the same person as Bodhisattva Powa Tseg (Accomplishing Confidence), and his consort Heroine Suwatre. At the place of his heart, Kancha, are Hero Mahabhairawa, who is the same person as Bodhi-sattva Ngensong Kunden (Liberating all Lower Realms), and his consort Heroine Hayakarna. At the place of his two tes-ticles, Himalaya, are Hero Virupaksha, who is the same per-son as Bodhisattva Drawa Chenkyiö (Web of Light), and his consort Heroine Khaganana. These sixteen Deities of the speech wheel are called the 'Heroes and Heroines of the vajra speech family' because they are a manifestation of all Buddhas' speech.

At the place of the tip of his sex organ, Pretapuri, are Hero Mahabala, who is the same person as Bodhisattva Daö Shönnu (Youthful Moonlight), and his consort Heroine Tzatrabega, who is a manifestation of Bodhisattva Gyenpung (Shoulder Ornament). At the place of his anus, Grihadewata, are Hero Ratnavajra, who is the same person as Bodhisattva Dorje Ö (Vajra Light), and his consort Heroine Khandarohi, who is a manifestation of Bodhisattva Sordang (Individual Liberator). At the place of his two thighs, Shauraktra, are Hero Hayagriva, who is the same person as Bodhisattva Nyimi Ökyi Nyingpo (Essence of Sunlight), and his consort Heroine Shaundini, who is a manifestation of Bodhisattva Macha Chenmo (Great Powerful One). At the place of his two calves, Suwanadvipa, are Hero Akashagarbha, who is the same person as Bodhisattva Dorje Öser (Vajra Light Rays), and his consort Heroine Tzatrawarmini, who is a manifestation of Bodhisattva Logyonma (One Wearing Leaves). At the place of his eight fingers and eight toes, Nagara, are Hero Shri Heruka, who is the same person as Bodhisattva Tuchen Tog (Powerful Attainment), and his consort Heroine Subira, who is a manifestation of Bodhisattva Dorje Lukugyü (Continuous Circle of Vajras). At the place of the tops of his feet, Sindhura, are Hero Pämanarteshvara, who is the same person as Bodhisattva Norsang (Excellent Wealth), and his consort Heroine Mahabala, who is a manifestation of Bodhisattva Chirdog Chenmo (Great Pacifier). At the place of his two thumbs and two big toes, Maru, are Hero Vairochana, who is the same person as Bodhisattva Sangden (Excellent Carer), and his consort Heroine Tzatrawartini, who is a manifestation of Bodhisattva Tsugtor Kharmo (White Ushnisha). At the place of his two knees, Kuluta, are Hero Vajrasattva, who is the same person as Bodhisattva Lodrö Gyatso (Ocean of Wisdom), and his consort Heroine Mahabire, who is a manifestation of Bodhisattva Dorje Jigma (Wrathful Vajra). These sixteen Deities of the body wheel are called the 'Heroes and Heroines of the vajra body family' because they are a manifestation of all Buddhas' body.

The twenty-four Heroes and the twenty-four Heroines listed above are distinguished only by their aspect and function. In essence all these Deities are a manifestation of definitive Heruka and no different from Heruka himself.

VISUALIZING THE EIGHT HEROINES OF THE DOORWAYS

The eight doors of the senses are: (1) the root of the tongue, (2) the navel, (3) the sex organ, (4) the anus, (5) the point between the eyebrows, (6) the two ears, (7) the two eyes, and (8) the two nostrils. The channel at the root of his tongue appears as Kakase, the manifestation of Bodhisattva Kaouri, who is the consort of Aparajita, one of the ten wrathful Deities. The channel at his navel appears as Ulukase, the manifestation of Bodhisattva Tzowri, who is the consort of the wrathful Deity Amritakundalini. The channel at the door of his sex organ appears as Shönase, the manifestation of Bodhisattva Bukase, who is the consort of the wrathful Deity Hayagriva. The channel at the door of his anus appears as Shukarase, the manifestation of Bodhisattva Petali, who is the consort of the wrathful Deity Yamantaka. The channel at the point between his eyebrows appears as Yamadhati, the manifestation of Bodhisattva Kamari, who is the consort of the wrathful Deity Niladanda. The channel at his two ears appears as Yamaduti, the manifestation of Bodhisattva Shawati, who is the consort of the wrathful Deity Takkiraja. The channel at his two eyes appears as Yamadangtrini, the manifestation of Bodhisattva Dzandali, who is the consort of the wrathful Deity Achala. The channel at his two nostrils appears as Yamamatani, the manifestation of Bodhisattva Tombini, who is the consort of the wrathful Deity Mahabala. These Heroines differ only in their aspect and function; in essence they are no different from Heruka himself.

The four Yoginis of the essence and the central Deity Heruka Father and Mother are the Deities of the great bliss wheel. These, together with the sixteen Deities of the heart wheel, the sixteen Deities of the speech wheel, the sixteen Deities of the body wheel, and the eight Deities of the commitment wheel (the eight Heroines of the doorways), are the sixty-two Deities of the body mandala. They all appear within basis Guru Heruka's body, which indicates that Guru Heruka is the synthesis of all Buddhas.

VISUALIZING THE OTHER HOLY BEINGS

From the heart of Guru Heruka, light radiates to his right where he emanates as Maitreya seated on a throne, lotus, and moon disc. Maitreya is in the aspect of the Enjoyment Body, adorned with ornaments and silk garments. He sits in the half-vajra posture. His body is orange, with one face and two hands held at the level of his heart in the gesture of turning the Wheel of Dharma. Between the thumb and index finger of each hand he holds the stem of a naga tree. Beside his right ear the flower of one of the stems blooms and supports a golden wheel. Beside his left ear the flower of the other stem blooms and supports a long-necked vase.

In front of Maitreya, on a lotus and moon disc, sits Arya Asanga. His legs are crossed in such a way that his left leg extends from under his right thigh with the sole of his foot facing outwards, and his right leg, crossed over his left, extends several inches beyond his left knee. His right hand is in the gesture of expounding Dharma and his left hand is in the gesture of meditative equipoise. He wears the three robes of an ordained person and a Pandit's hat. To his left is a spherical vessel. All the lineage Gurus of the vast path form a circle starting with Asanga and going clockwise around the central figure of Maitreya.

From the heart of Guru Heruka, light radiates to his left where he emanates as Manjushri seated on a throne, lotus, and moon disc. His body is the same colour as Maitreya's and he has the same posture except that instead of holding naga trees he holds the stems of upali flowers. The flower that blooms beside his right ear supports a wisdom sword, and the flower that blooms beside his left ear supports a text of the *Perfection of Wisdom Sutra in Eight Thousand Lines*. This posture is known as 'Manjushri Turning the Wheel of Dharma'.

In front of Manjushri sits Nagarjuna in the half-vajra posture, wearing the robes of an ordained person. His hands are in the gesture of expounding Dharma. He has a small crown-protusion and, arched over his head without touching it, is a canopy of seven snakes. All the lineage Gurus of the profound

Nagarjuna

path form a circle starting with Nagarjuna and going counter-clockwise around the central figure of Manjushri.

To the right of the lineage Gurus of the vast path sit the lineage Gurus of Kadam Lamrimpa, and to the left of the lineage Gurus of the profound path sit the lineage Gurus of Kadam Shungpawa. Behind the lineage Gurus of the vast path sit the lineage Gurus of Kadam Männgagpa. Each of these Kadampa Gurus sits on a lotus and moon disc.

From the heart of Guru Heruka, light radiates behind him where he emanates as Buddha Vajradhara, who in essence is our root Guru, seated on a throne, lotus, moon, and sun disc. Surrounding him are all the lineage Gurus of Heruka body mandala, from Ghantapa up to Kyabje Trijang Dorjechang Losang Yeshe.

From the heart of Guru Heruka, light radiates in front of him where he emanates as our principal Spiritual Guide sitting on a throne. We visualize him or her as radiant and youthful, without any physical imperfections. His right hand is in the gesture of expounding Dharma, indicating that he dispels the ignorance of his disciples. His left hand is in the gesture of meditative equipoise holding a life vase, indicating that he destroys the power death has over his disciples. These two, ignorance and death, are the greatest obstacles to our spiritual development. Ignorance prevents us from understanding Dharma, especially the instructions on superior seeing, which is the antidote to ignorance; and death destroys the very life that is the basis for practising Dharma. Surrounding our main Spiritual Guide, we visualize all the other Spiritual Guides who have taught us pure Dharma directly in this life.

In front of these groups of Gurus, we visualize the Deities of Highest Yoga Tantra. On the right is the assembly of Vajrabhairava, on the left the assembly of Guhyasamaja, and in the centre the assembly of Heruka. In front of these in successive rows are: Deities of Yoga Tantra, such as the assembly of Sarvavirti, the main Deity of Yoga Tantra; Deities of Performance Tantra, such as the assembly of Vairochana Deities; Deities of Action Tantra, such as Amitayus, Green Tara, and

White Tara; Buddhas of Sutra, such as the one thousand Buddhas of this Fortunate Aeon, the thirty-five Confession Buddhas, and the eight Medicine Buddhas; Sanghas of Sutra, including Bodhisattvas such as the eight Great Sons, Emanation Solitary Realizers such as the twelve Solitary Realizers, and Emanation Hearers such as the sixteen Foe Destroyers; Sanghas of Tantra such as the Heroes and Heroines of the twenty-four auspicious places, and supramundane Dharma Protectors such as Mahakala, Dharmaraja, Dorje Shugdän, Vaishravana, and Kalindewi.

We should believe that all these holy beings are actually present before us and that they are the manifestation of definitive Heruka. They are called the 'Field of Merit' because they are like a field from which we can harvest inner crops of merit and realizations.

To begin with we should not expect to perceive the Field of Merit clearly or in detail. We should be satisfied with simply perceiving a general image of the whole assembly of holy beings. Through meditating on this with strong faith again and again, our faith and merit will increase and we shall receive the blessings of the holy beings. As a result our mind will become purer, and when our mind is very pure we can receive a direct vision of these enlightened beings. We shall then have no doubt that we too shall become a pure being.

At this point we can practise three special meditations: (1) meditation on the assembly of the eight Heroines of the doorways at the places of the eight sense doors of Guru Heruka; (2) meditation on the assembly of the twenty-four Heroes and Heroines of the twenty-four places of Heruka's body; and (3) meditation on the assembly of the Deities of the great bliss wheel. To do these meditations we simply concentrate on the assemblies of Deities while remembering their significance. The first meditation is especially auspicious for the inward gathering of the winds that flow through the channels of our eight sense doors. The second meditation is especially auspicious for the inward gathering of the winds that flow through the channels of our twenty-four places. The third meditation is especially auspicious for all the inner winds to gather at the heart and dissolve into our indestructible drop. When this happens, we experience the clear light of bliss. In the extensive dedication prayer from the sadhana it says:

> Through meditating on the Goddesses of the doorways
> at the doors of the senses,
> May I reverse the winds through the doors of the
> senses;
> Through meditating on the Heroes and Heroines at
> the twenty-four places,
> May I gather the winds into the twenty-four channels;
>
> Through meditating on the Deities of the great bliss
> wheel on the petals of the Dharma Wheel,
> May I gather the winds into the eight channels
> Of the cardinal and intermediate directions at my heart,
> And then may I gather them into my central channel
> at the heart.

INVITING AND ABSORBING THE WISDOM BEINGS

The three places of the holy beings are marked as follows. The crown, the place of the body, is marked by a white letter OM, the seed of the body of all Buddhas; the throat, the place of the speech, is marked by a red letter AH, the seed of the speech of all Buddhas; and the heart, the place of the mind, is marked by a blue letter HUM, the seed of the mind of all Buddhas. This indicates that each being in the Field of Merit is the synthesis of all Buddhas.

From the letter HUM at Guru Heruka's heart, infinite rays of light radiate and invite all the Buddhas from their natural abode, the Dharmakaya, each in the aspect of the assembly of the entire Field of Merit. When we recite 'DZA' an entire assembly of wisdom beings comes above the crown of each commitment being; when we recite 'HUM' they dissolve into the commitment beings; when we recite 'BAM' they mix with the commitment beings; and when we recite 'HO' they are delighted to remain with the commitment beings.

Tantric practitioners have a commitment to visualize the Field of Merit, and so the visualized Field of Merit is called 'the commitment being'. The Field of Merit that we invite from the Buddha Lands is called 'the wisdom being'. The first is an imagined Field of Merit and the second is a naturally abiding Field of Merit.

OFFERING THE PRACTICE OF THE SEVEN LIMBS

One of the main purposes of visualizing the Field of Merit is to accumulate merit, purify negativities, and receive blessings. We do this by practising the seven limbs. The seven limbs are: (1) prostration, (2) offering, (3) confession, (4) rejoicing, (5) beseeching the Spiritual Guide not to pass away, (6) requesting the turning of the Wheel of Dharma, and (7) dedication. These are called 'limbs' because they support meditation, the main body of our practice. Just as our body is powerless if not supported by arms and legs, so our meditation has no power to produce authentic Dharma realizations unless it is supported by an accumulation of merit, purification of negativities, and blessings.

PROSTRATION

The practice of prostrations is a powerful method for purifying negative karma, disease, and obstacles, and for increasing our merit, our happiness, and our Dharma realizations. Temporarily, prostrations improve our physical health, and ultimately they cause us to attain the Form Body of a Buddha. Generating faith in the holy beings is mental prostration, reciting praises to them is verbal prostration, and showing them respect with our body is physical prostration. We can make physical prostrations by respectfully prostrating our whole body on the ground; by respectfully touching our palms, knees, and forehead to the ground; or by respectfully placing our palms together at the level of the heart with the tips of the fingers touching and the thumbs tucked inside so that our hands form the shape of a jewel.

To make prostrations to our root Guru, we begin by contemplating his or her pre-eminent qualities and kindness, and with a mind of wishing faith we recite the following prayer:

Vajra Holder, my jewel-like Guru,
Through whose kindness I can accomplish
The state of great bliss in an instant,
At your lotus feet humbly I bow.

Although our Spiritual Guide is likened to a jewel, no matter how precious external jewels may be, they have no power to give us true happiness or protect us from suffering. There is nothing in the external world that can compare with our Spiritual Guide. In the sadhana, the words 'jewel-like Guru' simply reveal that our Spiritual Guide is very precious. 'Vajra Holder' means that he or she is a manifestation of Buddha Vajradhara.

Compared to the lives of beings in the god realms, a human life is very short, like an instant. However, if we sincerely rely upon our Spiritual Guide, through his or her kindness we can accomplish the great bliss of Buddha Heruka and become an enlightened being in this short human life.

According to Highest Yoga Tantra, placing our hands together at the heart when we prostrate shows that we want to experience great bliss by dissolving the ten inner winds into the central channel at our heart. In this context, our ten fingers symbolize our ten inner winds, while placing the fingers together and tucking the thumbs inside symbolizes the inward gathering of the ten inner winds. Touching the point at the level of the heart symbolizes the dissolution of the ten inner winds into the central channel at our heart, and the jewel-like shape symbolizes the great bliss of Buddhahood. It is in order to receive these attainments that we prostrate to our root Guru.

To make a special prostration to Guru Heruka Father and Mother, we begin by contemplating his pre-eminent qualities through concentrating on the meaning of the following prayer:

As times become ever more impure
Your power and blessings ever increase,
And you care for us quickly, as swift as thought;
O Chakrasambara Father and Mother, to you I
    prostrate.

Now we make prostrations to the entire assembly of the
Field of Merit by concentrating on the meaning of the following prayer:

To the Gurus who abide in the three times and the
    ten directions,
The Three Supreme Jewels, and all other objects of
    prostration,
I prostrate with faith and respect, a melodious chorus
    of praise,
And emanated bodies as numerous as atoms in the
    world.

We generate deep faith that sincerely wishes to attain the
great bliss experienced by all the holy beings, which arises
through the dissolution of the inner winds into the central
channel at the heart. Then we imagine that from every pore
of our body we emanate another body, and that from every
pore of these bodies we emanate yet more bodies, until our
emanated bodies fill the entire world. While reciting the
prayer from the sadhana, we strongly believe that all these
countless bodies make prostrations to our root Guru, who is
inseparable from the assembly of Guru Heruka and all the
lineage Gurus, Yidams, Buddhas, Bodhisattvas, Dakas, Dakinis, and Dharma Protectors.

OFFERING

This has five parts:

1 Outer offerings
2 Inner offering
3 Secret offering
4 Thatness offering
5 Offering our spiritual practice

OUTER OFFERINGS

This has two parts:

1 The eight outer offerings
2 Offering the five objects of desire

THE EIGHT OUTER OFFERINGS

The eight outer offerings are water for drinking, water for bathing the feet, flowers, incense, lights, perfume, food, and music. The purpose of making these offerings to the Gurus, Yidams, Buddhas, and Bodhisattvas is to increase our collection of merit, or good fortune, and thereby create the main cause for our wishes to be fulfilled. In particular, by offering food and nectar we shall gain freedom from the suffering of poverty and experience the enjoyments of the Buddhas. By offering bathing water and perfume we shall become free from samsaric rebirths and attain the Form Body of a Buddha. By offering beautiful flowers we shall become free from sickness, ageing, and other bodily ailments, and we shall attain the special attributes of the body of a Buddha. By offering incense we create the cause to keep pure moral discipline and attain pure concentration. By offering lights we shall become free from the inner darkness of ignorance and attain omniscient wisdom. By offering beautiful music we create the cause never to have to hear unpleasant sounds but only to hear pleasant sounds, especially the sound of Dharma; and to receive only good news. Offering music is also a cause of attaining the speech of a Buddha. Knowing these benefits, we should try to make outer offerings every day, at least mentally.

To make water offerings we imagine that all the rivers, pools, lakes, and oceans throughout infinite worlds appear in the aspect of water for drinking, water for bathing, and perfume. As we do so, we recall that they are manifestations of their emptiness, their ultimate nature, inseparable from the wisdom of uncontaminated great bliss; that their function is to cause the holy beings to experience spontaneous great bliss; and that their aspect is that of the individual offering substances. In a similar way, when we offer all the flowers, incense, lights, food, and music that exist throughout infinite worlds we maintain the same recognition of their nature, function, and aspect. With this special knowledge we make the eight outer offerings.

From the letter HUM at our heart, we emanate infinite offering gods and goddesses, who are the nature of the exalted wisdom of uncontaminated great bliss and emptiness. They make infinite offerings of water for drinking, water for bathing the feet, flowers, incense, lights, perfume, food, and music to the assembly of Guru Heruka and to all the other holy beings in the Field of Merit.

OFFERING THE FIVE OBJECTS OF DESIRE

We offer these special offerings by concentrating on the meaning of the verses from the sadhana, beginning with:

> **All forms that exist throughout infinite realms transform
>   into a vast assembly of Rupavajra Goddesses,**
> **With smiling faces and beautiful bodies, pervading
>   the whole of space.**
> **I offer these to you Guru Father and Mother and to
>   the assembly of Deities;**
> **Please accept, and through the force of all forms that
>   exist appearing as Rupavajras,**
> **May I and all living beings receive unchanging great
>   bliss**
> **And complete the supreme concentration of the
>   union of great bliss and emptiness.**
> OM RUPA BENZ HUM HUM PHAT

We recall that not even the smallest atom of form exists from the side of the object and, by concentrating on this firm knowledge, we dissolve all appearances of form into emptiness, the ultimate nature of form. In the same way, we recall that sounds, smells, tastes, and tactile objects do not exist from their own side and, by concentrating on this firm knowledge, we dissolve all appearances of sounds, smells, tastes, and tactile objects into emptiness, their ultimate nature.

We then imagine that the ultimate nature of all forms that exist throughout infinite worlds appears in the aspect of countless Rupavajra Goddesses – female Deities, white in colour, holding mirrors reflecting the whole universe, who are born from omniscient wisdom mixed completely with the ultimate nature of all forms. The whole of space is pervaded by these beautiful goddesses, and we offer them to the assembly of Guru Heruka and all the holy beings in the Field of Merit.

We then imagine that the ultimate nature of all sounds that exist throughout infinite worlds appears in the aspect of countless Shaptavajra Goddesses – female Deities, blue in colour, holding flutes that spontaneously produce enchanting music, who are born from omniscient wisdom mixed completely with the ultimate nature of all sounds. The whole of space is pervaded by these beautiful goddesses, and we offer them to the assembly of Guru Heruka and the other holy beings.

We then imagine that the ultimate nature of all smells that exist throughout infinite worlds appears in the aspect of countless Gändhavajra Goddesses – female Deities, yellow in colour, holding beautiful jewelled containers filled with special perfumes whose fragrance pervades the whole world, who are born from omniscient wisdom mixed completely with the ultimate nature of all smells. The whole of space is pervaded by these beautiful goddesses, and we offer them to the assembly of Guru Heruka and the other holy beings.

With the same understanding, we offer infinite offerings of Rasavajra Goddesses – female Deities, red in colour, holding precious containers filled with nectar possessing three qualities – medicine nectar that cures all disease, life nectar that overcomes death, and wisdom nectar that destroys delusions – who are born from omniscient wisdom mixed completely with the ultimate nature of all tastes. We then offer infinite offerings of Parshavajra Goddesses – female Deities, green in colour, holding precious garments, who are born from omniscient wisdom mixed completely with the ultimate nature of all tactile objects.

These offerings have five functions. They cause us (1) to accumulate great merit, (2) to increase our knowledge of the

Shawari

profound view of emptiness, thereby accumulating a great collection of wisdom, (3) to develop and increase great bliss, (4) to purify ordinary appearances and conceptions, and (5) to gain the completion stage realization of isolated body.

Qualified practitioners of Highest Yoga Tantra have experience of the common paths of renunciation, bodhichitta, and the profound view of emptiness. If we have deep knowledge of emptiness, the ultimate nature of phenomena, it is not difficult to offer these eight outer offerings and five objects of desire. Even if we are not qualified at the moment, we can still train in these practices continually so that sooner or later we shall become a qualified practitioner.

Although this way of accumulating merit is a very special, higher practice, it is not a good sign if, despite the fact that we are making these mental and verbal offerings, we continue to have a miserly attitude towards our money and possessions, holding them very tightly and having no intention of using them to accumulate merit. We must have the intention to use our money and possessions to accumulate merit for the benefit of others and, every day if possible, offer actual water for drinking, water for bathing, flowers, incense, lights, perfume, food, and music. We should always dedicate all our activities to the happiness of all living beings.

INNER OFFERING

From our heart we emanate countless Rasavajra Goddesses and imagine that from the huge skullcup containing the inner nectar, as vast as an ocean, they scoop up nectar with their skullcups and offer it to the countless holy beings in the Field of Merit. At the same time, we recite the offering prayer from the sadhana: OM GURU HERUKA VAJRAYOGINI SAPARIWARA OM AH HUM. We hold the inner offering container in our right hand, around the level of our forehead, and then, as we say OM AH HUM, we dip our left ring finger into the nectar, flick a drop into space, and imagine that Guru Heruka Father and Mother and all the Field of Merit experience spontaneous great bliss.

SECRET OFFERING

We make this offering by concentrating on the essential meaning of the following prayer:

And I offer most attractive illusory mudras,
A host of messengers born from places, born from
mantra, and spontaneously born,
With slender bodies, skilled in the sixty-four arts of
love,
And possessing the splendour of youthful beauty.

By making this offering we create the cause to generate spontaneous great bliss ourself in the future by relying upon a consort, or mudra. The essence of Secret Mantra is to generate spontaneous great bliss by dissolving the inner winds within the central channel. This can be done to a limited extent through meditation alone, but to complete the practice in this life we need to accept an action mudra. Through completion stage meditation we can completely loosen the knots in the channel wheels at the crown, throat, navel, and secret place; and by relying upon vajra recitation we can partially loosen the knots at the heart channel wheel. However, we cannot completely loosen these knots by meditation alone. These will naturally loosen completely at death, but, if the practitioner wants this to happen before death, he or she must accept an action mudra. Through the force of the two central channels uniting during embrace, the downward-voiding wind of the consort will enter the practitioner's central channel, causing the knots at the heart channel wheel to loosen completely. The practitioner can then complete the path to enlightenment in that life.

The correct time to rely upon an action mudra is after having gained the experience of dissolving some of the inner winds within the central channel at the heart channel wheel. When through this practice we are able to perceive clearly the eight signs of dissolution from the mirage-like appearance to the clear light, and we have attained the experience of isolated body, isolated speech, and isolated mind, it is appropriate to enter into union with an action mudra.

A mudra is called a 'messenger' because he or she fulfils our wishes by bringing great bliss. There are three types of messenger: outer, inner, and secret. These are explained in detail in *Guide to Dakini Land*. In this context, an outer messenger is a knowledge consort. The verse from the sadhana mentions three types of outer messenger: those born from places, those born from mantra, and those who are spontaneously born. The first are Dakinis from the twenty-four holy places of Heruka, the second are messengers with realizations of generation stage or the first stages of completion stage, and the third are messengers with a realization of the union of clear light and illusory body that is either the union that needs learning or the Union of No More Learning.

We visualize countless action mudras of all three types emanating from our heart, merging into one, and dissolving into Vajravarahi, who is embracing Father Heruka. We imagine that through the force of this offering our Guru generates spontaneous great bliss. From his or her side, our Guru has no need of this offering because he or she already abides immovably in a state of great bliss; the purpose of making this offering is to create the cause for us to generate spontaneous great bliss in the future.

We should visualize all the knowledge women as youthful and extremely attractive. According to the words of the sadhana, these consorts are 'skilled in the sixty-four arts of love'. In the Sutras, Buddha explains sixty-four arts in connection with sports such as archery, but in the Tantras he explains sixty-four arts of love as methods for inducing spontaneous great bliss. There are eight basic arts: embracing, kissing, biting, scratching, enticing walking, whistling, performing the actions of a man, and lying on top. Each of these can be performed in eight different ways, making sixty-four arts in all.

In *Guhyasamaja Tantra* Vajradhara stresses how important it is for Tantric practitioners to make the four types of offering every day, and he places special emphasis on the secret offering as a method for generating great bliss.

THATNESS OFFERING

We make this offering by concentrating on the essential meaning of the prayer from the sadhana:

I offer you the supreme, ultimate bodhichitta,
A great exalted wisdom of spontaneous bliss free
  from obstructions,
Inseparable from the nature of all phenomena, the
  sphere of freedom from elaboration,
Effortless, and beyond words, thoughts, and
  expressions.

'Thatness' is emptiness, the ultimate nature of all phenomena. Strictly speaking we offer not emptiness but ultimate bodhichitta, which is a mind of spontaneous great bliss mixed inseparably with emptiness. We imagine that Guru Heruka generates this mind as a result of entering into union with the mudra offered to him during the secret offering. Although our Guru already has ultimate bodhichitta, we imagine that he or she generates it anew, as an auspicious cause for us to gain this realization in the future.

In Secret Mantra, the red and white drops that flow through the channels are sometimes called 'bodhichittas' because they are the basis for developing actual ultimate bodhichitta, spontaneous great bliss realizing emptiness directly. Without these drops, we would have no means of gaining any completion stage realization, let alone ultimate bodhichitta.

According to the words of the sadhana, Guru Heruka's exalted wisdom of spontaneous great bliss is 'free from obstructions', which means that it has completely abandoned both the delusion-obstructions and the obstructions to omniscience. Not all spontaneous great bliss is free from obstructions. When we first generate spontaneous great bliss our mind is still covered by obstructions, but by training in the five stages of completion stage these are gradually removed. When the mind is finally freed from both obstructions we attain enlightenment. Thus, the words of the sadhana indicate that Guru Heruka is a Buddha because his ultimate bodhichitta is free from obstructions.

The phrase, 'Inseparable from the nature of all phenomena, the sphere of freedom from elaboration', is very profound and difficult to understand without some experience of Secret Mantra. The term 'sphere' refers to emptiness, and the term 'elaboration' refers to inherent existence, so the meaning is that ultimate bodhichitta is inseparable from emptiness, lack of inherent existence. Once we have a rough understanding of emptiness, we should try to generate spontaneous great bliss by training in completion stage meditation. When our inner winds are gathered and dissolved within the central channel at our heart, our gross minds will cease and the very subtle mind of clear light will manifest. This mind is very peaceful and free from distracting conceptions. It is hundreds of times more powerful than the concentration described in the Sutra teachings. When this mind meditates on emptiness it easily mixes with it, like water mixing with water; and it feels as if the subject, our mind of clear light, and its object, emptiness, have become completely one.

The reason the clear light mind can mix so easily with emptiness is that it is totally free from conceptual distraction. When the inner winds are completely gathered and dissolved within the central channel, the gross inner winds are absorbed and so the gross minds that depend upon these winds cease to function. If there are no gross minds, there are no gross objects; thus, for the mind of clear light, gross objects do not exist. It is like when we fall asleep. At that time, because the gross minds of the waking state absorb, all the objects that appear to these minds disappear. For the sleeping or dreaming mind, the objects of our normal waking state do not exist. Being completely free from gross objects, the mind of clear light mixes with emptiness in space-like meditative equipoise. With respect to this mind, all phenomena are of one taste in space-like emptiness. Thus it is said that this mind is inseparable from the ultimate nature of all phenomena.

The mind that is described as ultimate bodhichitta in Sutra is not an actual ultimate bodhichitta because it still has subtle dualistic appearances. Therefore, to attain actual ultimate bodhichitta we need to engage in Secret Mantra practices.

Once we understand how the mind of ultimate bodhichitta is inseparable from the nature of all phenomena, we shall understand the real nature of the Guru. The actual Guru is definitive Vajradhara, or definitive Heruka. Vajradhara is sometimes called 'kyab dag' in Tibetan, which means 'pervading all natures'. This means that the ultimate bodhichitta that is Guru Vajradhara's Truth Body is inseparable from the nature of all phenomena. To appreciate this fully we also need to understand how the two truths are the same nature. This is more difficult to understand than emptiness itself because it is harder to abandon the mind grasping the two truths as separate entities than it is to abandon self-grasping. Bodhisattvas who have attained the union of meaning clear light and the illusory body, for example, have abandoned the latter but not the former. Only Buddhas are completely free from grasping the two truths as separate entities.

According to the sadhana, ultimate bodhichitta is 'beyond words, thoughts, and expressions'. This is because ultimate bodhichitta is necessarily a direct experience of emptiness, free from conceptuality. It is said that someone who has a direct experience of emptiness cannot adequately describe this experience in words, but can only point to it by means of analogies. Even so, great beings such as Je Tsongkhapa are able to give very clear descriptions of emptiness. Thus Changkya Rölpai Dorje praises Je Tsongkhapa, saying:

> Emptiness is said to be inexpressible, but you have described it as clearly as something seen with the eyes.

OFFERING OUR SPIRITUAL PRACTICE

The offering that delights our Spiritual Guide the most is putting his or her instructions into practice, which is why offering our spiritual practice is called an 'unsurpassed offering'. Whenever we practise Lamrim, Lojong, and the Vajrayana paths of Heruka and Vajrayogini, we are making a supreme offering.

There are seven special spiritual practices, presented in many Tantric sadhanas, that contain the very essence of Buddha's teachings. These are: (1) purification, (2) accumulating merit, (3) ultimate bodhichitta, (4) Mahayana refuge, (5) aspiring bodhichitta, (6) engaging bodhichitta, and (7) dedication. Remembering that these practices are the supreme offering, we should integrate them into our daily life.

We can make these seven offerings to our Spiritual Guide with the prayer from the sadhana:

I go for refuge to the Three Jewels
And confess individually all negative actions.
I rejoice in the virtues of all beings
And promise to accomplish a Buddha's enlightenment.

I go for refuge until I am enlightened
To Buddha, Dharma, and the Supreme Assembly,
And to accomplish the aims of myself and others
I shall generate the mind of enlightenment.

Having generated the mind of supreme
**   enlightenment,**
I shall invite all sentient beings to be my guests
And engage in the pleasing, supreme practices of
**   enlightenment.**
May I attain Buddhahood to benefit migrators.

These verses appear in many ritual sadhanas of both the lower and higher Tantras. The following explanation of the meaning of this prayer is given according to Highest Yoga Tantra. This prayer includes the essential practices necessary for making progress in our Mahayana training.

The meaning of the first two lines is that we need to purify our negativities by relying upon the Three Jewels. The third line indicates that we need to accumulate merit by rejoicing in all the special realizations and virtuous actions of Buddhas, Bodhisattvas, and other beings. With the fourth line we promise to accomplish the actual quick path to enlightenment, ultimate bodhichitta, the spontaneous great bliss that realizes emptiness directly, which is the very essence of Highest Yoga Tantra.

To engage successfully in the advanced practices for generating ultimate bodhichitta, meaning clear light, we first need to establish the firm foundation of the common paths. These are taught in the next two verses. The first two lines of the second verse, 'I go for refuge until I am enlightened to Buddha, Dharma, and the Supreme Assembly', reveal Mahayana refuge. The next two lines, 'And to accomplish the aims of myself and others I shall generate the mind of enlightenment', reveal aspiring bodhicitta. The third verse reveals engaging bodhichitta. To accomplish ultimate bodhichitta and great enlightenment we then need to engage in the meditations on generation stage and completion stage.

With the third verse we promise that, having generated and maintained bodhichitta, we shall engage in the pleasing, supreme practices of enlightenment – the practices of the six perfections; and that having completed this training we shall invite all living beings to our Buddha Land to enjoy the happiness of liberation. When we make this promise, we are generating engaging bodhichitta and we are taking the Bodhisattva vows. From this moment on, we should practise the six perfections sincerely and dedicate all our daily activities towards the happiness of others. The practice of dedication is revealed by the last line of the prayer. We then constantly pray every day with the following words from the sadhana:

May everyone be happy,
May everyone be free from misery,
May no one ever be separated from their happiness,
May everyone have equanimity, free from hatred and
attachment.

A detailed explanation of the remaining limbs of the seven-limbed prayer – confession, rejoicing, beseeching the Spiritual Guide not to pass away, requesting the turning of the Wheel of Dharma, and dedication – can be found in other books such as *Joyful Path of Good Fortune* and *Heart Jewel*.

OFFERING THE MANDALA

The practice of mandala offerings is very popular amongst practitioners of Mahayana Buddhism and is regarded as a very important practice. It is said that those who sincerely make mandala offerings will never experience poverty in this or future lives. Through her practice of making mandala offerings to Avalokiteshvara, the fully ordained nun Bhikshuni Palmo received a direct vision of the Buddha of Compassion. Through the practice of mandala offerings, Atisha received the blessings and a direct vision of Arya Tara, and Je Tsongkhapa received direct visions of all the enlightened beings in the Lamrim Field of Merit. After Je Tsongkhapa had passed away, Khädrubje, through his practice of making mandala offerings to Je Tsongkhapa, received a direct vision of him five times. These events demonstrate that the practice of mandala offerings is a powerful method for purifying our mind.

In *Guhyasamaja Tantra* Vajradhara says:

> Those who wish for attainments
> Should mentally and skilfully fill this universe
> With the seven precious objects.
> By offering them every day,
> Their wishes will be fulfilled.

This verse teaches the mandala offering. Although it explicitly mentions only seven points, implicitly it refers to the full thirty-seven-point mandala.

It is important for practitioners to obtain a traditional mandala set, which consists of a base, three rings, and a top jewel. The base and rings are used to support heaps of rice, or some other grain, which represent the various features of the mandala. Such simple things may seem useless to those who do not know their significance, but they can be very valuable in the hands of a practitioner who knows how to use them to accumulate a vast collection of merit.

To construct the thirty-seven-point mandala, we first take a little rice in our left hand and hold the mandala base with that hand. With our right hand we scoop up more rice and sprinkle a little onto the base. With the inside of our right wrist we rub the base three times clockwise, which symbolizes purification of the universal ground. As a result all rocky and uneven ground becomes smooth and level, and all

Luyipa

our delusions are purified. We then rub the base three times counter-clockwise and imagine that all the blessings of the body, speech, and mind of all the Buddhas gather into us. We think that the whole ground has been blessed and we recite the mantra for blessing the ground: OM VAJRA BHUMI AH HUM. We then sprinkle the rice that remains in our right hand onto the base and visualize that ground throughout the entire universe transforms into a pure golden ground.

While reciting OM VAJRA REKHE AH HUM we now put the largest ring on the base and, in a clockwise direction, pour a ring of rice inside it to symbolize the precious iron fence. We then place a heap of rice in the centre of the ring to symbolize Mount Meru, visualizing it as a huge mountain made of precious jewels. We then place another heap of rice in the east, the part of the mandala base nearest to us, to symbolize the eastern continent. Proceeding clockwise around the ring, we place heaps of rice in the three remaining cardinal directions to symbolize the southern, western, and northern continents.

We then place eight small heaps of rice to symbolize the eight sub-continents. Beginning with the eastern continent and proceeding in a clockwise direction, we place one heap a little to the left and one a little to the right of each continent.

We then place four small heaps of rice inside the eastern, southern, western, and northern continents to symbolize respectively the mountain of jewels, the wish-granting tree, the wish-granting cow, and the unsown harvest. We imagine that there are countless continents and sub-continents, each possessing their own special wealth of resources and riches.

We now put the second ring on top of the rice and place a heap of rice clockwise in each of the cardinal directions – east, south, west, and north – to symbolize respectively the precious wheel, the precious jewel, the precious queen, and the precious minister. We then place a heap of rice clockwise in each of the intermediate directions – south-east, south-west, north-west, and north-east – to symbolize respectively the precious elephant, the precious supreme horse, the precious general, and the great treasure vase. We imagine countless numbers of each of these filling all of space. Again we place heaps of rice clockwise in each of the four cardinal directions – east, south, west, and north – to symbolize the goddess of beauty, the goddess of garlands, the goddess of music, and the goddess of dance; and then clockwise in each of the four intermediate directions – south-east, south-west, north-west, and north-east – to symbolize the goddess of flowers, the goddess of incense, the goddess of light, and the goddess of scent. We imagine that there are countless offering gods and goddesses filling space.

We now put the third ring on top of the rice and place a heap of rice in the east for the sun, one in the west for the moon, one in the south for the precious umbrella, and one in the north for the banner of victory. We imagine that all of space is filled with innumerable precious objects.

As we place the top jewel, which is the last thing we place on the mandala, we imagine an abundance of other precious jewels and resources enjoyed by both humans and gods. In the space above Mount Meru are the environments of the desire realm gods and above these are the form realms. These god realms transform into Pure Lands and the enjoyments of the gods become pure enjoyments.

Having constructed the mandala, we take a little rice in our right hand and hold the base with both hands. We imagine that all the innumerable world systems and everything contained within them have completely transformed into Pure Lands and pure enjoyments. We imagine that all these are present on the base in our hands, and yet the base does not increase in size and the universe does not become smaller. Just as a mirror can reflect huge mountains, or a small television screen can show images of entire cities, so we imagine that the mandala in our hands contains the entire universe. We concentrate single-pointedly on these countless pure worlds, enjoyments, and beings, and with firm faith offer them all to our Gurus and the Buddhas.

While we construct this mandala, we recite the offering prayer from the sadhana. When we have recited the long mandala offering prayer we can continue, while still holding the base, to offer the twenty-three-point mandala. We do not need to construct a new mandala because the twenty-three precious objects are included among the precious objects of the thirty-seven-point mandala. The twenty-three precious objects are: Mount Meru, the four continents, the eight sub-continents, the seven precious objects (from the precious wheel up to the precious general), the treasure vase, the sun, and the moon.

To offer the twenty-three-point mandala, we recite the verse from the sadhana:

O Treasure of Compassion, my Refuge and Protector,
I offer you the mountain, continents, precious objects,
    treasure vase, sun and moon,
Which have arisen from my aggregates, sources, and
    elements
As aspects of the exalted wisdom of spontaneous
    bliss and emptiness.

With this verse we make outer, inner, secret, and thatness mandala offerings. We offer the outer mandala by visualizing the mountain, continents, precious objects, treasure vase, sun, and moon. We offer the inner mandala by mentally trans-forming our aggregates and elements into the form of the outer mandala. We offer the secret and thatness mandalas by imagining that our mind of indivisible bliss and emptiness transforms into the mandala. From the point of view of its having the nature of great bliss, the mandala is the secret mandala, and from the point of view of its being a manifes-tation of emptiness, it is the thatness mandala. If we wish to collect twenty-three-point mandalas as one of the great pre-liminary guides, we can construct them using the base, with or without the rings, and recite this verse.

Offering the mandala is the best method for freeing ourself from future poverty and for creating the cause of rebirth in a Buddha's Pure Land. By making mandala offerings we lessen our attachment to worldly enjoyments and posses-sions and accumulate a vast collection of merit. As a result we experience a gradual increase of our enjoyments, wealth, and good conditions. Our temporary wishes are fulfilled and finally we shall attain our ultimate goal, full enlightenment. If we wish to experience these benefits, we should familiarize ourself with the practice of offering the mandala.

Je Tsongkhapa was an enlightened being who did not need to accumulate merit, but to show a good example to other practitioners he offered a million mandalas during one of his long retreats in the south of central Tibet, in the cave called Ölga Chölung. For a base he used a flat stone, and through offering so many mandalas he rubbed the inside of his wrist until it was raw and bleeding.

If we are strongly attached to someone or something, we can imagine the object of our attachment on the mandala base, transform it into a pure object, and then offer it while praying, 'May I be free from all attachment.' In a similar way we can offer all the objects of our ignorance, anger, jealousy, pride, and so forth. While reciting the verse from the sadhana, we can offer all the objects of our delusions and pray to be free from those delusions.

To make mandala offerings as one of the great preliminary guides, we collect a hundred thousand mandala offerings. At the beginning of each session we offer a thirty-seven-point mandala, and we then collect seven-point mandalas. To construct and count seven-point mandala offerings we place a loosely threaded mala over the fingers of our left hand, take some rice in that hand, and then hold the mandala base with it. We then take some rice in our right hand and recite refuge and bodhichitta prayers while constructing the mandala. To do this we sprinkle a little rice on the base, and with the inside of the right wrist rub three times clockwise and three times counter-clockwise. We then place one heap of rice in the centre of the base, one in the east, one in the south, one in the west, and one in the north, to symbolize Mount Meru and the four continents. We then place a heap of rice in the east for the sun and one in the west for the moon. We then take a little rice in our right hand and hold the base with both hands while reciting the following mandala offering prayer:

The ground sprinkled with perfume and spread with flowers,
The Great Mountain, four lands, sun and moon,
Seen as a Buddha Land and offered thus,
May all beings enjoy such Pure Lands.

IDAM GURU RATNA MANDALAKAM NIRYATAYAMI

After reciting the prayer, we tip the rice towards us into a cloth on our lap. This is counted as one mandala offering and so we move one bead along the mala. We make as many mandala offerings as we wish during each session. At the end of the session, we make a long mandala offering of thirty-seven points and then dedicate our merit.

RECEIVING THE BLESSINGS OF THE FOUR EMPOWERMENTS

By receiving the blessings of the four empowerments every day, we can purify our broken Tantric vows and commitments and maintain the special blessings that we received directly from our root Guru when he or she granted the empowerment. Through this, our meditation on generation stage and completion stage will progress successfully.

We first make requests to Guru Heruka to bestow the blessings of the four empowerments by reciting three times the verse from the sadhana:

O Guru Heruka, the nature of the Truth Body,
I seek no refuge other than you.
Please purify all negativities of my three doors,
And bless me to attain the four bodies of great bliss.

The ultimate blessings of the four empowerments are the attainment of the four bodies of a Buddha: the two Form Bodies, the Emanation Body and Enjoyment Body; and the two Truth Bodies, the Nature Body and Wisdom Truth Body. These attainments depend upon progress in generation stage and completion stage meditations, which in turn depends upon receiving and maintaining the special blessings of the four empowerments.

Receiving the blessings of the four empowerments has four parts:

1 Receiving the vase empowerment
2 Receiving the secret empowerment
3 Receiving the wisdom-mudra empowerment
4 Receiving the precious word empowerment

RECEIVING THE VASE EMPOWERMENT

We imagine that due to our request Guru Heruka emanates from his heart Vajravarahi and the four Yoginis, who hold precious vases filled with wisdom nectar. They grant us the vase empowerment by pouring the nectar through our crown. Our body is filled with wisdom nectar, and this purifies all the defilements and obstructions of our body. We imagine that we experience great bliss, and thus we receive the blessings of the vase empowerment.

If we experience even a slight feeling of bliss through imagining the wisdom nectars pouring from the precious vases through our crown, this bliss is the actual vase empowerment. This empowerment causes us to accomplish the realizations of generation stage and the Emanation Body of a Buddha. It is called the 'vase empowerment' because it is granted by using a vase.

RECEIVING THE SECRET EMPOWERMENT

We imagine that as Guru Heruka Father and Mother engage in union, all the Heroes, the male Tantric Buddhas, enter Heruka's body through his mouth and melt into his white bodhichitta, the white drops; and all the Heroines, the female Tantric Buddhas, enter Vajravarahi's body through her mouth and melt into her red bodhichitta, the red drops. These white and red drops unite at the tip of Guru Heruka's sex organ, and Guru Heruka then places them on our tongue. Through tasting this secret substance, which is the nature of all the Heroes and Heroines, all the defilements and obstructions of our speech are purified. In particular, our channels, drops, and inner winds are purified. We imagine that we experience great bliss, and thus we receive the blessings of the secret empowerment.

If we experience even a slight feeling of bliss through imagining that we taste the white and red bodhichittas of Guru Heruka Father and Mother, this bliss is the actual secret empowerment. This empowerment causes us to accomplish the completion stage realization of illusory body, called the 'realization of conventional truth', and the Enjoyment Body of a Buddha. It is called the 'secret empowerment' because it is granted by using a secret substance.

RECEIVING THE WISDOM-MUDRA EMPOWERMENT

We imagine that a knowledge woman, who is an emanation of Vajravarahi, appears in front of us. Guru Heruka introduces her to us, saying:

This is a supremely qualified knowledge consort for you. By relying upon her, you should accomplish the Union of Buddha for the benefit of all living beings.

We promise to do this, and the emanation woman is delighted. We recall that no phenomenon exists from its own side and, by concentrating on this firm knowledge, we dissolve all our ordinary appearances into emptiness. From the state of emptiness we generate ourself as Heruka with a blue-coloured body, four faces, and twelve arms, embracing our consort Vajravarahi, who has a red-coloured body, one face, and two arms; and we engage in union. Through this, our bodhichitta melts. As it descends from our crown to our throat we experience joy, as it descends from our throat to our heart we experience supreme joy, as it descends from our heart to our navel we experience extraordinary joy, and as it descends from our navel to the tip of our sex organ we imagine that we are experiencing spontaneous great bliss inseparable from emptiness. At this point we have received the blessings of the wisdom-mudra empowerment.

If we experience any of the four joys through concentrating in the way described above, this is the actual wisdom-mudra empowerment. This empowerment purifies all the defilements and obstructions of our mind and causes us to accomplish the completion stage realization of meaning clear light, called the 'realization of ultimate truth', and the Truth Body of a Buddha. It is called the 'wisdom-mudra empowerment' because it is granted by our Guru giving us a wisdom mudra. In this context the term 'mudra' means Tantric consort. A wisdom mudra is a Tantric consort who is a manifestation of omniscient wisdom, whereas a knowledge woman (Tib. rigma) is a woman who is a Tantric consort.

RECEIVING THE PRECIOUS WORD EMPOWERMENT

In this empowerment, Guru Heruka gives us a special instruction on what the Union of No More Learning is and how to attain it. We imagine that we hear the following words directly:

When you received the third empowerment, the wisdom-mudra empowerment, you generated your body as Heruka's body. This is an imagined divine body. You also generated your mind as Heruka's mind, an imagined Deity mind. Finally, through continual practice of this meditation you will attain the actual body and mind of Heruka, the resultant union of the illusory body and the mind of great bliss and emptiness of a Buddha. This is the Union of No More Learning, the final goal.

Through hearing these words, we imagine that we experience great bliss, and through this we receive the blessings of the precious word empowerment.

If we experience a feeling of joy through imagining that we hear Guru Heruka's words, this is the actual word empowerment. This empowerment purifies all the defilements and obstructions of our body, speech, and mind together, and causes us to accomplish the union of Buddha Vajradhara's body and mind. It is called the 'word empowerment' because it is granted by instructions in the form of words.

REQUESTING THE LINEAGE GURUS

In the auspicious prayers in the sadhana, it says:

May there be the auspiciousness of a great treasury of blessings
Arising from the excellent deeds of all the root and lineage Gurus,

Who have accomplished the supreme attainment of
  Buddha Heruka
By relying upon the excellent, secret path of the King
  of Tantras.

As mentioned above, this prayer reveals that all the lineage
Gurus of these instructions, from Ghantapa up to Kyabje Trijang Dorjechang Losang Yeshe Rinpoche, are actual examples
of practitioners who have attained the Union of Buddha Heruka through the practice of Heruka body mandala. We now
rejoice deeply in their lives and accomplishments, and make
a strong determination to follow their example. With strong
faith we recite the request prayers from the sadhana, in particular requesting the lineage Gurus to bestow their blessings
so that we too can attain the Union of Buddha Heruka's holy
body and mind, and thereby benefit all living beings without
exception.

ACCOMPLISHING SPONTANEOUS GREAT BLISS BY DISSOLVING THE GURU INTO OURSELF

As a result of our sincere requests, we imagine that all the
other holy beings in the Field of Merit melt into light, gather
from the edges, and dissolve into our root Guru Heruka, the
Principal of the Field of Merit. Out of affection for us, our
root Guru develops the wish to unite with us, and from our
side too we strongly wish for this to happen. Then we imagine
that Guru Heruka becomes smaller from below and above,
diminishes to the size of a thumb, enters our crown, and
descends through our central channel to our heart, where he
mixes inseparably with our root mind. Since the essence of
Guru Heruka is the wisdom of spontaneous great bliss, we
think, 'Through mixing my root mind with Guru Heruka, my
mind transforms into spontaneous great bliss.' We meditate
single-pointedly on this experience of spontaneous great bliss
for as long as possible.

Darikapa

Bringing the Three Bodies into the Path

THE ACTUAL PRACTICE OF GENERATION STAGE

This has six parts:

1 What is generation stage?
2 Bringing the three bodies into the path
3 Checking meditation on the mandala and basis Heruka
4 Generating the mandala and Deities of the body mandala
5 Adorning our body with the armour Deities, inviting and absorbing the wisdom beings, and making offerings
6 The actual generation stage meditation

WHAT IS GENERATION STAGE?

Generation stage is defined as a realization of a creative yoga that purifies the three basic bodies and causes the three bodies of the path to ripen. It is called a 'creative yoga' because its object is generated, or created, by a mind of pure concentration. For example, when we perform self-generation as Heruka, there appears to our mind a form of Heruka with a blue-coloured body, four faces, and twelve arms; and this object is generated by our mind through the force of correct imagination. However, even though it is generated by mind, it exists. If we continue with this meditation, our mind will become more and more familiar with the object, and eventually we shall attain the actual body of Heruka; but if we do not first create it with our mind we shall never accomplish the actual body of Heruka in the future. In the same way that an artist begins with a rough outline of a picture and then continues painting until the picture is completed, so our generation stage meditation can be likened to an artist drawing a rough outline of a picture, and our completion stage meditation to the artist completing the picture.

When through the force of generation stage meditation the form of Heruka appears to our mind, this is an actual form. It is a form that is a phenomena source, a form that appears only to mental awareness. Later, when our concentrations of generation and completion stages are completed, we shall attain the actual form of Heruka, which we can see with our eye awareness. What was previously a form that is a phenomena source will now have become a form that is a form source, an actual object of eye awareness.

It is not only in Tantra that Buddha teaches how to generate objects with our mind that later become objects of the senses. In the *Vinaya Sutras* he says that monks who wish to overcome desirous attachment should visualize the ground covered with skeletons and see all things as impure. Some monks who practised this meditation sincerely saw skeletons directly with their eyes and impure things wherever they looked, and as a result they developed the strong wish to escape from samsara. We cannot say that their minds were wrong awarenesses, because the skeletons they saw were generated by pure concentration. To begin with, the skeletons were forms that are phenomena sources, but for the monks they later became actual form sources. In a similar way, people we dislike appear to us as unattractive but, if we later change our mind about them and come to like them, their appearance will also change and they will now appear to us as attractive. Only our mind has changed, but due to our mind changing the forms that appear to it also change. This shows how everything depends upon the mind. By contemplating these points we can understand what is meant by calling generation stage a 'creative yoga', and we can see how it is possible to generate ourself as Heruka through the power of pure concentration.

The definition also indicates that generation stage purifies the three basic bodies and causes the three bodies of the path to ripen. The three basic bodies are ordinary death, ordinary intermediate state (Tib. bardo), and ordinary rebirth. Ordinary death is known as the 'basic truth body'. It is not the actual Truth Body but is the basis for attaining the actual Truth Body because it is the basis for the practice of bringing death into the path of the Truth Body. Similarly, ordinary intermediate state is called the 'basic enjoyment body' because it is the basis for attaining the actual Enjoyment Body through the practice of bringing the intermediate state into the path; and ordinary rebirth is called the 'basic emanation body' because it is the basis for attaining the actual Emanation Body through the practice of bringing rebirth into the path. These three basic bodies are the bases to be purified. They are purified indirectly by the yogas of generation stage and directly by the yogas of completion stage.

For as long as we do not purify our ordinary death, intermediate state, and rebirth, we shall remain in samsara and there will be no possibility of our attaining Buddhahood. Up to now we have experienced these three states one after the other without interruption, like the turning of a wheel; and because of this we are trapped in samsara experiencing continuous suffering and problems. If we purify ordinary birth, death, and intermediate state, there will be no basis for us to experience suffering – we shall have attained liberation.

Even in the Sutras it says that we need to cut the continuum of birth, death, and intermediate state. What will happen if we cut the continuum of ordinary birth? Will we disappear and become like empty space? This is impossible. Even if we cut the continuum of ordinary rebirth, the continuum of our mind will remain; but instead of being thrown into a samsaric rebirth through the force of karma and delusion, we shall take rebirth through choice, either in a Pure Land or, out of compassion, in the human realm. It is the suffering of uncontrolled birth and death that will cease.

How do we purify ordinary death, intermediate state, and rebirth? Ordinary death is purified directly by the completion stage realization of ultimate example clear light; ordinary intermediate state is purified directly by the completion stage realization of illusory body; and ordinary rebirth is purified directly by the completion stage yoga of the gross Deity body attained after the realization of illusory body.

The clear light of completion stage is known as the 'path truth body', the illusory body of completion stage is known as the 'path enjoyment body', and the completion stage yoga of the gross Deity body is known as the 'path emanation body'. We cause these three path bodies to ripen by practising the three bringings of generation stage. The generation stage yoga of bringing ordinary death into the path of the Truth Body causes the completion stage realization of clear light to ripen; the generation stage yoga of bringing ordinary intermediate state into the path of the Enjoyment Body causes the completion stage realization of illusory body to ripen; and the generation stage yoga of bringing ordinary rebirth into the path of the Emanation Body causes the completion stage realization of the gross Deity body to ripen. The final result of purifying the three basic bodies by means of the three path bodies is the attainment of the three resultant bodies – the actual Truth Body, Enjoyment Body, and Emanation Body of a Buddha.

The Emanation Body is the gross body of a Buddha, the Enjoyment Body is the subtle body of a Buddha, and the Truth Body is the very subtle body of a Buddha. The Heruka that is imputed upon his gross body is called 'Emanation Body Heruka', the Heruka that is imputed upon his subtle body is called 'Enjoyment Body Heruka', and the Heruka that is imputed upon his very subtle body is called 'Truth Body Heruka'. The very subtle body of a Buddha, Truth Body, and Dharmakaya are synonymous.

BRINGING THE THREE BODIES INTO THE PATH

This has three parts:

1 Bringing death into the path of the Truth Body
2 Bringing the intermediate state into the path of the Enjoyment Body
3 Bringing rebirth into the path of the Emanation Body

BRINGING DEATH INTO THE PATH OF THE TRUTH BODY

Bringing death into the path of the Truth Body is a yoga, similar in aspect to the experience of death, that has the divine pride of being the Truth Body. We begin this practice by absorbing all external environments and their inhabitants. This helps us to overcome ordinary appearances and conceptions, and causes dualistic appearances to subside into emptiness. It also creates the cause for the inner winds to gather into the central channel, thereby laying the foundation for us to attain the clear light of the Truth Body.

Previously we dissolved Guru Heruka into our root mind at our heart and transformed our root mind into spontaneous great bliss. We now think that our root mind of great bliss is appearing in the form of a blue letter HUM at our heart, and we imagine that this letter HUM radiates powerful rays of light that reach all worlds and their beings. Everything melts into light, which gradually gathers back and dissolves into our body. We feel that all worlds and their beings have dissolved into us.

At this point we imagine that we experience the first of the eight signs that arise at the time of death, the mirage-like appearance. This sign arises due to the dissolution of the inner wind supporting our earth element. We meditate on this experience for a while, and then we imagine that our body gradually dissolves from below and above into the letter HUM at our heart. We think that nothing remains apart from the letter HUM, and we imagine that we perceive the smoke-like appearance that arises due to the dissolution of the inner wind supporting our water element. After meditating on this for a while, we imagine that the 'shabkyu' at the bottom of the letter HUM gradually dissolves upwards into the main letter HA, and that we perceive the sparkling-fireflies-like appearance that arises due to the dissolution of the inner wind supporting our fire element. After meditating on this for a while, we imagine that the main body of the letter HA gradually dissolves upwards into the horizontal line at its head, and that we perceive the candle-flame-like appearance that arises due to the inner wind supporting our wind element beginning to dissolve. After meditating on this for a while, we imagine that the horizontal line gradually dissolves upwards into the crescent moon, and that we experience the mind of white appearance that arises due to the complete dissolution of the inner wind supporting our wind element. After meditating on this for a while, we imagine that the crescent moon gradually dissolves upwards into the drop, and that we experience the mind of red increase that arises due to the dissolution of the inner wind supporting the mind of white appearance. After meditating on this for a while, we imagine that the drop gradually dissolves upwards into the nada, and that we experience the mind of black near-attainment that arises due to the dissolution of the inner wind supporting the mind of red increase. At this point we should feel that nothing exists apart from the nada. Then the nada itself gradually dissolves from the bottom upwards, the lower curve dissolving into the middle curve, the middle curve dissolving into the upper curve, and finally the upper curve dissolving into clear light emptiness. We imagine that we experience the eighth sign, the mind of clear light that arises due to the dissolution of the inner wind supporting the mind of black near-attainment.

At this stage, while we are meditating on the emptiness of all phenomena, one part of our mind should be contemplating four points: (1) we imagine that our mind is experiencing great bliss; (2) this mind of great bliss is mixed inseparably with emptiness; (3) this union of great bliss and emptiness is the Truth Body, the basis for imputing Heruka's I; and (4) on this basis we strongly think 'I am Truth Body Heruka.'

Principally we meditate on emptiness, but without forgetting these four points. Sometimes, without forgetting emptiness, we can emphasize meditation on the experience of great bliss, or we can emphasize meditation on the Truth Body, or meditation on the divine pride that thinks 'I am Truth Body Heruka.' We emphasize one point but we do so without forgetting the other three. Through this meditation we can transform our experience of death into the experience of the clear light of great bliss, the quick path of the Truth Body of a

Buddha. For this reason, this meditation is called 'bringing death into the path of the Truth Body'. This meditation is very powerful and performs the following functions: (1) it helps to overcome ordinary appearances and conceptions; (2) it causes dualistic appearances to subside into emptiness; (3) it indirectly purifies ordinary death; (4) it causes the completion stage realization of clear light to ripen; (5) it is a collection of wisdom; and (6) it sows in our mind a powerful potential to attain the actual Truth Body of a Buddha in the future.

Khädrubje said that even if we do not complete our training in generation stage and completion stage before we die, if we have experience of the meditation on bringing death into the path of the Truth Body of Heruka we shall be able to remember it when we die and, as a result, our consciousness will be transferred to Heruka's Pure Land. For sincere practitioners this meditation is the real transference of consciousness; they do not need to practise other types of transference.

Many practitioners have strong ordinary appearances and conceptions because they lack experience of emptiness, and due to this they experience great difficulties in their practice of Highest Yoga Tantra. If we do not understand emptiness, we should study qualified books such as *Heart of Wisdom* and *Ocean of Nectar* and listen to instructions from qualified Teachers. Without realizing emptiness there is no basis for authentic meditation on bringing death into the path of the Truth Body, and so it is not possible for us to cut the continuum of samsaric sufferings.

BRINGING THE INTERMEDIATE STATE INTO THE PATH OF THE ENJOYMENT BODY

Bringing the intermediate state into the path of the Enjoyment Body is a yoga, similar in aspect to the experience of the intermediate state, that is attained after bringing death into the path of the Truth Body, and that has the divine pride of being the Enjoyment Body.

After meditating for a while on the divine pride that thinks, 'I am Truth Body Heruka', one part of our mind should think:

*If I remain in this state, living beings will not be able to see
me and so I shall not be able to help them directly. Therefore,
I will arise in a Form Body for the benefit of all living beings.*

For ordinary beings the dream body arises out of the clear
light of sleep, and the intermediate state body arises out of
the clear light of death. For completion stage practitioners
the illusory body arises out of the realization of the mind of
clear light; and for Buddhas the Enjoyment Body arises out
of the clear light of the Truth Body. Therefore, at this stage
in the meditation we imagine that we arise out of the clear
light of the Truth Body as Enjoyment Body Heruka.

The Enjoyment Body can take many different forms. For
the purposes of this meditation we imagine that it arises in
the form of a tiny nada suspended in space. The nada is
white with a reddish tint. It has three curves, and its upper
tip is extremely fine. The three curves of the nada represent
the body, speech, and mind of the intermediate state being.
In this meditation it is not necessary to focus on the aspect
of the nada; rather we should emphasize developing divine
pride, thinking: 'I have purified the body, speech, and mind
of the intermediate state. Now I am Enjoyment Body Heruka.'
We meditate on this experience for a while. Through this meditation we can transform our experience of the intermediate
state into the experience of the illusory body, the quick path
of the Enjoyment Body of a Buddha. For this reason this meditation is called 'bringing the intermediate state into the path
of the Enjoyment Body'. It indirectly purifies ordinary intermediate state, causes the completion stage realization of illusory body to ripen, and sows in our mind a powerful potential
to attain the actual Enjoyment Body of a Buddha in the future.

BRINGING REBIRTH INTO THE PATH OF THE EMANATION BODY

Bringing rebirth into the path of the Emanation Body is a
yoga, similar in aspect to the experience of rebirth, that is
attained after bringing the intermediate state into the path of
the Enjoyment Body, and that has the divine pride of being
the Emanation Body.

While in the aspect of the nada in space, we should think:

Although I have arisen in a Form Body, the Enjoyment Body, only highly realized beings can see it. If I am going to benefit ordinary beings directly, I also need a gross Form Body. Therefore, I will take rebirth as an Emanation Body Heruka.

With this motivation we look down through space and see the place where we shall take rebirth. First we observe the protection circle, which consists of the vajra ground, fence, tent, and canopy. These are composed entirely of indestructible five-pronged vajras, the nature of Heruka's exalted wisdom. The vajra ground is vast, and is surrounded by the vajra fence, which is square in shape, also vast, and very high. On top of the vajra fence is the vajra canopy, which serves as a ceiling. Above this is the vajra tent, which is shaped like a Mongolian tent.

The vajras in the east are dark blue, in the north green, in the west red, and in the south yellow. They are joined together with no intervening space, like the shell of an egg, so that nothing can penetrate them. Around the outside – above, below, and all around – powerful fires of the five wisdoms, white, yellow, red, green, and blue in colour, swirl counterclockwise. Everything is the nature of the indivisible bliss and emptiness of Heruka. Our mind, the nada, observes the protection circle, regarding it as the Pure Land of Heruka in which we shall take rebirth.

Upon the vajra ground from a letter YAM comes a blue bow-shaped wind mandala; upon this from a letter RAM comes a red triangular fire mandala; upon this from a letter BAM comes a white circular water mandala; and upon this from a letter LAM comes a yellow square earth mandala. The wind mandala covers the entire vajra ground, the fire mandala fits within the bow of the wind mandala, the water mandala fits within the triangle of the fire mandala, and the earth mandala fits within the circle of the water mandala. We visualize the earth mandala as vast because it is the earth upon which stands Heruka's mandala. All four elements are the nature of Heruka's omniscient wisdom.

On top of the earth mandala from a letter SUM comes Mount Meru, which is square in shape, made of jewels, and extremely high. The eastern side is white, the northern yellow, the western red, and the southern blue. When Buddha first emanated the mandala of Heruka, he did so on top of Mount Meru, which is why we visualize the mandala on top of Mount Meru.

On top of Mount Meru from a letter PAM comes a sixty-four-petalled lotus, which covers the entire surface of the mountain. The petals in the east are white, in the north green, in the west red, and in the south yellow. Upon the centre of this lotus is a huge crossed five-pronged vajra. The central part of the vajra is blue, square in shape, and forms the vast floor of the mandala. The five prongs in the east are white, in the north green, in the west red, and in the south yellow. The centre of the vajra is completely covered by an eight-petalled lotus. The petals in the four cardinal directions are red, the petals in the south-east and north-west are yellow, the petal in the south-west is green, and the petal in the north-east is black. In the centre of the lotus is a moon mandala, white with a reddish tint, which has arisen from the Sanskrit vowels and consonants. We, in the aspect of the nada in space, observe these developments below us.

The protection circle, the four elements, Mount Meru, and the sixty-four-petalled lotus symbolize the place where we shall take rebirth as an Emanation Body. The vajra symbolizes the mother's body, and the eight-petalled lotus her womb. The white moon with a reddish tint symbolizes the union of the father's sperm and the mother's ovum. Its nature is wisdom but its substance is the white drops of Father Heruka and the red drops of Mother Vajravarahi. The white part of the moon is Heruka's mirror-like wisdom, and the red part is his wisdom of equality.

With the motivation to benefit all living beings, we, the nada in space, develop a strong wish to be reborn inside this union of Father Heruka's sperm and Mother Vajravarahi's ovum. Through the power of this motivation, we descend through space to the point just above the moon. Then, gradually, a drop develops from the nada, a crescent moon from the drop, a horizontal line from the crescent moon, a letter HA from the horizontal line, and a shabkyu from the letter HA. In this way a letter HUM develops in the centre of the moon. It is white with a reddish tint, and is the size of a man.

The nada descending to the centre of the moon symbolizes conception in the mother's womb, and the development of the HUM symbolizes the development of the baby inside the womb. The HUM is the nature of Heruka's wisdom of individual realization. We now think that we are just about to be born.

We visualize five-coloured lights radiating from the letter HUM in all directions, filling the whole of space. At the tips of the light rays are Deities of Heruka's mandala, who come to the crowns of all living beings and grant them empowerment, completely purifying their two obstructions. They all attain the state of Heruka, and their environments transform into Heruka's Pure Land. Then all these beings and their environments melt into light. At the same time, all the Heroes and Heroines are invited from all the Buddha Lands throughout the ten directions. They melt into red and white bodhichittas, and mix with the beings who have melted into light. This light gathers inwards until it dissolves into the nada of the HUM. As a result our mind, in the aspect of this HUM, becomes the nature of spontaneous great bliss. All worlds and their beings, and all Buddhas in the form of Heroes and Heroines, have dissolved into this HUM. This is Heruka's wisdom of accomplishing activities.

Now the moon, vowels, consonants, and HUM transform into the supporting mandala and supported Deities of Heruka, which appear fully and simultaneously. We imagine that we can see everything – the protection circle, the mandala, and all the Deities – perfectly clearly, and we think, 'Now I have been born as Emanation Body Heruka', and meditate on this feeling for a while. The protection circle, mandala, and Deities, appearing fully and simultaneously, are Heruka's wisdom of the Dharmadhatu. Although they appear as forms, in reality they are the nature of Heruka's omniscient wisdom.

Through this meditation we can transform our experience of rebirth into the experience of the gross Deity body, which is the quick path of the Emanation Body of a Buddha. For this reason it is called 'bringing rebirth into the path of the Emanation Body'. It indirectly purifies ordinary rebirth, causes the completion stage realization of the gross Deity body to ripen, and sows in our mind a powerful potential to attain the actual Emanation Body of a Buddha in the future. It is also the principal method for attaining rebirth in Keajra, Heruka's Pure Land.

Checking Meditation on the Mandala and Basis Heruka

Checking meditation on the mandala and basis Heruka has two parts:

1 Checking meditation
2 The symbolism of Heruka's body

CHECKING MEDITATION

To familiarize ourself with our new environment and new identity, we now do analytical meditation on the mandala and on ourself as basis Heruka. At the very edge of our new world, surrounding the protection circle, are the eight great charnel grounds. These are very similar to those described in *Guide to Dakini Land* except that in Vajrayogini practice they are inside the protection circle whereas in Heruka practice they are outside.

In each charnel ground there is a tree, at the foot of which there sits a directional guardian. Each directional guardian has four arms. With their first two hands they embrace their consort, and with their second two hands they hold aloft various objects and a skullcup. They each sit on a different mount and wear a silken scarf. Except for the guardians in the south and south-west, who wear a crown of three skulls, they all wear a golden five-lineage crown. At the top of each tree there is a regional guardian with the upper half of his body emerging from the branches. They each have the same face as the mounts of the directional guardians at the foot of their tree, and they hold a torma and a skullcup.

In each charnel ground there is a lake, in which there lives a naga holding a jewel. The nagas have half-human, half-serpent

Dingkiwa

bodies, with a canopy of snakes behind their head. They are of different colours, wear silken garments, and are adorned with jewelled ornaments. Above each lake there is a cloud. There is a mountain, at the summit of which there is a white stupa, and at the foot of which a wisdom fire blazes.

Throughout the charnel grounds are corpses in varying states of decay. Some are lying down, some standing up, some walking, and some crouching. Some are headless, some being eaten by animals, some impaled on stakes, some hanging by their hair from trees, and some half-consumed by fire. Wild birds and animals such as ravens, owls, vultures, wolves, jackals, and snakes inhabit the charnel grounds. Spirits, such as yellow givers of harm in tiger skins holding clubs, zombies, and terrifying naked cannibals, wander around uttering the sound 'Kili Kili'. Tantric practitioners such as Siddhas, Knowledge Holders, Yogis, and Yoginis also abide in the charnel grounds, keeping their commitments purely and single-pointedly practising Heruka's path. They are naked, with freely hanging hair, and are adorned with five mudras. They hold hand-drums, skullcups, and khatangas, and their crowns are adorned with skulls.

The eight directional guardians are: Indra, Vaishravana, Varuna, Yama, Agni, Kardava, Vayuni, and Ishvara. In addition to these there are two other directional guardians – Brahma, who protects the upper regions, and Bhumi, who protects the lower regions. We can sometimes include another five directional guardians – Surya, Chandra, Bhadra, Ganesh, and Vishnu – making fifteen in all. All fifteen directional guardians residing in the charnel grounds are emanations of Heruka appearing in mundane aspects; and whenever we offer the torma to the mundane Dakas and Dakinis we invite these guardians together with their retinues from the eight charnel grounds to receive it. All the beings abiding in the charnel grounds face the central Deity and instil the place with a sense of wonder.

The charnel grounds have great meaning. They are the nature of Heruka's omniscient wisdom, and all their features are emanated by Heruka to teach us how to practise the stages of the path of Sutra and Tantra. The corpses symbolize impermanence and the faults of samsara, particularly sickness, ageing, and death. The lake symbolizes conventional bodhichitta, the naga the six perfections and the ten perfections, and the jewel held by the naga the four ways of gathering disciples. Because corpses are ownerless they also symbolize selflessness. These features remind us to practise renunciation, bodhichitta, profound view, and the six perfections.

The wild animals symbolize generation stage realizations, and their eating the corpses teaches us to destroy our ordinary appearances and ordinary conceptions through the power of our generation stage practice.

The tree symbolizes the central channel, which is the basic object of completion stage meditation. The directional guardian at the foot of the tree symbolizes the downward-voiding wind just below the navel, and the regional guardian at the top of the tree symbolizes the life-supporting wind at the heart. The fire at the base of the mountain symbolizes the inner fire of tummo at the navel, and the cloud symbolizes the white bodhichittas in the crown chakra. The eight charnel grounds themselves, four in the cardinal directions and four in the intermediate directions, symbolize the four joys of serial and reverse order. The mountain symbolizes the immovable equipoise of spontaneous great bliss mixed with emptiness, and the stupa at the top of the mountain symbolizes the three bodies of a Buddha.

Completion stage meditation on tummo, or inner fire, causes the downward-voiding wind below our navel to reverse and flow up through the central channel, which in turn causes all our inner winds to gather into the central channel and dissolve into the life-supporting wind at our heart. This causes the white bodhichitta in our crown chakra to melt and descend through our central channel, giving rise to the four joys of serial and reverse order. The final joy, the mind of spontaneous great bliss, then mixes inseparably with emptiness and gradually abandons the two obstructions. When our mind is completely purified in this way, we attain the three resultant bodies of a Buddha – the Truth Body, Enjoyment Body, and Emanation Body. Thus, these aspects of the charnel grounds teach us how to attain full enlightenment by training in the yogas of completion stage. Milarepa once said, 'I have no need of books because everything around me teaches me Dharma.' In the same way, through simply contemplating the features of the charnel grounds, sincere Heruka practitioners develop a deep understanding of the phenomena of the basis, path, and result, and strong enthusiasm for practising the stages of the path of Sutra and Tantra.

Inside the circle of eight great charnel grounds is the protection circle of the vajra ground, fence, tent, and canopy, surrounded by five-coloured wisdom fires swirling counterclockwise. In the centre of these are the four elements, Mount Meru, the lotus, and the crossed vajra, all of which have been described previously.

Standing on the centre of the huge crossed vajra is the celestial mansion, which is constructed like a large square house with an elaborate entrance on each side. It is approached from the four directions by stairways that lead up through the prongs of the vajra to its ground floor. The jewelled walls have five layers, which from the outside in are coloured white, yellow, red, green, and blue. Around the top of the wall and overhanging it is a red jewelled moulding studded with rectangular, triangular, circular, and half-moon-shaped jewels. Upon this are four layers of golden bands, each separated by a series of supports made from six precious substances. Upon these, and extending beyond, are parallel rafters whose ends form the shape of sea-monsters, with full-length and half-length strings of pearls hanging from their mouths. Overhanging these are 'sharpu', special jewelled decorations, suspended from the eaves. Around the edge of the roof runs a white parapet in the shape of half lotus petals. This is adorned with eight victory banners embellished with beautiful creatures, and eight other banners, all set in golden vases. At all four corners of the roof monkeys sit on the parapet, holding parasols adorned at the top with a jewel, crescent moon, and blue half-vajra.

Around the outer foot of the wall runs a red ledge upon which stand sixteen offering goddesses of various colours and postures, each with three eyes and four arms. Each of the four entrances has an open porch leading into a short hallway, with a high double door leading into the main chamber. At the outer corners of the doorways and hallways, as well as at the four outer and four inner corners of the mansion, stand half-moons, upon which rest red jewels adorned at the top by vajras.

At the front of each entrance, upon square pedestals, four pillars set in vases support an eleven-tiered archway. Above each archway is a Dharma Wheel flanked right and left by a male and a female deer. Each archway is adorned with both types of banner, and with monkeys holding parasols. The eastern archway is decorated with white Dharma Wheels, the southern archway with yellow jewels, the western archway with red lotuses, and the northern archway with green swords. To the right and left of each archway, set in golden vases, are wish-granting trees bearing the seven precious possessions of a king. In the space around the celestial mansion are Siddhas, two on each side; and emerging from clouds are offering gods and goddesses holding garlands of flowers, making everything exquisitely beautiful.

Inside the celestial mansion are four concentric rings of eight pillars, which support the circular vajra beams underneath a four-stepped ceiling. On the very top of the mansion is a square lantern adorned with a golden roof and surmounted by an eight-faceted jewel and a five-pronged vajra. Inside this is a precious jewelled case containing the scriptures of the Heruka root Tantra.

The ceiling and floor of the mansion are white in the east, green in the north, red in the west, yellow in the south, and blue in the centre. On the floor is a four-tiered circular platform, each tier smaller than the one below it. Each of the three lower platforms is in the shape of a large wheel with eight petal-shaped spokes. On the lowest platform are the sixteen Deities of the body wheel, on the second platform are the sixteen Deities of the speech wheel, and on the third platform are the sixteen Deities of the heart wheel.

At the four inner corners of the mansion, and at the door-ways to each hallway, stand the eight Deities of the commitment wheel. In the very centre of the top platform is an eight-petalled lotus of various colours. Upon the petals in the cardinal directions stand the four Yoginis of the great bliss wheel, and upon the petals in the intermediate directions are skullcups brimming with five nectars. At the very centre of the lotus, standing on a sun mandala, we appear as the Blessed One Heruka, with a dark-blue body and four faces. We contemplate as follows:

My principal face is dark blue, the left face green, the back face red, and the right face yellow. Each face has three eyes and a rosary of five-pronged vajras on its forehead. My right leg is outstretched and treads on the head of black Bhairawa, who has four hands. His first two hands are pressed together, the second right hand holds a damaru, and the second left a sword. My bent left leg treads on the breast of red Kalarati, who has four hands. Her first two hands are pressed together, and the other two hold a skullcup and a khatanga. Both the beings beneath my feet have one face and three eyes, and are adorned with five mudras.

I have twelve arms. The first two embrace Vajravarahi, with my right hand holding a five-pronged vajra and my left hand a bell. The next two hands hold a bloody, white elephant skin stretched across my back; my right hand holds the left foreleg, and my left the left hind leg. Both these hands are in the threatening mudra with the tips of the outstretched fingers at the level of my eyebrows. My third right hand holds a damaru, the fourth an axe, the fifth a curved knife, and the sixth an upright three-pointed spear. My third left hand holds a khatanga marked with a vajra, the fourth a skullcup brimming with blood, the fifth a vajra noose, and the sixth a four-faced head of Brahma.

My hair is tied up in a topknot marked with a small crossed vajra of various colours. Each head is adorned with a crown of five human skulls strung together top and bottom with a rosary of black vajras. On the left side of my crown is a half moon, slightly tilted. My facial expressions change, and my four sets of four fangs are bared and terrifying. I display nine moods. The three physical moods of majesty, heroism, and menace are expressed by my body maintaining an air of majesty, my feet treading on Bhairawa and Kalarati, and the frown at the centre of my brow. The three verbal moods of laughter, wrath, and ferocity are expressed by the slight smile on my lips, my bared fangs, and my tongue curled back. The three mental moods of compassion, attentiveness, and serenity are expressed by my long almond-shaped eyes, my wide-open eyes, and my looking at the Mother from the corner of my eyes.

I wear a lower garment of a tiger skin, and a long necklace of fifty shrunken moist human heads strung together with human entrails. I am adorned with six bone ornaments: a crown ornament, ear ornaments, a necklace, bracelets and anklets, a heart ornament, and ashes of human bone smeared over my entire body. My hair is woven through the eight spokes of the crown ornament and gathered into a topknot which is surmounted by a nine-faceted jewel. The necklace, bracelets, and anklets are made of fragments of human bone embossed with vajras. I wear my heart ornament, the seraka, just below my Brahmin's thread, a three-knotted string hanging over my left shoulder. The front and back of the seraka consist of bone squares embossed with vajras, which are connected by strings of bone that go over the shoulders and under the arms.

The Father is embracing the Blessed Mother Vajravarahi, who has a red-coloured body, one face, two hands, and three eyes. She is naked with freely hanging hair and wears a lower garment made from fragments of skull. Her left hand, embracing the Father's neck, holds a skullcup brimming with the blood of the four maras. Her right hand in the threatening mudra brandishes a curved knife, opposing the malignant forces of the ten directions. Her body shines with a brilliance like that of the fire at the end of the aeon. Her two legs are clasped around the Father's thighs. She is the nature of blissful great compassion. Adorned with five mudras, she wears a crown of five shrunken human skulls and a necklace of fifty shrunken human skulls. Father and Mother abide in the centre of a fiercely blazing fire of exalted wisdom.

THE SYMBOLISM OF HERUKA'S BODY

Heruka's body, a manifestation of his omniscient wisdom, reveals all the phenomena of the basis that we need to abandon, the path that we need to practise, and the result that we need to accomplish. The dark-blue colour of his body symbolizes the Wisdom Truth Body, the head of Brahma the Nature Body, the skulls the Enjoyment Body, and the crossed vajra of various colours the Emanation Body. Thus, these features of Heruka's body teach the phenomena of the result, showing that Heruka has attained the four bodies of a Buddha and that we should strive to do the same. For this we need to abandon all objects to be abandoned, the phenomena of the basis, and practise all the stages of the path to enlightenment, the phenomena of the path.

Heruka's twelve arms teach us to abandon the cycle of twelve dependent-related links, samsara; the elephant skin to abandon the ignorance of self-grasping; and the lower garment of a tiger skin to abandon hatred. The axe teaches us to abandon all faults of body, speech, and mind; the curved knife to abandon conceptions grasping at extremes; and the three-pointed spear to abandon all imprints of the delusions of the three realms. The long necklace of fifty human heads teaches us to abandon ordinary appearances and conceptions by purifying the fifty inner winds; and the bared fangs teach us to overcome the four maras. Heruka's changing facial expressions teach us to turn away from wrong views and adopt correct views; and his treading on Bhairawa and Kalarati teaches us to abandon the two extremes of existence and non-existence, and the two extremes of samsara and solitary peace. Encouraging us to abandon the extreme of solitary peace implicitly teaches us to attain great compassion and practise the stages of the Mahayana path. Indeed, Heruka himself is the embodiment of Buddha's compassion. His six mudra-ornaments teach us to train in the six perfections, and his four faces teach us to realize emptiness by meditating on the four doors of perfect liberation – emptiness, signlessness, wishlessness, and non-production. Emptiness, in this context, refers to the emptiness of the nature of all functioning things, signlessness to the emptiness of their causes, wish-lessness to the emptiness of their effects, and non-production to the emptiness of all non-produced phenomena.

It is not enough simply to realize emptiness; we need to realize emptiness with a mind of spontaneous great bliss. This is symbolized by the skullcup brimming with blood. The blood symbolizes great bliss and the skullcup emptiness; together they symbolize the union of the two. The half moon on the left side of Heruka's crown symbolizes the white bodhichitta in the crown melting and descending through the central channel, giving rise to the experience of the great bliss of the four joys. The ashes smeared all over his body symbolize this bliss pervading his entire body. To complete our training in great bliss, we need to meditate with a consort, first with a visualized wisdom mudra and then with an actual action mudra; and this is symbolized by Heruka embracing Vajravarahi. Buddha's omniscient mind is the indivisible union of bliss and emptiness – his bliss appears as Heruka and his wisdom of emptiness as Vajravarahi. Heruka and Vajravarahi, therefore, are the same nature, and not two different people. Heruka holds a vajra symbolizing method and a bell symbol-izing wisdom; together these teach us that we need to accom-plish the union of method and wisdom.

In general, attachment is the source of our daily problems and thus an object to be abandoned, but in Highest Yoga Tantra, instead of abandoning it straightaway we transform it through the power of meditation. Therefore, Heruka wears an elephant skin teaching us to abandon ignorance and a tiger skin teaching us to abandon hatred, but there is nothing on his body teaching us to abandon attachment. We need some slight attachment in order to develop great bliss. When we develop bliss we mix this bliss with emptiness and use this mind to abandon all delusions, including attachment. If with a pure motivation we train sincerely in Highest Yoga Tantra, the power of our meditation will be stronger than the power of our attachment, and so even though we do not aban-don attachment right away, it will have no power to cause us problems.

We all have the seed of Herukahood, but without receiving the blessings of the Buddhas we shall not be able to ripen this seed. The sound of the damaru invokes all the Buddhas so that we can receive their blessings. The damaru itself symbolizes the blazing of the inner fire, and is played at the level of the navel; whereas the bell symbolizes clear light, and is played at the level of the heart.

The vajra noose teaches us that our mind should always be bound by bliss, and the khatanga teaches us to recognize that the ultimate bodhichitta of inseparable bliss and emptiness appears as Heruka's mandala and Deities. Whenever we practise Heruka generation stage meditation, we should always remember that everything is the nature of bliss and emptiness. In this way our meditation becomes an actual antidote to self-grasping.

Heruka's hair tied up in a topknot teaches us that the realizations of generation stage and completion stage, and all other good qualities, are accomplished gradually; we should not hope to gain all these realizations immediately. By training continually and sincerely, cherishing even our smallest insights, we shall gradually accomplish all realizations. Eventually we shall attain all Heruka's good qualities, such as his omniscient wisdom knowing all objects of the three times, symbolized by his three eyes, and his five exalted wisdoms, symbolized by the rosaries of five-pronged vajras.

By contemplating the symbolism of the features of Heruka's body, we should strive to improve our divine pride and clear appearance of ourself as Heruka. In the auspicious prayers in the sadhana it says: 'In the precious celestial mansions as extensive as the three thousand worlds'. This means that we should visualize the celestial mansion of Heruka as large as the entire universe, therefore it is without measurement. However, when we are drawing or building the mandala of Heruka we need to make it a specific size. This commentary explains how to accomplish the outer and inner mandala of Heruka through meditating on generation and completion stage, but it does not explain how to draw and build the mandala of Heruka.

Ghantapa

Generating the Mandala and Deities of the Body Mandala

Generating the mandala and Deities of the body mandala has two parts:

1 A preliminary explanation
2 The explanation of the actual practice

A PRELIMINARY EXPLANATION

In general, 'mandala' means 'celestial mansion', but it sometimes also refers to the assembly of Deities, who are known as the 'supported mandala'. When we visualize and meditate on a mandala and Deities in front of us we are accomplishing the in-front-generation; and when we generate and meditate on ourself as the Deity and our environment as the Deity's environment we are accomplishing the self-generation.

A ritual that is a method for accomplishing either the in-front-generation or the self-generation is called a 'sadhana' (Tib. drub thab), which literally means 'method for attainment'. There are many different Tantric sadhanas. Those that contain body mandala practices are more profound than those that do not, and among those that contain body mandala practices it is said that the body mandala practice of Heruka Father and Mother is the most profound. As Je Tsongkhapa says in his commentary to the Heruka sadhana (Tib. *Dö jo*), the profound realizations of completion stage depend upon the channels and drops being blessed by the Heroes and Heroines. Whereas in other body mandala practices it is the gross parts of our body that are generated as Deities, in the practice of Heruka body mandala the channels and drops are generated as Deities. In this way our channels and drops directly receive the blessings of the Heroes and Heroines. Therefore, the practice of Heruka body mandala is most important. The way of meditating on this practice and reciting the mantras is also very special.

Accomplishing the supporting mandala and the supported Deities of Heruka body mandala is the main practice of the instructions in this book. In general, there are four different ways of accomplishing a mandala:

(1) Simply through concentration
(2) In dependence upon a line drawing or painting as its basis of accomplishment
(3) In dependence upon a sand drawing as its basis of accomplishment
(4) In dependence upon the parts of a person's body as its basis of accomplishment

The Heruka body mandala is accomplished using the fourth method. We first need to generate the basis for accomplishing the body mandala, which we do by generating ourself as Heruka as described above. This Heruka is called 'basis Heruka' because the gross and subtle parts of his body are the basis for accomplishing the mandala and Deities of the body mandala. However, because basis Heruka is generated simply through the concentration of bringing the three bodies into the path it does not have a specific visual basis for accomplishing it.

What is a body mandala? A body mandala is an actual or imagined celestial mansion or assembly of Deities that is accomplished on the basis of the parts of a person's body. The parts of the body are generated as the celestial mansion or assembly of Deities. An actual body mandala is a celestial mansion or assembly of Deities that is the nature of the parts of the purified body of a Deity, or Tantric enlightened being.

Whenever we engage in the generation stage meditation of Heruka body mandala with clear appearance and divine pride, we accomplish an imagined Heruka body mandala in dependence upon its basis, the gross and subtle parts of the body of ourself generated as Heruka. With this basic foundation, when through completion stage meditation we attain meaning clear light, our imagined Heruka body mandala is completely purified through being dissolved into meaning clear light. Due to this, when we arise from meaning clear light we become an actual divine being with a divine body, the pure illusory body, similar in aspect to Heruka; and with a divine celestial mansion, similar in aspect to Heruka's actual mandala. This Heruka body mandala is superior to the imagined Heruka body mandala. It is called the 'nature Heruka body mandala of the path' because it arises naturally from meaning clear light, is not created by imagination, and is the main path to the resultant Heruka body mandala.

On the basis of attaining the nature Heruka body mandala of the path, when we completely abandon our subtle dualistic appearances through the force of the vajra-like concentration of meaning clear light we attain the resultant, or actual, Heruka body mandala. We become an actual Buddha Heruka, surrounded by the body mandala Deities, celestial mansion, protection circle, and charnel grounds, all of which are manifestations of omniscient wisdom. These all arise naturally and simultaneously from the vajra-like concentration of meaning clear light, which is our last mind as a sentient being. This is our final accomplishment. We lay the foundation for this accomplishment by engaging in generation stage meditation, and we complete it by engaging in the completion stage meditation of meaning clear light.

There are two ways to generate and meditate on Heruka body mandala: according to the common instructions, and according to the uncommon oral instructions. In this present commentary, the way we generate and meditate on the in-front-generation of the sixty-two Deities of Heruka body mandala when visualizing the Field of Merit in the practice of Guru yoga is explained according to the common instructions, but the way we generate and meditate on the self-generation of Heruka body mandala is explained according to the uncommon instructions. Kyabje Trijang Dorjechang, the lineage holder of the Heruka body mandala instructions, says that this is the main intention of Mahasiddha Ghantapa. This second way is most profound and blessed.

THE EXPLANATION OF THE ACTUAL PRACTICE

This has two parts:

1 Simultaneous generation of the entire supporting and supported Heruka body mandala
2 Checking meditation on this generation

SIMULTANEOUS GENERATION OF THE ENTIRE SUPPORTING AND SUPPORTED HERUKA BODY MANDALA

We concentrate on the meaning of the following words from the sadhana:

The gross parts of my body – the purified body of basis Heruka, and the subtle parts of my purified body – my channels and drops, appear in the form of seed-letters. These transform fully and all at once into the entire supporting and supported body mandala. Thus, I am Heruka Father and Mother, the nature of my white and red indestructible drop. I am surrounded by the Heroes and Heroines of the five wheels, the nature of my channels and drops. I reside at the centre of the celestial mansion, the nature of the gross parts of my body.

CHECKING MEDITATION ON THIS GENERATION

This has two parts:

1 Checking meditation on the gross parts of our body generated as Heruka's mandala
2 Checking meditation on the subtle parts of our body, the channels and drops, generated as the Deities

CHECKING MEDITATION ON THE GROSS PARTS OF OUR BODY GENERATED AS HERUKA'S MANDALA

The basis for accomplishing the celestial mansion of Heruka body mandala is the gross parts of the body of ourself generated as basis Heruka. We remember in detail as follows. Our two legs forming the shape of a bow transformed into the letter YAM, the seed of the wind mandala; the triangle at our secret place transformed into the letter RAM, the seed of the fire mandala; our round belly transformed into the letter BAM, the seed of the water mandala; our square-shaped chest transformed into the letter LAM, the seed of the earth mandala; our spine transformed into the letter SUM, the seed of the divine mountain, Mount Meru; the thirty-two channels at our crown transformed into the letter PAM, the seed of the divine lotus; and the trunk of our body transformed into the letter DHRUM, the seed of the celestial mansion. These seven letters, in nature Heruka's omniscient wisdom, transformed one on top of the other into the bow-shaped wind mandala, the three-cornered fire mandala, the circular water mandala, the square earth mandala, the divine mountain (Mount Meru), the divine lotus, and the square celestial mansion with four equal sides, the mandala of Heruka, exquisitely beautiful with adornments such as the jewelled moulding and strings of pearls. These seven arose simultaneously, fully and all at once. Beyond these is the protection circle surrounded by the eight charnel grounds.

While generating the celestial mansion of the body mandala, we imagined that the celestial mansion of the outer mandala (the mandala of basis Heruka) dissolved into it. The protection circle and the charnel grounds, however, remained as before for they are the same for both the outer mandala and the body mandala. Although the celestial mansion of the body mandala is different in nature to that of the outer mandala, it is exactly the same in aspect.

CHECKING MEDITATION ON THE SUBTLE PARTS OF OUR BODY, THE CHANNELS AND DROPS, GENERATED AS THE DEITIES

We remember in detail as follows. At the same time as generating the gross parts of our body as Heruka's mandala, we generated the subtle parts of our body as the sixty-two Deities of the body mandala. Thus, the supporting mandala and the supported Deities of the body mandala arose simultaneously, fully and all at once.

We imagined that the white bodhichitta at the centre of our heart channel wheel, like a drop of dew the size of a mustard seed, assumed the aspect of a letter HUM, which then transformed into the Blessed One Glorious Heruka, with four faces, twelve arms, and so forth. At our navel, the red tummo fire in the form of a red drop assumed the aspect of a letter BAM, which then transformed into the Blessed Mother Vajravarahi. As the nature of the red and white drops Heruka and Vajrayogini met at the very centre of the celestial mansion and entered into embrace.

The four channel petals of the heart channel wheel in the cardinal directions, which are the paths for the winds of the four elements, appeared in the aspect of the letters LAM, MAM, PAM, and TAM beginning clockwise in the east. These transformed beginning counter-clockwise in the east (in front of us) into dark-blue Dakini, in the north (to our left) into green Lama, in the west (behind us) into red Khandarohi, and in the south (to our right) into yellow Rupini. They each have one face with three eyes and bared fangs, and are naked with freely hanging hair. They each have two hands, the right holding a curved knife and the left a skullcup, with a khatanga held in the crook of their left elbow. They stand with their right leg outstretched and are adorned with five mudras. They wear a crown of five human skulls and a long necklace of fifty human skulls. The four channel petals of the heart channel wheel in the intermediate directions appeared in the aspect of four skullcups brimming with five nectars.

The four Yoginis in the cardinal directions are sometimes called the 'goddesses of the four elements' because they arise from the paths for the winds of the four elements. The visualized skullcups in the intermediate directions symbolize the goddesses of the four offerings: Rupavajra Goddess, Gändhavajra Goddess, Rasavajra Goddess, and Parshavajra Goddess. These offering goddesses in the form of the four skullcups brimming with five nectars arose from the four intermediate channel petals of the heart channel wheel. These channels are called the 'four channel petals of the offerings' because they are the paths for the winds of the four offering substances: form, smell, taste, and touch. As we purify the paths for the winds of the four elements and the paths for the winds of the four offering substances through meditation and recitation of Heruka body mandala, we also purify the inner winds flowing through these paths – the winds supporting our four elements and four transformed elements of form, smell, taste, and touch. As a result we experience all phenomena such as our environment, our enjoyments, and our body and mind as pure.

The central Deity Heruka Father and Mother and the four Yoginis in the cardinal directions are known as the 'Deities of the great bliss wheel'. Around them are the Deities of the heart wheel, speech wheel, body wheel, and commitment wheel.

We contemplate as follows. The twenty-four places of our body are: the hairline, the crown, the right ear, the back of the neck, the left ear, the point between the eyebrows, the two eyes, the two shoulders, the two armpits, the two breasts, the navel, the tip of the nose, the mouth, the throat, the heart, the two testicles, the tip of the sex organ, the anus, the two thighs, the two calves, the eight fingers and eight toes, the tops of the feet, the two thumbs and two big toes, and the two knees. These transformed simultaneously into the letters PU DZA OO AH GO RA DE MA, KA OH TRI KO KA LA KA HI, TRE GRI SOO SU NA SI MA KU respectively, and these transformed into the twenty-four places of Heruka in the form of the twenty-four petal-shaped spokes of the three wheels.

Thus, in the east is Puliramalaya, in the north Dzalandhara, in the west Odiyana, in the south Arbuta, in the south-east Godawari, in the south-west Rameshöri, in the north-west Dewikoti, and in the north-east Malawa. These are the eight places of the Deities of the heart wheel.

Around these are, in the east Kamarupa, in the north Ote, in the west Trishakune, in the south Kosala, in the south-east Kalinga, in the south-west Lampaka, in the north-west Kancha, and in the north-east Himalaya. These are the eight places of the Deities of the speech wheel.

Around these are, in the east Pretapuri, in the north Grihadewata, in the west Shauraktra, in the south Suwanadvipa, in the south-east Nagara, in the south-west Sindhura, in the north-west Maru, and in the north-east Kuluta. These are the eight places of the Deities of the body wheel.

We should strongly believe that the purified twenty-four places of our own body are appearing as the twenty-four holy places of Heruka. The channels of the twenty-four places of our body, each in the aspect of a letter BAM, transformed into the twenty-four Heroines, and the drops inside the twenty-four channels, each in the aspect of a letter HUM, transformed into the twenty-four Heroes.

We contemplate as follows. Thus, in the heart wheel, at the eastern spoke, Puliramalaya, the nature of my hairline, are Khandakapala and Partzandi. At the northern spoke, Dzalandhara, the nature of the place of my crown, are Mahakankala and Tzändriakiya. At the western spoke, Odiyana, the nature of the place of my right ear, are Kankala and Parbhawatiya. At the southern spoke, Arbuta, the nature of the place of the back of my neck, are Vikatadamshtri and Mahanasa. At the south-eastern spoke, Godawari, the nature of the place of my left ear, are Suraberi and Biramatiya. At the south-western spoke, Rameshöri, the nature of the place of the point between my eyebrows, are Amitabha and Karwariya. At the north-western spoke, Dewikoti, the nature of the place of my two eyes, are Vajraprabha and Lamkeshöriya. At the north-eastern spoke, Malawa, the nature of the place of my two shoulders, are Vajradeha and Drumatzaya. All the Deities of the heart wheel have blue-coloured bodies and are known as the 'Heroes and Heroines of the vajra mind family'.

In the speech wheel, at the eastern spoke, Kamarupa, the nature of the place of my two armpits, are Ankuraka and Airawatiya. At the northern spoke, Ote, the nature of the place of my two breasts, are Vajrajatila and Mahabhairawi. At the western spoke, Trishakune, the nature of the place of my navel, are Mahavira and Bayubega. At the southern spoke, Kosala, the nature of the place of the tip of my nose, are Vajrahumkara and Surabhakiya. At the south-eastern spoke, Kalinga, the nature of the place of my mouth, are Subhadra and Shamadewi. At the south-western spoke, Lampaka, the nature of the place of my throat, are Vajrabhadra and Suwatre. At the north-western spoke, Kancha, the nature of the place of my heart, are Mahabhairawa and Hayakarna. At the north-eastern spoke, Himalaya, the nature of the place of my two testicles, are Virupaksha and Khaganana. All the Deities of the speech wheel have red-coloured bodies and are known as the 'Heroes and Heroines of the vajra speech family'.

In the body wheel, at the eastern spoke, Pretapuri, the nature of the place of the tip of my sex organ, are Mahabala and Tzatrabega. At the northern spoke, Grihadewata, the nature of the place of my anus, are Ratnavajra and Khandarohi. At the western spoke, Shauraktra, the nature of the place of my two thighs, are Hayagriva and Shaundini. At the southern spoke, Suwanadvipa, the nature of the place of my two calves, are Akashagarbha and Tzatrawarmini. At the south-eastern spoke, Nagara, the nature of the place of my eight fingers and eight toes, are Shri Heruka and Subira. At the south-western spoke, Sindhura, the nature of the place of the tops of my feet, are Pämanarteshvara and Mahabala. At the north-western spoke, Maru, the nature of the place of my two thumbs and two big toes, are Vairochana and Tzatrawartini. At the north-eastern spoke, Kuluta, the nature of the place of my two knees, are Vajrasattva and Mahabire. All the Deities of the body wheel have white-coloured bodies and are known as the 'Heroes and Heroines of the vajra body family'.

All these Heroes and Heroines have one face, two hands, and three eyes; and their heads are adorned with a crown of five human skulls. The Heroes hold a vajra and bell, and embrace their consort. Their hair is tied up in a topknot, adorned with a vajra and a crescent moon. They have a rosary of vajras on their forehead and are adorned with six mudras. Wearing a long necklace of fifty human heads and a lower garment of a tiger skin, they stand with their right leg outstretched. The Heroines hold a curved knife and a skull-cup, and are entwined in embrace with the Heroes. Wearing a lower garment made from fragments of skull, and a necklace of fifty human skulls, they are adorned with five mudras.

The eight doors of the senses are: the root of the tongue, the navel, the sex organ, the anus, the point between the eyebrows, the two ears, the two eyes, and the two nostrils.

Dzalandharapa

The channels of the eight doors, each in the aspect of a letter HUM, transformed into the eight Heroines of the commitment wheel. We visualize these Goddesses surrounding the Deities of the body wheel. In the east is dark-blue Kakase; in the north green Ulukase; in the west red Shönase; in the south yellow Shukarase; in the south-east Yamadhati, who is blue on the right and yellow on the left; in the south-west Yamaduti, who is yellow on the right and red on the left; in the north-west Yamadangtrini, who is red on the right and green on the left; and in the north-east Yamamatani, who is green on the right and blue on the left. These Heroines have one face and two hands holding a curved knife and a skull-cup, and grip a khatanga with the crook of their left elbow. They are adorned with five mudras and stand on a corpse seat with their right leg outstretched. They wear a crown of five human skulls and a long necklace of fifty human skulls.

We should strongly believe that the purified channels and drops of our own body are appearing as the sixty-two Deities of Heruka's mandala. In summary, around the very edge of the mandala are the eight great charnel grounds; inside these is the protection circle; inside this is the celestial mansion, the nature of the gross parts of our purified body; and inside this are the Deities of the five wheels, the nature of the subtle parts of our purified body. Through meditating continually on the supporting mandala and supported Deities of the Heruka body mandala generated in this way, our channels and drops are gradually blessed by the Heroes and Heroines. Due to this all the winds flowing through the channels of the eight doors gather inwards, followed by the winds flowing through the channels of the twenty-four places. Finally all our inner winds gather into the central channel and dissolve into the white and red indestructible drop at our heart, and we experience spontaneous great bliss and emptiness.

Although this meditation belongs to generation stage, its function is nevertheless similar to that of completion stage meditation. This is an uncommon quality of Heruka body mandala generation stage. A Tibetan Heruka practitioner once wrote:

In the illusion-like holy temple of our body,
Abides the assembly of Heroes and Heroines, who
    are our channels and drops.
These are the supreme object for our merit,
So, my friend, please accumulate merit by making
    offerings to them.

This verse teaches that whenever Heruka body mandala practitioners see beautiful forms, hear beautiful sounds, experience
pleasant smells, taste delicious food or drink, and experience
smooth tactile objects, they can accumulate great merit by
offering these five objects of desire to the assembly of Heroes
and Heroines abiding in the holy temple of their body – the
celestial mansion of the body mandala accomplished through
correct imagination.

When we meditate on bringing rebirth into the path of the
Emanation Body as described above, we are generating and
meditating on the outer mandala. As this mandala is relatively easy to understand it is called the 'gross mandala'.
Because the body mandala is more profound and difficult to
understand it is called the 'subtle mandala'. It is also called
the 'inner mandala'. In fact, the celestial mansion of the body
mandala is the nature of the inner body, and so it is the inner
mandala. Its outer aspect is that of the celestial mansion, and
so from this point of view it is also the outer mandala. A
detailed explanation of how to train in meditation on the
body mandala will be given below.

**ADORNING OUR BODY WITH THE ARMOUR DEITIES,
INVITING AND ABSORBING THE WISDOM BEINGS,
AND MAKING OFFERINGS**

This has three parts:

1 Adorning our body, the bodies of Heruka Father and
  Mother of the body mandala, with the armour Deities
2 Inviting the wisdom beings, dissolving them into the
  commitment beings, and receiving the empowerment
3 Making offerings and praises to the self-generated
  Deities of the body mandala

ADORNING OUR BODY, THE BODIES OF HERUKA FATHER AND
MOTHER OF THE BODY MANDALA, WITH THE ARMOUR DEITIES

We imagine that on a moon mandala at our heart appears Hero Vajrasattva, the wrathful manifestation of Buddha Akshobya, in the form of white OM HA. On a sun mandala at our head, between the crown and hairline, appears Hero Vairochana, the wrathful manifestation of Buddha Vairochana, in the form of yellow NAMA HI. On a sun mandala at our crown appears Hero Pämanarteshvara, the wrathful manifestation of Buddha Amitabha, in the form of red SÖHA HU. On a sun mandala at our two shoulders appears Hero Shri Heruka, the wrathful manifestation of Buddha Vajradhara, in the form of black BOKE HE. On a sun mandala at our two eyes appears Hero Vajrasurya, the wrathful manifestation of Buddha Ratnasambhava, in the form of orange HUM HUM HO. On a sun mandala at our forehead appears Hero Paramashawa, the wrathful manifestation of Buddha Amoghasiddhi, in the form of green PHAT HAM. From all these seed-letters, or Deities, infinite rays of light radiate throughout our body. Without even the smallest gap, our entire body between the skin and flesh is pervaded by the six-coloured rays of light, which are the nature of the six Hero armour Deities. We should develop strong conviction that this inner protection circle directly protects us from the outer obstacles created by Ishvara or Behar spirits, and the inner obstacles caused by our delusions. We meditate on this conviction.

We then imagine that on a sun mandala at the navel of Vajravarahi appears Heroine Vajravarahi, the wrathful aspect of Vajravarahi herself, the consort of Buddha Akshobya, in the form of red OM BAM. On a sun mandala at her heart appears Heroine Yamani, the wrathful aspect of Lochana, the consort of Buddha Vairochana, in the form of blue HAM YOM. On a moon mandala at her throat appears Heroine Mohani, the wrathful aspect of Benzarahi, the consort of Buddha Amitabha, in the form of white HRIM MOM. On a sun mandala at her head appears Heroine Sachalani, the wrathful aspect of Vajradhatu Ishvara, the consort of Buddha Vajradhara, in the form of yellow HRIM HRIM. On a sun mandala at her crown appears Heroine Samtrasani, the wrathful aspect of Mamaki, the consort of Buddha Ratnasambhava, in the form of green HUM HUM. On a sun mandala at her forehead appears Heroine Chandika, the wrathful aspect of Tara, the consort of Buddha Amoghasiddhi, in the form of smoke-coloured PHAT PHAT. From all these seed-letters, or Deities, infinite rays of light radiate throughout her body. Without even the smallest gap, her entire body between the skin and flesh is pervaded by the six-coloured rays of light, in nature the six Heroine armour Deities.

By visualizing the mantras of these Deities, we are also visualizing the Deities themselves because they are the same nature. We should remember this in order to receive their protection. The armour Deities are specially emanated by Buddha Vajradhara to protect practitioners from hindrances and obstacles. They are described in detail in the burning offering sadhana, which can be found in Appendix II.

INVITING THE WISDOM BEINGS, DISSOLVING THEM INTO THE COMMITMENT BEINGS, AND RECEIVING THE EMPOWERMENT

At this point, we should have a rough generic image of the supporting mandala, by nature our purified gross body. We are standing in the very centre of the mandala in the form of Father Mother Heruka, the nature of our purified white and red indestructible drop, and are surrounded by the Heroes and Heroines of the five wheels, the nature of our purified channels and drops. Outside the mandala is the protection circle surrounded by the eight charnel grounds. Together the Deities, mandala, protection circle, and charnel grounds constitute the commitment beings – so called because it is our commitment to generate ourself in this aspect every day. We now need to invite the wisdom beings together with the empowering Deities, dissolve the wisdom beings into the commitment beings, and receive the empowerment.

A wisdom being is an actual living Buddha whose body is the nature of omniscient wisdom. In this practice we invite all the Buddhas of the ten directions as wisdom beings and dissolve them into ourself generated as the commitment being. The purpose of doing this is threefold: (1) it helps us to develop and maintain divine pride of being the Deity; (2) it helps us to integrate all other Deity practices into one practice, thus following Atisha's advice to Rinchen Sangpo as explained in *Guide to Dakini Land*; and (3) it causes the environment and the beings to receive the blessings of all the Buddhas.

When we invite the wisdom beings and dissolve them into us we should have no doubt that we are Heruka, for the actual wisdom beings will then enter and remain within our body, blessing our body, speech, and mind so that we gain realizations easily and swiftly. There are many accounts of worldly spirits entering into the bodies of oracles, so why can a holy being such as Heruka not enter into the body of a faithful practitioner? We should think, 'I am a Heruka oracle', and have complete confidence that the wisdom beings enter into us.

To invite the wisdom beings we begin by remembering bliss and emptiness, reciting aloud the mantra PHAIM, and performing the blazing mudra. Heruka pledged that when faithful practitioners perform these three actions with their body, speech, and mind, he will definitely come to them. If we are practising alone we can recite PHAIM quite loudly, but if we are practising in a group this is not necessary. The way to perform the blazing mudra is explained in *Guide to Dakini Land*.

We now visualize the three letters at our three places. At the centre of our crown chakra on a white wheel we visualize a white letter OM, the nature of all Buddhas' body; at the centre of our throat chakra on a red lotus we visualize a red letter AH, the nature of all Buddhas' speech; and at the centre of our heart chakra on a sun mandala we visualize a blue letter HUM, the nature of all Buddhas' mind. We imagine that from the letter HUM at our heart countless powerful rays of light radiate to the ten directions and invite all the Buddhas from their natural abode, the Dharmakaya, to the space above us, each in the aspect of the entire mandala and Deities of

115

Heruka body mandala. At the same time we invite the empowering Deities, the sixty-two Deities of Heruka's mandala, to
appear in the space above us.

Regarding the imagined Heruka Father and Mother, the
other Deities, the mandala, the protection circle, and the charnel grounds as the commitment beings, we now dissolve the
wisdom beings into the commitment beings while reciting
the mantra 'DZA HUM BAM HO' and performing the appropriate mudras. As we recite 'DZA' and perform the hooking
mudra we imagine that all the wisdom beings gather into a
single wisdom being in the aspect of the entire mandala and
Deities, directly above the commitment beings. As we recite
'HUM' and perform the binding mudra we imagine that the
wisdom beings dissolve into the commitment beings, like
milk that has been poured into water but not yet mixed with
it. As we recite 'BAM' and perform the iron chain mudra we
imagine that the wisdom beings and commitment beings mix
together completely and become one, like the milk and water
stirred together. Finally, as we recite 'HO' and perform the
bell mudra we imagine that this union of the wisdom beings
and commitment beings becomes completely stable, and that
the wisdom beings remain with delight. The way to perform
these four mudras is explained in *Guide to Dakini Land*. However, in Highest Yoga Tantra it does not matter if we do not
perform external mudras; what matters is that our faith and
imagination are strong.

After dissolving the wisdom beings we imagine that the
empowering Deities grant the empowerment. From the point
of view of uncommon appearances, when Buddha Shakyamuni
was born the five Buddha families of the ten directions anointed
his body with the five nectars. Here we imagine that we, the
newly born Buddha Heruka, receive a similar empowerment.

We visualize the empowering Deities of Heruka's mandala
in the space above us. The principal Deity Heruka consents
to grant the empowerment, and Vajravarahi and the four
Mothers – Lama, Khandarohi, Rupini, and Dakini – hold aloft
precious jewelled vases filled with the five wisdom nectars,
which they pour through the crowns of ourself – Heruka Father

and Mother – and all the other Deities of the mandala. The nectar enters through our crown chakra, filling our entire body and purifying all the obstructions and negative actions of our body, speech, and mind. The excess nectar flows up onto our crowns and transforms into various Deities. Heruka is adorned by Vajrasattva, Vajravarahi by Akshobya, the four Mothers by Ratnasambhava, the Deities of the heart wheel by Akshobya, the Deities of the speech wheel by Amitabha, the Deities of the body wheel by Vairochana, and the Deities of the commitment wheel by Amoghasiddhi. By receiving the empowerment in this way, the blessings of the vase empowerment that we received directly from our Spiritual Guide are restored and strengthened.

MAKING OFFERINGS AND PRAISES TO THE SELF-GENERATED DEITIES OF THE BODY MANDALA

In the root Tantra of Heruka, Vajradhara says:

Making offerings to ourself
Becomes an offering to all Buddhas.

During the practice of the three bringings, we dissolved all the Heroes and Heroines of the ten directions into our mind in the aspect of the letter HUM, which then transformed into ourself Heruka Father and Mother. Later, when we absorbed the wisdom beings, all Buddhas dissolved into and merged inseparably with ourself generated as Heruka. Therefore, the self-generation is the synthesis of all Buddhas, and so when we make offerings to the self-generation we are making offerings to all Buddhas.

Making offerings to ourself generated as the Deity is an especially powerful method for accumulating merit. If we maintain the awareness that we are Heruka throughout the day, then whatever we enjoy, such as food and drink, becomes an offering to the Deity. It is only in Secret Mantra that we have the opportunity to create merit in this way.

If we fail to make offerings to the self-generation, the power of our Secret Mantra practice will diminish. Je Tsongkhapa

117

Krishnapada

explained that a qualified Tantric practice is one characterized by four complete purities: complete purity of place, complete purity of body, complete purity of deeds, and complete
purity of enjoyments. In the practice of Heruka, complete
purity of place is the transformation of our environment into
Heruka's mandala, complete purity of body is the transformation of our body into Heruka's body, complete purity of
deeds is the practice of bestowing blessings upon living beings,
and complete purity of enjoyments is the viewing of every
enjoyment as an offering to the self-generation. If we omit
these offerings, our practice will not have the fourth complete
purity and so it will not be a fully qualified Tantric practice.
It will lack the full power, quality, and benefits of a Secret
Mantra practice.

The practice of making offerings and praises to the self-
generated Deities of the body mandala has five parts:

1 Blessing the offerings
2 Making the outer offerings
3 Making the inner offering
4 Making the secret and thatness offerings
5 Eight lines of praise

BLESSING THE OFFERINGS

This has two parts:

1 Blessing the inner offering
2 Blessing the outer offerings

Blessing the inner offering has five parts:

1 The benefits
2 The basis of the inner offering
3 The visual object of the inner offering
4 How to bless the inner offering
5 The significance of the inner offering

THE BENEFITS

The practice of inner offering is found only in Highest Yoga
Tantra. Inner offering can be used as an offering to the holy

beings, for ourself as in the yoga of experiencing nectar, or to avert external or internal obstacles. Blessing and tasting the inner offering is a cause of many levels of completion stage realization. Through this practice we can purify our five contaminated aggregates and elements and transform them into the five Buddha families, and we can purify the five delusions and transform them into the five omniscient wisdoms. Making the inner offering is a cause of increasing our life span, accumulating merit, and experiencing great bliss.

THE BASIS OF THE INNER OFFERING

The inner offering is so called because its basis is a collection of five meats and five nectars, all of which are inner substances, or substances derived from the bodies of sentient beings. Torma and tsog offerings are based upon external substances that are not obtained from the body and so they are called 'outer offerings'. For the inner offering, the basis and the visual object are different, whereas for the outer offerings they are the same.

THE VISUAL OBJECT OF THE INNER OFFERING

We set up in front of us a skullcup, or a vessel of similar shape, or any small container that has a lid. Into this container we pour black tea or alcohol, and into this we put a nectar pill that has been blessed by our Spiritual Guide or received from a Dharma practitioner of the same lineage as ourself. This is the visual object. Focusing on this, we proceed to bless the inner offering.

HOW TO BLESS THE INNER OFFERING

This has four parts:

1 Clearance
2 Purification
3 Generation
4 Transformation

CLEARANCE

Here, clearance means clearing or driving away obstacles such as harmful spirits who might interfere with the blessing of the inner offering. This is done by reciting the mantra OM KHANDAROHI HUM HUM PHAT. Among the many Deities of the Heruka mandala, the wrathful female Deity Khandarohi is the one responsible for dispelling obstacles and hindrances. She is also known as the 'goddess of action' and her mantra is called the 'action mantra'. While reciting this mantra, we imagine countless red Khandarohi Goddesses emanating from our heart. They disperse in all directions and drive away any negative forces that might obstruct the blessing of the inner offering. We then reabsorb the Goddesses into our heart.

PURIFICATION

In this context, purification means purifying our ordinary appearances and ordinary conceptions, including self-grasping, by means of meditation. We need to purify the ten substances before we can transform them into nectar. To do this we focus on the visual object of the inner offering and contemplate that it and all other phenomena, including ourself, are empty of inherent existence. At the same time, we recite the mantra: OM SÖBHAWA SHUDDHA SARWA DHARMA SÖBHAWA SHUDDHO HAM, followed by the phrase, 'Everything becomes emptiness.' The mantra summarizes the meditation on emptiness – OM refers to the visual object of the inner offering, SARWA DHARMA means 'all phenomena', and SÖBHAWA SHUDDHO means 'lack inherent existence'. The whole mantra, therefore, means: 'All phenomena, including the visual object of the inner offering, lack inherent existence.'

After reciting, 'Everything becomes emptiness', we meditate briefly on emptiness, lack of inherent existence. We imagine that all conventional appearances have dissolved into emptiness, identify this emptiness as lack of inherent existence, and then try to mix our mind with this emptiness.

GENERATION

This has two parts:

1 Generating the container
2 Generating the contained substances

GENERATING THE CONTAINER

We visualize:

From the state of emptiness appears a blue letter YAM. This is the seed of the wind element and its nature is the wisdom of great bliss and emptiness. The YAM transforms into a huge bow-shaped wind mandala, which is blue, and lies flat with its curved edge furthest from us. At both corners there is a white banner. The movement of the banners activates the wind mandala, causing the wind to blow.

Above the wind mandala appears a red letter RAM. This is the seed of the fire element and its nature is the wisdom of great bliss and emptiness. The RAM transforms into a triangular fire mandala, which is flat and red. One of its corners points towards us, directly above the straight edge of the wind mandala, and the other two corners are above the curved edge of the wind mandala. This red triangle, which is slightly smaller than the wind mandala, is the core of the fire mandala. When this core is fanned by the wind, red-hot flames blaze and cover the whole wind mandala.

Above the fire mandala appear three AH letters of different colours. The letter AH above the eastern point, the point closest to us, is white; the letter above the northern point, to our right, is red; and the letter above the southern point, to our left, is blue. These letters transform into three large human heads which are the same colours as the letters from which they developed.

Above the centre of the three heads appears a large white letter AH, which symbolizes emptiness. The AH transforms into a vast skullcup, white outside and red inside, which rests on top of the heads.

GENERATING THE CONTAINED SUBSTANCES

To generate the contained substances we should visualize the following:

Inside the skullcup the ten letters OM, KHAM, AM, TRAM, HUM, LAM, MAM, PAM, TAM, BAM appear instantaneously. Gradually these letters transform into the five meats and the five nectars. In the east, the part of the skullcup nearest to us, the white letter OM transforms into yellow excrement, which is marked by a radiant white OM, the seed-letter of Vairochana. In the north, to our right, the green letter KHAM transforms into white brains marked by a radiant green KHAM, the seed-letter of Amoghasiddhi. In the west the red letter AM transforms into white sperm marked by a radiant red AM, the seed-letter of Amitabha. In the south the yellow letter TRAM transforms into red blood marked by a radiant yellow TRAM, the seed-letter of Ratnasambhava. In the centre the blue letter HUM transforms into blue urine marked by a radiant blue HUM, the seed-letter of Akshobya.

In the south-east the white letter LAM transforms into the black corpse of a cow marked by a radiant white LAM, the seed-letter of Lochana. In the south-west the blue letter MAM transforms into the red corpse of a dog marked by a radiant blue MAM, the seed-letter of Mamaki. In the north-west the red letter PAM transforms into the white corpse of an elephant marked by a radiant red PAM, the seed-letter of Benzarahi. In the north-east the green letter TAM transforms into the green corpse of a horse marked by a radiant green TAM, the seed-letter of Tara. In the centre the red letter BAM transforms into a red human corpse marked by a radiant red BAM, the seed-letter of Vajravarahi.

All the corpses lie on their backs and are marked at the heart by their respective letters. The human corpse lies in the urine with its head pointing away from us. All the other corpses lie with their heads pointing towards the centre of the skullcup.

In summary, from inside the vast skullcup arise the ten letters – the seed-letters of the five Buddha Fathers and the five

Buddha Mothers. These ten letters transform into the ten inner substances that constitute the basis of the inner offering.

Those with no understanding of emptiness should not try to visualize the ten substances too clearly or they might feel that they are visualizing real excrement and urine, and instead of being able to transform it into nectar they will feel disgusted!

TRANSFORMATION

This has three parts:

1 Purifying faults
2 Transforming into nectar
3 Increasing

PURIFYING FAULTS

We contemplate:

Light rays radiate from the letter HUM at our heart and strike the two banners of the wind mandala, causing them to flutter. This causes the wind mandala to blow, which in turn causes the fire mandala to blaze. The heat from the fire mandala causes the ten seed-letters that mark the substances and the ten substances themselves to boil. They all melt together into a hot, orange liquid. As the letters mix with the ten substances, the unpleasant colours, tastes, and smells of the substances are purified.

TRANSFORMING INTO NECTAR

We contemplate:

Above the orange liquid appears a white letter HUM, which is the nature of Heruka's mind, the wisdom of indivisible great bliss and emptiness. The HUM transforms into a white upside-down khatanga. The substance of the khatanga is white bodhichitta and its nature is Heruka's mind.

Due to the heat of the boiling liquid below, the white khatanga begins to melt and drip into the skullcup, as butter melts when it is held close to steam. The melted white khatanga

124

swirls three times counter-clockwise inside the skullcup and then mixes completely with the liquid. The liquid becomes cool and sweet, and takes on the colour of mercury. Due to the mixing of the khatanga, the liquid transforms into nectar possessing three qualities: medicine nectar that prevents all diseases, life nectar that destroys death, and wisdom nectar that eradicates all delusions.

While we are imagining that the liquid is transforming into nectar with the three qualities, we need very firm and strong concentration.

INCREASING

Directly above the nectar, we visualize a row of Sanskrit vowels and consonants, which are white in colour. In the centre is the first vowel, the letter OM. Starting from the right of the OM and extending from right to left are the remaining vowels in the following sequence: A AA I II U UU RI RII LI LII E AI O AU AM AH. Starting to the left of the OM and extending from left to right are all the consonants in the following sequence: KA KHA GA GHA NGA CHA CHHA JA JHA NYA DA THA TA DHA NA DrA THrA TrA DHrA NA BA PHA PA BHA MA YA RA LA WA SHA KA SA HA KYA.

Above this row of white letters is a similar row of red letters, and above this is a row of blue letters. The letters of each row are the same, differing only in colour. All three rows of letters are made of radiant light.

We imagine that the row of white vowels and consonants gradually dissolves from both ends towards the centre and transforms into a white OM. In the same way, the row of red letters transforms into a red AH, and the row of blue letters transforms into a blue HUM. Now there is a white letter OM, a red letter AH, and a blue letter HUM, one above the other, above the nectar.

These three letters radiate brilliant light rays to the Buddha Lands of the ten directions, invoking the enjoyments of all the Buddhas, Heroes, and Yoginis, and drawing back all their wisdom nectars into the three letters. The blue HUM turns upside-down, descends, and dissolves into the nectar, followed in the same way by the red AH and the white OM. The three letters mix with the nectar, causing it to become inexhaustible. To stabilize the transformation of the nectar we recite OM AH HUM three times.

We engage in these inner offering practices while reciting the appropriate words from the sadhana. At the conclusion of the blessing, we should develop a strong conviction that in front of us there is a special wisdom nectar possessing the three qualities. This nectar can now be used either for our own purposes or to benefit others.

THE SIGNIFICANCE OF THE INNER OFFERING

When advanced meditators bless their inner offering they visualize the various stages as external transformations, but at the same time internally they engage in completion stage practices that correspond to the stages of the blessing. Knowing the symbolism of the inner offering, they use the process of blessing it to greatly enhance their completion stage practice.

The wind mandala symbolizes the downward-voiding winds that are located below the navel. The triangular-shaped fire mandala symbolizes the inner fire, or tummo, at the navel. The three human heads symbolize the minds of white appearance, red increase, and black near-attainment – the fifth, sixth, and seventh of the eight signs that occur when the winds have dissolved within the central channel. The skullcup symbolizes the mind of clear light, the eighth sign. The skullcup is white outside and red inside, symbolizing emptiness and great bliss respectively. The skullcup itself symbolizes the indivisible union of bliss and emptiness. The five nectars inside the skullcup symbolize the five contaminated aggregates, and the five meats symbolize the five elements – earth, water, fire, wind, and space, as well as the five principal delusions – confusion, miserliness, attachment, jealousy, and self-grasping. The contaminated aggregates and elements are the principal basis to be purified during completion stage practice. Their generation inside the skullcup of bliss and emptiness symbolizes their purification and transformation.

In general, meat symbolizes the flesh of the four maras that are slain by Tantric practitioners with the weapon of their wisdom. Each of the five meats also has a special significance. Cows are very dull and stupid, so the meat of the cow symbolizes confusion. Dog meat symbolizes miserliness because dogs are very possessive and miserly. Although a dog usually cannot enjoy its owner's possessions, it will nevertheless guard them diligently and attack anyone who threatens them. Elephant meat symbolizes attachment. Horse meat symbolizes jealousy because horses are very competitive. When they run together and one horse moves ahead, the others jealously chase after it. Human flesh symbolizes self-grasping because most humans have an inflated sense of their own importance. These delusions must be purified because they are the main cause of developing both contaminated aggregates and contaminated elements.

The fluttering of the banners on the wind mandala symbolizes the downward-voiding winds ascending. The blazing fire symbolizes the blazing of the inner fire. Through the blazing of the inner fire, the winds gather and dissolve within the central channel, inducing the three signs symbolized by the three human heads on top of the fire mandala. When the energy winds have completely dissolved within the central channel, the mind of clear light arises. This is symbolized by the skullcup on top of the three heads. Through meditating on the clear light the five contaminated aggregates are purified and transform into the five Buddha Fathers, and the five contaminated elements are purified and transform into the five Buddha Mothers. This is symbolized by the ten substances transforming into wisdom nectar.

In summary, blessing the inner offering indicates the basis that needs to be purified, the path that purifies, and the results of purification – the basis, path, and result of completion stage practice. When we have understood this, and can combine our understanding with the practice of blessing the inner offering, we shall begin to appreciate the real significance of this profound practice. Marpa Lotsawa said that tasting the nectar of his inner offering was more powerful

Tilopa

than receiving a hundred initiations from other Lamas. This may seem to be a boastful statement, but when we thoroughly understand the special qualities of the inner offering we shall realize the profound truth of Marpa's words.

When we bless our inner offering, the basis of the offering is the ten inner substances, but the visual object of the offering is a nectar pill dissolved in alcohol or tea. When we bless torma and tsog offerings, the visual object of the offerings and the basis of the offerings are the same, both having the aspect of nectar for eating. Apart from these differences, the four stages of clearance, purification, generation, and transformation are the same when blessing the inner offering, the tsog offerings, and the torma offerings.

BLESSING THE OUTER OFFERINGS

There are nine outer offerings to the self-generation: water for drinking, water for bathing the feet, water for the mouth, flowers, incense, light, perfume, food, and music. We set out the first eight in front of the shrine starting from our left. As mentioned before, there is no need to set anything out for the music offering because it is not visual form. For the first three offerings and the perfume offering we can set out water, and for the remainder we can set out the actual substances.

To bless the outer offerings, we begin by reciting OM KHAN-DAROHI HUM HUM PHAT and sprinkling a little inner offering over the substances with our left ring finger while visualizing countless wrathful Khandarohi Goddesses emanating from the letter HUM at our heart to all ten directions. These Goddesses drive away any spirits who may be trying to interfere with our practice of offerings. We then reabsorb the Goddesses into our heart.

Now we purify the substances by reciting the mantra OM SÖBHAWA SHUDDHA SARWA DHARMA SÖBHAWA SHUDDHO HAM while meditating on their lack of inherent existence. Having purified ordinary appearance and ordinary conception of the offerings by dissolving them into emptiness, we now generate pure offerings. We imagine that from the state of emptiness nine KAM letters instantaneously appear in the

space in front of us. These letters, which have the nature of
great bliss and emptiness, transform into nine skullcups.
Inside each skullcup a letter HUM appears. These letters, in
nature indivisible bliss and emptiness, transform into the
individual offerings: water for drinking, water for bathing
the feet, water for the mouth, and so on. Each offering has
three attributes: (1) its nature is the exalted union of great
bliss and emptiness, (2) its aspect is that of the individual
offering substance, and (3) its function is to cause those who
enjoy it to experience special, uncontaminated bliss.

Above each skullcup we visualize the three letters OM AH
HUM, one above the other, and we then recite the appropriate
blessing mantra. For each blessing mantra we insert the
Sanskrit name of the offering between OM and AH HUM. The
Sanskrit names of the nine outer offerings are: AHRGHAM,
water for drinking; PADÄM, water for bathing the feet; ÄNT-
ZAMANAM, water for the mouth; VAJRA PUPE, flowers; VAJRA
DHUPE, incense; VAJRA DIWE, lights; VAJRA GÄNDHE, perfume; VAJRA NEWIDE, food; and VAJRA SHAPTA, music. Thus,
to bless the nectar for drinking, for example, we recite the
blessing mantra OM AHRGHAM AH HUM.

After verbally blessing each offering in this way, we imagine
that the letter HUM above each skullcup dissolves into the
offering, followed by the letters AH and then OM. In this way
the offerings are blessed and transform into the nature of the
wisdom union of great bliss and emptiness possessing the
three attributes. While we recite the blessing mantra, we can
perform the accompanying hand gestures, or mudras, which
symbolize and bless each offering. These are described in
Guide to Dakini Land. As we recite the blessing mantra for the
music offering, we play the damaru and bell. As mentioned
before, the bell symbolizes clear light wisdom. We hold the
bell in our left hand and play it at the level of our heart to
symbolize the experience of clear light, which arises after the
inner winds have dissolved within the central channel at the
heart. To attain the wisdom of clear light through meditation,
we need to ignite the inner fire and cause it to increase, and
this is symbolized by playing the damaru. We hold the vajra

and damaru in our right hand. We play the damaru at the level of the navel because we ignite the inner fire by concentrating on our navel channel wheel. We begin by playing the damaru and imagining that it ignites our inner fire, and then we accompany it by playing the bell briefly, signifying the subsequent experience of clear light. Playing the instruments in this way sows in our mind a special potential to accomplish these attainments in the future.

The six additional outer offerings are also known by their Sanskrit names. They are: VAJRA ADARSHE, indestructible form – we imagine that all visual forms arise as Rupavajra Goddesses; VAJRA WINI, indestructible sound – all sounds arise as Shaptavajra Goddesses; VAJRA GÄNDHE, indestructible scents – all smells arise as Gändhavajra Goddesses; VAJRA RASE, indestructible tastes – all tastes arise as Rasavajra Goddesses; VAJRA PARSHE, indestructible objects of touch – all tactile objects arise as Parshavajra Goddesses; and VAJRA DHARME, indestructible phenomena – all other phenomena arise as Dharmadhatuvajra Goddesses.

MAKING THE OUTER OFFERINGS

We imagine that many offering goddesses emanate from our heart, take replica offerings from those blessed previously, and offer them to ourself generated as Heruka Father and Mother, and to all the other Deities of the body mandala. While visualizing this, we recite the offering mantras and perform the accompanying mudras. After making the nine offerings, we make the offerings of the six knowledge goddesses, Rupavajra and so forth, while reciting the offering mantras and performing the mudras.

MAKING THE INNER OFFERING

We imagine that many offering goddesses emanate from our heart and fill their skullcups with inner offering from the large skullcup of blessed nectar. As we recite the offering mantra, these goddesses offer the nectar to us generated as Heruka, and to all the other Deities. We take the inner offering with our left ring finger and taste it. We imagine that it blesses our channels, drops, and winds, and we experience great bliss. Through this practice, the blessings of the secret empowerment that we received directly from our Spiritual Guide are restored and strengthened.

MAKING THE SECRET AND THATNESS OFFERINGS

With strong divine pride of being Heruka in union with Vajravarahi, we imagine that through the force of our embrace the tummo at our navel blazes, causing the white bodhichitta in our crown to melt and descend through our central channel. As it descends from our crown to our throat we experience joy, as it descends from our throat to our heart we experience supreme joy, as it descends from our heart to our navel we experience extraordinary joy, and as it descends from our navel to the tip of our sex organ we generate spontaneous great joy. At the same time, we imagine that the Principal Deity Father and Mother, and all the retinue Deities of the body mandala, experience a special, exalted wisdom of bliss and emptiness.

Practising the secret offering is a very special method for generating spontaneous great bliss. Also, through this practice the blessings of the wisdom-mudra empowerment that we received directly from our Spiritual Guide are restored and strengthened.

EIGHT LINES OF PRAISE

This praise was taught by Vajradhara and it is an especially blessed practice. For practitioners of Heruka and Vajrayogini these words are the most supreme of all praises. Merely reciting these praises causes all the Deities of Heruka's mandala to draw closer to us and remain with us constantly. Practitioners of Heruka and Vajrayogini can regard anyone they meet as an emanation of Heruka or Vajrayogini and recite the eight lines of praise to them. By sincerely reciting these praises we swiftly purify our ordinary appearances and reach Heruka's Pure Land. Even if we are confronted with an aggressive and vicious criminal, we should not dwell upon ordinary appearances but regard him as an emanation of Heruka or Vajrayogini and silently make praises to him with these eight lines. If we gain familiarity with this practice we shall come to view all beings as pure. We can even extend this pure view to inanimate objects such as mountains, lakes, buildings, and the earth itself. We should not be misled by the external aspect of any object but should think that its real nature is the same as that of Heruka and Vajrayogini and then praise it with the eight lines. This helps us to overcome ordinary appearances and causes us to attain the Pure Land of Heruka.

As mentioned earlier, Heruka with a blue-coloured body, four faces, and twelve arms is interpretative Heruka. Definitive Heruka is Buddha's mind of great bliss mixed with emptiness. Since the ultimate nature of all phenomena is emptiness, definitive Heruka pervades all phenomena. In Tibetan, Heruka is sometimes called 'kyab dag' Heruka. 'Kyab' means 'pervasive' and 'dag' means 'nature', so 'kyab dag' means that all phenomena are pervaded by Heruka's nature. Therefore, from the point of view of ultimate nature, definitive Heruka pervades all phenomena and is the same nature as all phenomena. If we have deep understanding of this, there is great hope that we shall be able to perceive whatever appears to our mind as Heruka.

Although at this point in the sadhana we recite the eight lines of praise in Sanskrit, the following explanation will be based on the English translation. The letter OM at the beginning of each line symbolizes the body, speech, and mind of Heruka or Vajrayogini to whom we are offering praise. At the end of each line we recite HUM HUM PHAT. With the first HUM we make the request, 'Please grant me the mundane attainments such as increased wealth, life span, and merit.' With the second HUM we make the request, 'Please grant me the supramundane attainments such as the realization of spontaneous great bliss, the union that needs learning, and the Union of No More Learning.' With 'PHAT' we request the destruction of the outer, inner, and secret obstacles that prevent us from gaining these attainments.

The explanation of the eight lines of praise to the Father is given as follows:

OM I prostrate to the Blessed One, Lord of the Heroes
HUM HUM PHAT

When we praise Heruka with this line, we recall the pre-eminent qualities of his body by remembering the significance of his nine different moods of a Hero. These are: (1) his body displaying an air of majesty demonstrating his fearlessness; (2) his two legs treading on Bhairawa and Kalarati showing his complete control over samsaric rebirth and the self-cherishing mind; (3) his wrathful frown at the centre of his forehead showing that he destroys the enemies of the delusions; (4) his gently laughing manner showing that he subdues the power of the worldly deity Ishvara and all his retinues; (5) his four bared fangs showing that he destroys the four maras; (6) his tongue curled back showing that he pacifies subtle dualistic appearances; (7) his long almond-shaped eyes expressing his compassion for all living beings without exception; (8) his eyes opened attentively showing that out of compassion he is looking everywhere so as to care for all living beings; and (9) his serene eyes showing that he experiences spontaneous great bliss inseparably mixed with emptiness. Through this praise we develop wishing faith, sincerely wishing to attain Heruka's Form Body, and we request him to bestow the attainments of his holy body.

OM To you with a brilliance equal to the fire of the
great aeon HUM HUM PHAT

This line reveals the pre-eminent qualities of Heruka's speech. Just as the fire at the end of the great aeon has the power to destroy the entire world, so Heruka's speech has the power to destroy the ignorance of all living beings. Realizing this, we request him to bestow the attainments of his holy speech.

OM To you with an inexhaustible topknot HUM HUM
PHAT

This line reveals the pre-eminent qualities of Heruka's mind. Here, 'topknot' signifies Heruka's mind, which is inexhaustible

134

knowledge that knows all phenomena of the past, present, and future directly and simultaneously. Realizing this, we request him to bestow the attainments of his holy mind.

OM To you with a fearsome face and bared fangs
HUM HUM PHAT

This line reveals Heruka's pre-eminent qualities of abandonment and realization. His four bared fangs indicate that he has completely abandoned the four maras, and his wrathful four faces indicate that he has profound realizations of the four doors of liberation. We request him to bestow the attainments of these abandonments and realizations.

OM To you whose thousand arms blaze with light
HUM HUM PHAT

This line reveals Heruka's special deeds of benefiting others through peaceful actions. Out of compassion he benefits countless living beings with peaceful aspects, such as one-thousand-armed Avalokiteshvara. We request him to bestow the attainments of the Buddha of Compassion.

OM To you who hold an axe, an uplifted noose, a
spear, and a khatanga HUM HUM PHAT

This line reveals Heruka's special deeds of benefiting others through wrathful actions. Out of compassion he benefits countless living beings with wrathful aspects, such as twelve-armed Heruka holding an axe, an uplifted noose, a spear, a khatanga, and so forth. We request him to bestow the attainments of Buddha Heruka.

OM To you who wear a tiger-skin garment HUM HUM
PHAT

If the human beings of this world sincerely rely upon Heruka with strong faith, especially at this degenerate time, Heruka will bestow powerful blessings upon them to pacify anger and conflicts. To indicate this, he wears a tiger skin. We request him to bestow his blessings to help us to pacify our anger and achieve outer and inner peace.

OM I bow to you whose great smoke-coloured body
   dispels obstructions HUM HUM PHAT

The dark-blue-smoke colour of Heruka's body symbolizes
the eternal and unchanging nature of his Truth Body. This
line therefore reveals that the real nature of Heruka is the
Truth Body. From his Truth Body, countless emanations arise
and benefit countless living beings, dispelling their obstacles
and fulfilling their wishes. Thus, his Truth Body is the source
of all his deeds. We request him to bestow the attainment of
the Truth Body, definitive Heruka.

The explanation of the eight lines of praise to the Mother
is given as follows:

OM I prostrate to Vajravarahi, the Blessed Mother
   HUM HUM PHAT

All Buddhas have totally destroyed their ignorance through
the perfection of wisdom, and Vajravarahi, or Vajrayogini, is
the embodiment of the perfection of wisdom of all Buddhas.
The Tibetan translation of the Sanskrit name 'Vajravarahi' is
'Dorje Pagmo'. Here, 'pag' means pig. The pig is a symbol
of ignorance, which is why it is depicted at the very centre
of the Wheel of Life. By calling Vajrayogini 'Vajravarahi' we
are praising her as the essence of the perfection of wisdom
that destroys ignorance. She is the 'Blessed Mother' because
she has destroyed the four maras and possesses all the good
qualities of a Buddha.

OM To the Superior and powerful Knowledge Lady
   unconquered by the three realms HUM HUM PHAT

Here, 'Superior' refers to Vajrayogini's mind, which sees directly the ultimate nature of all phenomena; and 'powerful
Knowledge Lady' means that she has the power to bestow great
bliss upon Heruka and upon practitioners. 'Unconquered by
the three realms' means that she has abandoned all delusions
of the desire, form, and formless realms.

OM To you who destroy all fears of evil spirits with
   your great vajra HUM HUM PHAT

Here, 'great vajra' means spontaneous great bliss. Her wisdom of spontaneously born great bliss inseparable from emptiness destroys all harm from evil spirits.

OM To you with controlling eyes who remain as the
    vajra seat unconquered by others HUM HUM PHAT

Vajrayogini is the vajra seat of Heruka, who is always in union with her. While remaining unconquered by others, she can control them just by looking at them.

OM To you whose wrathful fierce form desiccates
    Brahma HUM HUM PHAT

Vajrayogini appears in the form of a wrathful, fierce Deity to subdue the pride of worldly gods such as Brahma and Indra.

OM To you who terrify and dry up demons, conquering
    those in other directions HUM HUM PHAT

Vajrayogini dries up the inner demons of ordinary appearances and ordinary conceptions through the blazing of her inner fire, and through this she conquers all external demons of the ten directions. If someone has no ordinary appearances and no ordinary conceptions, they cannot be harmed by external demons; therefore, they are said to have conquered them.

OM To you who conquer all those who make us dull,
    rigid, and confused HUM HUM PHAT

Vajrayogini enables us to overcome all harms inflicted by evil spirits who can interfere with our practice by causing us to become physically dull or heavy, verbally rigid – for example, unable to pronounce mantras clearly, or mentally confused about our practice.

OM I bow to Vajravarahi, the Great Mother, the Dakini
    consort who fulfils all desires HUM HUM PHAT

Because Vajrayogini is a manifestation of the perfection of wisdom, known as the 'Great Mother of all the Buddhas', she destroys the ignorance of all living beings and has the power to fulfil their wishes.

Naropa

The Actual Generation
Stage Meditation

The actual generation stage meditation has two parts:

1 A preliminary explanation
2 How to practise the actual generation stage
   meditation

A PRELIMINARY EXPLANATION

All the practices described so far are like limbs that support
the main body of actual generation stage meditation. When
through meditating on the three bringings we generate ourself as Heruka and develop divine pride, we need to change
the basis of imputation for our I. This is essential for accomplishing authentic realizations of generation stage. Thinking
'I am Heruka' on the basis of our ordinary body and mind
is a wrong awareness because our ordinary body and mind
are contaminated and therefore cannot be the basis for imputing Heruka. At this point we need to understand four things:

1 What is the basis of imputation for our I?
2 Why we need to change the basis of imputation
   for our I
3 How it is possible to change the basis of imputation
   for our I
4 How to change the basis of imputation for our I

WHAT IS THE BASIS OF IMPUTATION FOR OUR I?

What is a person's I or self? The I cannot be the body and
mind because the I is the possessor, and the body and mind
are the phenomena that are possessed. For example, when
we say, 'My body' or 'My mind', this indicates that we regard

ourself as the possessor of our body and mind. However, although the I is not the body and mind, when the thought 'I' arises naturally in our mind it does so only on the basis of perceiving our body or our mind. Thus, our body and mind are the basis for imputing our I.

WHY WE NEED TO CHANGE THE BASIS OF IMPUTATION FOR OUR I

When the thought 'I' arises within our mind, we automatically develop self-grasping that grasps at the I as existing from its own side. This self-grasping mind is the main cause of all the problems we experience and the root of samsara. Because our body and mind, which are the basis of imputation for our I, are contaminated aggregates, whenever we develop the thought 'I' we naturally develop the ignorance of self-grasping at the same time. For as long as we continue to use our present body and mind as the basis for imputing our I we shall never eradicate our ignorance of self-grasping, and so we shall continually have to experience suffering. For this reason we need to change the basis of imputation for our I.

HOW IT IS POSSIBLE TO CHANGE THE BASIS OF IMPUTATION FOR OUR I

In our previous lives we took countless bodies, and each time the basis of imputation for our I changed. When we were born human, the basis of imputation for our I was the body and mind of a human, and when we were born as an animal, the basis of imputation for our I was the body and mind of an animal. Even within one life the basis of imputation for our I changes many times. For instance, when we were a baby the basis of imputation for our I was a baby's body and mind, when we were a child the basis of imputation for our I was a child's body and mind, and when we grow old the basis of imputation for our I will be the body and mind of an old person.

We may feel that, even though we have had all these changes of body, there is no problem with regarding them all as bases of imputation for our 'I' because they are all of the same continuum; however, it is not so easy to understand how another's body, which does not belong to us, can become the basis of imputation for our I. To understand this we can consider the following. When we were conceived in our mother's womb, our body, which at that time was a pink yoghurt-like mixture of our mother's ovum and father's sperm, belonged to others. To begin with we had no thought of its being our body but later, as we became more familiar with the developing embryo, we came to regard it as our own body and gradually it became the basis of imputation for our I. This clearly indicates that, with familiarity, another's body can become the basis of imputation for our I. In other words, 'my body' and 'other's body' are like 'this mountain' and 'that mountain'; our view changes depending upon our relative position.

HOW TO CHANGE THE BASIS OF IMPUTATION FOR OUR I

We change the basis of imputation for our I by purifying the ordinary appearance of our body and mind through meditating on emptiness and then generating ourself as Heruka. Using Heruka's body and mind generated through correct imagination as the basis of imputation for our I, we strongly develop divine pride, thinking 'I am Heruka.' We continually familiarize ourself with the meditations on divine pride and clear appearance until eventually what was simply imagination becomes an actuality, and we experience the pure body and mind of Heruka. This is the special way of changing the basis of imputation for our I through practising the spiritual path. Unlike the normal changes in the basis of imputation for our I that occur from one life to the next due to karma, and which are the very process of samsara, this special method is the means for attaining release from samsara.

When we train in the three bringings, we should try not to forget the preceding stages as we progress to the next. Thus, when we progress from the first bringing to the second we should try not to forget that we experienced the aspect of death and that our mind transformed into Heruka's Truth Body; and when we progress to the third bringing we should not forget that we experienced the aspect of the intermediate state and attained Heruka's Enjoyment Body. Now, as we progress to the actual generation stage meditation, we should not forget that we experienced the aspect of rebirth and have attained Heruka's Emanation Body in his mandala. In particular, we should remember that our body of basis Heruka transformed into the mandala, that the very subtle white and red drop at our heart transformed into Heruka Father and Mother, and that our channels and drops transformed into the remaining Deities of the body mandala. If we keep all these recognitions fresh in our mind, we shall not find it difficult to engage in actual generation stage meditation.

How to practise actual generation stage meditation will now be explained under the following five headings:

1 Training in clear appearance
2 Training in divine pride
3 Training in tranquil abiding
4 Training in subtle generation stage
5 Training in the yoga of non-dual profundity and clarity

TRAINING IN CLEAR APPEARANCE

To begin with, we train in improving clear appearance of the mandala and the Deities. First we examine the eight charnel grounds until we have a rough mental image of them, and then, without forgetting these, we examine the five-coloured wisdom fires and the vajra ground, fence, tent, and canopy. Without forgetting these, we examine the four elements, Mount Meru, the lotus, and the crossed vajra. Then we examine the details of the celestial mansion, the Deities of the commitment wheel, the Deities of the body wheel, the Deities of the speech wheel, the Deities of the heart wheel, the four Yoginis, and finally ourself, Heruka Father and Mother in the centre. In this way we try to build up a composite image of the entire mandala and Deities. To make the image clearer we then repeat the process in reverse order, beginning with our crown ornament and checking all the details of our body, then the Deities of the five wheels and so on, all the way out to the charnel grounds. We continue like this, examining the mandala and Deities in both serial and reverse order, until we gain a mental image of the entire mandala and all the Deities. This is analytical meditation. Once we have an adequate mental image of the entire mandala and assembly of Deities, we try to hold this for as long as possible in single-pointed placement meditation.

There are four stages of meditation on the self-generation: seeking, finding, holding, and remaining. The first two are analytical meditation, and the second two are placement meditation. 'Seeking' means bringing to mind the details of the mandala and Deities through serial and reverse order checking meditation; 'finding' means perceiving a composite generic image of the entire mandala and Deities, that is, finding the object of generation stage meditation; 'holding' means holding this object of meditation through the power of mindfulness without forgetting it; and 'remaining' means fixing the mind single-pointedly on this generic image without distraction. If we train repeatedly in this meditation over a long period, we shall definitely improve our clear appearance. This will greatly help us to overcome our ordinary appearances.

When doing this kind of meditation we do not need to push, hoping to gain realizations quickly; rather, we should think of our meditation practice as lasting our whole life long, and practise gently and sincerely every day. Perhaps we shall complete our training in this life, perhaps we shall not; but, even if we do not, our meditation will not have been wasted. Each and every meditation we do places powerful potentials in our mind, which can be activated in our next life to produce their fruit of realizations. There are many stories of practitioners who have gained realizations with very little meditation, or even just by reciting mantras with faith. They were able to do this because they had placed powerful potentials in their mind through their practice in previous lives. For example, there is a story in *Heart Jewel* of how King Ajatashatru gained a direct realization of emptiness as a result of Manjushri disappearing as the king tried to offer him a cloak. Manjushri was able to help the king in this way because the king had already placed powerful potentials in his mind by practising purely in his previous life. We should not underestimate the importance of creating such potentials because without them it is impossible to gain authentic spiritual realizations. Therefore, we need not worry if our meditation does not show immediate results, but instead persevere happily and sincerely, in the knowledge that we shall definitely attain results in the future. This meditation in particular is a powerful cause to be reborn in the Pure Land of Heruka and Vajrayogini.

TRAINING IN DIVINE PRIDE

Divine pride is a special way of viewing ourself in which we imagine that we are a Tantric Deity and that our environment is his or her Pure Land. Although it is called 'pride', divine pride is not a delusion. It is utterly different from deluded pride. Deluded pride causes only rebirth in samsara whereas generating the divine pride of being Heruka leads only to liberation from samsara. If we maintain mindfulness throughout our practice of the three bringings, as explained above, then when the time comes to do actual generation stage meditation we shall already have some divine pride of being Heruka. Now we try to strengthen and stabilize our experience of divine pride through analytical and placement meditation. First we do analytical meditation on divine pride by contemplating as follows:

Previously I dissolved my ordinary body and mind into emptiness, and from the state of emptiness I arose as the Truth Body, Enjoyment Body, and Emanation Body of Heruka. I have taken rebirth as Emanation Body Heruka surrounded by all the other Deities in the mandala.

As a result of contemplating this, we develop a strong sense of actually being Heruka, and we hold this thought single-pointedly in placement meditation. To strengthen our divine pride we contemplate:

In the practice of inviting the wisdom beings, I invited all the Buddhas in the form of Heruka to dissolve into me. At that time, my body and mind and Heruka's body and mind became one. Therefore, there is no doubt that I am Heruka.

To meditate on divine pride, we first transform our mind into divine pride and then try to hold this mind single-pointedly, without distraction. Unlike meditation on emptiness or impermanence, where we focus on an object other than the mind itself, in this meditation the object of meditation is our own mind transformed into divine pride.

It is important to understand that the mind of divine pride is not a wrong awareness but a valid cognizer. When we meditate on divine pride we completely forget our ordinary body and mind and focus on the pure body and mind of Heruka, and it is upon this basis that we develop the divine pride of being Heruka. If we were to develop the thought 'I am Heruka' observing our ordinary body and mind, this would be a wrong awareness; but if we prevent all ordinary appearances and observe the pure body and mind of Heruka, this is a valid basis for imputing Heruka. Our mind of divine pride thinking 'I am Heruka' is a valid cognizer because it is generated by pure concentration and is a non-deceptive mind. For example, a person called 'Moon' is not the real moon but his thinking 'I am Moon' is correct and valid. Likewise, although at the moment we are not real Heruka, this mind of divine pride is a valid mind.

In general, everyone has pride in his or her identity, thinking, 'I am this' or 'I am that'. This ordinary pride is deluded pride and a wrong awareness because when we observe our ordinary contaminated aggregates they appear to us to be truly existent, and as a result we usually develop pride in a truly existent I. In reality there are no truly existent aggregates, and there is no truly existent I. The basis for imputing

I is changing all the time and so the I that we impute upon this basis is also changing; but due to our ignorance we are always grasping at this I as truly existent. The result of this ordinary deluded pride is that we experience uninterrupted ordinary death, intermediate state, and rebirth. If, instead of grasping at this impure I, we develop divine pride based on the pure body and mind of Heruka, there will be no basis for us to experience suffering. If we maintain divine pride of being Heruka, we shall remain happy and peaceful, we shall no longer commit any negative actions, we shall quickly and easily increase our spiritual realizations, and we shall be reborn in Heruka's Pure Land. Contemplating these points, we should think:

From this moment on I will give up my ordinary deluded pride, which is the cause of so much suffering, and always maintain the divine pride of being Heruka.

We may sometimes develop doubts, thinking, 'The body of Heruka is not my body, so how can I take it as the basis for imputing I?' To dispel this doubt we should remember that our present body is not ours either but simply borrowed from our parents. When our consciousness first entered our mother's womb we did not think of the fertilized ovum as being our body. Gradually, however, as the body formed in the womb we became more and more familiar with it and came to regard it as our own. We identify with our present body simply through the force of familiarity; there is no other reason why we should cling to it as ours. In a similar way, through repeatedly practising generation stage meditation on divine pride we shall gradually become familiar with the body of Heruka and come to regard it as ours.

When we practise generation stage meditation on Heruka, the appearing object is the imagined body of Heruka, a generic image of Heruka's body. As explained previously, this body is a form that is a phenomena source, a form that appears only to mental awareness, and so it is a valid basis for imputing Heruka. If we gain deep experience of this meditation, eventually we shall see our Heruka body with our eye awareness and it will become an actual visual form for us. Although the body of imagined Heruka is not the body of actual Heruka, it is a generic image of Heruka's body and so it can be a valid basis for imputing actual Heruka. There is debate as to whether generic images are permanent or impermanent.

For Tantric practitioners, the principal objects to be abandoned are ordinary conceptions and ordinary appearances. Divine pride overcomes ordinary conceptions and clear appearance overcomes ordinary appearances. The terms 'ordinary conception' and 'ordinary appearance' are best explained by the following example. Suppose there is a Heruka practitioner called John. Normally he sees himself as John, and his environment, enjoyments, body, and mind as John's. These appearances are ordinary appearances. The mind that assents to these ordinary appearances by holding them to be true is ordinary conception. Ordinary conceptions are obstructions to liberation and ordinary appearances are obstructions to omniscience. In general, all sentient beings, except Bodhisattvas who have attained the vajra-like concentration of the path of meditation, have ordinary appearances.

Now if John were to meditate on the generation stage of Heruka, strongly regarding himself as Heruka and believing his surroundings, experiences, body, and mind to be those of Heruka, at that time he would have the divine pride that prevents ordinary conceptions. If he were also to attain clear appearance of himself as Heruka, with the environment, enjoyments, body, and mind of Heruka, at that time he would have the clear appearance that prevents him from perceiving ordinary appearances.

At the beginning, ordinary conceptions are more harmful than ordinary appearance. How this is so is illustrated by the following analogy. Suppose a magician conjures up an illusion of a tiger in front of an audience. The tiger appears to both the audience and the magician, but whereas the audience believe that the tiger actually exists, and consequently become afraid, the magician does not assent to the appearance of tiger and so remains calm. The problem for the audience is not so much that a tiger appears to them, as their conception that the tiger actually exists. It is this conception rather than the mere appearance of the tiger that causes them to experience fear. If like the magician they had no conception that the tiger existed, then even though they still had an appearance of a tiger they would not be afraid. In the same way, even though things appear to us as ordinary, if we do not conceptually grasp them as ordinary this will not be so harmful. Similarly, it is less damaging to our spiritual development that our Spiritual Guide appears to us as ordinary and yet we hold him or her to be in essence a Buddha, than it is for our Spiritual Guide to appear to us as ordinary and for us to believe that he or she is ordinary. The conviction that our Spiritual Guide is a Buddha, even though he or she may appear to us as an ordinary person, helps our spiritual practice to progress rapidly.

TRAINING IN TRANQUIL ABIDING

It is very important for Secret Mantra practitioners to train in tranquil abiding, and the time to do this is during actual generation stage meditation. Detailed explanations of the stages of training in tranquil abiding can be found in *Joyful Path of Good Fortune* and *Meaningful to Behold*. What follows is a brief explanation of how to train in tranquil abiding during generation stage meditation.

The object of tranquil abiding is the same here as the object of generation stage meditation, namely the generic image of the entire supporting and supported mandala – the eight charnel grounds, the protection circle, the celestial mansion, the Deities of the five wheels, and ourself, Heruka Father and Mother. Therefore, when we are training in tranquil abiding we are sincerely practising generation stage meditation, and so this training is a powerful method for making progress in our generation stage meditation of improving clear appearance and divine pride.

To train in tranquil abiding, we practise the four stages of seeking, finding, holding, and remaining. First we practise seeking by engaging in the serial and reverse order checking meditation described above so as to bring to mind the entire mandala. When as a result of seeking we clearly perceive a rough generic image of the entire mandala, from the charnel grounds to ourself, the principal Deity Heruka, we have reached the second stage of tranquil abiding, finding. Having found our object of tranquil abiding, we hold it without forgetting. Through continual practice our concentration will develop until we reach the third stage, holding, so called because we are now able to hold the entire mandala single-pointedly for one minute without forgetting it. At this point we have attained the first mental abiding, placing the mind. Having attained the first mental abiding in one session, we need to repeat this meditation every day so that our concentration improves until we are able to remain single-pointedly on the entire mandala for five minutes without forgetting it. At this point we have reached the fourth stage, remaining, and attained the second mental abiding, continual placement.

Through continual training, when we reach the point at which every time we lose the object we are able immediately to recall it, we have attained the third mental abiding, replacement. When we can concentrate on the object without forgetting it for the whole session, we have attained the fourth mental abiding, close placement. We have now attained firmness with respect to gross generation stage. If at this point we engage in a retreat on tranquil abiding meditation it is possible that we shall attain the actual tranquil abiding of generation stage within six months. It is said that if a Heruka practitioner attains actual tranquil abiding on the generation stage of Heruka, he or she will definitely attain outer Dakini Land, the Pure Land of Buddha Heruka, in that life.

In *Lamp for the Path to Enlightenment*, Atisha says that we need to use the same object when training in tranquil abiding. His meaning is that we use the same object until we have attained firmness in our concentration, that is until the fourth mental abiding. On the fourth mental abiding we can see the entire mandala as clearly as we see things with our eyes. The power of our mindfulness is complete but there is still a danger of mental sinking and mental excitement. To overcome these, and to complete our training in tranquil abiding, we switch to meditation on subtle generation stage.

As mentioned before, the purpose of training in generation stage is to lay the foundation for completion stage realizations. Once we have attained firmness in gross generation stage, if we then switch to subtle generation stage this will greatly help us in gathering our inner winds into the central channel, and thereby prepare us for completion stage realizations.

The focal point for subtle generation stage meditation of Heruka is inside the central channel at the tip of the sex organ. We meditate as follows. Our mind in the aspect of the letter HUM at our heart transforms into a transparent blue drop, the size of a small pea, which descends through our central channel to the tip of the sex organ. Inside the drop we visualize the entire supporting and supported mandala of Heruka. We should think that we can see the whole mandala very clearly, rather as we can see a whole room reflected in a small water bubble; and we feel that our mind has become one with the mind of the Heruka in the centre of that mandala. We then do placement meditation on this mandala and drop.

How can we know when we have completed our training in generation stage? There are four levels of generation stage practitioners:

(1) Beginners
(2) Practitioners in whom some wisdom has descended
(3) Practitioners with some power over wisdom
(4) Practitioners with complete power over wisdom

Beginners are generation stage practitioners who meditate principally on gross generation stage and can visualize the individual parts of the mandala and Deity clearly, but not the mandala in its entirety. Practitioners in whom some wisdom has descended are able to visualize the entire mandala very clearly and so are closer than beginners to the wisdom being. Practitioners with some power over wisdom are able to visualize the entire object of subtle generation stage clearly and are now very close to the wisdom being. Some practitioners at this level are able to bring their winds into the central channel through the force of meditating on subtle generation stage, and thereby directly enter completion stage. Complete power over wisdom is attained when we have perfect mastery of both gross and subtle generation stage.

When we are able to remain concentrated on the entire object of gross generation stage without mental sinking or mental excitement for four hours, we have attained firmness in gross generation stage; and when we can remain on this object for as long as we like, for months or even for years, we have completed gross generation stage. When we are able to remain concentrated on the entire object of subtle generation stage without mental sinking or mental excitement for four hours, we have attained firmness in subtle generation stage; and when we can remain on this object for as long as we like, we have completed subtle generation stage.

TRAINING IN THE YOGA OF NON-DUAL PROFUNDITY AND CLARITY

This is a special way of meditating on generation stage that is more profound than the relatively simple one described above, and that acts as the antidote to self-grasping as well as to ordinary appearance and ordinary conception. We begin by practising the simple generation stage meditation explained above, and as our wisdom and concentration improve we gradually transform this into training in the yoga of non-dual profundity and clarity.

'Clarity' refers to the entire mandala appearing clearly, and 'profundity' refers to realizing its emptiness. The yoga of non-dual profundity and clarity is a concentration to which the mandala and Deities appear clearly and that simultaneously cognizes the emptiness of these phenomena. Thus, what appears to this concentration are the mandala and Deities, and what is conceived is their emptiness of inherent existence.

For example, if due to pressing our eyeball we were to see two moons in the sky, their very appearance would remind us that in reality there are not two moons. Similarly, for a practitioner who is familiar with emptiness and clarity, the clear appearance of the mandala and Deities reminds him or her that in reality the mandala and Deities do not exist from their own side. This one concentration realizes both the clear appearance of the mandala and Deities and their lack of true existence. Since this concentration realizes that clear appearance and its emptiness, or profundity, are of one nature, it is called the 'yoga of non-dual profundity and clarity'. Both conventional truths, the mandala and Deities, and ultimate truths, the emptiness of all phenomena, are the objects of this one single concentration, which accumulates both a collection of merit and a collection of wisdom, and thereby creates the cause to attain both the Form Body and the Truth Body of a Buddha.

Perceiving the Deities and mandala clearly while at the same time realizing their emptiness helps us to understand that the appearance of the mandala and Deities develops from the mind of concentration, just as dream objects develop from the mind of sleep. Through this we can understand that the mind of concentration and its objects are the same nature. This experience is essential for gaining the higher realizations of Highest Yoga Tantra.

Although the object of this meditation is the same as that of tranquil abiding on generation stage, the way of meditating is different. We train in the yoga of non-dual profundity and clarity as follows. First we remember that when Guru Heruka dissolved into our mind at our heart, our mind transformed into spontaneous great bliss; and we now recall this experience of bliss. With this mind of bliss we practise the serial and reverse order checking meditation and perceive clearly the generic image of the entire mandala and Deities; and at the same time we develop the divine pride of being Heruka. With our blissful mind we then meditate on the clear appearance of the entire mandala and on divine pride, while at the same time realizing the lack of inherent existence of all phenomena. Thus, our concentration possesses four characteristics: (1) it experiences bliss, (2) it meditates on clear appearance, (3) it meditates on divine pride, and (4) it realizes the emptiness of all phenomena.

Through continual training in this meditation, our mind of concentration will gradually realize that the clear appearance of the mandala and Deities, and their emptiness, or profundity, are non-dual. With this realization we have accomplished the yoga of non-dual profundity and clarity; and with our mind of bliss we experience the two truths, conventional truth and ultimate truth, to be of one nature. We clearly realize that form and the emptiness of form are of one nature, that sound and the emptiness of sound are of one nature, and so on. With this experience, during the meditation break we try to remember and recognize that everything appearing to our mind is the nature of emptiness. Since the emptiness of all phenomena and the great bliss of Heruka are inseparable, everything that appears to us is the nature of the great bliss of definitive Heruka. With this understanding, we shall view every phenomenon that appears to us as the nature of definitive Heruka. By maintaining this view day and night, our ordinary appearances and conceptions will cease and we shall quickly attain enlightenment.

Malgyur Lodrö Drag

The Concluding Practices

The concluding practices has four parts:

1 Mantra recitation
2 Torma offerings
3 Dissolution and generating the action Deities
4 Dedication

MANTRA RECITATION

The practice of training in mantra recitation is called the 'yoga of the vajra speech'. It is a special method for purifying our ordinary speech and for gaining the realizations of vajra recitation and the vajra speech of a Buddha. Through mantra recitation we can pacify the outer and inner obstacles of both ourself and others, and increase our good fortune and spiritual realizations. We can gather all the necessary conditions for spiritual development, and benefit many beings through peaceful or wrathful actions conjoined with the recitation of mantra.

The practice of mantra recitation will now be explained under the following five headings:

1 The mantras to be recited
2 Blessing the mala
3 Long mantra recitation
4 Short mantra recitation
5 Explanation of close retreat

THE MANTRAS TO BE RECITED

'Mantra' literally means 'mind protection'. Training in mantra protects our mind from ordinary appearances and ordinary conceptions, which are the main causes of mental and physical suffering. In general, mantra can be either recitation or meditation. Mantra recitation that is conjoined with special meditation or concentration protects our mind from ordinary appearances and conceptions.

In the root Tantra of Heruka, Buddha Vajradhara explains many different mantras to be recited, and four of these, known as 'the four precious mantras', are particularly blessed. These are: (1) the root mantras of the Father and Mother, (2) the essence mantras of the Father and Mother, (3) the close essence mantras of the Father and Mother, and (4) the mantras of the armour Deities of the Father and Mother. As times become more impure, the blessings and power of these mantras become stronger and stronger. With other Deities, however, as times become more impure the power of their mantras decreases.

In Tibet, some Lamas used to give special blessing cords to their followers, and because some of these followers believed that just by wearing these cords they would be released from suffering, they called them 'liberating merely by wearing'. Others believed in a scripture they called 'liberating merely by hearing', and still others in a special object used by their Lamas, which they called 'liberating merely by seeing'. Other scholars and Lamas, however, are sceptical about these things. They say that the real 'liberating merely by wearing' and 'liberating merely by hearing' are the four precious mantras of Heruka, and that the real 'liberating merely by seeing' are qualified Heruka body mandala practitioners. They say this because Buddha Vajradhara himself said this.

THE ROOT MANTRA OF THE FATHER

In the root Tantra of Heruka, Vajradhara praises in particular the root mantra of the Father:

On this earth, there are the four precious ones,
And of these the root mantra is the most profound.

The root mantra of Heruka reveals the essence of the practice of generation stage and completion stage of Heruka Tantra; it is a condensation of the entire Heruka Tantra. We need to understand its real meaning, not merely the words. Because many of Buddha's Tantric scriptures, especially those of Highest Yoga Tantra, are secret teachings, their real meaning is not revealed directly and we can discover it only by relying upon authentic commentaries. If, for example, we neglect to study the commentaries written by Mahasiddha Ghantapa and Je Tsongkhapa, but try to understand how to practise Heruka body mandala solely through reading Buddha's scriptures, we shall not succeed.

The essential meaning of the root mantra of the Father is expressed as follows:

Through verbal or mental recitation of the profound
    root mantra
And remembering great bliss and emptiness,
O Glorious Heruka, please pacify the fire of harmful
    actions and obstructions,
And their root, the true-grasping of all living beings.

Through the power of valid reasons and scriptures,
Realizing that phenomena, like reflections, do not
    truly exist,
But exist as mere name and mere imputation,
Please pacify all ordinary appearances and
    conceptions.

Through investigating the reality of conventional
    things,
Realizing that it is the middle way, inconceivable and
    inexpressible,
Like finding gold among stones,
Please pacify all conceptions grasping at extremes.

By penetrating the vajra with the lotus of the
    messenger the HAM at my crown melts,
And all the Deities of my channels and drops are
    satiated
With the great bliss concentrating on emptiness;
Please pacify all gross and subtle dualistic appearances.

Through generating the imagined new moon clear
    light
By gathering the secret substance, the white and red
    bodhichittas, at the centre of the lotus,
And through training in the union of this clear light
    and the imagined illusory body,
Please bestow the union of the actual full moon clear
    light and illusory body.

O Glorious Heruka,
You enjoy the supreme pure illusory body and clear
    light of great bliss.
With your fire of omniscient great wisdom,
Please consume and destroy the maras of delusions
    and contaminated aggregates.

You who wear a necklace of human heads strung
    together with human entrails,
Please hook, catch, and destroy the lord of death
    residing at the seventh lower level,
The fearsome, poisonous snake of self-grasping,
And the contaminated aggregates of living beings.

Obstructed by the stains of ignorance, they do not
    know reality –
That everything is a manifestation of emptiness and
    the nature of great bliss;
O Glorious Heruka, please bestow your blessings
    upon all living beings
To lead them to great bliss and emptiness and the
    Union of No More Learning.

The root mantra of Heruka is called the 'root mantra of
the Heroes' because it contains the mantras of all twenty-four
Heroes; KARA KARA, for instance, is the mantra of Khandakapala, KURU KURU the mantra of Mahakankala, and so forth.
The individual mantras of the twenty-four Heroes are therefore the parts of the root mantra of Heruka. The function of
these mantras is to purify the twenty-four drops and winds
that flow through the twenty-four channels. The twenty-four

channels are generated as the twenty-four Heroines, and the twenty-four drops as the twenty-four Heroes. We meditate on these Deities and then recite the root mantra of Heruka, requesting the Principal of all Heroes – Heruka himself – and the twenty-four Heroes to purify our channels, drops, and winds.

THE ROOT MANTRA OF THE MOTHER

When we recite this mantra – the root mantra of Vajravarahi, the Principal of all Heroines – we are calling the supreme enlightened being Vajravarahi, who is the same as Vajrayogini, and requesting her to pacify the maras of our delusions and to purify our channels, drops, and winds. Remembering the pre-eminent qualities of her body and mind, with wishing faith we request her to bestow attainments and help us to progress swiftly along the paths to enlightenment. While concentrating on this meaning, we recite the mantra. A detailed explanation of the pre-eminent qualities of Vajrayogini's body and mind can be found in *Guide to Dakini Land*.

As a result of reciting the root mantras of the Father and Mother with strong faith, all the Heroes and Heroines residing in the twenty-four places of Heruka quickly gather into our channels and drops. Our channels and drops are blessed and purified, which enables us to experience spontaneous great bliss. When our channels, drops, and inner winds are completely purified, so are the appearances to our mind. Delusions and ordinary conceptions cease, and we experience the completely pure environment, enjoyments, body, and mind of Buddha Heruka.

According to Highest Yoga Tantra, samsara and all the sufferings of samsara arise from impure appearances to mind, which in turn arise from impure inner winds. Therefore, impure inner winds are the root of samsara. Through practising Heruka body mandala, our channels and drops are blessed by the Heroes and Heroines, and thus our inner winds are purified. When our inner winds are completely pure, only pure appearances arise, and the sufferings of samsara cease. This is one of the special pre-eminent qualities of Heruka body mandala practice.

The essence mantra of Heruka is OM SHRI VAJRA HE HE RU RU KAM HUM HUM PHAT DAKINI DZALA SHAMBARAM SÖHA. It is called the 'essence mantra' because its main function is to accomplish definitive Heruka, the very essence of Heruka Tantra practice. To start with we accomplish an imagined definitive Heruka, and on this basis, through continual practice, we eventually, attain meaning clear light, the nature definitive Heruka of the path. Finally we accomplish the resultant definitive Heruka.

The emptiness of Heruka's mind is his Nature Truth Body, his mind of great bliss is his Wisdom Truth Body, and the Heruka that is imputed upon these Truth Bodies is definitive Heruka. In Heruka's Truth Body, all phenomena are simultaneously gathered into one nature, emptiness, and completely purified. This is the meaning of 'Chakrasambara'. 'Chakra' means 'wheel of all phenomena' and 'sambara' here means 'gathered together'. The meaning of the essence mantra is as follows:

OM symbolizes Heruka's body, speech, and mind.

SHRI VAJRA HE HE RU RU KAM is the request: 'O Glorious Heruka please listen to me.'

HUM HUM PHAT is the request: 'Please pacify all outer and inner obstacles.'

DAKINI DZALA SHAMBARAM is the request: 'Please bestow the attainments of the wheel of all phenomena gathered and purified in the Dharmakaya.' DAKINI indicates the inner Dakini of the Dharmakaya, DZALA indicates the wheel of all phenomena, and SHAMBARAM means that all phenomena are gathered and purified in the Dharmakaya.

SÖHA is the request: 'Please help me to build the foundation of all attainments by blessing my mental continuum.'

When we recite this mantra, we are requesting Glorious Heruka to pacify all our obstacles and bestow the attainment of Chakrasambara, the wheel of all phenomena gathered and purified in the ultimate truth of the Dharmakaya. Because this mantra is the very essence of Heruka Tantra, precious Lamas advise Heruka practitioners to recite it day and night.

THE CLOSE ESSENCE MANTRA OF THE FATHER

The meaning of the close essence mantra of Heruka, OM HRIH HA HA HUM HUM PHAT, is as follows:

OM symbolizes Heruka's body, speech, and mind.

HRIH HA HA HUM HUM indicate the five exalted wisdoms of all the Buddhas appearing in the form of the Deities of the five wheels of Heruka body mandala. Therefore, when we recite this mantra we are requesting Heruka to help us to accomplish the Deities of the five wheels as well as the mandala.

PHAT is the request: 'Please pacify all outer and inner obstacles.'

When we meditate on generation stage with clear appearance and divine pride, we have accomplished the imagined Deities of the five wheels together with the entire mandala. When we recite the close essence mantra, we are requesting Heruka to help us to accomplish the actual supported Deities and supporting mandala.

In summary, in the practice of reciting the essence mantra we emphasize accomplishing Truth Body Heruka, and in the practice of reciting the close essence mantra we emphasize accomplishing Form Body Heruka. Throughout these practices our motivation is compassion for all living beings. By continually practising these meditations and recitations with deep faith and conviction, we shall attain the Truth and Form Bodies of a Buddha, and thereby be in a position to fulfil our compassionate intention to benefit all living beings.

THE ESSENCE MANTRA OF THE MOTHER

The meaning of the essence mantra of Vajravarahi, OM VAJRA BEROTZANIYE HUM HUM PHAT SÖHA, is as follows:

OM symbolizes Vajravarahi's body, speech, and mind.

VAJRA BEROTZANIYE means 'Vajra Form Dakini', and indicates that Vajravarahi is the nature of the vajra body of all Buddhas. Here 'vajra' refers to great bliss inseparable from emptiness.

HUM HUM is a request to Vajravarahi: 'Please grant me the mundane and supramundane attainments.'

PHAT is the request: 'Please pacify all outer and inner obstacles.'

SÖHA is the request: 'Please help me to build the foundation of all attainments by blessing my mental continuum.'

When we recite this mantra we are first calling our most precious Mother Vajravarahi with 'OM', and then making the following request:

O Holy Mother Vajravarahi, I wish to attain the vajra body of the Buddhas for the benefit of all living beings. For this purpose, please bestow the mundane attainments of increased good fortune, life span, wealth, and other necessary conditions; and the supramundane attainments of renunciation, bodhichitta, the profound view of emptiness, generation stage, and completion stage. Please pacify all outer and inner obstacles and bless my mental continuum.

THE CLOSE ESSENCE MANTRA OF THE MOTHER

The meaning of the close essence mantra of Vajravarahi, OM SARWA BUDDHA DAKINIYE VAJRA WARNANIYE HUM HUM PHAT SÖHA, is as follows:

OM symbolizes Vajravarahi's body, speech, and mind.

SARWA BUDDHA DAKINIYE VAJRA WARNANIYE means the vajra mind and vajra speech of all Buddhas, and so reveals that Vajravarahi is the embodiment of all Buddhas' vajra mind and vajra speech.

HUM HUM is a request to Vajravarahi: 'Please grant me the mundane and supramundane attainments.'

PHAT is the request: 'Please pacify all outer and inner obstacles.'

SÖHA is the request: 'Please help me to build the foundation of all attainments by blessing my mental continuum.'

When we recite this mantra, we are making the following request:

> O Holy Mother Vajravarahi, I wish to attain the vajra mind and vajra speech of the Buddhas for the benefit of all living beings. For this purpose, please bestow the mundane and supramundane attainments, pacify all obstacles, and bless my mental continuum.

In this context, 'vajra' means omniscient great bliss. The real nature of Buddha's body, speech, and mind is omniscient great bliss, and so they are called 'vajra body', 'vajra speech', and 'vajra mind'. Vajrayogini's mantra, known as the 'three-OM mantra', is the union of the essence and close essence mantras of Vajravarahi, arranged in a special way for the recitation of Vajravarahi's mantras. A detailed explanation of Vajrayogini's mantra can be found in *Guide to Dakini Land*.

THE SIX ARMOUR MANTRAS OF THE FATHER AND MOTHER

The main function of the armour Deities and their mantras is to protect Heruka practitioners from obstacles to their concentration on generation stage and completion stage caused by the outer maras of evil spirits and the inner maras of delusions. We do not directly visualize the armour Deities themselves, but simply the letters of their mantras at various places on the body of ourself generated as Heruka and Vajravarahi. We recognize these mantras as the actual Deities, and then with faith and conviction we recite the mantras requesting them to protect our meditation.

With OM OM HA HUM HUM PHAT we request Hero Vajrasattva, the wrathful aspect of Buddha Akshobya; with OM NAMA HI HUM HUM PHAT we request Hero Vairochana, the wrathful aspect of Buddha Vairochana; with OM SÖHA HU

HUM HUM PHAT we request Hero Pämanarteshvara, the wrathful aspect of Buddha Amitabha; with OM BOKE HE HUM HUM PHAT we request Hero Glorious Heruka, the wrathful aspect of Buddha Vajradhara; with OM HUM HUM HO HUM HUM PHAT we request Hero Vajrasurya, the wrathful aspect of Buddha Ratnasambhava; and with OM PHAT HAM HUM HUM PHAT we request Hero Paramashawa, the wrathful aspect of Buddha Amoghasiddhi.

With OM OM BAM HUM HUM PHAT we request Heroine Vajravarahi, the wrathful aspect of Buddha Vajravarahi, the consort of Buddha Akshobya; with OM HAM YOM HUM HUM PHAT we request Heroine Yamani, the wrathful aspect of Lochana, the consort of Buddha Vairochana; with OM HRIM MOM HUM HUM PHAT we request Heroine Mohani, the wrathful aspect of Benzarahi, the consort of Buddha Amitabha; with OM HRIM HRIM HUM HUM PHAT we request Heroine Sachalani, the wrathful aspect of Vajradhatu Ishvara, the consort of Buddha Vajradhara; with OM HUM HUM HUM HUM PHAT we request Heroine Samtrasani, the wrathful aspect of Mamaki, the consort of Buddha Ratnasambhava; and with OM PHAT PHAT HUM HUM PHAT we request Heroine Chandika, the wrathful aspect of Tara, the consort of Buddha Amoghasiddhi.

THE MANTRAS OF THE FOUR YOGINIS OF
THE GREAT BLISS WHEEL

These mantras are the name mantras of Vajradakini, Vajralama, Khandarohi, and Vajrarupini, who are the manifestations of the four Mothers of the five Buddha families – Lochana, Tara, Benzarahi, and Mamaki respectively. When we recite these mantras, we are calling these Deities and requesting them to bestow the mundane and supramundane attainments and to pacify all outer and inner obstacles.

THE MANTRAS OF THE TWENTY-FOUR HEROES

As mentioned before, these mantras are the parts of the root mantra of Heruka. When we recite them, we are calling the individual Heroes such as Khandakapala and requesting them to bestow their blessings upon our channels, drops, and inner winds, and to pacify all outer and inner obstacles.

THE MANTRAS OF THE TWENTY-FOUR HEROINES

These mantras are the name mantras of the twenty-four Heroines. When we recite them, we are calling the individual Heroines such as Partzandi and requesting them to bestow their blessings upon our channels, drops, and inner winds, and to pacify all outer and inner obstacles.

THE MANTRAS OF THE DEITIES OF THE COMMITMENT WHEEL

The mantras of the eight Deities of the commitment wheel are the name mantras of these Deities. We request them principally to pacify obstacles to our life, including danger from fire, water, earth, and wind, as well as harm from humans and non-humans.

When Vajradhara emanated the supporting and supported mandala of Heruka on top of Mount Meru, he appeared as the Principal of the mandala in the form of Heruka with his consort Vajravarahi. Heruka asked the sixty Heroes and Heroines of his retinue to take on various responsibilities, and they promised to do so. The main responsibility of the four Yoginis of the great bliss wheel, and the twenty-four Heroines of the heart wheel, speech wheel, and body wheel, is to help qualified Heruka practitioners to accomplish spontaneous great bliss. The main responsibility of the twenty-four Heroes of the heart wheel, speech wheel, and body wheel is to bestow blessings upon the channels, drops, and inner winds of Heruka practitioners. The main responsibility of the Deities of the commitment wheel is to pacify the obstacles of Heruka practitioners. There is one Heroine in particular, called 'Khandarohi', who took on the responsibility of pacifying the obstacles of practitioners whenever they engaged in any of the four actions, and so she is also called 'action Deity'. Because she is one of the four Yoginis of the great bliss wheel, as well as one of the twenty-four Heroines, she also helps practitioners to accomplish great bliss.

BLESSING THE MALA

Although it is common in many religions to use a mala, or rosary, for reciting prayers or mantras, the way of using it differs. According to Highest Yoga Tantra, we first need to bless the mala and then we can use it for three purposes: (1) for counting mantra recitations, (2) for receiving blessings, and (3) for bestowing blessings on others. In the practice of Heruka body mandala, we bless the mala by generating each bead as the Deity Pämanarteshvara, who is one of the six armour Deities of Father Heruka and is by nature the speech of all Buddhas. He has a red-coloured body with one face and four arms. His first right hand holds a lotus, and his second a damaru. His first left hand holds a bell, and his second a skullcup; and with his left shoulder he supports a khatanga. To bless the mala, we first purify it by meditating on its emptiness while reciting, 'the mala becomes emptiness.' We then imagine that from the state of emptiness each bead appears in its own aspect but with the nature of Pämanarteshvara, the vajra speech of all Buddhas.

Having blessed the mala, we recite the mantras. We begin by hanging the mala over either the ring finger or the index finger of our left hand, holding it either at the level of our heart or our navel. We recite the mantra once and move the first bead in towards us with our thumb. We imagine that from the emptiness of this bead there arises a Heruka who dissolves into our heart or navel, and we receive the blessings of all the Buddhas. Without forgetting this special feeling, we repeat this for each bead. Through reciting the mantras in this way every day, our mala gradually becomes a very powerful and blessed object with which we can bestow blessings to increase others' merit and good fortune, to avert their obstacles, and to pacify their unhappy or negative minds. We can also perform the healing action of touching a person's crown with our blessed mala while making special prayers for their welfare.

LONG MANTRA RECITATION

The visualization for the recitation of the root mantras, the essence mantras, and the close essence mantras of the Father and Mother is as follows. We begin by focusing on the letter HUM at our heart and recognizing it as the nature of Heruka's wisdom of great bliss and emptiness, the source of all the mantras of the Deities of Heruka body mandala. As we recite the root mantra of Heruka, we imagine that from the lower tip of the letter HUM comes a rosary of mantra letters, blue in colour, the nature of wisdom light. This descends through our central channel, leaves through the tip of our vajra, enters the consort's bhaga, ascends through her central channel, leaves through her mouth, enters our mouth, descends, and dissolves back into the HUM at our heart. We then repeat this process, observing the mantra circling through the central channels of ourself and Vajravarahi. While focusing on this visualization, we verbally or mentally recite the mantra as a request to Heruka to bestow profound realizations and pacify outer and inner obstacles. We focus on a similar visualization while reciting the root mantra of Vajravarahi, and the essence and close essence mantras of the Father and Mother.

This visualization is very special. It helps us to maintain divine pride and clear appearance, and causes us to generate great bliss. If our concentration is clear and strong, it also causes the inner winds to gather into and dissolve within the central channel. Without forgetting this visualization, we recite the mantras as a request to pacify obstacles and to bestow attainments.

If we take the words of the root mantras of the Father and Mother literally, it may appear that we are requesting Heruka and Vajravarahi to hook, catch, kill, eat, or destroy someone! In reality however we are requesting Heruka Father and Mother to pacify our outer and inner obstacles and destroy the enemy of the delusions.

The way to recite the mantras of the armour Deities has already been explained. The visualization for reciting the mantras of the sixty retinue Deities is as follows:

Je Tsongkhapa

Standing on a sun seat at the heart of each Deity is a letter HUM or BAM surrounded by the mantra to be recited. From the letter in the centre of the encircling mantra, assemblies of mandala Deities radiate and fulfil the welfare of all living beings. They gather back and dissolve into the central letter, repeatedly radiating and gathering back.

SHORT MANTRA RECITATION

We may not always have time to practise long mantra recitation, or we may be a beginner who finds reciting the long mantra too difficult or complicated. If this is the case we can practise short mantra recitation. To do this, we should recite only the essence mantras and the close essence mantras of the Father and Mother, the mantras of the four Yoginis of the great bliss wheel, the mantras of the Deities of the heart wheel, speech wheel, body wheel, and commitment wheel, and the condensed essence mantra of the sixty retinue Deities.

While focusing on the visualization described above, we practise reciting the essence mantra of the Father as follows. First we imagine that our mind is experiencing great bliss mixed with emptiness, and we perceive nothing other than this union of great bliss and emptiness. Using this union as the basis for imputing Heruka, we think 'I am Truth Body Heruka' and meditate on the divine pride of being definitive Heruka. Without forgetting divine pride, we recite the essence mantra as a request to Heruka to help us to complete the attainment of definitive Heruka as our ultimate refuge. In this way our recitation becomes the uncommon refuge practice of Highest Yoga Tantra that brings resultant refuge into the path. When we first practise this mantra recitation we accomplish an imagined definitive Heruka, which is like the new moon. At the same time, by reciting the mantra we are requesting Heruka to help us to complete the attainment of definitive Heruka so that finally our imagined definitive Heruka becomes the actual definitive Heruka, which is like the full moon.

If our experience of emptiness is weak, while we are reciting one part of our mind should think:

Since beginningless time everything has been the same nature as emptiness. Nothing, not even the smallest atom, exists from the side of the object. This is ultimate truth.

If our experience of bliss is weak we should strengthen it by recalling the visualization for reciting the mantras of the Principal Deities described in the sadhana, or at the very least we should remember that we, Heruka, are in embrace with Vajravarahi. Experiencing the union of great bliss and emptiness, we strongly think, 'I am Truth Body Heruka', and while maintaining this divine pride we recite the mantra.

The visualization and way of reciting the close essence mantra of the Father, the essence and close essence mantras of the Mother, and the mantras of the retinues are the same as those described above.

EXPLANATION OF CLOSE RETREAT

In general, the most important thing is to practise the sadhana every day of our life. During our sessions, we should emphasize meditation and recitation, in particular becoming familiar with the three bringings, divine pride, and clear appearance. Out of meditation, we should integrate our meditational experiences into our daily activities so that we can transform our daily life into the paths of Highest Yoga Tantra.

It is also important to engage in retreat from time to time to gain a deeper experience of our daily practice. We can do a simple retreat at any time, even for just a few days or weeks. During retreat we stop all busy minds and distractions. For this purpose we stop daily business, meaningless talk, reading newspapers, listening to the radio, watching television, and so forth, and remain with a quiet and happy mind day and night.

A close retreat is so called because it is a retreat in which we practise special methods that cause us to draw closer to the attainments of a Tantric Deity. There are three types of close retreat: (1) a close retreat of signs, (2) a close retreat of time, and (3) a close retreat of numbers. We engage in a close retreat of signs when we remain in retreat until a correct sign of attainment manifests. We engage in a close retreat of time when we do a retreat for a definite period of time, such as six months; or alternatively when we do either a long or short close retreat every year at the same time.

There are two types of close retreat of numbers: a close retreat of actions, and a great close retreat. There are also two types of close retreat of actions: a long close retreat of actions, and a short close retreat of actions. On a long close retreat of actions of Heruka we recite the essence mantras of the Father and Mother three hundred thousand times, the close essence mantras of the Father and Mother ten thousand times, and the essence mantras of the sixty retinues ten thousand times each. On a short close retreat of actions of Heruka we recite the essence mantras of the Father and Mother one hundred thousand times, the close essence mantras of the Father and Mother ten thousand times, and the condensed essence mantra of the sixty retinues ten thousand times. For a close retreat of actions it is not necessary to count the root mantras of the Father and Mother or the mantras of the armour Deities.

To conclude both long and short close retreats of actions we recite ten thousand wisdom-descending mantras. This mantra is: OM SHRI VAJRA HE HE RU RU KAM HUM HUM PHAT DAKINI DZALA SHAMBARAM VAJRA BEROTZANIYE HUM HUM PHAT HUM HA ADZE SÖHA. While reciting this mantra, we visualize countless rays of blue light radiating from our heart to the ten directions and inviting all the Buddhas in the form of Heruka. These dissolve into our body like a heavy shower of rain falling into an ocean. With strong conviction we think that we have received the blessings of all the Buddhas, and we imagine that our mind and body transform into the nature of omniscient wisdom.

To complete a successful close retreat of actions we need to do four things:

1 The preparations
2 The preliminary practices
3 The actual retreat
4 The fire puja

THE PREPARATIONS

There are two types of preparation: inner and outer. The most important inner preparation is to understand clearly how to meditate on the three bringings and the actual generation stage, how to practise the mantra recitations, and how to begin, progress on, and complete the whole retreat. We do this by studying the commentary and receiving advice from Teachers or other qualified practitioners. In particular, we need to cultivate and maintain a pure motivation and strong faith in this holy Dharma and in our Spiritual Teacher from whom we received the empowerments and instructions.

Once we have made these inner preparations, we make the outer preparations. If the place where we are living is quiet, peaceful, and free from specific obstacles, we do not need to look elsewhere; but if this is not the case we need to find a suitable location and meditation room for our retreat that is free from obstacles and where it is easy to find the necessary conditions. We then clean our meditation room, and prepare our shrine and meditation seat, or cushion. This should be very comfortable and stable because on a close retreat of actions we need to recite all the mantra recitations on the same seat without moving it. If possible it should face the shrine. If for any reason we find it difficult to sit on the floor, we can use a chair as our meditation seat.

THE PRELIMINARY PRACTICES

On the morning of the day that our retreat begins, we once again clean our meditation room and the area around it. In front of a shrine containing statues or pictures of our Spiritual Guide, Buddha Shakyamuni, Je Tsongkhapa, Heruka, and Dharmapala Dorje Shugdän, we set out tormas, outer offerings, and tsog offerings. On a small table in front of our meditation seat we arrange our inner offering, vajra, bell, damaru, mala, and sadhana. Then in the afternoon, before supper, we engage in the actual preliminary practices. We sit on our meditation seat and first practise the *Heart Jewel* sadhana with Lamrim meditation, especially the meditation on bodhichitta, to pacify obstacles, receive blessings, and generate a pure motivation. Then, while concentrating on its meaning, we practise the Heruka retreat sadhana, *Heruka Retreat Preliminary Jewel*, which can be found in Appendix II.

THE ACTUAL RETREAT

After finishing the preliminary practices, we relax until the evening when, with a happy mind, we start the first session of our retreat. We recite the *Essence of Vajrayana* sadhana from going for refuge up to the auspicious prayers, including the tsog offering, while concentrating on its meaning; and afterwards we practise the yoga of sleep. The following morning we practise the yoga of rising and the yoga of experiencing nectar, and then we do the first session of the day. If we do four sessions each day, the first session should be finished before breakfast, the second before lunch, the third before supper, and the fourth before we go to bed. In the first three sessions we do not need to offer the tormas or recite the extensive dedication prayers, and in the last three sessions we do not need to do the meditation and recitation of Vajrasattva or bless the inner offering.

During every session it is most important to prevent our mind from being distracted to other objects such as our normal activities, friends, and enjoyments; and also to prevent ourself from falling asleep. We should do our sessions with a joyful mind, having strong faith in the supreme Buddha, Guru Heruka Father and Mother, the holy Dharma of these profound Heruka body mandala instructions, and the supreme Sangha, the assembly of Heroes and Heroines.

Between sessions we should improve our experience of renunciation, bodhichitta, and the profound view of emptiness by reading, contemplating, and meditating on the precious practices of Lamrim and Lojong. Without doing this, it will be very difficult for us to maintain a pure motivation and so our Tantric meditation will become powerless. We should also read again and again the commentary to the practice of Heruka body mandala until we gain a deep understanding of the entire meaning of the sadhana.

Once we have concluded our retreat, and before we perform the fire puja, we need to complete a full session of the sadhana every day without missing even one day.

THE FIRE PUJA

The purpose of performing the fire puja, or burning offering, after our retreat is to purify the many mistakes we made during the retreat. For example, we may not have done our retreat correctly as a result of ignoring the instructions on what we should and should not do. We may have created non-virtuous mental actions by developing anger, wrong views, and negative thoughts towards our Teachers, spiritual friends, or other people. We may have done our whole retreat with a distracted mind or impure motivation, and we may have developed many doubts about Dharma. During the sessions we may have had no concentration at all, nor even a single positive mind. We may have spent most of the time during sessions under the influence of dullness or sleep. We may have had no faith in Buddha, Dharma, or Sangha, and no conviction in the instructions. We may have failed to recite the mantras correctly or with feeling. We can purify all these mistakes by performing the fire puja.

During the fire puja, we offer thirteen different substances to the supramundane Fire Deities – Heruka and his retinues – and to the mundane Fire Deity. Making these offerings is a cause of increasing our wealth, resources, good fortune, life span, physical health, mental peace, and the power of our actions. In particular, it is a powerful purification of downfalls, mistaken actions, and all inauspiciousness. We should learn how to prepare the offerings and the mandala and how to do the actual puja. If we have no knowledge of these, we need to find qualified assistants within the same lineage. A more detailed explanation of the fire puja can be found in *Guide to Dakini Land*.

Once we have completed a close retreat of actions and a fire puja, we have the opportunity to engage in self-initiation. Through this we can renew our Tantric vows if they have degenerated, and we can also benefit many living beings by performing ritual actions such as pacifying, increasing, controlling, and wrathful actions. Therefore, this retreat is called 'close retreat of actions'. The self-initiation sadhana, *Union of No More Learning*, can be found in Appendix II.

On a great close retreat of Heruka, we recite the essence mantra of the Father ten million times; the essence mantra of the Mother four hundred thousand times; the close essence mantras of the Father and Mother, the root mantras of the Father and Mother, and the armour mantras of the Father and Mother one thousand times; and the essence mantras of the sixty retinues ten thousand times. We recite the wisdom-descending mantra one hundred thousand times, and then we engage in the extensive burning offering.

TORMA OFFERINGS

The torma offering is a special offering of food made to the in-front-generated Deities with the request that they bestow upon us siddhis, or attainments. In the *Heruka Tantra* it says:

Without powerful torma offerings
You cannot swiftly accomplish siddhis;
Thus, previous Buddhas praised torma offerings.

The Tibetan term 'torma' is composed of the two words 'tor' and 'ma'. 'Tor' indicates that we should spend everything we own on these offerings, and 'ma', which literally means 'mother', indicates that we should love all living beings as a mother loves her children. Nowadays it is impossible to find a practitioner who will spend everything he or she owns on a torma offering, but from the word 'tor' we should understand that the torma offering is very important and that it would be worthwhile to spend everything on it. The meaning of 'ma' reveals that our motivation for making torma offerings should be love and compassion for all living beings. Because we wish to benefit all living beings, we make the torma offerings as a request to Guru Heruka and his retinues to bestow the attainment of full enlightenment.

The explanation of the torma offering has three parts:

1 Blessing the tormas
2 Inviting the guests of the tormas
3 The actual torma offering

BLESSING THE TORMAS

We bless the tormas in the same way as we bless the inner offering except for two differences. First, the basis for accomplishing the torma offering is an outer substance set out in front of the shrine, whereas the basis for accomplishing the inner offering is the inner substances of the five meats and the five nectars. Second, in the torma offering the basis is transformed into the nectar of food, whereas in the inner offering the basis is transformed into nectar for drinking.

INVITING THE GUESTS OF THE TORMAS

Verbally we recite PHAIM, physically we perform the blazing mudra, and mentally we imagine that we are experiencing great bliss and emptiness. We imagine that from the letter HUM at our heart infinite light rays emanate and invite all the Buddhas in the form of the assembly of the Deities of the five wheels from their natural abode, the Dharmakaya; and all the directional guardians, regional guardians, and so forth from the eight charnel grounds.

We visualize the assembly of the Deities of the five wheels in the space in front of us inside our celestial mansion. At the outermost edge is a circle of the eight Goddesses of the commitment wheel, inside this is a circle of the eight Heroes and Heroines of the body wheel, inside this is a circle of the eight Heroes and Heroines of the speech wheel, inside this is a circle of the eight Heroes and Heroines of the heart wheel, inside this are the four Yoginis of the great bliss wheel, and in the very centre are Guru Heruka Father and Mother. We imagine that the purified channels and drops of Guru Heruka are appearing in the form of the Deities of the five wheels. This is the in-front-generation of the Deities of Heruka body mandala.

When we invite the directional guardians and so forth, we are inviting the eleven great assemblies of mundane Dakas and Dakinis from each charnel ground. These are the assemblies of gods, nagas, givers of harm, cannibals, evil spirits, hungry ghosts, flesh-eaters, crazy-makers, forgetful-makers, dakas, and female spirits. Because they have the aspect of worldly gods and spirits, they are called 'mundane Dakas and Dakinis', but in essence they are manifestations of Heruka. We now visualize the eleven assemblies of each charnel ground gathering as our guests at the borders of their charnel ground, together with all the spirits throughout the world.

THE ACTUAL TORMA OFFERING

To make the torma offering, we imagine that countless Rasavajra Goddesses emanate from the letter HUM at our heart, take replica tormas from the tormas that were blessed, and offer these first to the Principal Father and Mother and the four Yoginis, then to the other supramundane guests, and finally to the mundane guests. The actual torma offering therefore has four parts:

1 Offering the principal torma
2 Offering the torma to the Deities of the heart wheel, speech wheel, and body wheel
3 Offering the torma to the Deities of the commitment wheel
4 Offering the torma to the mundane Dakas and Dakinis, and to all the spirits throughout the world

OFFERING THE PRINCIPAL TORMA

With the mudra of holding the torma container, which is described in *Guide to Dakini Land*, we recite three times the offering mantra: OM VAJRA AH RA LI HO: DZA HUM BAM HO: VAJRA DAKINI SAMAYA TÖN TRISHAYA HO. With the first recitation we offer the torma to Guru Heruka, with the second we offer it to Vajravarahi, and with the third we offer it to the four Yoginis. The meaning of the mantra is as follows:

OM means that we are calling the guests of the torma.

VAJRA refers to the torma itself, which is the nature of great bliss inseparable from emptiness.

AH RA LI HO means 'Please enjoy.'

DZA: we imagine the nectar reaches the tongues of the guests.

HUM: the nectar reaches their throats.

BAM: it reaches their hearts.

HO: they experience spontaneous great bliss.

VAJRA DAKINI here means 'O Space Enjoyer'.

SAMAYA TÖN means 'Through your compassionate equanimity'.

TRISHAYA HO means 'Please care for me.'

'Space Enjoyers' are Dakas and Dakinis – Tantric male and female Buddhas. The Tibetan word for Space Enjoyer is 'kha-dro' – 'kha' means 'space-like Dharmakaya', the Nature Truth Body of the Buddhas, and 'dro' means 'enjoyer'. Tantric Buddhas are called 'Space Enjoyers' because they enjoy their Nature Truth Body, which is space-like emptiness. They are also called 'Heroes' and 'Heroines' because they are completely victorious over the four maras. Explanations of the four maras can be found in *Ocean of Nectar* and *Heart of Wisdom*.

OFFERING THE TORMA TO THE DEITIES OF THE HEART WHEEL, SPEECH WHEEL, AND BODY WHEEL

With the mudra of holding the torma container, we recite once the root mantra of the Heroes, requesting each of the Heroes and Heroines to enjoy our offerings and bestow siddhis. We imagine that Rasavajra Goddesses take nectar food from the blessed nectar of the torma and serve it to the twenty-four Heroes and Heroines, such as Hero Khandakapala and Heroine Partzandi.

OFFERING THE TORMA TO THE DEITIES OF THE COMMITMENT WHEEL

With the mudra of holding the torma container, we recite twice the 'VAJRA AH RA LI' mantra, and imagine that Rasavajra Goddesses serve the nectar food of the torma. With the first recitation we offer the torma to the four Goddesses in the cardinal directions, Kakase, Ulukase, Shönase, and Shukarase; and with the second recitation we offer it to the four Goddesses in the intermediate directions, Yamadhati, Yamaduti, Yamadangtrini, and Yamamatani.

We then make the eight outer offerings, the inner offering, the secret and thatness offerings, and the eight lines of praise to the Father and Mother, followed by requests to the assembly of supramundane Deities for the fulfilment of wishes.

OFFERING THE TORMA TO THE MUNDANE DAKAS AND DAKINIS, AND TO ALL THE SPIRITS THROUGHOUT THE WORLD

We meditate on the real nature of these countless mundane beings – their lack of true existence – and then imagine that from the state of emptiness they each arise in the aspect of Heruka with one face and two arms, embracing his consort. With the mudra of holding the torma container, we recite twice the offering mantra beginning, 'OM KHA KHA, KHAHI KHAHI . . . ', and imagine that countless Rasavajra Goddesses serve the nectar food of the torma to all these mundane guests. With the first recitation we offer the torma to the mundane guests in the four cardinal directions, and with the second recitation we offer it to the mundane guests in the four intermediate directions. We then make the eight outer offerings and the inner offering; and, because we have generated all the worldly spirits as Heruka, we can also offer them the eight lines of praise to the Father and Mother. We then recite the request prayer from the sadhana.

This special way of making offerings to the worldly spirits causes their minds to become peaceful and virtuous. In this way, their intention to harm living beings ceases and we are freed from many obstacles and dangers. It is said that this practice of making torma offerings to the mundane guests is very beneficial both for individuals and for society in general. If we have bad dreams or physical or mental difficulties, we can sincerely practise the yoga of torma offerings of Heruka or Vajrayogini.

To purify any mistakes we made during our session, we recite Heruka's one-hundred-letter mantra once, and then recall divine pride thinking, 'I am Truth Body Heruka', by reciting 'OM YOGA SHUDDHA SARWA DHARMA YOGA SHUDDHO HAM'. This means, 'I am the nature of the yoga of the complete purity of all phenomena', and refers to Buddha's Truth Body, the Dharmakaya. We then recite 'VAJRA MU', which means that the mundane guests return to their own places. Finally, we imagine that the assembly of supramundane guests dissolves into us.

DISSOLUTION AND GENERATING THE ACTION DEITIES

Through training in the following meditation, we shall gain the deep knowledge that clearly understands the ultimate nature of samsara and nirvana to be the same – mere lack of inherent existence. Understanding this will enable us to make rapid progress in both generation stage and completion stage.

Immediately after the clear light of death of our previous life ceased, we experienced the first moment of the mind of this life and perceived the appearance of black near-attainment of reverse order. Gradually from this mind developed all the gross minds that perceive the appearances of this life, such as our environment, enjoyments, body, and mind; and we came to experience various pleasant, unpleasant, and neutral feelings. When we die, all our gross minds will dissolve back into the clear light of death and all appearances of this world will vanish.

Similarly, when we meditate on bringing death into the path of the Truth Body, we imagine that all ordinary appearances dissolve into the clear light of death, and that from this mind gross minds perceiving the pure environment, enjoyments, body, and mind of Heruka develop. Later, in this meditation on dissolution, these gross minds dissolve back into the clear light of emptiness. Everything we perceived during generation stage meditation, the mandala and Deities, has disappeared, and once again we experience only the clear light of emptiness. This process of manifestation and dissolution of the mind and its objects shows very clearly that nothing in samsara or nirvana exists from its own side; they exist only as mere appearances to mind.

We do this meditation by following the sadhana. We visualize as follows:

The charnel grounds and protection circle dissolve into the celestial mansion. The celestial mansion dissolves into the Deities of the commitment wheel. They dissolve into the Deities of the body wheel. They dissolve into the Deities of the speech wheel. They dissolve into the Deities of the heart wheel. They dissolve into the four Yoginis of the great bliss wheel. They dissolve into me, the Principal Deity Father and Mother, the nature of the white and red indestructible drop. I, the Principal Deity Father and Mother, also melt into light and dissolve into the letter HUM at my heart, in nature the emptiness of the Dharmakaya.

At this point we perceive nothing other than the emptiness of the Dharmakaya. We meditate on this emptiness for a short while and then we generate the action Deities. We imagine:

From the state of emptiness, our world arises as Heruka's Pure Land, Keajra. I and all sentient beings arise as the Blessed One Heruka, with a blue-coloured body, one face, and two arms embracing Vajravarahi.

We feel that we have fulfilled both our own purpose and that of all other living beings. We should keep this view during the meditation break throughout the day and the night.

We adorn our body with the armour Deities as an inner protection circle as explained on pages 113-4, and then recite the mantra emanating from the four faces to prevent any harm from spirits. We then complete the session with the dedication and auspicious prayers from the sadhana.

HOW TO PRACTISE DURING THE MEDITATION BREAK

During the meditation break, we should continually maintain our experience of the divine pride of being Heruka, together with the pure environment and enjoyments that we accomplished during the meditation session. We should always maintain the special recognition that everything we see or hear is a manifestation of definitive Heruka. Full experience of this special recognition prevents us from damaging or breaking our Tantric vows and commitments, and is a powerful method for preventing ordinary appearances and conceptions. If we can prevent ordinary appearances and conceptions during the meditation break, there is no doubt that during our meditation session our generation stage meditation will progress quickly towards the final result.

Heruka practitioners should regard whatever they see or hear as a manifestation of Heruka and then praise it with the eight lines of praise. Whenever they enjoy beautiful forms, sounds, food, drink, or any other enjoyment, they should regard these as offerings to themselves generated as Heruka, the synthesis of all Buddhas. We should constantly recall that when we engaged in the practice of generating the action Deities we generated ourself and all sentient beings as the Blessed One Heruka. We believe that this appearance is valid and that our normal ordinary appearance is incorrect and deceptive. By thinking in this way, we prevent ordinary appearances and conceptions during the meditation break.

How quickly our practice progresses during the meditation session and the meditation break depends upon how well we understand the instructions. Therefore, during the meditation break we should study the commentaries, improve our understanding of the instructions on generation stage and completion stage, and make a determination to put our understanding into practice.

The results of Highest Yoga Tantra practice depend upon our motivation, and so we should cultivate and maintain a pure motivation, free from self-cherishing. In these degenerate times it is impossible to maintain such a motivation without the sincere practice of Lamrim, and for this reason qualified Tantric Masters advise their disciples to keep Lamrim as their daily practice. For example, suppose there is a sincere Heruka practitioner called Mary. Whenever she thinks, 'I am Mary', she should practise renunciation, the three types of love, compassion, and bodhichitta; and whenever she thinks, 'I am Heruka', she should engage in the practice of Heruka Tantra.

PART TWO

Completion Stage

Je Phabongkhapa

Preliminary Explanation

The explanation of completion stage will be given under three headings:

1 An introduction to completion stage
2 The preliminary practices
3 The actual practice of completion stage

AN INTRODUCTION TO COMPLETION STAGE

As mentioned before, generation stage is like drawing the basic outline of a picture and completion stage is like completing the picture. Whereas the principal objects of generation stage meditation – the mandala and Deities – are generated by imagination, the principal objects of completion stage meditation – the channels, drops, and winds – already exist within our body and so there is no need to generate them through the power of imagination. Therefore, completion stage is not a creative yoga but a yoga of learning developed in dependence upon the inner winds entering, abiding, and dissolving within the central channel through the force of meditation. A detailed explanation of the meaning of completion stage can be found in *Tantric Grounds and Paths*.

According to the system of Ghantapa, there are five stages to the completion stage practice of Heruka. The purpose of the first stage – blessing the self – is to control the inner winds; and the purpose of the second stage – the vajra of various qualities – is to control the drops. In dependence upon these two stages, we can gain the initial realization of the union of spontaneous great bliss and emptiness by relying upon mudras on the third stage – filling with jewels. In dependence upon this, on the fourth stage – dzöladhara – through tummo meditation we can improve the realization of great bliss and emptiness that we gained on the third stage. In dependence upon this, we can attain the union of illusory body and meaning clear light, and thereby enter the fifth stage – inconceivability. From this stage, we shall directly reach the stage of the Union of No More Learning, Buddhahood.

Before engaging in the practice of these five stages, we need to understand the basic objects of meditation – the channels, drops, and winds – and the actual stages of the paths. There are three main channels: the central channel, the right channel, and the left channel; and six principal channel wheels: the crown channel wheel, the throat channel wheel, the heart channel wheel, the navel channel wheel, the secret place channel wheel, and the channel wheel of the sex organ.

The central channel is like the pole of an umbrella, running through the centre of each of the channel wheels, and the right and left channels run either side of it. The central channel is pale blue on the outside and has four attributes: (1) it is very straight, like the trunk of a plantain tree, (2) inside it is an oily red colour, like pure blood, (3) it is very clear and transparent, like a candle flame, and (4) it is very soft and flexible, like a lotus petal. The central channel is located exactly midway between the left and right halves of the body, but is closer to the back than the front. Immediately in front of the spine, there is the life channel, which is quite thick; and in front of this is the central channel. It begins at the point between the eyebrows, from where it ascends in an arch to the crown of the head, and then descends in a straight line to the tip of the sex organ.

Either side of the central channel, with no intervening space, are the right and left channels. The right channel is red in colour and the left is white. The right channel begins at the tip of the right nostril and the left channel at the tip of the left nostril. From there, they both ascend in an arch to the crown of the head, either side of the central channel. From the crown of the head down to the navel, these three main channels are straight and adjacent to one another. As the left channel continues down below the level of the navel, it curves a little to the right, separating slightly from the central channel and rejoining it at the tip of the sex organ. There it functions to hold and release sperm, blood, and urine. As the right channel continues down below the level of the navel, it curves a little to the left and terminates at the tip of the anus, where it functions to hold and release faeces and so forth.

The right and left channels coil around the central channel at various places, thereby forming the so-called 'channel knots'. The four places at which these knots occur are, in ascending order, the navel channel wheel, the heart channel wheel, the throat channel wheel, and the crown channel wheel. At each of these places, except at the heart level, there is a twofold knot formed by a single coil of the right channel and a single coil of the left. As the right and left channels ascend to these places they coil around the central channel by crossing in front and then looping around it. They then continue upward to the level of the next knot. At the heart the same thing happens, except that here there is a sixfold knot formed by three overlapping loops of each of the flanking channels. At the beginning, it is sufficient simply to become familiar with the description and visualization of the three channels.

We then need to become familiar with the drops, particularly the indestructible drop. In this context, drops are the essence of our blood and sperm; sometimes they are also called 'bodhichittas'. As just explained, at the heart channel wheel there is a sixfold knot formed by the right and left channels coiling around the central channel and constricting it. This is the most difficult knot to loosen, but when it is loosened through meditation we shall develop great power – the realization of clear light. Because the central channel at the heart is constricted by this sixfold knot, it is blocked like a tube of bamboo. Inside the central channel, at the very centre of this sixfold knot, there is a very small vacuole, and inside this is a drop called the 'indestructible drop'. It is the size of a small pea, with the upper half white in colour and the lower half red. The substance of the white half is the very clear essence of sperm, and the substance of the red half is the very clear essence of blood. This drop, which is very pure and subtle, is the very essence of all drops. All the ordinary red and white drops throughout the body originally come from this drop.

The indestructible drop is rather like a small pea that has been cut in half, slightly hollowed out, and then rejoined. It is called the 'indestructible drop' because its two halves never separate until we die. When we die, all the inner winds dissolve into the indestructible drop, and this causes the drop to open. As the two halves separate, our consciousness immediately leaves our body and goes to the next life.

Inside the indestructible drop resides the indestructible wind and mind, which is the union of our very subtle wind and our very subtle mind. The very subtle wind is our own body, or continuously residing body; and the very subtle mind is our own mind, or continuously residing mind. The union of these two is called the 'indestructible wind and mind'. Our indestructible wind and mind have never separated since beginningless time, and they will never separate in the future. The potential possessed by the combination of our very subtle body and mind to communicate is our very subtle speech, which is our own speech. This will become a Buddha's speech in the future. In short, inside the indestructible drop is our own body, speech, and mind, which in the future will become the enlightened body, speech, and mind of a Buddha.

Inner winds are essential for the functioning of our body and mind. Their main role, however, is to act as mounts for the various minds. Altogether there are ten types of inner wind – the five root and the five branch winds. The five root winds are: (1) the life-supporting wind, (2) the downward-voiding wind, (3) the upward-moving wind, (4) the equally-abiding wind, and (5) the pervading wind. The five branch winds are: (1) the moving wind, (2) the intensely-moving wind, (3) the perfectly-moving wind, (4) the strongly-moving wind, and (5) the definitely-moving wind. A detailed explanation of these winds can be found in *Clear Light of Bliss.*

We should check what the central channel and indestructible drop look like and where they are located, and become familiar with these.

THE PRELIMINARY PRACTICES

The essential preliminary practices for successful completion stage meditation are meditation on the common paths – renunciation, bodhichitta, and the correct view of emptiness – as well as purifying negativities and obstacles, accumulating great merit, and receiving special blessings. We should spend some time every day practising these, and sometimes we should do a special retreat on the preliminary practices.

When emphasizing the practice of generation stage according to the sadhana *Essence of Vajrayana*, after generating ourself as the action Deity we regard all the practices from going for refuge up to generating as the action Deity as preliminary practices for completion stage meditation. We then engage in the first meditation of the five stages of completion stage, meditating on the stage of blessing the self, as described in the sadhana.

Later, when emphasizing the practice of completion stage, we can follow the preliminary practices from the sadhana, from going for refuge up to the end of Guru yoga, as preliminary practices for our completion stage meditation. Once we have imagined that Guru Heruka has become of one taste with our mind at our heart, we can engage in the practice of any of the five stages of completion stage meditation.

At the end of each session, we recite the following dedication prayers while concentrating on their meaning:

For the sake of all living beings
May I become Heruka;
And then lead every living being
To Heruka's supreme state.

May I gain the realizations of the five stages of the
profound path

Of the secret meaning of the King of Mother Tantras
As clearly explained by Mahasiddha Ghantapa;
And thus may I accomplish the state of Glorious
　　Heruka in this life.

Through the stage of blessing the self,
With my mind absorbed in vajra recitation on the
　　winds inseparable from mantra
And on the letter HUM at the centre of my heart
　　chakra,
May I completely release the channel knots at my
　　heart.

Through the stage of the vajra of various qualities,
Observing the tiny HUM and the moon, sun, and drop
At the centre of the vajra at the lower and upper tips
　　of my central channel,
May I attain stable spontaneous bliss, and may my
　　bodhichittas increase.

Through the pure fire induced by the whirling touch
　　of the four beautiful goddesses –
The commitment mudra, action mudra, phenomenon
　　mudra, and Mahamudra –
Melting the drops of my seventy-two thousand
　　channels,
May I complete the stage of filling with jewels.

Through holding the drop of the five families
　　enclosed within the vase breath,
Inside the phenomena source at dzöladhara at my
　　secret place,
And through the strong movement of the blazing
　　and dripping of AH and HAM,
May I receive the stream of blessings of all the
　　compassionate Conquerors.

By relying upon the outer and inner methods,
Such as the three enjoyments and the two
　　concentrations,

May I attain the inseparable union of illusory body
and clear light,
And thus complete the stage of inconceivability.

In short, may I never be separated from Venerable
Guru Father and Mother,
But always come under their loving care and receive
their blessings.
In this way, may I swiftly complete all the grounds
and paths,
And quickly attain the state of Heruka.

Kyabje Trijang Rinpoche

The Five Stages of Completion Stage

THE ACTUAL PRACTICE OF COMPLETION STAGE

The actual practice of completion stage will now be explained
under the following five headings:

1 The stage of blessing the self
2 The stage of the vajra of various qualities
3 The stage of filling with jewels
4 The stage of dzöladhara
5 The stage of inconceivability

THE STAGE OF BLESSING THE SELF

This has two parts:

1 The stage of blessing the self with seed
2 The stage of blessing the self without seed

THE STAGE OF BLESSING THE SELF WITH SEED

This has three parts:

1 Meditation on the central channel
2 Meditation on the indestructible drop
3 Meditation on the indestructible wind and mind

The first two meditations are preparations, and the third is
the actual meditation on blessing the self with seed.

MEDITATION ON THE CENTRAL CHANNEL

We contemplate as follows:

*My central channel is located exactly midway between the
left and right halves of my body, but is closer to the back than*

the front. Immediately in front of the spine, there is the life channel, which is quite thick; and in front of this is the central channel. It begins at the point between my eyebrows, from where it ascends in an arch to the crown of my head, and then descends in a straight line to the tip of my sex organ. It is pale blue in colour on the outside, and it is an oily red colour on the inside. It is clear and transparent, and very soft and flexible.

At the very beginning we can, if we wish, visualize the central channel as being fairly wide, and then gradually visualize it as becoming thinner and thinner until finally we are able to visualize it as being the width of a drinking straw. We contemplate like this repeatedly until we perceive a generic image of our central channel. We then focus on the central channel at the level of our heart and feel that our mind is inside the central channel. We meditate single-pointedly on this without distraction.

MEDITATION ON THE INDESTRUCTIBLE DROP

Having gained some experience of the central channel at the heart, we then meditate on the indestructible drop. We contemplate as follows:

Inside my central channel at my heart level, there is a very small vacuole. Inside this is my indestructible drop. It is the size of a small pea, with the upper half white in colour, and the lower half red. It resembles a pea that has been cut in half, slightly hollowed out, and then rejoined. It is the very essence of all drops and is very pure and subtle. Even though it is the substance of blood and sperm, it has a very clear nature, like a tiny ball of crystal that radiates five-coloured rays of light.

We contemplate like this repeatedly until we perceive a clear generic image of our indestructible drop and its location, and we meditate on this without distraction.

MEDITATION ON THE INDESTRUCTIBLE WIND AND MIND

We contemplate as follows:

Inside the indestructible drop is my indestructible wind and mind in the aspect of a tiny letter HUM, the size of a mustard seed. It is reddish-white in colour and radiates five-coloured rays of light. Its nature is my Guru, who is the synthesis of all the Buddhas, its substance is my indestructible wind and mind, and its shape is that of a letter HUM, symbolizing Heruka's mind.

We think of the indestructible drop as being like a house, and of our indestructible wind and mind in the aspect of a letter HUM as being like a person inhabiting that house. We contemplate like this repeatedly until we perceive the letter HUM inside the indestructible drop at the centre of the heart channel wheel.

We then concentrate principally on the nada at the tip of the HUM. This is red at the top and reddish-white at the bottom. It is radiating red light and dripping nectar. We imagine that the five winds that flow through the five doors of the senses, such as the moving wind, and the five minds, such as the eye awareness, dissolve into the nada; and we feel that our mind has entered into the nada. We then meditate on the nada single-pointedly. If we find this difficult, to help us to absorb our mind into the nada we can think of the nada as being extremely dense and heavy.

If we do this meditation repeatedly, when we attain the second mental abiding our inner winds will enter into our central channel. Later, when we attain the fourth mental abiding, our winds will enter, abide, and dissolve within the central channel and we shall actually experience the eight signs of dissolution from the mirage-like-appearance up to the clear light.

As explained in *Clear Light of Bliss*, there are ten doors through which the winds can enter the central channel. According to this system we choose the heart channel wheel. It is important always to do this meditation gently, without pushing. Some people say that we should not begin our practice of completion stage meditation at the heart because it can cause sickness such as wind disease, but Je Tsongkhapa praised this practice highly. He said that because the object of meditation, the HUM, is the essence of Heruka, this will prevent us from receiving any obstacles. If we do this meditation peacefully and regularly over a long period of time, it will definitely cause our winds to dissolve within our central channel and lead to a very clear and vivid experience of clear light.

Ghantapa said:

We should meditate single-pointedly
On the indestructible drop that always abides at our
    heart.
Those who are familiar with this meditation
Will definitely develop exalted wisdom.

Here 'exalted wisdom' means the wisdom of the clear light of bliss experienced when the knots at the heart channel wheel are loosened. Of all the knots in the central channel, these are the most difficult to loosen; but if from the beginning of our completion stage practice we concentrate on our heart channel wheel, this will help us to loosen these knots. This meditation, therefore, is a powerful method for gaining qualified completion stage realizations.

Why is this meditation called 'blessing the self with seed'? 'Self' here refers to the indestructible wind and mind, which are our actual body and mind and therefore the basis for imputing our actual self. Through this meditation our very subtle wind and mind are blessed, and as a result our very subtle mind transforms into the clear light of bliss. 'Seed' here refers to the letter HUM, the seed-letter of Heruka.

Until we receive signs that our five winds are actually entering, abiding, and dissolving within our central channel, we simply imagine that this is happening. We imagine that we perceive the eight signs from the mirage-like appearance up to the clear light, and then fix our mind single-pointedly on this imagined clear light. We try to perceive only clear light emptiness, and on the basis of this experience develop the divine pride of being Truth Body Heruka. This is called 'mixing with the Truth Body during waking'.

After a while we imagine that we rise from the emptiness of the Truth Body in the aspect of a white Heruka, and we develop the divine pride of being Enjoyment Body Heruka. This is called 'mixing with the Enjoyment Body during waking'.

Before beginning our meditation on completion stage, we generated ourself as a blue Heruka with one face and two arms. Although we stopped focusing on this Heruka as an object of meditation, we did not dissolve the visualization and so it has been present throughout the first two mixings, rather as our gross body continues to exist throughout the process of sleeping and dreaming even though it is not an object of the sleeping and dreaming minds. The white Heruka now enters through the crown of the blue Heruka. This blue Heruka is the commitment being, and the white Heruka who enters into him is the wisdom being. The white Heruka remains at the heart of the blue Heruka. We focus on the body of the blue Heruka and develop divine pride of being Emanation Body Heruka. This is called 'mixing with the Emanation Body during waking'. We then rise from meditation and engage in the activities of the meditation break with the divine pride of being Emanation Body Heruka.

In one session we can practise these three mixings once, three times, or seven times, depending upon our time and capacity. This practice of the three mixings is very similar to the three bringings of generation stage. The completion stage practice of bringing the three bodies into the path is the same as the practice of the three mixings. If we gain experience of the three mixings during waking, we can go on to practise them during sleep, and then during death. The way to do this is explained in *Clear Light of Bliss*.

In summary, meditating on the nada at the tip of the HUM at the heart channel wheel and practising the three mixings causes our inner winds to enter, abide, and dissolve within our central channel, leading to a very sharp and vivid experience of clear light. Before we gain the actual realizations, we train in the three mixings using our imagination. Once we have experience of the mixings during waking and sleeping, when we come to die we shall be able to practise the three mixings during death. We shall then die with a peaceful and happy mind and be able to choose our next rebirth. Eventually, we shall attain the resultant bodies of a Buddha.

THE STAGE OF BLESSING THE SELF WITHOUT SEED

On this stage we practise vajra recitation, which is a special method for controlling the inner winds. As mentioned before, the main purpose of blessing the self is to control the inner winds. Blessing the self with seed lays the foundation for blessing the self without seed, or vajra recitation. We begin by visualizing the central channel and the indestructible drop as before, but, instead of visualizing the seed-letter HUM inside the drop, we now visualize only a nada, which in nature is our very subtle wind. This is why this practice is said to be 'without seed'.

This tiny three-curved nada, white in colour and as fine as the tip of a hair, is the nature of the very subtle life-supporting wind at our heart. We focus on the nada and then imagine that from the nada our life-supporting wind rises gently through our central channel, like white incense smoke. As it ascends it makes the sound HUM. We should feel that the wind itself makes this sound, and that our mind is simply listening to it. Gradually the life-supporting wind reaches the centre of the throat channel wheel. We hold it there for a while, still making the sound HUM, and then allow it to descend slowly. As it descends it makes the sound OM. Finally it reaches the centre of the heart channel wheel and dissolves into the nada. It remains there for a short time, making the sound AH. Then again the life-supporting wind ascends to the throat making the sound HUM, descends making the sound OM, and abides at the nada making the sound AH. We should repeat this cycle several times. Finally we concentrate single-pointedly only on the wind abiding at the nada at the heart, making the sound AH.

When we have gained some familiarity with this meditation, we modify it as follows. We begin as before but, when the wind ascends, instead of it remaining at the throat we allow it to continue without interruption to the crown, all the time making the sound HUM. It remains at the crown very briefly and then descends slowly back to the heart, making the sound OM. Then it abides at the heart for a while, making the sound AH. We repeat this cycle several times. Finally we concentrate only on the wind abiding at the heart, making the sound AH.

When we have gained some familiarity with this second meditation, we imagine that the life-supporting wind rises from the indestructible wind, which is in the form of the nada, and goes all the way to the nostrils without stopping at the throat or crown; and that as it ascends it makes the sound HUM. It remains at the nostrils very briefly and then returns slowly to the heart, making the sound OM, and remains at the heart, making the sound AH. We repeat this cycle several times, and end by focusing single-pointedly on the sound AH at the heart.

Through this meditation, our experience of the inner winds entering, abiding, and dissolving within our central channel will be much stronger than before, and we shall perceive the eight signs from the mirage-like appearance up to the clear light more clearly than before. Until this actually happens, we should imagine that it does. Either way, we should meditate single-pointedly on the clear light of bliss mixed with emptiness, and, focusing on this union, develop the divine pride of being Truth Body Heruka. Then, as before, we arise in the form of a white Heruka and develop the divine pride of being Enjoyment Body Heruka. This white Heruka enters through the crown of the blue Heruka generated at the beginning of the session, and abides at his heart; and we develop the divine pride of being Emanation Body Heruka. We can either end the session at this point and engage in the activities of the meditation break, or we can repeat the whole cycle again.

Vajra recitation has two main functions: (1) to control our inner winds by uniting them with mantra, and (2) to loosen the central channel knots at the heart. With respect to the first function, when we do this meditation it is important to think that our inner winds have transformed into mantra, making the sound HUM, OM, and AH. The very subtle wind is the root of all speech, including mantra. All our normal gross speech depends upon gross inner winds, which develop from the very subtle inner wind. When we generate ourself as the Deity, we regard our speech as the mantra of the Deity. By training in vajra recitation we gradually purify our inner winds. As our inner winds become pure, our mind becomes pure, and in this way we gain more control over our inner winds and hence our minds. When through the force of meditation we gain the ability to cause our inner winds to enter, abide, and dissolve within the central channel, easily and without obstacles, we can say that we are controlling our inner winds. However, there are many levels of controlling the inner winds. It is taught that practitioners who have completed vajra recitation can mix their inner winds with external winds throughout the world, gathering them all into the central channel and transforming all winds into the mantra OM AH HUM. Through controlling the winds in this way, they attain many special miracle powers.

With respect to the second function, through vajra recitation we can loosen the central channel knots at the heart, but not completely. To loosen these knots completely we need either to wait until death or to rely upon an action mudra. When we loosen the heart channel knots completely through completion stage practice, we attain the isolated mind of ultimate example clear light; and when we rise from the equipoise of ultimate example clear light, we attain the illusory body. This is an actual divine body, not one generated by imagination. In summary, to attain the actual divine body we need to attain ultimate example clear light, and to do this we need to loosen the knots of the heart channel wheel through training in vajra recitation.

When we attain stable concentration on vajra recitation in conjunction with the life-supporting wind, we can then do vajra recitation in conjunction with the five branch winds that flow through the doors of the senses. For example, the first branch wind, the moving wind, arises from our very subtle wind and flows up to our eye organ, causing our eye awareness to move to its object, visual form, thereby enabling us to see. Without this wind, we would have no eye awareness. At present this wind is impure, and so our eye awareness is impure and we see only an impure world. However, if we purify our moving wind our eye awareness will become pure, and we shall see the Pure Lands of Buddhas.

To purify the moving wind, we concentrate on the moving wind rising from the nada inside the indestructible drop, flowing up to the two eyes, descending again, and abiding inside the indestructible drop, making the sounds HUM, OM, and AH. When we gain deep experience of this meditation, we attain eye clairvoyance. Similarly, through gaining deep experience of vajra recitation on the second branch wind, the intensely-moving wind, which supports ear awareness, we attain ear clairvoyance. Further explanation on how to do these meditations and how to mix external winds with our inner winds can be found in *Tantric Grounds and Paths*.

THE STAGE OF THE VAJRA OF VARIOUS QUALITIES

Through training in the stages of blessing the self with seed, we shall gain an initial experience of the inner winds dissolving within the central channel. Through training in the stages of blessing the self without seed, we deepen this experience until we attain the actual clear light realization. This clear light, however, is not yet fully qualified because at this stage we have still not completely loosened the knots at the heart channel wheel. To experience the fully qualified clear light, or ultimate example clear light, we need to rely upon an action mudra. However, relying upon an action mudra can only lead to this realization if we already have the ability to control our drops, or bodhichitta. When the bodhichitta melts in our channels and reaches the tip of our sex organ, if we have the ability to hold it there without releasing it while experiencing bliss, for as long as we wish, we have control over our drops. We achieve this ability through training in the two stages of the vajra of various qualities. The first step in attaining ultimate example clear light, therefore, is training in the stage of the vajra of various qualities.

The explanation of the stage of the vajra of various qualities has two parts:

1 The stage of the vajra of various qualities with seed
2 The stage of the vajra of various qualities without seed

THE STAGE OF THE VAJRA OF VARIOUS QUALITIES
WITH SEED

We begin by visualizing our central channel clearly, and imagining that, because we have generated ourself as Heruka in union with Vajravarahi, the lower tips of our central channels are joined. We visualize the Father's central channel protruding slightly from his vajra and joining the Mother's central channel inside her bhaga. Inside the part of the Father's central channel that protrudes beyond his vajra, we visualize Heruka's mind of great bliss in the form of a tiny one-pronged vajra, which is white with a shade of red, and the size of a grain of barley. In the centre of the vajra, we visualize Heruka's Truth Body in the form of a minute blue letter HUM. The white part of the vajra is white bodhichitta and the red part is red bodhichitta; the substance of the vajra is therefore the drops, but its real nature is great bliss. We visualize it to remind ourself of the experience of great bliss.

We now imagine that our mind, together with the indestructible drop at the heart, descends through the central channel and dissolves into the letter HUM in the centre of the tiny vajra. It is essential to feel that our entire mind has dissolved into the HUM. We then meditate single-pointedly on the vajra while experiencing great bliss for as long as possible. Finally, we imagine that the vajra and HUM transform into the aspect of the indestructible drop, which then ascends slowly through the central channel. When it reaches the vital point at the centre of our navel channel wheel, we hold it there for a short time, concentrating single-pointedly without distraction. The drop then continues to ascend through the central channel until it reaches the very centre of the heart channel wheel, its own location. We hold it there with strong concentration until we perceive the eight signs. Finally we meditate on the clear light of bliss and emptiness with the divine pride of being Truth Body Heruka. We complete the three mixings as before and then conclude the session. We need to repeat this meditation many times to control the drops and to stabilize great bliss.

THE STAGE OF THE VAJRA OF VARIOUS QUALITIES WITHOUT SEED

For this meditation, we visualize the one-pronged vajra, now the size of a pea, just inside the upper tip of the central channel, at the point between the eyebrows. However, we do not visualize a seed-letter HUM in the centre of the vajra, which is why this stage is called 'without seed'.

Our mind, together with the indestructible drop at the heart, ascends through the central channel to our crown and then travels down to the point between the eyebrows, where it reaches the centre of the vajra. The white part of the drop transforms into a moon seat, and on top of this the red part of the drop transforms into a sun seat. On top of the sun seat we visualize Buddha Akshobya in the form of a tiny blue drop, the size of a mustard seed. In front of this we visualize Buddha Vairochana in the form of a tiny white drop, to the left Buddha Amoghasiddhi in the form of a green drop, behind Buddha Amitabha in the form of a red drop, and to the right Buddha Ratnasambhava in the form of a yellow drop. We then imagine that our entire mind dissolves into this cluster of five drops, the size of a small pea, and we hold it there without distraction.

When we are about to conclude the meditation, we imagine that the vajra dissolves into the moon, which dissolves into the sun. This dissolves into the white drop, this into the green drop, this into the red drop, this into the yellow drop, and this into the blue drop at the centre, the nature of Akshobya-Heruka. Radiating five-coloured wisdom light to bless our drops, the blue drop ascends slowly through our central channel to the very centre of our crown channel wheel. We hold it here and meditate single-pointedly for a while. This causes the bodhichitta in our crown to increase. After a while, the drop descends slowly to the very centre of our throat channel wheel, and we hold it there for a while. Then it descends to the very centre of our heart channel wheel, where we meditate on it until we perceive the eight signs. Finally we complete the three mixings as before and conclude the session. We need to repeat this meditation until we gain the ability to control the drops and to stabilize great bliss.

It is said that this stage is called the 'vajra of various qualities' because by meditating on the vajra in different places we can attain various types of clairvoyance. In this context, the vajra is the inner vajra, the union of great bliss and emptiness. We can use this meditation to purify the eye element, ear element, mentality element, and so forth, and thereby attain eye clairvoyance that is able to see divine beings and divine environments directly, ear clairvoyance that can hear the speech of divine beings, and many other good qualities. To do this, we first engage in meditation on the stage of the vajra of various qualities as described above, and meditate on the union of great bliss and emptiness while regarding it as the Dharmakaya. Then we strongly imagine that all our defiled eye elements, ear elements, mentality elements, and so forth are purified, and we achieve the divine eye, divine ear, and so forth. By continually training in this way, we can gain the special realizations of clairvoyance.

THE STAGE OF FILLING WITH JEWELS

Here, 'jewels' refers to the four joys, which are real wish-fulfilling inner jewels. Since the function of this third stage is to fill our body with the experience of the four joys, it is called 'filling with jewels'. We do this practice in dependence upon the four mudras: the commitment mudra, the action mudra, the phenomenon mudra, and the Mahamudra. Je Tsongkhapa said that the practice of the first mudra is the preliminary practice, the second the actual practice, the third the subsequent practice, and the fourth the result.

The first mudra, the commitment mudra, is the visualized consort, or wisdom mudra. During the wisdom-mudra empowerment, the Vajra Master gives us a consort who is an emanation of Vajravarahi, and a commitment to accomplish great bliss in dependence upon this wisdom mudra. Therefore, the visualized consort is known as the 'commitment mudra'. Relying upon a wisdom mudra is a preliminary for relying upon an action mudra. If our meditation on relying upon a wisdom mudra causes our inner winds to gather and dissolve within the central channel and we experience great bliss, this is a correct sign that we can now have the confidence to rely upon an action mudra. An action mudra is an actual consort who has received the empowerment of our personal Deity, is keeping the Tantric commitments, and has perfect knowledge of the instructions.

Once we have completely loosened the central channel knots at our heart through the power of relying upon the action mudra, when we subsequently meditate on inner fire we shall generate powerful spontaneous great bliss. Because for us the phenomenon of inner fire meditation performs a function similar to that of a consort, it is called the 'phenomenon mudra'. The realization of the union of great bliss and emptiness is called 'Mahamudra', or 'great seal', which means 'great indestructible truth'. When our continuously residing mind transforms into spontaneous great bliss that realizes emptiness through a generic image, it is called 'ultimate example clear light'. The term 'ultimate' reveals that it is a fully qualified clear light, and 'example' means that we can use this realization as an example to understand how we can accomplish the actual meaning clear light, the union of great bliss and emptiness. Through meditating continually on ultimate example clear light, it will transform into meaning clear light. Ultimate example clear light is therefore an example that illustrates its meaning, namely meaning clear light. Meaning clear light is a continuously residing mind that is the nature of spontaneous great bliss realizing emptiness directly.

As a preliminary to the practice of the stage of filling with jewels, we emphasize both the secret offering to ourself generated as Heruka, and the practice of relying upon the wisdom mudra as explained in the section on receiving the wisdom-mudra empowerment. Once we have the ability to control our drops, and a deep experience of the inner winds dissolving within our central channel, we can then practise relying upon the action mudra.

There are two ways to do this practice. The first is to meditate on the emptiness of both ourself and our consort, and then, from the state of emptiness, to generate ourself as Heruka and our consort as Vajravarahi, free from ordinary appearances and conceptions. With strong divine pride of ourself as Heruka and our consort as Vajravarahi, we engage in union and gradually generate the four joys. Finally we meditate on spontaneous great bliss and emptiness single-pointedly for as long as possible.

To practise the second way, with strong divine pride of ourself as Heruka, and free from ordinary appearances and conceptions, we simply believe that our consort is a manifestation of Vajravarahi, engage in union, generate the four joys, and finally meditate on spontaneous great bliss and emptiness.

THE STAGE OF DZÖLADHARA

The Sanskrit word 'dzöladhara' means 'holding the blazing'. 'Dzöla' means 'blazing', and 'dhara' means 'holding'. This meditation on the stages of dzöladhara is so called because it holds its object, the blazing of the tummo fire, single-pointedly. Through this meditation practitioners improve their realization of spontaneous great bliss and emptiness gained on the third stage until their continuously residing mind becomes the mind of spontaneous great bliss realizing emptiness. Initially this realization is ultimate example clear light and gradually it transforms into meaning clear light. Some texts say 'dzalendhara' instead of 'dzöladhara', but the meaning is the same.

The actual practice of the stage of dzöladhara has eight parts:

1 Visualizing the central channel
2 Visualizing the letters
3 Igniting the inner fire
4 Causing the fire to blaze
5 Causing the dripping of the bodhichitta
6 Causing the special blazing of the fire
7 Causing the special dripping of the bodhichitta
8 Meditating on spontaneous bliss and emptiness

VISUALIZING THE CENTRAL CHANNEL

We visualize the central channel as explained above on pages 195-6.

VISUALIZING THE LETTERS

At the very centre of our secret place channel wheel, located four finger-widths below the navel, we visualize a tiny phenomena source. Inside the phenomena source on a sun seat, our root mind, which is inseparable from Heruka's mind, appears in the aspect of a pea-sized cluster of five drops. In front is a white drop, the nature of Buddha Vairochana; on the left is a green drop, the nature of Buddha Amoghasiddhi; at the back is a red drop, the nature of Buddha Amitabha; on the right is a yellow drop, the nature of Buddha Ratnasambhava; and at the centre is a blue drop, the nature of Buddha Akshobya.

Inside the central blue drop, we visualize our inner fire in the form of a very tiny red letter short-AH. At the very centre of our crown channel wheel, we visualize a white upsidedown letter HAM, the nature of our white bodhichitta. At the very centre of our heart channel wheel, we visualize an upsidedown letter HUM, white with a shade of red, the nature of our white and red indestructible drop. We briefly contemplate the letter HAM at our crown, the letter HUM at our heart, and the letter short-AH at our secret place, and finally we meditate on the short-AH.

IGNITING THE INNER FIRE, CAUSING THE FIRE TO BLAZE, AND SO FORTH, UP TO MEDITATING ON SPONTANEOUS BLISS AND EMPTINESS

When a man and woman engage in ordinary sexual intercourse, due to the tip of the man's penis touching the tip of the woman's vagina they penetrate each other's central channel and, as a result, the downward-voiding wind located at their secret places rises upwards. This causes the inner fire located at their navels to blaze, and the white or red drops to melt and flow through their channels, but not the central channel. Through this, they experience contaminated bliss for a very short time. When qualified practitioners of the third stage, filling with jewels, rely upon an action mudra, their activity is in general similar to ordinary sexual intercourse, but their inner heat blazes in the central channel rather than the side channels and so the drops melt and flow inside the central channel instead of being quickly ejaculated. As a result, they experience pure spontaneous great bliss for a long time. Here, on the fourth stage of completion stage, dzöladhara, practitioners generate and increase their experience of spontaneous great bliss by meditating on tummo. On this stage, igniting the inner fire and causing it to blaze are both accomplished through vase breathing meditation at the secret place.

We practise vase breathing meditation as follows. We inhale gently through both nostrils and imagine that we draw all the winds located in the upper part of our body down to just above the five drops inside the central channel at the secret place. We then slightly and gently constrict the two lower doors, the anus and sex organ, and draw all the winds of the lower part of our body up to just below the five drops. Our mind inside the five drops is now enclosed within the upper and lower winds like a precious object inside an amulet box. We then stop breathing and, while keeping the upper and lower winds at the secret place, hold our concentration single-pointedly on the short-AH within the central blue drop. One part of our mind thinks that the short-AH is about to blaze. This is called 'igniting the inner fire'. Just before we start to feel discomfort, we exhale very gently through both nostrils, with our mind still remaining on the short-AH.

We then repeat the vase breath and, concentrating on the short-AH, think that an intensely hot and thin needle-like flame blazes from it. This is called 'causing the fire to blaze'. This in turn causes the upside-down letter HUM at our heart to melt and drip onto the fire. This is called 'dripping of the bodhichitta'. The fire then blazes more intensely and gets even hotter, as when oil is poured onto a fire. This is called 'special blazing of the fire'. This increase in heat causes the upside-down letter HAM at our crown to melt, and from this the white bodhichitta drips through our central channel. This is called 'special dripping of the bodhichitta'.

As the white bodhichitta melts and slowly drips, we experience spontaneous great bliss. When the bodhichitta eventually drips onto the tummo fire at our secret place, the fire dims slightly for a short while, but our experience of spontaneous great bliss becomes even more intense. Then the fire blazes even more powerfully, as when molten butter drips onto a fire. As a result, the tummo fire blazes at the secret place, mixing with the rays of light from the five drops – the five Buddha families – and passes through all the channels in our body. It consumes all defiled drops and gathers all pure drops into the bodhichitta at our crown. From here the bodhichitta continually drips through the central channel and we experience spontaneous great bliss for a long time. We meditate on this inseparable bliss and emptiness. This is the eighth part, 'meditating on spontaneous bliss and emptiness'.

THE STAGE OF INCONCEIVABILITY

On the stage of dzöladhara we attain the complete and fully qualified clear light that is the nature of spontaneous great bliss realizing emptiness. When we rise from this meditative equipoise, we attain the illusory body, which is the actual divine body. This body is not created by imagination but is an actual body. Its substantial cause is the indestructible wind that is the mount of the mind of ultimate example clear light. Its aspect is a white-coloured Heruka with consort, together with the entire mandala. The illusory body that the practitioner attains on this stage is the impure illusory body because the practitioner has not yet abandoned the delusions and so he or she is still not a Superior being, and because his or her mind of clear light of bliss does not yet realize emptiness directly.

To realize emptiness directly with the very subtle mind of spontaneous great bliss, the practitioner progresses to the meditations of the fifth stage, inconceivability. Here, 'inconceivability' refers to attainments that cannot be experienced by those who are not Superior beings. Examples of inconceivability are meaning clear light, the union of meaning clear light and illusory body of the path, and the union of a Buddha's Form Body and Truth Body. The first is the union of great bliss and emptiness, the second is the union that needs learning, and the third is the Union of No More Learning. Through practising the meditations of the fifth stage, practitioners attain these three types of union.

The actual practice has two parts:

1 Relying upon the consort
2 Engaging in the two concentrations

RELYING UPON THE CONSORT

There are three ways of relying upon the consort. The first is relying upon the action mudra by practising enjoyments with elaborations, such as King Indrabodhi's way of relying upon the consort. The second is relying upon the action mudra by practising enjoyments without elaborations, such as Ghantapa's way of relying upon the consort. The third is relying upon the wisdom mudra alone, such as Gyälwa Ensapa's way of relying upon the consort. Through any of these three practices, practitioners of the fifth stage first accomplish the union of great bliss and emptiness, then the union that needs learning, and finally the Union of No More Learning.

ENGAGING IN THE TWO CONCENTRATIONS

In the first of these, we concentrate on dissolving first all worlds and then all their inhabitants into the clear light of emptiness, and then we meditate on the union of the clear light of bliss and emptiness. In the second, we concentrate on dissolving all worlds and their inhabitants simultaneously into the clear light of emptiness, and then we meditate on the union of the clear light of bliss and emptiness.

Through engaging in either of these concentrations, the practitioner of the fifth stage attains meaning clear light. When the practitioner arises from meaning clear light, he or she attains the pure illusory body – the vajra body – and engages in the practices of subsequent attainment. In the next session, when meaning clear light manifests through engaging in either of the two concentrations, the practitioner attains the union of meaning clear light and pure illusory body, and meditates on meaning clear light for as long as he or she wishes. Through continually meditating on meaning clear light, both during sleep and while awake, this meaning clear light eventually becomes the direct antidote to the very subtle dualistic appearances. It is then called the 'vajra-like concentration of the path of meditation', which is the last moment of the mind of a sentient being. In the next moment, the practitioner becomes a Buddha by attaining the Union of No More Learning.

Geshe Kelsang Gyatso Rinpoche

Dedication

Through the great merit accumulated by writing this book, may everyone receive the precious opportunity to practise this holy Dharma. In this way, may all the suffering in this world that arises from fighting, famine, and so forth cease completely. May everyone experience permanent world peace by gaining permanent inner peace. Finally, may all living beings attain the ultimate happiness of full enlightenment.

Appendix I
The Condensed Meaning of
the Commentary

The Condensed Meaning of the Commentary

The commentary to the Highest Yoga Tantra practice of Heruka body mandala has three parts:

1 The preliminary explanation
2 The explanation of the practice
3 Dedication

The preliminary explanation has five parts:

1 The pre-eminent qualities of Heruka
2 The origin of these instructions
3 The benefits of practising these instructions
4 Examples of previous practitioners who accomplished attainments through these instructions
5 The qualifications of a sincere Heruka practitioner

The explanation of the practice has two parts:

1 Generation stage
2 Completion stage

Generation stage has two parts:

1 How to practise during the meditation session
2 How to practise during the meditation break

How to practise during the meditation session has three parts:

1 The preliminary practices
2 The actual practice of generation stage
3 The concluding practices

The preliminary practices has six parts:

1 Going for refuge and generating bodhichitta
2 Receiving blessings
3 Purifying our own mind, body, and speech
4 Purifying other beings, the environment, and enjoyments
5 Purifying non-virtues, downfalls, and obstacles
6 Guru yoga

Going for refuge and generating bodhichitta has four parts:

1 The causes of going for refuge
2 Visualizing the objects of refuge
3 The way of going for refuge
4 Generating aspiring and engaging bodhichitta

Purifying our own mind, body, and speech has three parts:

1 Purifying our own mind
2 Purifying our own body
3 Purifying our own speech

Purifying non-virtues, downfalls, and obstacles has two parts:

1 Why we need to purify non-virtuous actions and downfalls
2 The actual practice of purification

The actual practice of purification has four parts:

1 The power of regret
2 The power of reliance
3 The power of the opponent force
4 The power of promise

Guru yoga has two parts:

1 A general explanation
2 The actual practice of Guru yoga

The actual practice of Guru yoga has six parts:

1 Visualizing the commitment beings of the Field of Merit, and inviting and absorbing the wisdom beings
2 Offering the practice of the seven limbs
3 Offering the mandala
4 Receiving the blessings of the four empowerments
5 Requesting the lineage Gurus
6 Accomplishing spontaneous great bliss by dissolving the Guru into ourself

Visualizing the commitment beings of the Field of Merit, and inviting and absorbing the wisdom beings has two parts:

1 Visualizing the commitment beings of the Field of Merit
2 Inviting and absorbing the wisdom beings

Visualizing the commitment beings of the Field of Merit has three parts:

1 Visualizing basis Guru Heruka
2 Visualizing Guru Heruka of the body mandala
3 Visualizing the other holy beings

Visualizing Guru Heruka of the body mandala has two parts:

1 Visualizing the Principal
2 Visualizing the retinues

Visualizing the retinues has three parts:

1 Visualizing the four Yoginis of the essence
2 Visualizing the Heroes and Heroines of the twenty-four places
3 Visualizing the eight Heroines of the doorways

Offering the practice of the seven limbs has seven parts:

1 Prostration
2 Offering
3 Confession
4 Rejoicing
5 Beseeching the Spiritual Guide not to pass away

6 Requesting the turning of the Wheel of Dharma
7 Dedication

Offering has five parts:

1 Outer offerings
2 Inner offering
3 Secret offering
4 Thatness offering
5 Offering our spiritual practice

Outer offerings has two parts:

1 The eight outer offerings
2 Offering the five objects of desire

Receiving the blessings of the four empowerments has four parts:

1 Receiving the vase empowerment
2 Receiving the secret empowerment
3 Receiving the wisdom-mudra empowerment
4 Receiving the precious word empowerment

The actual practice of generation stage has six parts:

1 What is generation stage?
2 Bringing the three bodies into the path
3 Checking meditation on the mandala and basis Heruka
4 Generating the mandala and Deities of the body mandala
5 Adorning our body with the armour Deities, inviting and absorbing the wisdom beings, and making offerings
6 The actual generation stage meditation

Bringing the three bodies into the path has three parts:

1 Bringing death into the path of the Truth Body
2 Bringing the intermediate state into the path of the Enjoyment Body
3 Bringing rebirth into the path of the Emanation Body

Checking meditation on the mandala and basis Heruka has two parts:

1 Checking meditation
2 The symbolism of Heruka's body

Generating the mandala and Deities of the body mandala has two parts:

1 A preliminary explanation
2 The explanation of the actual practice

The explanation of the actual practice has two parts:

1 Simultaneous generation of the entire supporting and supported Heruka body mandala
2 Checking meditation on this generation

Checking meditation on this generation has two parts:

1 Checking meditation on the gross parts of our body generated as Heruka's mandala
2 Checking meditation on the subtle parts of our body, the channels and drops, generated as the Deities

Adorning our body with the armour Deities, inviting and absorbing the wisdom beings, and making offerings has three parts:

1 Adorning our body, the bodies of Heruka Father and Mother of the body mandala, with the armour Deities
2 Inviting the wisdom beings, dissolving them into the commitment beings, and receiving the empowerment
3 Making offerings and praises to the self-generated Deities of the body mandala

Making offerings and praises to the self-generated Deities of the body mandala has five parts:

1 Blessing the offerings
2 Making the outer offerings
3 Making the inner offering
4 Making the secret and thatness offerings
5 Eight lines of praise

Blessing the offerings has two parts:

1 Blessing the inner offering
2 Blessing the outer offerings

Blessing the inner offering has five parts:

1 The benefits
2 The basis of the inner offering
3 The visual object of the inner offering
4 How to bless the inner offering
5 The significance of the inner offering

How to bless the inner offering has four parts:

1 Clearance
2 Purification
3 Generation
4 Transformation

Generation has two parts:

1 Generating the container
2 Generating the contained substances

Transformation has three parts:

1 Purifying faults
2 Transforming into nectar
3 Increasing

The actual generation stage meditation has two parts:

1 A preliminary explanation
2 How to practise the actual generation stage meditation

A preliminary explanation has four parts:

1 What is the basis of imputation for our I?
2 Why we need to change the basis of imputation
   for our I
3 How it is possible to change the basis of imputation
   for our I
4 How to change the basis of imputation for our I

How to practise the actual generation stage meditation has five parts:

1 Training in clear appearance
2 Training in divine pride
3 Training in tranquil abiding
4 Training in subtle generation stage
5 Training in the yoga of non-dual profundity and clarity

The concluding practices has four parts:

1 Mantra recitation
2 Torma offerings
3 Dissolution and generating the action Deities
4 Dedication

Mantra recitation has five parts:

1 The mantras to be recited
2 Blessing the mala
3 Long mantra recitation
4 Short mantra recitation
5 Explanation of close retreat

Explanation of close retreat has four parts:

1 The preparations
2 The preliminary practices
3 The actual retreat
4 The fire puja

Torma offerings has three parts:

1 Blessing the tormas
2 Inviting the guests of the tormas
3 The actual torma offering

The actual torma offering has four parts:

1 Offering the principal torma
2 Offering the torma to the Deities of the heart wheel, speech wheel, and body wheel

3 Offering the torma to the Deities of the commitment wheel

4 Offering the torma to the mundane Dakas and Dakinis, and to all the spirits throughout the world

Completion stage has three parts:

1 An introduction to completion stage
2 The preliminary practices
3 The actual practice of completion stage

The actual practice of completion stage has five parts:

1 The stage of blessing the self
2 The stage of the vajra of various qualities
3 The stage of filling with jewels
4 The stage of dzöladhara
5 The stage of inconceivability

The stage of blessing the self has two parts:

1 The stage of blessing the self with seed
2 The stage of blessing the self without seed

The stage of blessing the self with seed has three parts:

1 Meditation on the central channel
2 Meditation on the indestructible drop
3 Meditation on the indestructible wind and mind

The stage of the vajra of various qualities has two parts:

1 The stage of the vajra of various qualities with seed
2 The stage of the vajra of various qualities without seed

The stage of filling with jewels has four parts:

1 Commitment mudra
2 Action mudra
3 Phenomenon mudra
4 Mahamudra

The stage of dzöladhara has eight parts:

1 Visualizing the central channel
2 Visualizing the letters
3 Igniting the inner fire
4 Causing the fire to blaze
5 Causing the dripping of the bodhichitta
6 Causing the special blazing of the fire
7 Causing the special dripping of the bodhichitta
8 Meditating on spontaneous bliss and emptiness

The stage of inconceivability has two parts:

1 Relying upon the consort
2 Engaging in the two concentrations

Appendix II
Sadhanas

CONTENTS

Vajra Hero Yoga

———

A BRIEF ESSENTIAL PRACTICE OF HERUKA
BODY MANDALA SELF-GENERATION

&

CONDENSED SIX-SESSION YOGA

Introduction

Those who are unable to recite the extensive sadhana, *Essence of Vajrayana*, can begin with this brief essential yoga of Heruka body mandala self-generation. The detailed meaning of this practice should be understood from the extensive sadhana and its commentary, *Essence of Vajrayana*.

It is most important to improve our faith, and conviction in this practice through careful reading of its commentary. With a clear understanding and strong faith we can enjoy this very essential practice of Highest Yoga Tantra and attain the ultimate goal of human life.

Vajra Hero Yoga

THE PRELIMINARY PRACTICES

Visualizing the objects of refuge and the Field of Merit

In the space before me appear Guru Heruka Father
and Mother, surrounded by the assembly of direct and
lineage Gurus, Yidams, Buddhas, Bodhisattvas, Heroes,
Dakinis, and Dharma Protectors.

Going for refuge and generating aspiring bodhichitta

Eternally I shall go for refuge
To Buddha, Dharma, and Sangha.
For the sake of all living beings
I shall become Heruka.   (3x)

Generating engaging bodhichitta

To lead all mother living beings to the state of ultimate
    happiness,
I shall attain as quickly as possible, in this very life,
The state of the Union of Buddha Heruka.
For this purpose I shall practise the stages of Heruka's
    path.   (3x)

Guru Yoga

Prayer of seven limbs

With my body, speech, and mind, humbly I prostrate,
And make outer, inner, and secret offerings.
I confess my wrong deeds from all time,
And rejoice in the virtues of all.
Please stay until samsara ceases,
And turn the Wheel of Dharma for us.
I dedicate all virtues to the great enlightenment of Heruka.

Offering the mandala

The ground sprinkled with perfume and spread with
    flowers,
The Great Mountain, four lands, sun and moon,
Seen as a Buddha Land and offered thus,
May all beings enjoy such Pure Lands.

I offer without any sense of loss
The objects that give rise to my attachment, hatred,
    and confusion,
My friends, enemies, and strangers, our bodies and
    enjoyments;
Please accept these and bless me to be released directly
    from the three poisons.

IDAM GURU RATNA MANDALAKAM NIRYATAYAMI

Requesting our root Guru

As times become ever more impure,
Your power and blessings ever increase,
And you care for us quickly, as swift as thought;
O my root Guru Heruka Father and Mother, please bestow
    your blessings.   (3x)

Accomplishing spontaneous great bliss by dissolving the Guru into oneself

The Field of Merit gathers gradually from the edges and dissolves into my root Guru Heruka. Out of delight he comes to my crown, descends through my central channel, and becomes of one taste with my mind at my heart. I experience spontaneous great bliss.

THE ACTUAL PRACTICE OF GENERATION STAGE

Bringing death into the path of the Truth Body

Light rays from the HUM at my heart melt all worlds and beings into light. This dissolves into me, and I in turn gradually melt into light from below and above and dissolve into the HUM at my heart. The letter HUM dissolves in stages from the bottom up into the nada. The nada becomes smaller and smaller and dissolves into clear light emptiness. I am Truth Body Heruka.

Bringing the intermediate state into the path of the Enjoyment Body

From the state of emptiness my mind appears in the form of a nada. I am Enjoyment Body Heruka.

Bringing rebirth into the path of the Emanation Body

From YAM, RAM, BAM, LAM, SUM, PAM arise the four elements, Mount Meru, and the lotus. In the centre of the lotus, from the vowels and consonants, arises a reddish-white moon, the nature of the red and white bodhichittas of Guru Heruka Father and Mother. I, the nada, enter the centre of the moon and gradually transform into the aspect of a HUM.

Five-coloured lights radiate from the HUM and lead all living beings to the state of Chakrasambara. At the same time all the Heroes and Heroines are invited from the Buddha Lands of the ten directions. They all melt into light and dissolve into the HUM, which becomes the nature of spontaneous joy. The moon, vowels, consonants, and HUM completely transform, and the Deities of the body mandala together with the mandala arise fully and all at once. I am Emanation Body Heruka.

Thus I am Heruka with a blue-coloured body, four faces, and twelve arms, the nature of my white indestructible drop. I am embracing Vajravarahi, the nature of my red indestructible drop. I am surrounded by the Heroes and Heroines of the five wheels, who are the nature of my purified channels and drops. I reside in the mandala, the celestial mansion, which is the nature of my purified gross body.

Inviting the wisdom beings, dissolving them into the commitment beings, and receiving the empowerment

PHAIM
My three places are marked by the three letters. Light rays radiate from the letter HUM and invite all the Buddhas of the ten directions in the same aspect as those visualized, together with the empowering Deities. All the wisdom beings gather into one complete supporting and supported mandala.

DZA HUM BAM HO
The wisdom beings become inseparable from the commitment beings.

The empowering Deities grant the empowerment, my body is filled with nectar, and I experience bliss. The excess nectar on the crowns completely transforms, and the Principal is adorned by Vajrasattva, Vajravarahi by Akshobya, the four Mothers by Ratnasambhava, the Deities of the heart wheel by Akshobya, the Deities of the speech wheel by Amitabha, the Deities of the body wheel by Vairochana, and the Deities of the commitment wheel by Amoghasiddhi.

Making offerings and praise to the self-generated Deities of the body mandala

Countless breathtakingly beautiful offering and praising goddesses emanate from my heart and make offerings and praise to me as Heruka Father and Mother.

Outer offerings

OM AHRGHAM PARTITZA SÖHA
OM PADÄM PARTITZA SÖHA
OM ÄNTZAMANAM PARTITZA SÖHA
OM VAJRA PUPE AH HUM SÖHA
OM VAJRA DHUPE AH HUM SÖHA
OM VAJRA DIWE AH HUM SÖHA
OM VAJRA GÄNDHE AH HUM SÖHA
OM VAJRA NEWIDE AH HUM SÖHA
OM VAJRA SHAPTA AH HUM SÖHA

OM AH VAJRA ADARSHE HUM
OM AH VAJRA WINI HUM
OM AH VAJRA GÄNDHE HUM
OM AH VAJRA RASE HUM
OM AH VAJRA PARSHE HUM
OM AH VAJRA DHARME HUM

Inner offering

OM HUM BAM RIM RIM LIM LIM, KAM KHAM GAM GHAM NGAM, TSAM TSHAM DZAM DZHAM NYAM, TrAM THrAM DrAM DHrAM NAM, TAM THAM DAM DHAM NAM, PAM PHAM BAM BHAM, YAM RAM LAM WAM, SHAM KAM SAM HAM HUM HUM PHAT OM AH HUM

Secret and thatness offerings

I, the Principal Father and Mother, enter into the union of embrace. The bodhichitta melts, and as it descends from my crown to my throat I experience joy, as it descends from my throat to my heart I experience supreme joy, as it descends from my heart to my navel I experience extraordinary joy, and as it descends from my navel to the tip of my jewel I generate spontaneous great bliss inseparable from emptiness. The Principal and all the retinue experience a special, exalted wisdom of bliss and emptiness.

Praise

To Glorious Heruka Father and Mother,
The nature of all the Buddhas' compassion,
And to all the Heroes and Heroines of the five wheels,
Respectfully I prostrate.

At this point, (1) while experiencing great bliss and emptiness, (2) we meditate on the clear appearance of the mandala and Deities, and (3) we meditate on divine pride, while (4) recognizing that the Deities are the nature of our purified channels and drops, and that the mandala is the nature of our purified gross body.

In this way, we train sincerely in one single concentration on gross or subtle generation stage possessing these four characteristics. Holding the fourth characteristic – recognizing the Deities as the nature of our purified channels and drops, and the mandala as the nature of our purified gross body – makes this concentration an actual body mandala meditation.

Then, when we need to rest from meditation, we can practise mantra recitation.

Blessing the mala

The mala becomes emptiness. From the state of emptiness each bead appears in its own aspect, the nature of Pämanarteshvara, the vajra speech of all Buddhas.

Mantra recitation

Visualization

The mantra to be recited descends from the letter HUM at my heart, leaves through the tip of my vajra, enters the consort's bhaga, ascends, leaves through her mouth, enters my mouth, descends, and dissolves back into the HUM. Then again it circles as before, leaving and re-entering my central channel. My four mouths, and all the Deities of the retinue, recite the mantras.

Recite the following mantras as many times as you can:

The essence mantra of the Father

OM SHRI VAJRA HE HE RU RU KAM HUM HUM PHAT
   DAKINI DZALA SHAMBARAM SÖHA

The close essence mantra of the Father

OM HRIH HA HA HUM HUM PHAT

The essence mantra of the Mother

OM VAJRA BEROTZANIYE HUM HUM PHAT SÖHA

The close essence mantra of the Mother

OM SARWA BUDDHA DAKINIYE VAJRA WARNANIYE HUM
   HUM PHAT SÖHA

The condensed essence mantra of the sixty retinue Deities

OM RIM RIM LIM LIM, KAM KHAM GAM GHAM NGAM,
TSAM TSHAM DZAM DZHAM NYAM, TrAM THrAM DrAM
DHrAM NAM, TAM THAM DAM DHAM NAM, PAM PHAM
BAM BHAM, YAM RAM LAM WAM, SHAM KAM SAM HAM
HUM HUM PHAT

*At this point you can, if you wish, make torma offerings and
tsog offerings. These can be found in the extensive sadhana,*
Essence of Vajrayana.

Dedication

Thus, through my virtues from correctly performing
   the offerings, praises, recitations, and meditations
Of the generation stage of Glorious Heruka,
May I complete all the stages
Of the common and uncommon paths.

For the sake of all living beings,
May I become Heruka;
And then lead every living being
To Heruka's supreme state.

And if I do not attain this supreme state in this life,
At my deathtime may I be met by the venerable Father
   and Mother and their retinue,
With clouds of breathtaking offerings, heavenly music,
And many excellent, auspicious signs.

Then, at the end of the clear light of death,
May I be led to Pure Dakini Land,
The abode of the Knowledge Holders who practise the
   supreme path;
And there may I swiftly complete this profound path.

May the most profound practice and instruction of Heruka,
Practised by millions of powerful Yogis, greatly increase;
And may it remain for a very long time without
   degenerating,
As the main gateway for those seeking liberation.

May the Heroes, Dakinis, and their retinues
Abiding in the twenty-four supreme places of this world,
Who possess unobstructed power for accomplishing this
   method,
Never waver from always assisting practitioners.

Auspicious prayers

May there be the auspiciousness of a great treasury
   of blessings
Arising from the excellent deeds of all the root and
   lineage Gurus,
Who have accomplished the supreme attainment of
   Buddha Heruka
By relying upon the excellent, secret path of the King
   of Tantras.

May there be the auspiciousness of the great excellent
   deeds of the Three Jewels –
The holy Buddha Jewel, the pervading nature Heruka;
The ultimate, great, secret Dharma Jewel, the scriptures
   and realizations of Heruka Tantra;
And the supreme Sangha Jewel, the assemblies of
   Heruka's retinue Deities.

Through all the great good fortune there is
In the precious, celestial mansions as extensive as the
   three thousand worlds,
Adorned with ornaments like the rays of the sun and
   the moon,
May all worlds and their beings have happiness,
   goodness, glory, and prosperity.

Condensed Six-session Yoga

Everyone who has received a Highest Yoga Tantra empowerment has a commitment to practise six-session Guru yoga. If we are very busy, we can fulfil our six-session commitment by doing the following practice six times each day. First we recall the nineteen commitments of the five Buddha families that are listed below, and then, with a strong determination to keep these commitments purely, we recite the Condensed Six-session Yoga *that follows.*

THE NINETEEN COMMITMENTS OF THE FIVE BUDDHA FAMILIES

The six commitments of the family of Buddha Vairochana

1 To go for refuge to Buddha
2 To go for refuge to Dharma
3 To go for refuge to Sangha
4 To refrain from non-virtue
5 To practise virtue
6 To benefit others

The four commitments of the family of Buddha Akshobya

1 To keep a vajra to remind us of great bliss
2 To keep a bell to remind us of emptiness
3 To generate ourself as the Deity
4 To rely sincerely upon our Spiritual Guide

The four commitments of the family of Buddha Ratnasambhava

1 To give material help
2 To give Dharma
3 To give fearlessness
4 To give love

The three commitments of the family of Buddha Amitabha

1 To rely upon the teachings of Sutra
2 To rely upon the teachings of the two lower classes of Tantra
3 To rely upon the teachings of the two higher classes of Tantra

The two commitments of the family of Buddha Amoghasiddhi

1 To make offerings to our Spiritual Guide
2 To strive to maintain purely all the vows we have taken

CONDENSED SIX-SESSION YOGA

I go for refuge to the Guru and Three Jewels.
Holding vajra and bell I generate as the Deity and make offerings.
I rely upon the Dharmas of Sutra and Tantra and refrain from all non-virtuous actions.
Gathering all virtuous Dharmas, I help all living beings through the practice of the four givings.

All nineteen commitments are referred to in this verse. The words, 'I go for refuge to the . . . Three Jewels', refer to the first three commitments of the family of Buddha Vairochana – to go for refuge to Buddha, to go for refuge to Dharma, and to go for refuge to Sangha. The word, 'Guru', refers to the fourth commitment of the family of Buddha Akshobya – to rely sincerely upon our Spiritual Guide.

The words, 'Holding vajra and bell I generate as the Deity', refer to the first three commitments of the family of Buddha Akshobya – to keep a vajra to remind us of great bliss, to keep a bell to remind us of emptiness, and to generate ourself as the Deity. The words, 'and make offerings', refer to the first commitment of the family of Buddha Amoghasiddhi – to make offerings to our Spiritual Guide.

The words, 'I rely upon the Dharmas of Sutra and Tantra', refer to the three commitments of the family of Buddha Amitabha – to rely upon the teachings of Sutra, to rely upon the teachings of the two lower classes of Tantra, and to rely upon the teachings of the two higher classes of Tantra. The words, 'and refrain from all non-virtuous actions', refer to the fourth commitment of the family of Buddha Vairochana – to refrain from non-virtue.

The words, 'Gathering all virtuous Dharmas', refer to the fifth commitment of the family of Buddha Vairochana – to practise virtue. The words, 'I help all living beings', refer to the sixth commitment of the family of Buddha Vairochana – to benefit others. The words, 'through the practice of the four givings', refer to the four commitments of the family of Buddha Ratnasambhava – to give material help, to give Dharma, to give fearlessness, and to give love.

Finally, the entire verse refers to the second commitment of the family of Buddha Amoghasiddhi – to strive to maintain purely all the vows we have taken.

More detail on the vows and commitments of Secret Mantra can be found in the book Tantric Grounds and Paths.

Colophon: This sadhana was compiled from traditional sources by Venerable Geshe Kelsang Gyatso.

Essence of Vajrayana

HERUKA BODY MANDALA SELF-GENERATION
SADHANA ACCORDING TO THE SYSTEM OF
MAHASIDDHA GHANTAPA

Introduction

Those who have received the empowerment and commentary of Heruka body mandala, and who have a sincere wish to gain deep realizations of the generation and completion stages of Heruka body mandala, can practise this sadhana, which is the very essence of Vajrayana.

For the purposes of daily practice, in front of a shrine containing a statue or picture of Heruka you should set out three tormas. These can either be made in the traditional way according to the illustration on page 488, or can consist simply of any clean, fresh food such as honey or cakes. The central torma is for the Deities of the great bliss wheel – Heruka Father and Mother and the four Yoginis; the torma to its left is for the supramundane retinues of Heruka; and the torma to its right is for the mundane retinues of Heruka.

In front of the tormas, set out three rows of offerings. The first row, nearest the shrine, is for the supramundane in-front-generated Deities, and the second row is for the mundane Dakas and Dakinis. Both these rows start from the left side of the shrine, your right, and include AHRGHAM, PADÄM, PUPE, DHUPE, DIWE, GÄNDHE, and NEWIDE. Nothing is set out for the SHAPTA offering because music is not a visual object. The third row, which is for the self-generated Deities, starts from the right side of the shrine and includes AHRGHAM, PADÄM, ÄNTZAMANAM, PUPE, DHUPE, DIWE, GÄNDHE, and NEWIDE.

When making a tsog offering, this can be set out at any suitable place in front of the shrine, and can consist of clean, fresh foods such as cakes, biscuits, honey, and fruit. You can also offer a tsog offering torma made in the traditional way according to the illustration on page 489. If you do not have time to practise extensive self-generation, you can make the tsog offering in conjunction with the brief sadhana entitled *Assembly of Good Fortune*. More information on tsog offerings can be found in *Guide to Dakini Land*.

On a small table in front of your meditation seat, arrange from left to right your inner offering, vajra, bell, damaru, and mala. In front of these, place your sadhana text. Then, with a pure motivation and a happy mind, begin the actual practice. Do not worry if initially you are unable to prepare the shrine and the offerings as described here; the important thing is simply to practise the sadhana with a pure mind and strong faith.

Essence of Vajrayana

THE PRELIMINARY PRACTICES

Visualizing the objects of refuge

In the space before me appear Guru Heruka Father and
Mother, surrounded by the assembly of direct and lineage
Gurus, Yidams, Buddhas, Bodhisattvas, Heroes, Dakinis,
and Dharma Protectors.

Going for refuge and generating aspiring bodhichitta

Eternally I shall go for refuge
To Buddha, Dharma, and Sangha.
For the sake of all living beings
I shall become Heruka.   (3x)

Generating engaging bodhichitta

To lead all mother living beings to the state of ultimate
     happiness,
I shall attain as quickly as possible, in this very life,
The state of the Union of Buddha Heruka.
For this purpose I shall practise the stages of Heruka's
     path.   (3x)

Receiving blessings

Guru Heruka Father and Mother together with all the
other objects of refuge dissolve into me, and I receive
their blessings.

Vajrasattva Father and Mother

Purifying our own mind, body, and speech

From the state of bliss and emptiness I arise as Heruka
with a blue-coloured body, one face, and two hands,
holding vajra and bell, and embracing Vajravarahi. I stand
with my right leg outstretched.

OM SHRI VAJRA HE HE RU RU KAM HUM HUM PHAT DAKINI
DZALA SHAMBARAM SÖHA

My mind has transformed into the union of bliss and
emptiness, my body into Heruka's body, and my speech
into Heruka's mantra.

Purifying other beings, the environment, and enjoyments

Light rays from the letter HUM at my heart
Purify all worlds and their beings.
Everything becomes immaculately pure,
Completely filled with a vast array of offerings,
The nature of exalted wisdom and bestowing
     uncontaminated bliss.

Purifying non-virtues, downfalls, and obstacles

On my crown on a lotus and moon seat sit Vajrasattva Father
and Mother. They are inseparable from the wisdom beings.

O Guru Vajrasattva please listen to me.
There is great danger that I may die before I purify my
     negativities.
So with the water of your compassion
Please purify all my non-virtues and downfalls.

Recite the mantra:

OM VAJRA HERUKA SAMAYA, MANU PALAYA, HERUKA
TENO PATITA, DRIDHO ME BHAWA, SUTO KAYO ME BHAWA,
SUPO KAYO ME BHAWA, ANURAKTO ME BHAWA, SARWA
SIDDHI ME PRAYATZA, SARWA KARMA SUTZA ME, TZITAM
SHRIYAM KURU HUM, HA HA HA HA HO BHAGAWÄN,
VAJRA HERUKA MA ME MUNTSA, HERUKA BHAWA, MAHA
SAMAYA SATTÖ AH HUM PHAT   (7x, 21x, etc.)

Heruka Father and Mother

As a result of my request, lights and nectars flow down from the mantra rosary at his heart and purify all the negativities and obstructions of my body, speech, and mind.

Vajrasattva Father and Mother dissolve into me and bless my mental continuum.

Guru yoga

Visualizing the commitment beings of the Field of Merit, and inviting and absorbing the wisdom beings

In the space before me on a lotus and sun, treading on Bhairawa and Kalarati, is my root Guru Heruka. He has a dark-blue body like a lapis mountain, four faces, and twelve arms. His principal face is dark blue, the left face green, the back face red, and the right face yellow. His two principal hands embrace Vajravarahi and hold a vajra and bell. Two hands hold an elephant skin, two hands hold a damaru and a khatanga, two hands hold an axe and a skullcup of blood, two hands hold a curved knife and a vajra noose, and two hands hold a three-pointed spear and a four-faced head of Brahma.

He displays the nine moods and wears six bone ornaments. His crown is adorned with a half moon and a crossed vajra. He wears a long necklace of fifty human heads, the nature of wisdom, and a lower garment of a tiger skin. He stands with his right leg outstretched, in the centre of a mass of blazing fire. Vajravarahi is red in colour and adorned with five mudras. She holds a curved knife and a skullcup, and is entwined in embrace with Heruka.

In the centre of the Principal Deity's body, the gross parts of which symbolize the four elements, Mount Meru, and the celestial mansion, his actual white and red drop inside his heart chakra appears as Heruka and Vajravarahi embracing each other. The channel petals of the elements in the four directions appear as the four Yoginis, and the channel petals in the intermediate directions appear as skullcups filled with nectars. At the twenty-four places of Heruka in the upper and lower parts of his body are the twenty-four Heroes, the nature of the drops, embracing the twenty-four Heroines, the nature of the channels; and at the doors of his senses are the eight Goddesses of the doorways.

They are surrounded by a vast assembly of direct and lineage Gurus, Yidams, Buddhas, Bodhisattvas, Heroes, Dakinis, and Dharma Protectors. Their three places are marked by the three letters. Light rays radiate from the letter HUM and invite the assembly of wisdom beings.

DZA HUM BAM HO
The wisdom beings become inseparable from the commitment beings.

Prostration

Vajra Holder, my jewel-like Guru,
Through whose kindness I can accomplish
The state of great bliss in an instant,
At your lotus feet humbly I bow.

As times become ever more impure,
Your power and blessings ever increase,
And you care for us quickly, as swift as thought;
O Chakrasambara Father and Mother, to you I prostrate.

To the Gurus who abide in the three times and the ten
    directions,
The Three Supreme Jewels, and all other objects of
    prostration,
I prostrate with faith and respect, a melodious chorus of
    praise,
And emanated bodies as numerous as atoms in the world.

The eight outer offerings

The exalted wisdom of uncontaminated bliss and
  emptiness,
Appearing in the aspect of infinite offering goddesses
Of all the water for drinking, water for bathing,
Flowers, incense, lights, perfume, food, and music
  throughout infinite worlds,
I offer to you Guru Heruka, glorious Father and Mother,
To the Heroes and Heroines of the great bliss wheel,
And to those of the heart, speech, body, and commitment
  wheels;
Please bestow the attainments of outer and inner Dakini
  Land.

OM GURU HERUKA VAJRAYOGINI SAPARIWARA AHRGHAM
  PARTITZA SÖHA
PADÄM PARTITZA SÖHA
VAJRA PUPE AH HUM SÖHA
VAJRA DHUPE AH HUM SÖHA
VAJRA DIWE AH HUM SÖHA
VAJRA GÄNDHE AH HUM SÖHA
VAJRA NEWIDE AH HUM SÖHA
VAJRA SHAPTA AH HUM SÖHA

Offering the five objects of desire

All forms that exist throughout infinite realms transform
  into a vast assembly of Rupavajra Goddesses,
With smiling faces and beautiful bodies, pervading the
  whole of space.
I offer these to you Guru Father and Mother and to the
  assembly of Deities;
Please accept, and through the force of all forms that exist
  appearing as Rupavajras,
May I and all living beings receive unchanging great bliss
And complete the supreme concentration of the union of
  great bliss and emptiness.
OM RUPA BENZ HUM HUM PHAT

All sounds that exist throughout infinite realms transform
into a vast assembly of Shaptavajra Goddesses,
Singing sweet songs and playing the lute, pervading the
whole of space.
I offer these to you Guru Father and Mother and to the
assembly of Deities;
Please accept, and through the force of all sounds that exist
appearing as Shaptavajras,
May I and all living beings receive unchanging great bliss
And complete the supreme concentration of the union of
great bliss and emptiness.
OM SHAPTA BENZ HUM HUM PHAT

All smells that exist throughout infinite realms transform
into a vast assembly of Gāndhavajra Goddesses,
Filling all directions with beautiful smells, pervading the
whole of space.
I offer these to you Guru Father and Mother and to the
assembly of Deities;
Please accept, and through the force of all smells that exist
appearing as Gāndhavajras,
May I and all living beings receive unchanging great bliss
And complete the supreme concentration of the union of
great bliss and emptiness.
OM GÄNDHE BENZ HUM HUM PHAT

All tastes that exist throughout infinite realms transform
into a vast assembly of Rasavajra Goddesses,
Holding jewelled vessels brimming with nectar, pervading
the whole of space.
I offer these to you Guru Father and Mother and to the
assembly of Deities;
Please accept, and through the force of all tastes that exist
appearing as Rasavajras,
May I and all living beings receive unchanging great bliss
And complete the supreme concentration of the union of
great bliss and emptiness.
OM RASA BENZ HUM HUM PHAT

All tactile objects that exist throughout infinite realms
    transform into a vast assembly of Parshavajra Goddesses,
Who steal the mind with supremely soft touch, pervading
    the whole of space.
I offer these to you Guru Father and Mother and to the
    assembly of Deities;
Please accept, and through the force of all touch that exists
    appearing as Parshavajras,
May I and all living beings receive unchanging great bliss
And complete the supreme concentration of the union of
    great bliss and emptiness.
OM PARSHE BENZ HUM HUM PHAT

Inner offering

OM GURU HERUKA VAJRAYOGINI SAPARIWARA OM AH HUM

Secret offering

And I offer most attractive illusory mudras,
A host of messengers born from places, born from mantra,
    and spontaneously born,
With slender bodies, skilled in the sixty-four arts of love,
And possessing the splendour of youthful beauty.

Thatness offering

I offer you the supreme, ultimate bodhichitta,
A great exalted wisdom of spontaneous bliss free from
    obstructions,
Inseparable from the nature of all phenomena, the sphere
    of freedom from elaboration,
Effortless, and beyond words, thoughts, and expressions.

Offering our spiritual practice

I go for refuge to the Three Jewels
And confess individually all negative actions.
I rejoice in the virtues of all beings
And promise to accomplish a Buddha's enlightenment.

I go for refuge until I am enlightened
To Buddha, Dharma, and the Supreme Assembly,
And to accomplish the aims of myself and others
I shall generate the mind of enlightenment.

Having generated the mind of supreme enlightenment,
I shall invite all sentient beings to be my guests
And engage in the pleasing, supreme practices of
    enlightenment.
May I attain Buddhahood to benefit migrators.

May everyone be happy,
May everyone be free from misery,
May no one ever be separated from their happiness,
May everyone have equanimity, free from hatred and
    attachment.

Confession, rejoicing, beseeching the Spiritual Guide not to pass away, requesting the turning of the Wheel of Dharma, and dedication

I confess my wrong deeds from all time,
And rejoice in the virtues of all.
Please stay until samsara ceases,
And turn the Wheel of Dharma for us.
Through the power of my entire collection of virtue
May I swiftly attain the Union of Heruka.

Offering the mandala

OM VAJRA BHUMI AH HUM
Great and powerful golden ground,
OM VAJRA REKHE AH HUM
At the edge the iron fence stands around the outer circle.
In the centre Mount Meru the king of mountains,
Around which are four continents:
In the east Purvavideha, in the south Jambudipa,
In the west Aparagodaniya, in the north Uttarakuru.
Each has two sub-continents:
Deha and Videha, Tsamara and Abatsamara,

Satha and Uttaramantrina, Kurava and Kaurava.
The mountain of jewels, the wish-granting tree,
The wish-granting cow, and the harvest unsown.
The precious wheel, the precious jewel,
The precious queen, the precious minister,
The precious elephant, the precious supreme horse,
The precious general, and the great treasure vase.
The goddess of beauty, the goddess of garlands,
The goddess of music, the goddess of dance,
The goddess of flowers, the goddess of incense,
The goddess of light, and the goddess of scent.
The sun and the moon, the precious umbrella,
The banner of victory in every direction.
In the centre all treasures of both gods and men,
An excellent collection with nothing left out.
I offer this to you my kind root Guru and lineage Gurus,
To all of you sacred and glorious Gurus;
Please accept with compassion for migrating beings,
And having accepted please grant us your blessings.

O Treasure of Compassion, my Refuge and Protector,
I offer you the mountain, continents, precious objects,
    treasure vase, sun and moon,
Which have arisen from my aggregates, sources, and
    elements
As aspects of the exalted wisdom of spontaneous bliss
    and emptiness.

I offer without any sense of loss
The objects that give rise to my attachment, hatred, and
    confusion,
My friends, enemies, and strangers, our bodies and
    enjoyments;
Please accept these and bless me to be released directly
    from the three poisons.

IDAM GURU RATNA MANDALAKAM NIRYATAYAMI

Receiving the blessings of the four empowerments

Requesting the empowerments

O Guru Heruka, the nature of the Truth Body,
I seek no refuge other than you.
Please purify all negativities of my three doors,
And bless me to attain the four bodies of great bliss.   (3x)

Receiving the vase empowerment

Having been requested single-pointedly in this way,
Vajravarahi and the four Yoginis grant the vase
empowerment. This purifies all obstructions of my body,
and I am empowered to attain the gross and subtle
generation stages and the Emanation Body.

Receiving the secret empowerment

Guru Father and Mother enter into union and I taste their
secret substance. This purifies all obstructions of my speech,
channels, and winds, and I am empowered to attain the
completion stage of illusory body and the Enjoyment Body.

Receiving the wisdom-mudra empowerment

I receive Vajravarahi as my consort, and through embracing
her I generate the exalted wisdoms of the four joys. This
purifies all obstructions of my mind, and I am empowered
to attain the completion stage of clear light and the Truth
Body.

Receiving the precious word empowerment

Through listening to the words of instruction I understand
the meaning of union – the union of the illusory body and
the mind of bliss and emptiness. This purifies all obstructions
of my body, speech, and mind, and I am empowered to
attain the Union of Vajradhara.

Requesting the lineage Gurus

O Blessed One Chakrasambara, Great Mother Vajrayogini,
Mahasiddha Ghantapa, Kurmapada, Dzalandarapa,
Krishnapada, Guhyapa, Vijayapada, Tilopa, and Naropa,
I request you, please bestow Union in this life.

O Pamtingpa Brothers, Lokya Sherab Tseg,
Malgyur Lodrö Drag, Kunga Nyingpo, Master Sönam
  Tsemo,
Venerable Dragpa Gyaltsän, Kunga Gyaltsän, Drogön
  Chögyäl Pagpa,
Shangtön Könchogpäl, Nasa Dragpugpa, and Lamadampa
  Sönam Gyaltsän,
I request you, please bestow Union in this life.

O Venerable Tsongkhapa, Khädrub Geleg Pälsang,
Baso Chökyi Gyaltsän, Mahasiddha Dharmavajra, Gyalwa
  Ensäpa,
Khädrub Sangye Yeshe, Panchen Losang Chögyän,
  Könchog Gyaltsän,
Changkya Ngawang Chöndän, Drubwang Losang
  Chöndzin, and Changkya Rölpai Dorje,
I request you, please bestow Union in this life.

O Venerable Losang Nyendrag, Jetsun Losang Tugje,
Jampäl Tsultrim, Lhatsün Jampäl Dorje, Great Yogi Yeshe
  Döndrub,
Kelsang Tendzin Khädrub, Mahasiddha Päma Dorje,
Je Phabongkhapa Dechen Nyingpo, and Heruka Losang
  Yeshe,
I request you, please bestow Union in this life.

And especially to you, most precious Lama Kelsang
  Gyatso,
Who reveal all the sublime, profound essential practices
For receiving swiftly the great blessings of Heruka,
I request you, please bestow Union in this life.

The appearances of this life are as fleeting as a flash of
   lightning,
And samsara's enjoyments are as deceptive as a
   demoness's smile;
Please bless me to realize this and generate from the
   depths of my heart
A strong and powerful renunciation longing for liberation.

Since I cannot bear the torment of living beings, my
   mothers,
Who have fallen into the blazing abyss of suffering,
Please bless me to develop a spontaneous bodhichitta
Striving for complete enlightenment for their sake.

Please bless me to complete the practice
Of the profound yoga of the two stages of the glorious
   body mandala –
The ultimate, excellent path of Mother Tantra
And the supreme practice by which millions have passed
   beyond sorrow.

And after my death may the Blessed One Heruka,
Together with the assembly of Heroes and Yoginis,
Accompanied by the sound of heavenly music,
Lead me to the city of Pure Dakini Land.

In short, throughout all my lives,
May I always come under the loving care of Guru Heruka.
May I swiftly complete all the grounds and paths
And attain the state of Buddha Heruka.

Accomplishing spontaneous great bliss by dissolving the Guru into oneself

The Field of Merit gathers gradually from the edges and
dissolves into my root Guru Heruka. Out of delight he
comes to my crown, descends through my central channel,
and becomes of one taste with my mind at my heart.
I experience spontaneous great bliss.

THE ACTUAL PRACTICE OF GENERATION STAGE

Bringing death into the path of the Truth Body

Light rays from the HUM at my heart melt all worlds and beings into light. This dissolves into me, and I in turn gradually melt into light from below and above and dissolve into the HUM at my heart. The letter HUM dissolves in stages from the bottom up into the nada. The nada becomes smaller and smaller and dissolves into clear light emptiness. I am Truth Body Heruka.

Bringing the intermediate state into the path of the Enjoyment Body

From the state of emptiness my mind appears in the form of a nada. I am Enjoyment Body Heruka.

Bringing rebirth into the path of the Emanation Body

From YAM, RAM, BAM, LAM, SUM, PAM arise the four elements, Mount Meru, and the lotus. In the centre of the lotus, from the vowels and consonants, arises a reddish-white moon, the nature of the red and white bodhichittas of Guru Heruka Father and Mother. I, the nada, enter the centre of the moon and gradually transform into the aspect of a HUM.

Five-coloured lights radiate from the HUM and lead all living beings to the state of Chakrasambara. At the same time all the Heroes and Heroines are invited from the Buddha Lands of the ten directions. They all melt into light and dissolve into the HUM, which becomes the nature of spontaneous joy. The moon, vowels, consonants, and HUM completely transform, and the supported Deities and supporting mandala arise fully and all at once. I am Emanation Body Heruka.

Checking meditation on the mandala and basis Heruka

Furthermore, there is the celestial mansion, which is square with four doorways. The jewelled walls have five layers coloured white, yellow, red, green, and blue from the outside in. Around the top of the wall is a red jewelled moulding studded with square, triangular, and other-shaped jewels. Upon this are four layers of golden bands. Upon these, and extending beyond, are rafters whose ends form the shape of sea-monsters, with full and half-length strings of pearls hanging from their mouths. Overhanging these are sharpu, special jewelled decorations, suspended from the eaves. Above these is a parapet in the shape of half lotus petals. It is adorned with eight victory banners and eight other banners, all set in golden vases, and parasols on top of the four outer corners.

Around the outer foot of the wall runs a red ledge for the objects of desire. Upon this stand goddesses of various colours and postures making offerings. At the outer corners of the doorways and hallways, as well as at the four outer and four inner corners of the mansion, stand half moons, upon which rest red jewels adorned at the top by vajras.

At the front of each entrance, upon square pedestals, four pillars set in vases support a square, eleven-tiered archway. Above each archway is a Dharma Wheel flanked right and left by a male and a female deer. To the right and left of each archway, set in golden vases, are wish-granting trees bearing the seven precious possessions of a king. In the space around are Siddhas, and emerging from clouds are offering gods and goddesses holding garlands of flowers, making everything exquisitely beautiful.

Beyond this is the protection circle of a fence of vajras of various sizes, and so forth. Surrounding the protection circle are five-coloured vajra fires blazing like the fire of the aeon. They swirl counter-clockwise, covering all directions – above, below, and all around. Beyond these are the eight great charnel grounds. In each charnel ground there is a tree, at the foot of which there sits a directional guardian. At the top of the tree there is a regional guardian with the upper half of his body emerging from the branches. There is a lake, in which there lives a naga, and above each lake there is a cloud. There is a mountain, on top of which there is a white stupa, and there is a wisdom fire.

Throughout the charnel grounds wild birds and animals such as ravens, owls, vultures, wolves, jackals, and snakes wander around; and spirits such as givers of harm, zombies, and cannibals utter the sound 'Kili Kili'. There are also Yogis and Yoginis such as those who have accomplished attainments, and Knowledge Holders keeping their commitments purely. They are all single-pointedly practising Heruka's path. They are naked, with freely hanging hair, and are adorned with five mudras. They hold hand-drums, skullcups, and khatangas, and their crowns are adorned with skulls. All the beings abiding in the charnel grounds instil the place with a sense of wonder.

Inside the celestial mansion eight pillars support vajra beams adorning the ceiling. The roof is surmounted at its crest by a precious jewel and a vajra. The ceiling and floor are white in the east, green in the north, red in the west, yellow in the south, and blue in the centre. In the very centre is a lotus of various colours and a sun mandala.

On the sun mandala at the centre of the lotus I arise as the Blessed One Heruka, with a dark-blue body and four faces. My principal face is dark blue, the left face green, the back face red, and the right face yellow. Each face has three eyes and a rosary of five-pronged vajras on its forehead. My right leg is outstretched and treads on the head of black Bhairawa, who has four hands. His first two hands are pressed together, the second right hand holds a damaru, and the second left a sword. My bent left

leg treads on the breast of red Kalarati, who has four
hands. Her first two hands are pressed together, and the
other two hold a skullcup and a khatanga. Both the beings
beneath my feet have one face and three eyes, and are
adorned with five mudras.

I have twelve arms. The first two embrace Vajravarahi,
with my right hand holding a five-pronged vajra and my
left hand a bell. The next two hands hold a bloody, white
elephant skin stretched across my back; my right hand
holds the left foreleg, and my left the left hind leg. Both
these hands are in the threatening mudra with the tips of
the outstretched fingers at the level of my eyebrows. My
third right hand holds a damaru, the fourth an axe, the
fifth a curved knife, and the sixth an upright three-pointed
spear. My third left hand holds a khatanga marked with a
vajra, the fourth a skullcup brimming with blood, the fifth
a vajra noose, and the sixth a four-faced head of Brahma.

My hair is tied up in a topknot marked with a crossed
vajra. Each head is adorned with a crown of five skulls
strung together top and bottom with a rosary of black
vajras. On the left side of my crown is a half moon,
slightly tilted. My facial expressions change, and my four
sets of four fangs are bared and terrifying. I display nine
moods: three physical moods of majesty, heroism, and
menace; three verbal moods of laughter, wrath, and ferocity;
and three mental moods of compassion, attentiveness, and
serenity. I wear a lower garment of a tiger skin, and a long
necklace of fifty human heads strung together with human
entrails. Adorned with six mudras, my entire body is
smeared with ashes of human bone.

Embracing the Blessed One is the Blessed Mother
Vajravarahi, who has a red-coloured body, one face, two
hands, and three eyes. She is naked with freely hanging
hair and wears a lower garment made from fragments of
skull. Her left hand, embracing the Father's neck, holds a
skullcup brimming with the blood of the four maras. Her
right hand in the threatening mudra brandishes a curved

knife, opposing the malignant forces of the ten directions. Her body shines with a brilliance like that of the fire of the aeon. Her two legs are clasped around the Father's thighs. She is the nature of blissful great compassion. Adorned with five mudras, she wears a crown of five human skulls and a necklace of fifty human skulls. Father and Mother abide in the centre of a fiercely blazing fire of exalted wisdom.

Simultaneous generation of the entire supporting and supported Heruka body mandala

The gross parts of my body – the purified body of basis Heruka, and the subtle parts of my purified body – my channels and drops, appear in the form of seed-letters. These transform fully and all at once into the entire supporting and supported body mandala. Thus, I am Heruka Father and Mother, the nature of my white and red indestructible drop. I am surrounded by the Heroes and Heroines of the five wheels, the nature of my channels and drops. I reside at the centre of the celestial mansion, the nature of the gross parts of my body.

Checking meditation on the gross parts of our body generated as Heruka's mandala

Remember in detail as follows:

My two legs forming the shape of a bow are the bow-shaped wind mandala. The triangle at my secret place is the three-cornered fire mandala. My round belly is the circular water mandala. My square-shaped chest is the square earth mandala. My spine is Mount Meru. The thirty-two channels at my crown are the lotus. The trunk of my body, the upper and lower parts of which are equal in size, is the square celestial mansion with four equal sides, the mandala of Heruka, exquisitely beautiful with adornments such as the jewelled moulding and strings of pearls. The eight parts of my limbs are the eight pillars. Beyond these is the protection circle surrounded by the eight charnel grounds.

Checking meditation on the subtle parts of our body, the channels and drops, generated as the Deities

Remember in detail as follows:

The white bodhichitta at the centre of the Dharma Wheel inside the central channel at my heart is like a drop of dew. This drop, the size of a mustard seed, in aspect the letter HUM, transformed into the Blessed One Glorious Heruka, with four faces and twelve arms. At my navel the red tummo fire in the form of the red drop, in aspect the letter BAM, transformed into the Blessed Mother Vajravarahi. As the nature of the red and white drops they met at the very centre of the celestial mansion and entered into embrace.

At my heart the four channel petals in the cardinal directions, which are the paths for the winds of the four elements, in aspect the letters LAM, MAM, PAM, TAM beginning clockwise in the east (in front of me), transformed, beginning counter-clockwise in the east (in front of me) into dark-blue Dakini, in the north (to my left) into green Lama, in the west (behind me) into red Khandarohi, and in the south (to my right) into yellow Rupini. They each have one face with three eyes and bared fangs, and are naked with freely hanging hair. They each have two hands, the right holding a curved knife and the left a skullcup, with a khatanga held in the crook of their left elbow. They stand with their right leg outstretched and are adorned with five mudras. They wear a crown of five human skulls and a long necklace of fifty human skulls. These are Deities of the great bliss wheel. The four channel petals of the offerings in the intermediate directions transformed into four skullcups brimming with five nectars.

Surrounding these, in three concentric circles, my twenty-four places such as the hairline and crown, in aspect the twenty-four letters PU DZA and so forth, transformed into the twenty-four places of Heruka in the form of the twenty-four petal-shaped spokes of the wheels. The channels of the twenty-four places, each in the aspect of a letter BAM, transformed into the twenty-four Heroines. The drops

inside these channels, each in the aspect of a letter HUM,
transformed into the twenty-four Heroes.

Thus, in the heart wheel, at the eastern spoke, Puliramalaya,
the nature of my hairline, are Khandakapala and Partzandi.
At the northern spoke, Dzalandhara, the nature of my crown,
are Mahakankala and Tzändriakiya.
At the western spoke, Odiyana, the nature of my right ear,
are Kankala and Parbhawatiya.
At the southern spoke, Arbuta, the nature of the back of
my neck, are Vikatadamshtri and Mahanasa.
At the south-eastern spoke, Godawari, the nature of my
left ear, are Suraberi and Biramatiya.
At the south-western spoke, Rameshöri, the nature of the
point between my eyebrows, are Amitabha and Karwariya.
At the north-western spoke, Dewikoti, the nature of my
two eyes, are Vajraprabha and Lamkeshöriya.
At the north-eastern spoke, Malawa, the nature of my two
shoulders, are Vajradeha and Drumatzaya.

All the Deities of the heart wheel have blue-coloured
bodies and are known as the Heroes and Heroines of the
vajra mind family.

In the speech wheel, at the eastern spoke, Kamarupa, the
nature of my two armpits, are Ankuraka and Airawatiya.
At the northern spoke, Ote, the nature of my two breasts,
are Vajrajatila and Mahabhairawi.
At the western spoke, Trishakune, the nature of my navel,
are Mahavira and Bayubega.
At the southern spoke, Kosala, the nature of the tip of my
nose, are Vajrahumkara and Surabhakiya.
At the south-eastern spoke, Kalinga, the nature of my
mouth, are Subhadra and Shamadewi.
At the south-western spoke, Lampaka, the nature of my
throat, are Vajrabhadra and Suwatre.
At the north-western spoke, Kancha, the nature of my
heart, are Mahabhairawa and Hayakarna.

At the north-eastern spoke, Himalaya, the nature of my
two testicles, are Virupaksha and Khaganana.

All the Deities of the speech wheel have red-coloured
bodies and are known as the Heroes and Heroines of the
vajra speech family.

In the body wheel, at the eastern spoke, Pretapuri, the
nature of the tip of my sex organ, are Mahabala and
Tzatrabega.

At the northern spoke, Grihadewata, the nature of my
anus, are Ratnavajra and Khandarohi.

At the western spoke, Shauraktra, the nature of my two
thighs, are Hayagriva and Shaundini.

At the southern spoke, Suwanadvipa, the nature of my
two calves, are Akashagarbha and Tzatrawarmini.

At the south-eastern spoke, Nagara, the nature of my
eight fingers and eight toes, are Shri Heruka and Subira.

At the south-western spoke, Sindhura, the nature of the
tops of my feet, are Pämanarteshvara and Mahabala.

At the north-western spoke, Maru, the nature of my two
thumbs and two big toes, are Vairochana and
Tzatrawartini.

At the north-eastern spoke, Kuluta, the nature of my two
knees, are Vajrasattva and Mahabire.

All the Deities of the body wheel have white-coloured
bodies and are known as the Heroes and Heroines of the
vajra body family.

All these Heroes and Heroines have one face, two hands,
and three eyes; and their heads are adorned with a crown
of five human skulls. The Heroes hold a vajra and bell, and
embrace their consort. Their hair is tied up in a topknot,
adorned with a vajra and a crescent moon. They have a
rosary of vajras on their forehead and are adorned with
six mudras. Wearing a long necklace of fifty human heads
and a lower garment of a tiger skin, they stand with their
right leg outstretched. The Heroines hold a curved knife
and a skullcup, and are entwined in embrace with the

Heroes. Wearing a lower garment made from fragments of skull and a necklace of fifty human skulls, they are adorned with five mudras.

Around the Deities of the body wheel, the channels of my eight doors of the senses, such as the channel of the root of my tongue, each in the aspect of a letter HUM, transformed into the eight Heroines. In the east is dark-blue Kakase; in the north green Ulukase; in the west red Shönase; in the south yellow Shukarase; in the south-east Yamadhati, who is blue on the right and yellow on the left; in the south-west Yamaduti, who is yellow on the right and red on the left; in the north-west Yamadangtrini, who is red on the right and green on the left; and in the north-east Yamamatani, who is green on the right and blue on the left. These Heroines have one face and two hands holding a curved knife and a skullcup, and grip a khatanga with the crook of their left elbow. They are adorned with five mudras and stand on a corpse seat with their right leg outstretched. They wear a crown of five human skulls and a long necklace of fifty human skulls.

Thus, I am Heruka Father and Mother, the nature of my white and red indestructible drop, surrounded by the Heroes and Heroines of the five wheels, who are the nature of my channels and drops.

Adorning our body, the bodies of Heruka Father and Mother of the body mandala, with the armour Deities

At my heart on a moon mandala appears white OM HA, the nature of Vajrasattva; at my head on a sun, yellow NAMA HI, the nature of Vairochana; at my crown on a sun, red SÖHA HU, the nature of Pämanarteshvara; at my two shoulders on a sun, black BOKE HE, the nature of Glorious Heruka; at my two eyes on a sun, orange HUM HUM HO, the nature of Vajrasurya; and at my forehead on a sun, green PHAT HAM, the nature of Paramashawa.

At the Principal Mother's navel on a sun mandala appears red OM BAM, the nature of Vajravarahi; at her heart on a sun, blue HAM YOM, the nature of Yamani; at her throat on a moon, white HRIM MOM, the nature of Mohani; at her head on a sun, yellow HRIM HRIM, the nature of Sachalani; at her crown on a sun, green HUM HUM, the nature of Samtrasani; and at her forehead on a sun, smoke-coloured PHAT PHAT, the nature of Chandika.

Inviting the wisdom beings, dissolving them into the commitment beings, and receiving the empowerment

PHAIM
My three places are marked by the three letters. Light rays radiate from the letter HUM and invite all the Buddhas of the ten directions in the same aspect as those visualized, together with the empowering Deities. All the wisdom beings gather into one complete supporting and supported mandala.

DZA HUM BAM HO
The wisdom beings become inseparable from the commitment beings.

The empowering Deities grant the empowerment, my body is filled with nectar, and I experience bliss. The excess nectar on the crowns completely transforms, and the Principal is adorned by Vajrasattva, Vajravarahi by Akshobya, the four Mothers by Ratnasambhava, the Deities of the heart wheel by Akshobya, the Deities of the speech wheel by Amitabha, the Deities of the body wheel by Vairochana, and the Deities of the commitment wheel by Amoghasiddhi.

Making offerings and praises to the self-generated Deities of the body mandala

Blessing the inner offering

OM KHANDAROHI HUM HUM PHAT
OM SÖBHAWA SHUDDHA SARWA DHARMA SÖBHAWA
   SHUDDHO HAM
Everything becomes emptiness.

From the state of emptiness, from YAM comes wind, from
RAM comes fire, from AH a grate of three human heads.
Upon this from AH appears a broad and expansive skullcup.
Inside from OM, KHAM, AM, TRAM, HUM come the five
nectars; from LAM, MAM, PAM, TAM, BAM come the five
meats, each marked by these letters. The wind blows, the
fire blazes, and the substances inside the skullcup melt.
Above them from HUM there arises a white, upside-down
khatanga, which falls into the skullcup and melts whereby
the substances take on the colour of mercury. Above them
three rows of vowels and consonants, standing one above
the other, transform into OM AH HUM. From these, light
rays draw the nectar of exalted wisdom from the hearts of
all the Tathagatas, Heroes, and Yoginis of the ten directions.
When this is added the contents increase and become vast.
OM AH HUM   (3x)

Blessing the outer offerings

OM KHANDAROHI HUM HUM PHAT
OM SÖBHAWA SHUDDHA SARWA DHARMA SÖBHAWA
    SHUDDHO HAM
Everything becomes emptiness.

From the state of emptiness, from KAMs come broad and
expansive skullcups, inside which from HUMs come water
for drinking, water for bathing, water for the mouth,
flowers, incense, lights, perfume, food, and music. By
nature emptiness, they have the aspect of the individual
offering substances, and function as objects of enjoyment
of the six senses to bestow special, uncontaminated bliss.

OM AHRGHAM AH HUM
OM PADÄM AH HUM
OM ÄNTZAMANAM AH HUM
OM VAJRA PUPE AH HUM
OM VAJRA DHUPE AH HUM
OM VAJRA DIWE AH HUM
OM VAJRA GÄNDHE AH HUM

OM VAJRA NEWIDE AH HUM
OM VAJRA SHAPTA AH HUM

Making the offerings

Countless breathtakingly beautiful offering and praising goddesses emanate from my heart and make offerings and praises to me as Heruka Father and Mother.

Outer offerings

OM AHRGHAM PARTITZA SÖHA
OM PADÄM PARTITZA SÖHA
OM ÄNTZAMANAM PARTITZA SÖHA
OM VAJRA PUPE AH HUM SÖHA
OM VAJRA DHUPE AH HUM SÖHA
OM VAJRA DIWE AH HUM SÖHA
OM VAJRA GÄNDHE AH HUM SÖHA
OM VAJRA NEWIDE AH HUM SÖHA
OM VAJRA SHAPTA AH HUM SÖHA

OM AH VAJRA ADARSHE HUM
OM AH VAJRA WINI HUM
OM AH VAJRA GÄNDHE HUM
OM AH VAJRA RASE HUM
OM AH VAJRA PARSHE HUM
OM AH VAJRA DHARME HUM

Inner offering

OM HUM BAM RIM RIM LIM LIM, KAM KHAM GAM GHAM NGAM, TSAM TSHAM DZAM DZHAM NYAM, TrAM THrAM DrAM DHrAM NAM, TAM THAM DAM DHAM NAM, PAM PHAM BAM BHAM, YAM RAM LAM WAM, SHAM KAM SAM HAM HUM HUM PHAT OM AH HUM

Secret and thatness offerings

I, the Principal Father and Mother, enter into the union of embrace. The bodhichitta melts, and as it descends from my crown to my throat I experience joy, as it descends from my

throat to my heart I experience supreme joy, as it descends
from my heart to my navel I experience extraordinary joy,
and as it descends from my navel to the tip of my jewel I
generate spontaneous great bliss inseparable from emptiness.
The Principal and all the retinue experience a special, exalted
wisdom of bliss and emptiness.

Eight lines of praise to the Father

OM NAMO BHAGAWATE WIRE SHAYA HUM HUM PHAT
OM MAHA KÄLWA AHGNI SAMNI BHAYA HUM HUM PHAT
OM DZATA MUGUTRA KORTAYA HUM HUM PHAT
OM DHAMKHATRA KARA LOTRA BHIKHANA MUKAYA HUM
    HUM PHAT
OM SAHARA BHUNDZA BHASURAYA HUM HUM PHAT
OM PARASHUWA SHODHÄDA SHULA KHATAMGA DHARINE
    HUM HUM PHAT
OM BHÄGADZINAM WARA DHARAYA HUM HUM PHAT
OM MAHA DHUMBA ÄNDHAKARA WAWUKAYA HUM HUM
    PHAT

Eight lines of praise to the Mother

OM NAMO BHAGAWATI VAJRA VARAHI BAM HUM HUM
    PHAT
OM NAMO ARYA APARADZITE TRE LOKYA MATI BIYE SHÖRI
    HUM HUM PHAT
OM NAMA SARWA BUTA BHAYA WAHI MAHA VAJRE HUM
    HUM PHAT
OM NAMO VAJRA SANI ADZITE APARADZITE WASHAM
    KARANITRA HUM HUM PHAT
OM NAMO BHRAMANI SHOKANI ROKANI KROTE KARALENI
    HUM HUM PHAT
OM NAMA DRASANI MARANI PRABHE DANI PARADZAYE
    HUM HUM PHAT
OM NAMO BIDZAYE DZAMBHANI TAMBHANI MOHANI
    HUM HUM PHAT
OM NAMO VAJRA VARAHI MAHA YOGINI KAME SHÖRI
    KHAGE HUM HUM PHAT

The offering and praising goddesses dissolve into the HUM at my heart.

At this point, (1) with a mind of great bliss, (2) meditate on the clear appearance of the mandala and Deities, and (3) meditate on divine pride, while (4) realizing the lack of inherent existence of all phenomena. In this way, train sincerely in one single concentration on gross or subtle generation stage possessing these four characteristics. Then, when you need to rest from meditation, you can practise mantra recitation.

THE CONCLUDING PRACTICES

Blessing the mala

The mala becomes emptiness. From the state of emptiness each bead appears in its own aspect, the nature of Pämanarteshvara, the vajra speech of all Buddhas.

Mantra recitation

You can practise either the long or the short mantra recitation.

Long mantra recitation

Visualization for reciting the mantras of the Principal Deities

The mantra to be recited descends from the letter HUM at my heart, leaves through the tip of my vajra, enters the consort's bhaga, ascends, leaves through her mouth, enters my mouth, descends, and dissolves back into the HUM. Then again it circles as before, leaving and re-entering my central channel. My four mouths, and all the Deities of the retinue, recite the mantras.

The root mantra of the Father

OM KARA KARA, KURU KURU, BÄNDHA BÄNDHA, TrASAYA
TrASAYA, KYOMBHAYA KYOMBHAYA, HROM HROM, HRAH
HRAH, PHAIM PHAIM, PHAT PHAT, DAHA DAHA, PATSA
PATSA, BHAKYA BHAKYA BASA RUDHI ÄNTRA MALA
WALAMBINE, GRIHANA GRIHANA SAPTA PATALA GATA
BHUDZAMGAM SARWAMPA TARDZAYA TARDZAYA,
AKANDYA AKANDYA, HRIM HRIM, GYÖN GYÖN, KYAMA
KYAMA, HAM HAM, HIM HIM, HUM HUM, KILI KILI, SILI
SILI, HILI HILI, DHILI DHILI, HUM HUM PHAT

The root mantra of the Mother

OM VAJRA VARAHI, PROTANGE PROTANGE, HANA HANA
PARANÄM, KING KINI KING KINI, DHUNA DHUNA VAJRA
HA TE, SHOKAYA SHOKAYA, VAJRA KHATANGA KAPALA
DHARINI, MAHA BISHITA MAMSA SANI, MANU KÄNTAR
PARI TESANI DHANA RASI RAMALA KARAMDAM DHARANI,
SUMBHANI SUMBHA, HANA HANA PARANÄM SARWA
PASHA WANÄM, MAHA MANÄ TSEDANI, KROMAMURTE
KAM KARA KARALINI, MAHA MUDRE, SHRI HERUKA,
DEWASÄ TRAMA HIKI, SAHARU SHIRE, SAHARA BAHAWE,
SHATA SAHA SANANE DZÖLITA, TEDZA SEDZÖLA MUKE
SAMGALA LOTSANI, VAJRA SHÖRIRE, VAJRA SANI, MILITA
TSILITA, HE HE, HUM HUM, KHA KHA, DHURU DHURU,
MURU MURU, ADETE MAHA YOGINI, PATITA SIDDHE,
TERADHAM TERADHAM, GARAM GARAM, HE HE, HA HA,
BHIME HASA HASA BIRI, HA HA, HE HE, HUM HUM,
TERLOKYA BINA SHANI SHATA SAHA SAKOTI, TATHAGATA,
PARIWARE, HUM HUM PHAT, SAHA RUPEKHA GADZA RUPE
AH, TERLOKYA UDHARE SAMUTA MEKALE, TRASA TRASA
HUM HUM PHAT, BIRA DETE HUM HUM, HA HA, MAHA
PASHU MOHANI YOGI SHÖRI TAM, DAKINI SARWA LOKANI
BÄNDHANI SADYA PRADYA KARINI HUM HUM PHAT,
BHUTA TRASANI MAHA BIRA PARA MAHASIDDHA, YOGI
SHÖRI PHAT, HUM HUM PHAT SÖHA

The essence mantra of the Father

OM SHRI VAJRA HE HE RU RU KAM HUM HUM PHAT DAKINI
DZALA SHAMBARAM SÖHA

The close essence mantra of the Father

OM HRIH HA HA HUM HUM PHAT

The essence mantra of the Mother

OM VAJRA BEROTZANIYE HUM HUM PHAT SÖHA

The close essence mantra of the Mother

OM SARWA BUDDHA DAKINIYE VAJRA WARNANIYE HUM
HUM PHAT SÖHA

The extensive armour mantras

The armour mantras of the Father

OM OM HA HUM HUM PHAT
OM NAMA HI HUM HUM PHAT
OM SÖHA HU HUM HUM PHAT
OM BOKE HE HUM HUM PHAT
OM HUM HUM HO HUM HUM PHAT
OM PHAT HAM HUM HUM PHAT

The armour mantras of the Mother

OM OM BAM HUM HUM PHAT
OM HAM YOM HUM HUM PHAT
OM HRIM MOM HUM HUM PHAT
OM HRIM HRIM HUM HUM PHAT
OM HUM HUM HUM HUM PHAT
OM PHAT PHAT HUM HUM PHAT

The condensed armour mantra

OM OM HA, NAMA HI, SÖHA HU, BOKE HE, HUM HUM HO,
PHAT HAM, OM BAM, HAM YOM, HRIM MOM, HRIM HRIM,
HUM HUM, PHAT PHAT, HUM HUM PHAT

Visualization for reciting the retinue mantras

Standing on a sun seat at the heart of each Deity is a letter HUM or BAM surrounded by the mantra to be recited. From the letter in the centre of the encircling mantra, assemblies of mandala Deities radiate and fulfil the welfare of all living beings. They gather back and dissolve into the central letter.

Recite the mantras while repeatedly radiating and gathering back.

The mantras of the four Yoginis of the great bliss wheel

OM DAKINIYE HUM HUM PHAT
OM LAME HUM HUM PHAT
OM KHANDAROHI HUM HUM PHAT
OM RUPINIYE HUM HUM PHAT

The mantras of the Deities of the heart wheel

OM KARA KARA HUM HUM PHAT, OM PARTZANDI HUM HUM PHAT, OM KURU KURU HUM HUM PHAT, OM TZÄNDRIAKIYE HUM HUM PHAT, OM BÄNDHA BÄNDHA HUM HUM PHAT, OM PARBHAWATIYE HUM HUM PHAT, OM TrASAYA TrASAYA HUM HUM PHAT, OM MAHANASE HUM HUM PHAT, OM KYOMBHAYA KYOMBHAYA HUM HUM PHAT, OM BIRAMATIYE HUM HUM PHAT, OM HROM HROM HUM HUM PHAT, OM KARWARIYE HUM HUM PHAT, OM HRAH HRAH HUM HUM PHAT, OM LAMKESHÖRIYE HUM HUM PHAT, OM PHAIM PHAIM HUM HUM PHAT, OM DRUMATZAYE HUM HUM PHAT

The mantras of the Deities of the speech wheel

OM PHAT PHAT HUM HUM PHAT, OM AIRAWATIYE HUM HUM PHAT, OM DAHA DAHA HUM HUM PHAT, OM MAHABHAIRAWI HUM HUM PHAT, OM PATSA PATSA HUM HUM PHAT, OM BAYUBEGE HUM HUM PHAT, OM BHAKYA BHAKYA BASA RUDHI ÄNTRA MALA WALAMBINE HUM

HUM PHAT, OM SURABHAKIYE HUM HUM PHAT, OM
GRIHANA GRIHANA SAPTA PATALA GATA BHUDZAMGAM
SARWAMPA TARDZAYA TARDZAYA HUM HUM PHAT, OM
SHAMADEWI HUM HUM PHAT, OM AKANDYA AKANDYA
HUM HUM PHAT, OM SUWATRE HUM HUM PHAT, OM HRIM
HRIM HUM HUM PHAT, OM HAYAKARNE HUM HUM PHAT,
OM GYÖN GYÖN HUM HUM PHAT, OM KHAGANANE HUM
HUM PHAT

The mantras of the Deities of the body wheel

OM KYAMA KYAMA HUM HUM PHAT, OM TZATRABEGE
HUM HUM PHAT, OM HAM HAM HUM HUM PHAT, OM
KHANDAROHI HUM HUM PHAT, OM HIM HIM HUM HUM
PHAT, OM SHAUNDINI HUM HUM PHAT, OM HUM HUM
HUM HUM PHAT, OM TZATRAWARMINI HUM HUM PHAT,
OM KILI KILI HUM HUM PHAT, OM SUBIRE HUM HUM PHAT,
OM SILI SILI HUM HUM PHAT, OM MAHABALE HUM HUM
PHAT, OM HILI HILI HUM HUM PHAT, OM TZATRAWARTINI
HUM HUM PHAT, OM DHILI DHILI HUM HUM PHAT, OM
MAHABIRE HUM HUM PHAT

The mantras of the Deities of the commitment wheel

OM KAKASE HUM HUM PHAT, OM ULUKASE HUM HUM
PHAT, OM SHÖNASE HUM HUM PHAT, OM SHUKARASE
HUM HUM PHAT, OM YAMADHATI HUM HUM PHAT, OM
YAMADUTI HUM HUM PHAT, OM YAMADANGTRINI HUM
HUM PHAT, OM YAMAMATANI HUM HUM PHAT

The condensed essence mantra of the sixty retinue Deities

OM RIM RIM LIM LIM, KAM KHAM GAM GHAM NGAM,
TSAM TSHAM DZAM DZHAM NYAM, TrAM THrAM DrAM
DHrAM NAM, TAM THAM DAM DHAM NAM, PAM PHAM
BAM BHAM, YAM RAM LAM WAM, SHAM KAM SAM HAM
HUM HUM PHAT

Short mantra recitation

If you wish to practise short mantra recitation you should recite only the essence mantras and the close essence mantras of the Father and Mother, the mantras of the four Yoginis of the great bliss wheel, the mantras of the Deities of the heart wheel, speech wheel, body wheel, and commitment wheel, and the condensed essence mantra of the sixty retinue Deities.

Purifying any mistakes made during mantra recitation with the hundred-letter mantra of Heruka

OM VAJRA HERUKA SAMAYA, MANU PALAYA, HERUKA TENO PATITA, DRIDHO ME BHAWA, SUTO KAYO ME BHAWA, SUPO KAYO ME BHAWA, ANURAKTO ME BHAWA, SARWA SIDDHI ME PRAYATZA, SARWA KARMA SUTZA ME, TZITAM SHRIYAM KURU HUM, HA HA HA HA HO BHAGAWÄN, VAJRA HERUKA MA ME MUNTSA, HERUKA BHAWA, MAHA SAMAYA SATTÖ AH HUM PHAT

Blessing the tormas

OM KHANDAROHI HUM HUM PHAT
OM SÖBHAWA SHUDDHA SARWA DHARMA SÖBHAWA
    SHUDDHO HAM
Everything becomes emptiness.

From the state of emptiness, from YAM comes wind, from RAM comes fire, from AH a grate of three human heads. Upon this from AH appears a broad and expansive skullcup. Inside from OM, KHAM, AM, TRAM, HUM come the five nectars; from LAM, MAM, PAM, TAM, BAM come the five meats, each marked by these letters. The wind blows, the fire blazes, and the substances inside the skullcup melt. Above them from HUM there arises a white, upside-down khatanga, which falls into the skullcup and melts whereby the substances take on the colour of mercury. Above them three rows of vowels and consonants, standing one above the other, transform into OM AH HUM. From these, light rays draw the nectar of exalted wisdom from the hearts of

all the Tathagatas, Heroes, and Yoginis of the ten directions.
When this is added the contents increase and become vast.
OM AH HUM   (3x)

Inviting the guests of the tormas

PHAIM
Light rays radiate from the letter HUM on the sun seat
at my heart and invite to the space before me the entire
assembly of the Deities of Chakrasambara together with
his mundane retinues, such as the directional guardians
who reside in the eight charnel grounds.

OM AHRGHAM PARTITZA SÖHA
OM PADÄM PARTITZA SÖHA
OM VAJRA PUPE AH HUM SÖHA
OM VAJRA DHUPE AH HUM SÖHA
OM VAJRA DIWE AH HUM SÖHA
OM VAJRA GÄNDHE AH HUM SÖHA
OM VAJRA NEWIDE AH HUM SÖHA
OM VAJRA SHAPTA AH HUM SÖHA

From a white HUM in the tongue of each Deity, there
arises a white, three-pronged vajra, through which they
partake of the nectar of the torma by drawing it through
straws of light the thickness of only a grain of barley.

Offering the principal torma

OM VAJRA AH RA LI HO: DZA HUM BAM HO: VAJRA DAKINI
SAMAYA TÖN TRISHAYA HO   (3x)

*With the first recitation offer the torma to the Principal
Father, with the second to the Principal Mother, and with the
third to the four Yoginis, beginning in the east and offering
counter-clockwise.*

Offering the torma to the Deities of the heart wheel, speech wheel, and body wheel

OM KARA KARA, KURU KURU, BÄNDHA BÄNDHA, TrASAYA
TrASAYA, KYOMBHAYA KYOMBHAYA, HROM HROM, HRAH

HRAH, PHAIM PHAIM, PHAT PHAT, DAHA DAHA, PATSA
PATSA, BHAKYA BHAKYA BASA RUDHI ÄNTRA MALA
WALAMBINE, GRIHANA GRIHANA SAPTA PATALA GATA
BHUDZAMGAM SARWAMPA TARDZAYA TARDZAYA,
AKANDYA AKANDYA, HRIM HRIM, GYÖN GYÖN, KYAMA
KYAMA, HAM HAM, HIM HIM, HUM HUM, KILI KILI, SILI
SILI, HILI HILI, DHILI DHILI, HUM HUM PHAT

Offering the torma to the Deities of the commitment wheel

OM VAJRA AH RA LI HO: DZA HUM BAM HO: VAJRA DAKINI
SAMAYA TÖN TRISHAYA HO   (2x)

Outer offerings

OM AHRGHAM PARTITZA SÖHA
OM PADÄM PARTITZA SÖHA
OM VAJRA PUPE AH HUM SÖHA
OM VAJRA DHUPE AH HUM SÖHA
OM VAJRA DIWE AH HUM SÖHA
OM VAJRA GÄNDHE AH HUM SÖHA
OM VAJRA NEWIDE AH HUM SÖHA
OM VAJRA SHAPTA AH HUM SÖHA

OM AH VAJRA ADARSHE HUM
OM AH VAJRA WINI HUM
OM AH VAJRA GÄNDHE HUM
OM AH VAJRA RASE HUM
OM AH VAJRA PARSHE HUM
OM AH VAJRA DHARME HUM

Inner offering

OM HUM BAM RIM RIM LIM LIM, KAM KHAM GAM GHAM
NGAM, TSAM TSHAM DZAM DZHAM NYAM, TrAM THrAM
DrAM DHrAM NAM, TAM THAM DAM DHAM NAM, PAM
PHAM BAM BHAM, YAM RAM LAM WAM, SHAM KAM SAM
HAM HUM HUM PHAT OM AH HUM

Secret and thatness offerings

Through Father and Mother uniting in embrace, all the principal and retinue Deities enjoy a special experience of great bliss and emptiness.

Eight lines of praise to the Father

OM I prostrate to the Blessed One, Lord of the Heroes HUM HUM PHAT

OM To you with a brilliance equal to the fire of the great aeon HUM HUM PHAT

OM To you with an inexhaustible topknot HUM HUM PHAT

OM To you with a fearsome face and bared fangs HUM HUM PHAT

OM To you whose thousand arms blaze with light HUM HUM PHAT

OM To you who hold an axe, an uplifted noose, a spear, and a khatanga HUM HUM PHAT

OM To you who wear a tiger-skin garment HUM HUM PHAT

OM I bow to you whose great smoke-coloured body dispels obstructions HUM HUM PHAT

Eight lines of praise to the Mother

OM I prostrate to Vajravarahi, the Blessed Mother HUM HUM PHAT

OM To the Superior and powerful Knowledge Lady unconquered by the three realms HUM HUM PHAT

OM To you who destroy all fears of evil spirits with your great vajra HUM HUM PHAT

OM To you with controlling eyes who remain as the vajra seat unconquered by others HUM HUM PHAT

OM To you whose wrathful fierce form desiccates Brahma HUM HUM PHAT

OM To you who terrify and dry up demons, conquering those in other directions HUM HUM PHAT

OM To you who conquer all those who make us dull, rigid, and confused HUM HUM PHAT

OM I bow to Vajravarahi, the Great Mother, the Dakini consort who fulfils all desires HUM HUM PHAT

Requesting the fulfilment of wishes

You who have destroyed equally attachment to samsara
    and solitary peace, as well as all conceptualizations,
Who see all things that exist throughout space;
O Protector endowed with strong compassion, may I be
    blessed by the waters of your compassion,
And may the Dakinis take me into their loving care.

Offering the torma to the mundane Deities

The directional guardians, regional guardians, nagas, and
so forth, who reside in the eight great charnel grounds,
instantly enter into the clear light, and arise in the form of
the Deities of Heruka in the aspect of Father and Mother.
From a white HUM in the tongue of each guest, there
arises a white, three-pronged vajra, through which they
partake of the essence of the torma by drawing it through
straws of light the thickness of only a grain of barley.

OM KHA KHA, KHAHI KHAHI, SARWA YAKYA RAKYASA,
BHUTA, TRETA, PISHATSA, UNATA, APAMARA, VAJRA
DAKA, DAKI NÄDAYA, IMAM BALING GRIHANTU, SAMAYA
RAKYANTU, MAMA SARWA SIDDHI METRA YATZANTU,
YATIPAM, YATETAM, BHUDZATA, PIWATA, DZITRATA,
MATI TRAMATA, MAMA SARWA KATAYA, SÄDSUKHAM
BISHUDHAYE, SAHAYEKA BHAWÄNTU, HUM HUM PHAT
PHAT SÖHA   (2x)

*With the first recitation offer the torma to the guests in the
cardinal directions, and with the second to the guests in the
intermediate directions.*

Outer offerings

OM AHRGHAM PARTITZA SÖHA
OM PADÄM PARTITZA SÖHA
OM VAJRA PUPE AH HUM SÖHA
OM VAJRA DHUPE AH HUM SÖHA
OM VAJRA DIWE AH HUM SÖHA

OM VAJRA GĀNDHE AH HUM SŌHA
OM VAJRA NEWIDE AH HUM SŌHA
OM VAJRA SHAPTA AH HUM SŌHA

Inner offering

To the mouths of the directional guardians, regional guardians, nagas, and so forth, OM AH HUM

Requests

You the entire gathering of gods,
The entire gathering of nagas,
The entire gathering of givers of harm,
The entire gathering of cannibals,
The entire gathering of evil spirits,
The entire gathering of hungry ghosts,
The entire gathering of flesh-eaters,
The entire gathering of crazy-makers,
The entire gathering of forgetful-makers,
The entire gathering of dakas,
The entire gathering of female spirits,
All of you without exception
Please come here and listen to me.
O Glorious attendants, swift as thought,
Who have taken oaths and heart commitments
To guard the doctrine and benefit living beings,
Who subdue the malevolent and destroy the dark forces
With terrifying forms and inexhaustible wrath,
Who grant results to yogic actions,
And who have inconceivable powers and blessings,
To you eight types of guest I prostrate.

I request all of you together with your consorts, children,
    and servants
To grant me the fortune of all the attainments.
May I and other practitioners
Have good health, long life, power,
Glory, fame, fortune,
And extensive enjoyments.

Please grant me the attainments
Of pacifying, increasing, controlling, and wrathful actions.
O Guardians, always assist me.
Eradicate all untimely death, sicknesses,
Harm from spirits, and hindrances.
Eliminate bad dreams,
Ill omens, and bad actions.

May there be happiness in the world, may the years be
    good,
May crops increase, and may Dharma flourish.
May all goodness and happiness come about,
And may all wishes be accomplished.

*At this point you can, if you wish, make the tsog offering.
This starts on page 297.*

Purifying any mistakes made during this practice with the hundred-letter mantra of Heruka

OM VAJRA HERUKA SAMAYA, MANU PALAYA, HERUKA
TENO PATITA, DRIDHO ME BHAWA, SUTO KAYO ME BHAWA,
SUPO KAYO ME BHAWA, ANURAKTO ME BHAWA, SARWA
SIDDHI ME PRAYATZA, SARWA KARMA SUTZA ME, TZITAM
SHRIYAM KURU HUM, HA HA HA HA HO BHAGAWÄN,
VAJRA HERUKA MA ME MUNTSA, HERUKA BHAWA, MAHA
SAMAYA SATTÖ AH HUM PHAT

OM YOGA SHUDDHA SARWA DHARMA YOGA SHUDDHO HAM

VAJRA MU

The mundane beings return to their own places, and the
assembly of the Deities of the in-front-generation dissolve
into me.

Dissolution and generating the action Deities

The charnel grounds and protection circle dissolve into the
celestial mansion. The celestial mansion dissolves into the
Deities of the commitment wheel. They dissolve into the

Two-armed Heruka

Deities of the body wheel. They dissolve into the Deities
of the speech wheel. They dissolve into the Deities of the
heart wheel. They dissolve into the four Yoginis of the
great bliss wheel. They dissolve into me, the Principal
Deity Father and Mother, the nature of the white and red
indestructible drop. I, the Principal Deity Father and Mother,
also melt into light and dissolve into the letter HUM at my
heart, in nature the emptiness of the Dharmakaya.

From the state of emptiness, our world arises as Heruka's
Pure Land, Keajra. I and all sentient beings arise as the
Blessed One Heruka, with a blue-coloured body, one face,
and two arms embracing Vajravarahi.

Meditating on the first of the five stages of completion stage, the stage of blessing the self

Inside my central channel, in the centre of the Dharma
Wheel at my heart, is a drop the size of a small pea. Its
upper half is white and its lower half is red, and it radiates
five-coloured rays of light. At its centre is a tiny letter HUM,
white with a shade of red, the nature of Heruka. The minute
three-curved nada of the HUM, as fine as the tip of a hair, is
red at the top and reddish-white at the bottom. The nature
of great bliss, it is extremely bright, radiates red light, and
drips nectar. My mind mixes inseparably with the nada.

Adorning our body with the armour Deities

At my heart on a moon mandala appears white OM HA,
the nature of Vajrasattva; at my head on a sun, yellow
NAMA HI, the nature of Vairochana; at my crown on a sun,
red SÖHA HU, the nature of Pämanarteshvara; at my two
shoulders on a sun, black BOKE HE, the nature of Glorious
Heruka; at my two eyes on a sun, orange HUM HUM HO,
the nature of Vajrasurya; and at my forehead on a sun,
green PHAT HAM, the nature of Paramashawa.

At the Principal Mother's navel on a sun mandala appears
red OM BAM, the nature of Vajravarahi; at her heart on a

sun, blue HAM YOM, the nature of Yamani; at her throat
on a moon, white HRIM MOM, the nature of Mohani; at her
head on a sun, yellow HRIM HRIM, the nature of Sachalani;
at her crown on a sun, green HUM HUM, the nature of
Samtrasani; and at her forehead on a sun, smoke-coloured
PHAT PHAT, the nature of Chandika.

The mantra emanating from the four faces

OM SUMBHANI SUMBHA HUM HUM PHAT
OM GRIHANA GRIHANA HUM HUM PHAT
OM GRIHANA PAYA GRIHANA PAYA HUM HUM PHAT
OM ANAYA HO BHAGAWÄN BYÄ RADZA HUM HUM PHAT

Dedication

You can recite either the extensive or the brief dedication.

Extensive dedication

Through the virtues I have collected and shall collect,
May I rely sincerely upon my holy Spiritual Guide,
The supreme source of all the attainments
And of all the good fortune I experience.

The Spiritual Guide's instructions clearly explain
The freedom and endowment of this precious human
   form, its great meaning, and how difficult it is to find,
How easy it is to die, the dangers of lower rebirth,
And how going for refuge and observing actions and
   effects protect us.

Through contemplating these well, and gaining deep
   experience,
May I firmly maintain the basis of the stages of the path;
And through understanding that samsara is as essenceless
   as a plantain tree,
May I always maintain renunciation.

Out of compassion, unable to bear the sufferings of
   mother living beings,
With a mind seeking only the attainment of supreme
   enlightenment,
May I maintain perfectly the vows of the aspiring and
   engaging minds,
And train sincerely in the six perfections and the four
   ways of gathering.

Having become a pure vessel through the common paths,
   may I receive the four empowerments
That place the potentials to attain the four bodies,
Purify the four types of defilement,
And empower me to meditate on the two stages.

By practising sincerely everything that was taught,
May I maintain perfectly the vows and commitments
Taken at that time, in front of the witnesses –
The Gurus, Buddhas, Bodhisattvas, Heroes, and Dakinis.

Thus may I always maintain purely the nineteen
   commitments of the five Buddha families:
The six commitments of Buddha Vairochana –
To go for refuge to Buddha, Dharma, and Sangha,
Refrain from non-virtue, practise virtue, and benefit others;

The four commitments of Buddha Akshobya –
To keep a vajra and bell, generate myself as the Deity, and
   rely sincerely upon my Spiritual Guide;
The four commitments of Buddha Ratnasambhava –
To give material help, Dharma, fearlessness, and love;

The three commitments of Buddha Amitabha –
To rely upon the teachings of Sutra and of the two lower
   and two higher classes of Tantra;
And the two commitments of Buddha Amoghasiddhi –
To make offerings to my Spiritual Guide, and strive to
   maintain purely all the vows I have taken.

Realizing that the practice of generation stage
Causes me to receive the special care of my Yidam
    throughout all my lives,
Receive the blessings of the holy Deities,
Ripen my mental continuum to generate all the
    completion stages,

And purify the defilements of ordinary appearance and
    conception;
Through practising it sincerely in four sessions
May I gain the generation stage realization
Of perceiving all objects that appear as manifestations of
    the Deity.

Through practising the yoga of three purifications
May I receive the blessings of Heruka's body, speech, and
    mind,
Purify my body, speech, and mind, together with all
    obstacles,
And complete a great collection of merit.

Gathering all elaborations into clear light,
Arising from that in the form of a nada,
Entering the centre of the reddish-white moon,
Within which the vowels and consonants appear like a
    reflection,

And from that completing the entire mandala of Heruka;
Understanding the meaning of this, and meditating on the
    three bringings,
May I attain the Truth Body, Enjoyment Body, and
    Emanation Body
At the time of death, bardo, and rebirth.

May I gain the realization of the vajra body –
The channel wheels and so forth that are the objects to be
    penetrated –
Symbolized by the four elements, Mount Meru, and the lotus,
Which are the supreme place within which Heruka is
    complete.

Meditating with perfect knowledge in four sessions
On the blazing red drop from the navel
Meeting the dripping white drop from the crown
Within the central channel at my heart,

Which is the method for generating definitive Heruka,
Symbolized by the gathering of white and red
Within the moon at the centre of the lotus;
May I gain these realizations of completion stage.

Through meditating in four sessions
On the outer mandala and body mandala of Heruka,
Which arise from bringing rebirth into the path of the
    Emanation Body,
May I complete clear appearance of the outer and inner
    mandalas of gross and subtle generation stage.

Through meditating on the Goddesses of the doorways
    at the doors of the senses,
May I reverse the winds through the doors of the senses;
Through meditating on the Heroes and Heroines at the
    twenty-four places,
May I gather the winds into the twenty-four channels;

Through meditating on the Deities of the great bliss wheel
    on the petals of the Dharma Wheel,
May I gather the winds into the eight channels
Of the cardinal and intermediate directions at my heart,
And then may I gather them into my central channel at
    the heart.

Through meditating on the inner venerable Father
    and Mother,
May my red and white drops enter into embrace,
And then may I ripen fully my virtuous roots
For generating the supreme completion stages.

May I gain the realizations of the five stages of the
    profound path
Of the secret meaning of the King of Mother Tantras

As clearly explained by Mahasiddha Ghantapa;
And thus may I accomplish the state of Glorious Heruka
in this life.

Through the stage of blessing the self,
With my mind absorbed in vajra recitation on the winds
inseparable from mantra
And on the letter HUM at the centre of my heart chakra,
May I completely release the channel knots at my heart.

Through the stage of the vajra of various qualities,
Observing the tiny HUM and the moon, sun, and drop
At the centre of the vajra at the lower and upper tips of
my central channel,
May I attain stable spontaneous bliss, and may my
bodhichittas increase.

Through the pure fire induced by the whirling touch of
the four beautiful goddesses –
The commitment mudra, action mudra, phenomenon
mudra, and Mahamudra –
Melting the drops of my seventy-two thousand channels,
May I complete the stage of filling with jewels.

Through holding the drop of the five families enclosed
within the vase breath,
Inside the phenomena source at dzöladhara at my secret
place,
And through the strong movement of the blazing and
dripping of AH and HAM,
May I receive the stream of blessings of all the
compassionate Conquerors.

By relying upon the outer and inner methods
Such as the three enjoyments and the two concentrations,
May I attain the inseparable union of illusory body and
clear light,
And thus complete the stage of inconceivability.

In short, may I never be separated from Venerable Guru
  Father and Mother,
But always come under their loving care and receive their
  blessings.
In this way, may I swiftly complete all the grounds and
  paths
And quickly attain the state of Heruka.

Brief dedication

Thus, through my virtues from correctly performing
  the offerings, praises, and recitations
Of the generation stage of Glorious Heruka,
May I complete all the stages
Of the common and uncommon paths.

For the sake of all living beings,
May I become Heruka;
And then lead every living being
To Heruka's supreme state.

And if I do not attain this supreme state in this life,
At my deathtime may I be met by the venerable Father
  and Mother and their retinue,
With clouds of breathtaking offerings, heavenly music,
And many excellent, auspicious signs.

Then, at the end of the clear light of death,
May I be led to Pure Dakini Land,
The abode of the Knowledge Holders who practise the
  supreme path;
And there may I swiftly complete this profound path.

May the most profound practice and instruction of Heruka,
Practised by millions of powerful Yogis, greatly increase;
And may it remain for a very long time without
  degenerating,
As the main gateway for those seeking liberation.

May the Heroes, Dakinis, and their retinues
Abiding in the twenty-four supreme places of this world,
Who possess unobstructed power for accomplishing this
   method,
Never waver from always assisting practitioners.

Auspicious prayers

May there be the auspiciousness of a great treasury
   of blessings
Arising from the excellent deeds of all the root and
   lineage Gurus,
Who have accomplished the supreme attainment of
   Buddha Heruka
By relying upon the excellent, secret path of the King
   of Tantras.

May there be the auspiciousness of the great excellent
   deeds of the Three Jewels –
The holy Buddha Jewel, the pervading nature Heruka;
The ultimate, great, secret Dharma Jewel, the scriptures
   and realizations of Heruka Tantra;
And the supreme Sangha Jewel, the assemblies of
   Heruka's retinue Deities.

Through all the great good fortune there is
In the precious, celestial mansions as extensive as the
   three thousand worlds,
Adorned with ornaments like the rays of the sun and
   the moon,
May all worlds and their beings have happiness,
   goodness, glory, and prosperity.

THE TSOG OFFERING FOR
HERUKA BODY MANDALA

Blessing the outer and inner offerings, the environment and beings, and the substances of the tsog offering

OM AH HUM   (3x)

By nature exalted wisdom, having the aspect of the inner offering and the individual offering substances, and functioning as objects of enjoyment of the six senses to generate a special, exalted wisdom of bliss and emptiness, inconceivable clouds of outer, inner, and secret offerings, commitment substances, and attractive offerings, cover all the ground and fill the whole of space.

EH MA HO Great manifestation of exalted wisdom.
All realms are vajra realms
And all places are great vajra palaces
Endowed with vast clouds of Samantabhadra's offerings,
An abundance of all desired enjoyments.
All beings are actual Heroes and Heroines.
Everything is immaculately pure,
Without even the name of mistaken impure appearance.

HUM All elaborations are completely pacified in the state of the Truth Body. The wind blows and the fire blazes. Above, on a grate of three human heads, AH within a qualified skullcup, OM the individual substances blaze. Above these stand OM AH HUM, each ablaze with its brilliant colour. Through the wind blowing and the fire blazing, the substances melt. Boiling, they swirl in a great vapour. Masses of light rays from the three letters radiate to the ten directions and invite the three vajras together with nectars. These dissolve separately into the three letters. Melting into nectar, they blend with the mixture. Purified, transformed, and increased,
EH MA HO They become a blazing ocean of magnificent delights.

OM AH HUM   (3x)

Inviting the guests of the tsog offering

PHAIM
From the sacred palace of the Dharmakaya,
Great Master, holder of the supreme lineage of the
 Vajrayana,
Who fulfil our hopes for all the attainments,
O Assembly of root and lineage Gurus, please come
 to this place.

From the twenty-four holy places throughout the world,
O Glorious Heruka, whose nature is the compassion of all
 the Buddhas,
And all the Heroes and Heroines of these places,
Please come here to bestow the attainments that we
 long for.

From the pure and impure lands of the ten directions,
O Assembly of Yidams, Buddhas, Bodhisattvas, and
 Dharma Protectors,
And all the beings of samsara and nirvana,
Please come here as guests of this tsog offering.

OM GURU VAJRADHARA CHAKRASAMBARA SÄMANDALA
DEWA SARWA BUDDHA BODHISATTÖ SAPARIWARA EH
HAYE HI VAJRA SAMAYA DZA DZA

PÄMA KAMALAYE TÖN

Making the tsog offering

HO This ocean of tsog offering of uncontaminated nectar,
Blessed by concentration, mantra, and mudra,
I offer to please my kind root Guru Vajradhara Heruka
 Father and Mother.
OM AH HUM
Delighted by enjoying these magnificent objects of desire,
EH MA HO
Please bless me so that I may attain outer and inner
 Dakini Land.

HO This ocean of tsog offering of uncontaminated nectar,
Blessed by concentration, mantra, and mudra,
I offer to please the four Yoginis of the great bliss wheel.
OM AH HUM
Delighted by enjoying these magnificent objects of desire,
EH MA HO
Please bless me so that I may attain spontaneous great
    bliss.

HO This ocean of tsog offering of uncontaminated nectar,
Blessed by concentration, mantra, and mudra,
I offer to please the Heroes and Heroines of the vajra
    mind.
OM AH HUM
Delighted by enjoying these magnificent objects of desire,
EH MA HO
Please bless me so that I may experience delight with the
    messengers of the vajra mind family.

HO This ocean of tsog offering of uncontaminated nectar,
Blessed by concentration, mantra, and mudra,
I offer to please the Heroes and Heroines of the vajra
    speech.
OM AH HUM
Delighted by enjoying these magnificent objects of desire,
EH MA HO
Please bless me so that I may experience delight with the
    messengers of the vajra speech family.

HO This ocean of tsog offering of uncontaminated nectar,
Blessed by concentration, mantra, and mudra,
I offer to please the Heroes and Heroines of the vajra
    body.
OM AH HUM
Delighted by enjoying these magnificent objects of desire,
EH MA HO
Please bless me so that I may experience delight with the
    messengers of the vajra body family.

Dorje Shugdän

HO This ocean of tsog offering of uncontaminated nectar,
Blessed by concentration, mantra, and mudra,
I offer to please the Deities of the commitment wheel.
OM AH HUM
Delighted by enjoying these magnificent objects of desire,
EH MA HO
Please bless me so that I may pacify all obstacles.

HO This ocean of tsog offering of uncontaminated nectar,
Blessed by concentration, mantra, and mudra,
I offer to please all other Yidams, Buddhas, Bodhisattvas,
    and Dharma Protectors.
OM AH HUM
Delighted by enjoying these magnificent objects of desire,
EH MA HO
Please bless me so that I may attain all the realizations of
    Sutra and Tantra.

HO This ocean of tsog offering of uncontaminated nectar,
Blessed by concentration, mantra, and mudra,
I offer to please the assembly of mother sentient beings.
OM AH HUM
Delighted by enjoying these magnificent objects of desire,
EH MA HO
May suffering and mistaken appearance be pacified.

Outer offerings

OM AHRGHAM PARTITZA SÖHA
OM PADÄM PARTITZA SÖHA
OM VAJRA PUPE AH HUM SÖHA
OM VAJRA DHUPE AH HUM SÖHA
OM VAJRA DIWE AH HUM SÖHA
OM VAJRA GÄNDHE AH HUM SÖHA
OM VAJRA NEWIDE AH HUM SÖHA
OM VAJRA SHAPTA AH HUM SÖHA

Inner offering

OM HUM BAM RIM RIM LIM LIM, KAM KHAM GAM GHAM
NGAM, TSAM TSHAM DZAM DZHAM NYAM, TrAM THrAM
DrAM DHrAM NAM, TAM THAM DAM DHAM NAM, PAM
PHAM BAM BHAM, YAM RAM LAM WAM, SHAM KAM SAM
HAM HUM HUM PHAT OM AH HUM

Secret and thatness offerings

Through Father and Mother uniting in embrace, all the
principal and retinue Deities enjoy a special experience
of great bliss and emptiness.

Eight lines of praise to the Father

OM I prostrate to the Blessed One, Lord of the Heroes
   HUM HUM PHAT
OM To you with a brilliance equal to the fire of the great
   aeon HUM HUM PHAT
OM To you with an inexhaustible topknot HUM HUM PHAT
OM To you with a fearsome face and bared fangs HUM
   HUM PHAT
OM To you whose thousand arms blaze with light HUM
   HUM PHAT
OM To you who hold an axe, an uplifted noose, a spear,
   and a khatanga HUM HUM PHAT
OM To you who wear a tiger-skin garment HUM HUM PHAT
OM I bow to you whose great smoke-coloured body
   dispels obstructions HUM HUM PHAT

Eight lines of praise to the Mother

OM I prostrate to Vajravarahi, the Blessed Mother HUM
   HUM PHAT
OM To the Superior and powerful Knowledge Lady
   unconquered by the three realms HUM HUM PHAT
OM To you who destroy all fears of evil spirits with your
   great vajra HUM HUM PHAT

OM To you with controlling eyes who remain as the vajra
seat unconquered by others HUM HUM PHAT

OM To you whose wrathful fierce form desiccates Brahma
HUM HUM PHAT

OM To you who terrify and dry up demons, conquering
those in other directions HUM HUM PHAT

OM To you who conquer all those who make us dull,
rigid, and confused HUM HUM PHAT

OM I bow to Vajravarahi, the Great Mother, the Dakini
consort who fulfils all desires HUM HUM PHAT

Making the tsog offering to the Vajra Master

EH MA HO Great circle of tsog!
O Great Hero we understand
That, following in the path of the Sugatas of the three
times,
You are the source of all attainments.
Forsaking all minds of conceptualization,
Please continuously enjoy this circle of tsog.
AH LA LA HO

The Master's reply

OM With a nature inseparable from the three vajras
I generate as the Guru-Deity.
AH This nectar of uncontaminated exalted wisdom and
bliss,
HUM Without stirring from bodhichitta
I partake to delight the Deities dwelling in my body.
AH HO MAHA SUKHA

Song of the Spring Queen

HUM All you Tathagatas,
Heroes, Yoginis,
Dakas, and Dakinis,
To all of you I make this request:
O Heruka who delight in great bliss,
You engage in the Union of spontaneous bliss,

By attending the Lady intoxicated with bliss
And enjoying in accordance with the rituals.
AH LA LA, LA LA HO, AH I AH, AH RA LI HO
May the assembly of stainless Dakinis
Look with loving affection and accomplish all deeds.

HUM All you Tathagatas,
Heroes, Yoginis,
Dakas, and Dakinis,
To all of you I make this request:
With a mind completely aroused by great bliss
And a body in a dance of constant motion,
I offer to the hosts of Dakinis
The great bliss from enjoying the lotus of the mudra.
AH LA LA, LA LA HO, AH I AH, AH RA LI HO
May the assembly of stainless Dakinis
Look with loving affection and accomplish all deeds.

HUM All you Tathagatas,
Heroes, Yoginis,
Dakas, and Dakinis,
To all of you I make this request:
You who dance with a beautiful and peaceful manner,
O Blissful Protector and the hosts of Dakinis,
Please come here before me and grant me your blessings,
And bestow upon me spontaneous great bliss.
AH LA LA, LA LA HO, AH I AH, AH RA LI HO
May the assembly of stainless Dakinis
Look with loving affection and accomplish all deeds.

HUM All you Tathagatas,
Heroes, Yoginis,
Dakas, and Dakinis,
To all of you I make this request:
You who have the characteristic of the liberation of great
    bliss,
Do not say that deliverance can be gained in one lifetime
Through various ascetic practices having abandoned great
    bliss,

But that great bliss resides in the centre of the supreme
   lotus.
AH LA LA, LA LA HO, AH I AH, AH RA LI HO
May the assembly of stainless Dakinis
Look with loving affection and accomplish all deeds.

HUM All you Tathagatas,
Heroes, Yoginis,
Dakas, and Dakinis,
To all of you I make this request:
Like a lotus born from the centre of a swamp,
This method, though born from attachment, is unstained
   by the faults of attachment.
O Supreme Dakini, through the bliss of your lotus,
Please quickly bring liberation from the bonds of samsara.
AH LA LA, LA LA HO, AH I AH, AH RA LI HO
May the assembly of stainless Dakinis
Look with loving affection and accomplish all deeds.

HUM All you Tathagatas,
Heroes, Yoginis,
Dakas, and Dakinis,
To all of you I make this request:
Just as the essence of honey in the honey source
Is drunk by swarms of bees from all directions,
So through your broad lotus with six characteristics
Please bring satisfaction with the taste of great bliss.
AH LA LA, LA LA HO, AH I AH, AH RA LI HO
May the assembly of stainless Dakinis
Look with loving affection and accomplish all deeds.

Blessing the remaining tsog offering

HUM Impure mistaken appearances are purified in
   emptiness,
AH Great nectar accomplished from exalted wisdom,
OM It becomes a vast ocean of desired enjoyment.
OM AH HUM   (3x)

Giving the remaining tsog offering to the spirits

HO This ocean of remaining tsog offering of
   uncontaminated nectar,
Blessed by concentration, mantra, and mudra,
I offer to please the assembly of oath-bound guardians.
OM AH HUM
Delighted by enjoying these magnificent objects of desire,
EH MA HO
Please perform perfect actions to help practitioners.

Send out the remainder of the tsog offering to the spirits.

HO
O Guests of the remainder together with your retinues
Please enjoy this ocean of remaining tsog offering.
May those who spread the precious doctrine,
The holders of the doctrine, their benefactors, and others,
And especially I and other practitioners
Have good health, long life, power,
Glory, fame, fortune,
And extensive enjoyments.
Please grant me the attainments
Of pacifying, increasing, controlling, and wrathful actions.
You who are bound by oaths please protect me
And help me to accomplish all the attainments.
Eradicate all untimely death, sicknesses,
Harm from spirits, and hindrances.
Eliminate bad dreams,
Ill omens, and bad actions.

May there be happiness in the world, may the years be
   good,
May crops increase, and may Dharma flourish.
May all goodness and happiness come about,
And may all wishes be accomplished.

By the force of this bountiful giving,
May I become a Buddha for the sake of living beings;
And through my generosity may I liberate
All those not liberated by previous Buddhas.

Colophon: This sadhana was compiled from traditional sources by Venerable Geshe Kelsang Gyatso. The verse to Geshe Kelsang Gyatso in *Requesting the lineage Gurus* was composed at the request of Geshe Kelsang's faithful disciples by the glorious Dharma Protector, Düldzin Dorje Shugdän. We requested permission from Geshe Kelsang to include this verse in the sadhana to express our heartfelt gratitude for his kindness; and for the use, in group or individual practice, of practitioners who have received initiation from him.

Condensed Essence of Vajrayana

CONDENSED HERUKA BODY MANDALA
SELF-GENERATION SADHANA

Condensed Essence of Vajrayana

Those unable to practise the long sadhana, Essence of Vajra-yana, *can start by practising this condensed sadhana. Through gaining familiarity with this, they should then gradually change to the practice of the long sadhana.*

THE PRELIMINARY PRACTICES

Visualizing the objects of refuge

In the space before me appear Guru Heruka Father and Mother, surrounded by the assembly of direct and lineage Gurus, Yidams, Buddhas, Bodhisattvas, Heroes, Dakinis, and Dharma Protectors.

Going for refuge and generating aspiring bodhichitta

Eternally I shall go for refuge
To Buddha, Dharma, and Sangha.
For the sake of all living beings
I shall become Heruka.　　(3x)

Generating engaging bodhichitta

To lead all mother living beings to the state of ultimate
　　happiness,
I shall attain as quickly as possible, in this very life,
The state of the Union of Buddha Heruka.
For this purpose I shall practise the stages of Heruka's
　　path.　　(3x)

Receiving blessings

Guru Heruka Father and Mother together with all the other objects of refuge dissolve into me, and I receive their blessings.

THE ACTUAL PRACTICE OF GENERATION STAGE

Bringing death into the path of the Truth Body

Light rays from the HUM at my heart melt all worlds and beings into light. This dissolves into me, and I in turn gradually melt into light from below and above and dissolve into the HUM at my heart. The letter HUM dissolves in stages from the bottom up into the nada. The nada becomes smaller and smaller and dissolves into clear light emptiness. I am Truth Body Heruka.

Bringing the intermediate state into the path of the Enjoyment Body

From the state of emptiness my mind appears in the form of a nada. I am Enjoyment Body Heruka.

Bringing rebirth into the path of the Emanation Body

From YAM, RAM, BAM, LAM, SUM, PAM arise the four elements, Mount Meru, and the lotus. In the centre of the lotus, from the vowels and consonants, arises a reddish-white moon, the nature of the red and white bodhichittas of Guru Heruka Father and Mother. I, the nada, enter the centre of the moon and gradually transform into the aspect of a HUM.

Five-coloured lights radiate from the HUM and lead all living beings to the state of Chakrasambara. At the same time all the Heroes and Heroines are invited from the Buddha Lands of the ten directions. They all melt into light and dissolve into the HUM, which becomes the nature of spontaneous joy. The moon, vowels, consonants, and HUM completely transform, and the supported Deities and supporting mandala arise fully and all at once. I am Emanation Body Heruka.

Checking meditation on the mandala and basis Heruka

Furthermore, there is the celestial mansion, which is square with four doorways. The jewelled walls have five layers coloured white, yellow, red, green, and blue from the outside in. Around the top of the wall is a red jewelled moulding studded with square, triangular, and other-shaped jewels. Upon this are four layers of golden bands. Upon these, and extending beyond, are rafters whose ends form the shape of sea-monsters, with full and half-length strings of pearls hanging from their mouths. Overhanging these are sharpu, special jewelled decorations, suspended from the eaves. Above these is a parapet in the shape of half lotus petals. It is adorned with eight victory banners and eight other banners, all set in golden vases, and parasols on top of the four outer corners.

Around the outer foot of the wall runs a red ledge for the objects of desire. Upon this stand goddesses of various colours and postures making offerings. At the outer corners of the doorways and hallways, as well as at the four outer and four inner corners of the mansion, stand half moons, upon which rest red jewels adorned at the top by vajras.

At the front of each entrance, upon square pedestals, four pillars set in vases support a square, eleven-tiered archway. Above each archway is a Dharma Wheel flanked right and left by a male and a female deer. To the right and left of each archway, set in golden vases, are wish-granting trees bearing the seven precious possessions of a king. In the space around are Siddhas, and emerging from clouds are offering gods and goddesses holding garlands of flowers, making everything exquisitely beautiful.

313

Beyond this is the protection circle of a fence of vajras of
various sizes, and so forth. Surrounding the protection circle
are five-coloured vajra fires blazing like the fire of the aeon.
They swirl counter-clockwise, covering all directions – above,
below, and all around. Beyond these are the eight great
charnel grounds. In each charnel ground there is a tree,
at the foot of which there sits a directional guardian. At
the top of the tree there is a regional guardian with the
upper half of his body emerging from the branches. There
is a lake, in which there lives a naga, and above each lake
there is a cloud. There is a mountain, on top of which
there is a white stupa, and there is a wisdom fire.

Throughout the charnel grounds wild birds and animals
such as ravens, owls, vultures, wolves, jackals, and snakes
wander around; and spirits such as givers of harm, zombies,
and cannibals utter the sound 'Kili Kili'. There are also
Yogis and Yoginis such as those who have accomplished
attainments, and Knowledge Holders keeping their
commitments purely. They are all single-pointedly
practising Heruka's path. They are naked, with freely
hanging hair, and are adorned with five mudras. They
hold hand-drums, skullcups, and khatangas, and their
crowns are adorned with skulls. All the beings abiding
in the charnel grounds instil the place with a sense of
wonder.

Inside the celestial mansion eight pillars support vajra
beams adorning the ceiling. The roof is surmounted at its
crest by a precious jewel and a vajra. The ceiling and floor
are white in the east, green in the north, red in the west,
yellow in the south, and blue in the centre. In the very
centre is a lotus of various colours and a sun mandala.

On the sun mandala at the centre of the lotus I arise as
the Blessed One Heruka, with a dark-blue body and four
faces. My principal face is dark blue, the left face green,
the back face red, and the right face yellow. Each face has
three eyes and a rosary of five-pronged vajras on its

forehead. My right leg is outstretched and treads on the
head of black Bhairawa, who has four hands. His first
two hands are pressed together, the second right hand
holds a damaru, and the second left a sword. My bent left
leg treads on the breast of red Kalarati, who has four
hands. Her first two hands are pressed together, and the
other two hold a skullcup and a khatanga. Both the beings
beneath my feet have one face and three eyes, and are
adorned with five mudras.

I have twelve arms. The first two embrace Vajravarahi,
with my right hand holding a five-pronged vajra and my
left hand a bell. The next two hands hold a bloody, white
elephant skin stretched across my back; my right hand
holds the left foreleg, and my left the left hind leg. Both
these hands are in the threatening mudra with the tips of
the outstretched fingers at the level of my eyebrows. My
third right hand holds a damaru, the fourth an axe, the
fifth a curved knife, and the sixth an upright three-pointed
spear. My third left hand holds a khatanga marked with a
vajra, the fourth a skullcup brimming with blood, the fifth
a vajra noose, and the sixth a four-faced head of Brahma.

My hair is tied up in a topknot marked with a crossed
vajra. Each head is adorned with a crown of five skulls
strung together top and bottom with a rosary of black
vajras. On the left side of my crown is a half moon,
slightly tilted. My facial expressions change, and my four
sets of four fangs are bared and terrifying. I display nine
moods: three physical moods of majesty, heroism, and
menace; three verbal moods of laughter, wrath, and ferocity;
and three mental moods of compassion, attentiveness, and
serenity. I wear a lower garment of a tiger skin, and a long
necklace of fifty human heads strung together with human
entrails. Adorned with six mudras, my entire body is
smeared with ashes of human bone.

Embracing the Blessed One is the Blessed Mother
Vajravarahi, who has a red-coloured body, one face, two

hands, and three eyes. She is naked with freely hanging hair and wears a lower garment made from fragments of skull. Her left hand, embracing the Father's neck, holds a skullcup brimming with the blood of the four maras. Her right hand in the threatening mudra brandishes a curved knife, opposing the malignant forces of the ten directions. Her body shines with a brilliance like that of the fire of the aeon. Her two legs are clasped around the Father's thighs. She is the nature of blissful great compassion. Adorned with five mudras, she wears a crown of five human skulls and a necklace of fifty human skulls. Father and Mother abide in the centre of a fiercely blazing fire of exalted wisdom.

Simultaneous generation of the entire supporting and supported Heruka body mandala

The gross parts of my body – the purified body of basis Heruka, and the subtle parts of my purified body – my channels and drops, appear in the form of seed-letters. These transform fully and all at once into the entire supporting and supported body mandala. Thus, I am Heruka Father and Mother, the nature of my white and red indestructible drop. I am surrounded by the Heroes and Heroines of the five wheels, the nature of my channels and drops. I reside at the centre of the celestial mansion, the nature of the gross parts of my body.

Checking meditation on the gross parts of our body generated as Heruka's mandala

Remember in detail as follows:

My two legs forming the shape of a bow are the bow-shaped wind mandala. The triangle at my secret place is the three-cornered fire mandala. My round belly is the circular water mandala. My square-shaped chest is the square earth mandala. My spine is Mount Meru. The thirty-two channels at my crown are the lotus. The trunk of my body, the upper and lower parts of which are equal in size, is the square celestial mansion with four equal sides, the mandala of Heruka, exquisitely beautiful with adornments such as the jewelled moulding and strings of pearls. The eight parts of my limbs are the eight pillars. Beyond these is the protection circle surrounded by the eight charnel grounds.

Checking meditation on the subtle parts of our body, the channels and drops, generated as the Deities

Remember in detail as follows:

The white bodhichitta at the centre of the Dharma Wheel inside the central channel at my heart is like a drop of dew. This drop, the size of a mustard seed, in aspect the letter HUM, transformed into the Blessed One Glorious Heruka, with four faces and twelve arms. At my navel the red tummo fire in the form of the red drop, in aspect the letter BAM, transformed into the Blessed Mother Vajravarahi. As the nature of the red and white drops they met at the very centre of the celestial mansion and entered into embrace.

At my heart the four channel petals in the cardinal directions, which are the paths for the winds of the four elements, in aspect the letters LAM, MAM, PAM, TAM beginning clockwise in the east (in front of me), transformed, beginning counter-clockwise in the east (in front of me) into dark-blue Dakini, in the north (to my left) into green Lama, in the west (behind me) into red Khandarohi, and in the south (to my right) into yellow Rupini. They each have one face with three eyes and bared fangs, and are naked with freely hanging hair. They each have two hands, the right holding a curved knife and the left a skullcup, with a khatanga held in the crook of their left elbow. They stand with their right leg outstretched and are adorned with five mudras. They wear a crown of five human skulls and a long necklace of fifty human skulls. These are Deities of the great bliss wheel. The four channel petals of the offerings in the intermediate directions transformed into four skullcups brimming with five nectars.

Surrounding these, in three concentric circles, my twenty-four places such as the hairline and crown, in aspect the twenty-four letters PU DZA and so forth, transformed into the twenty-four places of Heruka in the form of the twenty-four petal-shaped spokes of the wheels. The channels of the twenty-four places, each in the aspect of a letter BAM, transformed into the twenty-four Heroines. The drops inside these channels, each in the aspect of a letter HUM, transformed into the twenty-four Heroes.

Thus, in the heart wheel, at the eastern spoke, Puliramalaya, the nature of my hairline, are Khandakapala and Partzandi.
At the northern spoke, Dzalandhara, the nature of my crown, are Mahakankala and Tzändriakiya.
At the western spoke, Odiyana, the nature of my right ear, are Kankala and Parbhawatiya.
At the southern spoke, Arbuta, the nature of the back of my neck, are Vikatadamshtri and Mahanasa.
At the south-eastern spoke, Godawari, the nature of my left ear, are Suraberi and Biramatiya.
At the south-western spoke, Rameshöri, the nature of the point between my eyebrows, are Amitabha and Karwariya.
At the north-western spoke, Dewikoti, the nature of my two eyes, are Vajraprabha and Lamkeshöriya.
At the north-eastern spoke, Malawa, the nature of my two shoulders, are Vajradeha and Drumatzaya.

All the Deities of the heart wheel have blue-coloured bodies and are known as the Heroes and Heroines of the vajra mind family.

In the speech wheel, at the eastern spoke, Kamarupa, the nature of my two armpits, are Ankuraka and Airawatiya.
At the northern spoke, Ote, the nature of my two breasts, are Vajrajatila and Mahabhairawi.
At the western spoke, Trishakune, the nature of my navel, are Mahavira and Bayubega.
At the southern spoke, Kosala, the nature of the tip of my nose, are Vajrahumkara and Surabhakiya.

At the south-eastern spoke, Kalinga, the nature of my
   mouth, are Subhadra and Shamadewi.
At the south-western spoke, Lampaka, the nature of my
   throat, are Vajrabhadra and Suwatre.
At the north-western spoke, Kancha, the nature of my
   heart, are Mahabhairawa and Hayakarna.
At the north-eastern spoke, Himalaya, the nature of my
   two testicles, are Virupaksha and Khaganana.

All the Deities of the speech wheel have red-coloured
bodies and are known as the Heroes and Heroines of the
vajra speech family.

In the body wheel, at the eastern spoke, Pretapuri, the
   nature of the tip of my sex organ, are Mahabala and
   Tzatrabega.
At the northern spoke, Grihadewata, the nature of my
   anus, are Ratnavajra and Khandarohi.
At the western spoke, Shauraktra, the nature of my two
   thighs, are Hayagriva and Shaundini.
At the southern spoke, Suwanadvipa, the nature of my
   two calves, are Akashagarbha and Tzatrawarmini.
At the south-eastern spoke, Nagara, the nature of my
   eight fingers and eight toes, are Shri Heruka and Subira.
At the south-western spoke, Sindhura, the nature of the
   tops of my feet, are Pämanarteshvara and Mahabala.
At the north-western spoke, Maru, the nature of my two
   thumbs and two big toes, are Vairochana and
   Tzatrawartini.
At the north-eastern spoke, Kuluta, the nature of my two
   knees, are Vajrasattva and Mahabire.

All the Deities of the body wheel have white-coloured
bodies and are known as the Heroes and Heroines of the
vajra body family.

All these Heroes and Heroines have one face, two hands,
and three eyes; and their heads are adorned with a crown
of five human skulls. The Heroes hold a vajra and bell, and

embrace their consort. Their hair is tied up in a topknot, adorned with a vajra and a crescent moon. They have a rosary of vajras on their forehead and are adorned with six mudras. Wearing a long necklace of fifty human heads and a lower garment of a tiger skin, they stand with their right leg outstretched. The Heroines hold a curved knife and a skullcup, and are entwined in embrace with the Heroes. Wearing a lower garment made from fragments of skull and a necklace of fifty human skulls, they are adorned with five mudras.

Around the Deities of the body wheel, the channels of my eight doors of the senses, such as the channel of the root of my tongue, each in the aspect of a letter HUM, transformed into the eight Heroines. In the east is dark-blue Kakase; in the north green Ulukase; in the west red Shönase; in the south yellow Shukarase; in the south-east Yamadhati, who is blue on the right and yellow on the left; in the south-west Yamaduti, who is yellow on the right and red on the left; in the north-west Yamadangtrini, who is red on the right and green on the left; and in the north-east Yamamatani, who is green on the right and blue on the left. These Heroines have one face and two hands holding a curved knife and a skullcup, and grip a khatanga with the crook of their left elbow. They are adorned with five mudras and stand on a corpse seat with their right leg outstretched. They wear a crown of five human skulls and a long necklace of fifty human skulls.

Thus, I am Heruka Father and Mother, the nature of my white and red indestructible drop, surrounded by the Heroes and Heroines of the five wheels, who are the nature of my channels and drops.

Adorning our body, the bodies of Heruka Father and Mother of the body mandala, with the armour Deities

At my heart on a moon mandala appears white OM HA, the nature of Vajrasattva; at my head on a sun, yellow

NAMA HI, the nature of Vairochana; at my crown on a sun, red SÖHA HU, the nature of Pämanarteshvara; at my two shoulders on a sun, black BOKE HE, the nature of Glorious Heruka; at my two eyes on a sun, orange HUM HUM HO, the nature of Vajrasurya; and at my forehead on a sun, green PHAT HAM, the nature of Paramashawa.

At the Principal Mother's navel on a sun mandala appears red OM BAM, the nature of Vajravarahi; at her heart on a sun, blue HAM YOM, the nature of Yamani; at her throat on a moon, white HRIM MOM, the nature of Mohani; at her head on a sun, yellow HRIM HRIM, the nature of Sachalani; at her crown on a sun, green HUM HUM, the nature of Samtrasani; and at her forehead on a sun, smoke-coloured PHAT PHAT, the nature of Chandika.

Inviting the wisdom beings, dissolving them into the commitment beings, and receiving the empowerment

PHAIM
My three places are marked by the three letters. Light rays radiate from the letter HUM and invite all the Buddhas of the ten directions in the same aspect as those visualized, together with the empowering Deities. All the wisdom beings gather into one complete supporting and supported mandala.

DZA HUM BAM HO
The wisdom beings become inseparable from the commitment beings.

The empowering Deities grant the empowerment, my body is filled with nectar, and I experience bliss. The excess nectar on the crowns completely transforms, and the Principal is adorned by Vajrasattva, Vajravarahi by Akshobya, the four Mothers by Ratnasambhava, the Deities of the heart wheel by Akshobya, the Deities of the speech wheel by Amitabha, the Deities of the body wheel by Vairochana, and the Deities of the commitment wheel by Amoghasiddhi.

Making offerings and praises to the self-generated Deities of the body mandala

Countless breathtakingly beautiful offering and praising goddesses emanate from my heart and make offerings and praises to me as Heruka Father and Mother.

Outer offerings

OM AHRGHAM PARTITZA SÖHA
OM PADÄM PARTITZA SÖHA
OM ÄNTZAMANAM PARTITZA SÖHA
OM VAJRA PUPE AH HUM SÖHA
OM VAJRA DHUPE AH HUM SÖHA
OM VAJRA DIWE AH HUM SÖHA
OM VAJRA GÄNDHE AH HUM SÖHA
OM VAJRA NEWIDE AH HUM SÖHA
OM VAJRA SHAPTA AH HUM SÖHA

OM AH VAJRA ADARSHE HUM
OM AH VAJRA WINI HUM
OM AH VAJRA GÄNDHE HUM
OM AH VAJRA RASE HUM
OM AH VAJRA PARSHE HUM
OM AH VAJRA DHARME HUM

Inner offering

OM HUM BAM RIM RIM LIM LIM, KAM KHAM GAM GHAM NGAM, TSAM TSHAM DZAM DZHAM NYAM, TrAM THrAM DrAM DHrAM NAM, TAM THAM DAM DHAM NAM, PAM PHAM BAM BHAM, YAM RAM LAM WAM, SHAM KAM SAM HAM HUM HUM PHAT OM AH HUM

Secret and thatness offerings

I, the Principal Father and Mother, enter into the union of embrace. The bodhichitta melts, and as it descends from my crown to my throat I experience joy, as it descends from my throat to my heart I experience supreme joy, as it descends from my heart to my navel I experience extraordinary joy, and as it descends from my navel to the tip of my jewel I generate spontaneous great bliss inseparable from emptiness. The Principal and all the retinue experience a special, exalted wisdom of bliss and emptiness.

Eight lines of praise to the Father

OM NAMO BHAGAWATE WIRE SHAYA HUM HUM PHAT
OM MAHA KÄLWA AHGNI SAMNI BHAYA HUM HUM PHAT
OM DZATA MUGUTRA KORTAYA HUM HUM PHAT
OM DHAMKHATRA KARA LOTRA BHIKHANA MUKAYA HUM
    HUM PHAT
OM SAHARA BHUNDZA BHASURAYA HUM HUM PHAT
OM PARASHUWA SHODHÄDA SHULA KHATAMGA DHARINE
    HUM HUM PHAT
OM BHÄGADZINAM WARA DHARAYA HUM HUM PHAT
OM MAHA DHUMBA ÄNDHAKARA WAWUKAYA HUM HUM
    PHAT

Eight lines of praise to the Mother

OM NAMO BHAGAWATI VAJRA VARAHI BAM HUM HUM
    PHAT
OM NAMO ARYA APARADZITE TRE LOKYA MATI BIYE SHÖRI
    HUM HUM PHAT
OM NAMA SARWA BUTA BHAYA WAHI MAHA VAJRE HUM
    HUM PHAT
OM NAMO VAJRA SANI ADZITE APARADZITE WASHAM
    KARANITRA HUM HUM PHAT
OM NAMO BHRAMANI SHOKANI ROKANI KROTE KARALENI
    HUM HUM PHAT
OM NAMA DRASANI MARANI PRABHE DANI PARADZAYE
    HUM HUM PHAT
OM NAMO BIDZAYE DZAMBHANI TAMBHANI MOHANI
    HUM HUM PHAT
OM NAMO VAJRA VARAHI MAHA YOGINI KAME SHÖRI
    KHAGE HUM HUM PHAT

The offering and praising goddesses dissolve into the HUM at my heart.

At this point, (1) with a mind of great bliss, (2) meditate on the clear appearance of the mandala and Deities, and (3) meditate on divine pride, while (4) realizing the lack of inherent existence of all phenomena. In this way, train sincerely in one single concentration on gross or subtle generation stage possessing these four characteristics. Then, when you need to rest from meditation, you can practise mantra recitation.

THE CONCLUDING PRACTICES

Blessing the mala

The mala becomes emptiness. From the state of emptiness each bead appears in its own aspect, the nature of Pämanarteshvara, the vajra speech of all Buddhas.

Mantra recitation

Visualization for reciting the mantras of the Principal Deities

The mantra to be recited descends from the letter HUM at my heart, leaves through the tip of my vajra, enters the consort's bhaga, ascends, leaves through her mouth, enters my mouth, descends, and dissolves back into the HUM. Then again it circles as before, leaving and re-entering my central channel. My four mouths, and all the Deities of the retinue, recite the mantras.

The essence mantra of the Father

OM SHRI VAJRA HE HE RU RU KAM HUM HUM PHAT DAKINI DZALA SHAMBARAM SÖHA

The close essence mantra of the Father

OM HRIH HA HA HUM HUM PHAT

The essence mantra of the Mother

OM VAJRA BEROTZANIYE HUM HUM PHAT SÖHA

The close essence mantra of the Mother

OM SARWA BUDDHA DAKINIYE VAJRA WARNANIYE HUM
HUM PHAT SÖHA

Visualization for reciting the retinue mantras

Standing on a sun seat at the heart of each Deity is a letter
HUM or BAM surrounded by the mantra to be recited. From
the letter in the centre of the encircling mantra, assemblies
of mandala Deities radiate and fulfil the welfare of all
living beings. They gather back and dissolve into the
central letter.

*Recite the mantras while repeatedly radiating and
gathering back.*

The mantras of the four Yoginis of the great bliss wheel

OM DAKINIYE HUM HUM PHAT
OM LAME HUM HUM PHAT
OM KHANDAROHI HUM HUM PHAT
OM RUPINIYE HUM HUM PHAT

The mantras of the Deities of the heart wheel

OM KARA KARA HUM HUM PHAT, OM PARTZANDI HUM
HUM PHAT, OM KURU KURU HUM HUM PHAT, OM
TZÄNDRIAKIYE HUM HUM PHAT, OM BÄNDHA BÄNDHA
HUM HUM PHAT, OM PARBHAWATIYE HUM HUM PHAT, OM
TrASAYA TrASAYA HUM HUM PHAT, OM MAHANASE HUM
HUM PHAT, OM KYOMBHAYA KYOMBHAYA HUM HUM
PHAT, OM BIRAMATIYE HUM HUM PHAT, OM HROM HROM
HUM HUM PHAT, OM KARWARIYE HUM HUM PHAT, OM
HRAH HRAH HUM HUM PHAT, OM LAMKESHÖRIYE HUM
HUM PHAT, OM PHAIM PHAIM HUM HUM PHAT, OM
DRUMATZAYE HUM HUM PHAT

The mantras of the Deities of the speech wheel

OM PHAT PHAT HUM HUM PHAT, OM AIRAWATIYE HUM
HUM PHAT, OM DAHA DAHA HUM HUM PHAT, OM
MAHABHAIRAWI HUM HUM PHAT, OM PATSA PATSA HUM
HUM PHAT, OM BAYUBEGE HUM HUM PHAT, OM BHAKYA
BHAKYA BASA RUDHI ÄNTRA MALA WALAMBINE HUM
HUM PHAT, OM SURABHAKIYE HUM HUM PHAT, OM
GRIHANA GRIHANA SAPTA PATALA GATA BHUDZAMGAM
SARWAMPA TARDZAYA TARDZAYA HUM HUM PHAT, OM
SHAMADEWI HUM HUM PHAT, OM AKANDYA AKANDYA
HUM HUM PHAT, OM SUWATRE HUM HUM PHAT, OM HRIM
HRIM HUM HUM PHAT, OM HAYAKARNE HUM HUM PHAT,
OM GYÖN GYÖN HUM HUM PHAT, OM KHAGANANE HUM
HUM PHAT

The mantras of the Deities of the body wheel

OM KYAMA KYAMA HUM HUM PHAT, OM TZATRABEGE
HUM HUM PHAT, OM HAM HAM HUM HUM PHAT, OM
KHANDAROHI HUM HUM PHAT, OM HIM HIM HUM HUM
PHAT, OM SHAUNDINI HUM HUM PHAT, OM HUM HUM
HUM HUM PHAT, OM TZATRAWARMINI HUM HUM PHAT,
OM KILI KILI HUM HUM PHAT, OM SUBIRE HUM HUM PHAT,
OM SILI SILI HUM HUM PHAT, OM MAHABALE HUM HUM
PHAT, OM HILI HILI HUM HUM PHAT, OM TZATRAWARTINI
HUM HUM PHAT, OM DHILI DHILI HUM HUM PHAT, OM
MAHABIRE HUM HUM PHAT

The mantras of the Deities of the commitment wheel

OM KAKASE HUM HUM PHAT, OM ULUKASE HUM HUM
PHAT, OM SHÖNASE HUM HUM PHAT, OM SHUKARASE
HUM HUM PHAT, OM YAMADHATI HUM HUM PHAT, OM
YAMADUTI HUM HUM PHAT, OM YAMADANGTRINI HUM
HUM PHAT, OM YAMAMATANI HUM HUM PHAT

The condensed essence mantra of the sixty retinue Deities

OM RIM RIM LIM LIM, KAM KHAM GAM GHAM NGAM,
TSAM TSHAM DZAM DZHAM NYAM, TrAM THrAM DrAM
DHrAM NAM, TAM THAM DAM DHAM NAM, PAM PHAM
BAM BHAM, YAM RAM LAM WAM, SHAM KAM SAM HAM
HUM HUM PHAT

Purifying any mistakes made during mantra recitation with the hundred-letter mantra of Heruka

OM VAJRA HERUKA SAMAYA, MANU PALAYA, HERUKA
TENO PATITA, DRIDHO ME BHAWA, SUTO KAYO ME BHAWA,
SUPO KAYO ME BHAWA, ANURAKTO ME BHAWA, SARWA
SIDDHI ME PRAYATZA, SARWA KARMA SUTZA ME, TZITAM
SHRIYAM KURU HUM, HA HA HA HA HO BHAGAWÄN,
VAJRA HERUKA MA ME MUNTSA, HERUKA BHAWA, MAHA
SAMAYA SATTÖ AH HUM PHAT

Dissolution and generating the action Deities

The charnel grounds and protection circle dissolve into the
celestial mansion. The celestial mansion dissolves into the
Deities of the commitment wheel. They dissolve into the
Deities of the body wheel. They dissolve into the Deities
of the speech wheel. They dissolve into the Deities of the
heart wheel. They dissolve into the four Yoginis of the
great bliss wheel. They dissolve into me, the Principal
Deity Father and Mother, the nature of the white and red
indestructible drop. I, the Principal Deity Father and Mother,
also melt into light and dissolve into the letter HUM at my
heart, in nature the emptiness of the Dharmakaya.

From the state of emptiness, our world arises as Heruka's
Pure Land, Keajra. I and all sentient beings arise as the
Blessed One Heruka, with a blue-coloured body, one face,
and two arms embracing Vajravarahi.

The mantra emanating from the four faces

OM SUMBHANI SUMBHA HUM HUM PHAT
OM GRIHANA GRIHANA HUM HUM PHAT
OM GRIHANA PAYA GRIHANA PAYA HUM HUM PHAT
OM ANAYA HO BHAGAWÄN BYÄ RADZA HUM HUM PHAT

Dedication

Thus, through my virtues from correctly performing
    the offerings, praises, and recitations
Of the generation stage of Glorious Heruka,
May I complete all the stages
Of the common and uncommon paths.

For the sake of all living beings,
May I become Heruka;
And then lead every living being
To Heruka's supreme state.

And if I do not attain this supreme state in this life,
At my deathtime may I be met by the venerable Father
    and Mother and their retinue,
With clouds of breathtaking offerings, heavenly music,
And many excellent, auspicious signs.

Then, at the end of the clear light of death,
May I be led to Pure Dakini Land,
The abode of the Knowledge Holders who practise the
    supreme path;
And there may I swiftly complete this profound path.

May the most profound practice and instruction of Heruka,
Practised by millions of powerful Yogis, greatly increase;
And may it remain for a very long time without
    degenerating,
As the main gateway for those seeking liberation.

May the Heroes, Dakinis, and their retinues
Abiding in the twenty-four supreme places of this world,
Who possess unobstructed power for accomplishing this
    method,
Never waver from always assisting practitioners.

Auspicious prayers

Through all the great good fortune there is
In the precious, celestial mansions as extensive as the
three thousand worlds,
Adorned with ornaments like the rays of the sun and
the moon,
May all worlds and their beings have happiness,
goodness, glory, and prosperity.

Colophon: This sadhana has been extracted from
the long sadhana *Essence of Vajrayana.*

Assembly of Good Fortune

THE TSOG OFFERING FOR
HERUKA BODY MANDALA

Introduction

For practitioners of Highest Yoga Tantra in general, and of Heruka and Vajrayogini in particular, the tsog offering is very important for renewing commitments and averting obstacles. It is a special method through which they come under the care and guidance of the Dakas and Dakinis who bestow completion stage realizations. Through making the tsog offering, their wealth, merit, and great bliss will greatly increase. The tsog offering is a principal method for attaining both outer and inner Pure Dakini Land.

A 'tsog' is an assembly of Heroes and Heroines. When you make a tsog offering, you should regard both those to whom the offering is made and those who are making the offering as Heroes and Heroines. When you gather together in a group to make a tsog offering, it is very important to regard each other as Heroes and Heroines. If you are doing this puja alone, you should visualize yourself surrounded by all living beings in the aspect of Heroes and Heroines.

Practitioners of Heruka and Vajrayogini have a commitment to make tsog offerings on the two 'tenth' days – ten days after the new moon and ten days after the full moon – the tenth and twenty-fifth days of the month according to the Buddhist calendar. Khädrubje received a vision of Heruka in which Heruka said to him, 'Practitioners who sincerely make the tsog offering on the two tenth days of each month without missing will definitely be born in Pure Dakini Land.'

The substances of the tsog offering can be set out at any suitable place in front of the shrine, and can consist of clean, fresh foods such as cakes, biscuits, honey, and fruit. You can also offer a tsog offering torma made in the traditional way according to the illustration on page 489.

There are two ways to make the tsog offering of Heruka body mandala: in conjunction with this brief sadhana, or, if you have time to practise extensive self-generation, in conjunction with the sadhana *Essence of Vajrayana*. More information on tsog offerings can be found in *Guide to Dakini Land*.

If possible, you should arrange your inner offering, vajra, bell, and damaru on a small table in front of your meditation seat. Then, with a pure motivation and a happy mind, begin the actual practice.

Assembly of Good Fortune

Visualizing the objects of refuge

In the space before me appear Guru Heruka Father and Mother, surrounded by the assembly of direct and lineage Gurus, Yidams, Buddhas, Bodhisattvas, Heroes, Dakinis, and Dharma Protectors.

Going for refuge and generating aspiring bodhichitta

Eternally I shall go for refuge
To Buddha, Dharma, and Sangha.
For the sake of all living beings
I shall become Heruka.   (3x)

Generating engaging bodhichitta

To lead all mother living beings to the state of ultimate
      happiness,
I shall attain as quickly as possible, in this very life,
The state of the Union of Buddha Heruka.
For this purpose I shall practise the stages of Heruka's
      path.   (3x)

Receiving blessings

Guru Heruka Father and Mother together with all the other objects of refuge dissolve into me, and I receive their blessings.

Purifying our own mind, body, and speech

From the state of bliss and emptiness I arise as Heruka with a blue-coloured body, one face, and two hands, holding vajra and bell, and embracing Vajravarahi. I stand with my right leg outstretched.

OM SHRI VAJRA HE HE RU RU KAM HUM HUM PHAT DAKINI DZALA SHAMBARAM SÖHA

My mind has transformed into the union of bliss and emptiness, my body into Heruka's body, and my speech into Heruka's mantra.

Purifying other beings, the environment, and enjoyments

Light rays from the letter HUM at my heart
Purify all worlds and their beings.
Everything becomes immaculately pure,
Completely filled with a vast array of offerings,
The nature of exalted wisdom and bestowing
    uncontaminated bliss.

Blessing the outer and inner offerings, the environment and beings, and the substances of the tsog offering

OM AH HUM   (3x)

By nature exalted wisdom, having the aspect of the inner offering and the individual offering substances, and functioning as objects of enjoyment of the six senses to generate a special, exalted wisdom of bliss and emptiness, inconceivable clouds of outer, inner, and secret offerings, commitment substances, and attractive offerings, cover all the ground and fill the whole of space.

EH MA HO Great manifestation of exalted wisdom.
All realms are vajra realms
And all places are great vajra palaces
Endowed with vast clouds of Samantabhadra's offerings,
An abundance of all desired enjoyments.
All beings are actual Heroes and Heroines.
Everything is immaculately pure,
Without even the name of mistaken impure appearance.

HUM All elaborations are completely pacified in the state
of the Truth Body. The wind blows and the fire blazes.
Above, on a grate of three human heads, AH within a
qualified skullcup, OM the individual substances blaze.
Above these stand OM AH HUM, each ablaze with its
brilliant colour. Through the wind blowing and the fire
blazing, the substances melt. Boiling, they swirl in a great
vapour. Masses of light rays from the three letters radiate
to the ten directions and invite the three vajras together
with nectars. These dissolve separately into the three
letters. Melting into nectar, they blend with the mixture.
Purified, transformed, and increased,
EH MA HO They become a blazing ocean of magnificent
delights.

OM AH HUM   (3x)

Inviting the guests of the tsog offering

PHAIM
From the sacred palace of the Dharmakaya,
Great Master, holder of the supreme lineage of the
   Vajrayana,
Who fulfil our hopes for all the attainments,
O Assembly of root and lineage Gurus, please come
   to this place.

From the twenty-four holy places throughout the world,
O Glorious Heruka, whose nature is the compassion of all
   the Buddhas,
And all the Heroes and Heroines of these places,
Please come here to bestow the attainments that we
   long for.

From the pure and impure lands of the ten directions,
O Assembly of Yidams, Buddhas, Bodhisattvas, and
   Dharma Protectors,
And all the beings of samsara and nirvana,
Please come here as guests of this tsog offering.

OM GURU VAJRADHARA CHAKRASAMBARA SÄMANDALA
DEWA SARWA BUDDHA BODHISATTÖ SAPARIWARA EH
HAYE HI VAJRA SAMAYA DZA DZA

PÄMA KAMALAYE TÖN

Making the tsog offering

HO This ocean of tsog offering of uncontaminated nectar,
Blessed by concentration, mantra, and mudra,
I offer to please my kind root Guru Vajradhara Heruka
    Father and Mother.
OM AH HUM
Delighted by enjoying these magnificent objects of desire,
EH MA HO
Please bless me so that I may attain outer and inner
    Dakini Land.

HO This ocean of tsog offering of uncontaminated nectar,
Blessed by concentration, mantra, and mudra,
I offer to please the four Yoginis of the great bliss wheel.
OM AH HUM
Delighted by enjoying these magnificent objects of desire,
EH MA HO
Please bless me so that I may attain spontaneous great
    bliss.

HO This ocean of tsog offering of uncontaminated nectar,
Blessed by concentration, mantra, and mudra,
I offer to please the Heroes and Heroines of the vajra
    mind.
OM AH HUM
Delighted by enjoying these magnificent objects of desire,
EH MA HO
Please bless me so that I may experience delight with the
    messengers of the vajra mind family.

HO This ocean of tsog offering of uncontaminated nectar,
Blessed by concentration, mantra, and mudra,
I offer to please the Heroes and Heroines of the vajra
    speech.

OM AH HUM
Delighted by enjoying these magnificent objects of desire,
EH MA HO
Please bless me so that I may experience delight with the
    messengers of the vajra speech family.

HO This ocean of tsog offering of uncontaminated nectar,
Blessed by concentration, mantra, and mudra,
I offer to please the Heroes and Heroines of the vajra body.
OM AH HUM
Delighted by enjoying these magnificent objects of desire,
EH MA HO
Please bless me so that I may experience delight with the
    messengers of the vajra body family.

HO This ocean of tsog offering of uncontaminated nectar,
Blessed by concentration, mantra, and mudra,
I offer to please the Deities of the commitment wheel.
OM AH HUM
Delighted by enjoying these magnificent objects of desire,
EH MA HO
Please bless me so that I may pacify all obstacles.

HO This ocean of tsog offering of uncontaminated nectar,
Blessed by concentration, mantra, and mudra,
I offer to please all other Yidams, Buddhas, Bodhisattvas,
    and Dharma Protectors.
OM AH HUM
Delighted by enjoying these magnificent objects of desire,
EH MA HO
Please bless me so that I may attain all the realizations of
    Sutra and Tantra.

HO This ocean of tsog offering of uncontaminated nectar,
Blessed by concentration, mantra, and mudra,
I offer to please the assembly of mother sentient beings.
OM AH HUM
Delighted by enjoying these magnificent objects of desire,
EH MA HO
May suffering and mistaken appearance be pacified.

Outer offerings

OM AHRGHAM PARTITZA SÖHA
OM PADÄM PARTITZA SÖHA
OM VAJRA PUPE AH HUM SÖHA
OM VAJRA DHUPE AH HUM SÖHA
OM VAJRA DIWE AH HUM SÖHA
OM VAJRA GÄNDHE AH HUM SÖHA
OM VAJRA NEWIDE AH HUM SÖHA
OM VAJRA SHAPTA AH HUM SÖHA

Inner offering

OM HUM BAM RIM RIM LIM LIM, KAM KHAM GAM GHAM
NGAM, TSAM TSHAM DZAM DZHAM NYAM, TrAM THrAM
DrAM DHrAM NAM, TAM THAM DAM DHAM NAM, PAM
PHAM BAM BHAM, YAM RAM LAM WAM, SHAM KAM SAM
HAM HUM HUM PHAT OM AH HUM

Secret and thatness offerings

Through Father and Mother uniting in embrace, all the
principal and retinue Deities enjoy a special experience
of great bliss and emptiness.

Eight lines of praise to the Father

OM I prostrate to the Blessed One, Lord of the Heroes
    HUM HUM PHAT
OM To you with a brilliance equal to the fire of the great
    aeon HUM HUM PHAT
OM To you with an inexhaustible topknot HUM HUM PHAT
OM To you with a fearsome face and bared fangs HUM
    HUM PHAT
OM To you whose thousand arms blaze with light HUM
    HUM PHAT
OM To you who hold an axe, an uplifted noose, a spear,
    and a khatanga HUM HUM PHAT
OM To you who wear a tiger-skin garment HUM HUM PHAT
OM I bow to you whose great smoke-coloured body
    dispels obstructions HUM HUM PHAT

Eight lines of praise to the Mother

OM I prostrate to Vajravarahi, the Blessed Mother HUM
HUM PHAT
OM To the Superior and powerful Knowledge Lady
unconquered by the three realms HUM HUM PHAT
OM To you who destroy all fears of evil spirits with your
great vajra HUM HUM PHAT
OM To you with controlling eyes who remain as the vajra
seat unconquered by others HUM HUM PHAT
OM To you whose wrathful fierce form desiccates Brahma
HUM HUM PHAT
OM To you who terrify and dry up demons, conquering
those in other directions HUM HUM PHAT
OM To you who conquer all those who make us dull,
rigid, and confused HUM HUM PHAT
OM I bow to Vajravarahi, the Great Mother, the Dakini
consort who fulfils all desires HUM HUM PHAT

Making the tsog offering to the Vajra Master

EH MA HO Great circle of tsog!
O Great Hero we understand
That, following in the path of the Sugatas of the three
times,
You are the source of all attainments.
Forsaking all minds of conceptualization,
Please continuously enjoy this circle of tsog.
AH LA LA HO

The Master's reply

OM With a nature inseparable from the three vajras
I generate as the Guru-Deity.
AH This nectar of uncontaminated exalted wisdom and
bliss,
HUM Without stirring from bodhichitta
I partake to delight the Deities dwelling in my body.
AH HO MAHA SUKHA

Song of the Spring Queen

HUM All you Tathagatas,
Heroes, Yoginis,
Dakas, and Dakinis,
To all of you I make this request:
O Heruka who delight in great bliss,
You engage in the Union of spontaneous bliss,
By attending the Lady intoxicated with bliss
And enjoying in accordance with the rituals.
AH LA LA, LA LA HO, AH I AH, AH RA LI HO
May the assembly of stainless Dakinis
Look with loving affection and accomplish all deeds.

HUM All you Tathagatas,
Heroes, Yoginis,
Dakas, and Dakinis,
To all of you I make this request:
With a mind completely aroused by great bliss
And a body in a dance of constant motion,
I offer to the hosts of Dakinis
The great bliss from enjoying the lotus of the mudra.
AH LA LA, LA LA HO, AH I AH, AH RA LI HO
May the assembly of stainless Dakinis
Look with loving affection and accomplish all deeds.

HUM All you Tathagatas,
Heroes, Yoginis,
Dakas, and Dakinis,
To all of you I make this request:
You who dance with a beautiful and peaceful manner,
O Blissful Protector and the hosts of Dakinis,
Please come here before me and grant me your blessings,
And bestow upon me spontaneous great bliss.
AH LA LA, LA LA HO, AH I AH, AH RA LI HO
May the assembly of stainless Dakinis
Look with loving affection and accomplish all deeds.

HUM All you Tathagatas,
Heroes, Yoginis,
Dakas, and Dakinis,
To all of you I make this request:
You who have the characteristic of the liberation of great
    bliss,
Do not say that deliverance can be gained in one lifetime
Through various ascetic practices having abandoned great
    bliss,
But that great bliss resides in the centre of the supreme
    lotus.
AH LA LA, LA LA HO, AH I AH, AH RA LI HO
May the assembly of stainless Dakinis
Look with loving affection and accomplish all deeds.

HUM All you Tathagatas,
Heroes, Yoginis,
Dakas, and Dakinis,
To all of you I make this request:
Like a lotus born from the centre of a swamp,
This method, though born from attachment, is unstained
    by the faults of attachment.
O Supreme Dakini, through the bliss of your lotus,
Please quickly bring liberation from the bonds of samsara.
AH LA LA, LA LA HO, AH I AH, AH RA LI HO
May the assembly of stainless Dakinis
Look with loving affection and accomplish all deeds.

HUM All you Tathagatas,
Heroes, Yoginis,
Dakas, and Dakinis,
To all of you I make this request:
Just as the essence of honey in the honey source
Is drunk by swarms of bees from all directions,
So through your broad lotus with six characteristics
Please bring satisfaction with the taste of great bliss.
AH LA LA, LA LA HO, AH I AH, AH RA LI HO
May the assembly of stainless Dakinis
Look with loving affection and accomplish all deeds.

Blessing the remaining tsog offering

HUM Impure mistaken appearances are purified in
    emptiness,
AH Great nectar accomplished from exalted wisdom,
OM It becomes a vast ocean of desired enjoyment.
OM AH HUM   (3x)

Giving the remaining tsog offering to the spirits

HO This ocean of remaining tsog offering of
    uncontaminated nectar,
Blessed by concentration, mantra, and mudra,
I offer to please the assembly of oath-bound guardians.
OM AH HUM
Delighted by enjoying these magnificent objects of desire,
EH MA HO
Please perform perfect actions to help practitioners.

Send out the remainder of the tsog offering to the spirits.

HO
O Guests of the remainder together with your retinues
Please enjoy this ocean of remaining tsog offering.
May those who spread the precious doctrine,
The holders of the doctrine, their benefactors, and others,
And especially I and other practitioners
Have good health, long life, power,
Glory, fame, fortune,
And extensive enjoyments.
Please grant me the attainments
Of pacifying, increasing, controlling, and wrathful actions.
You who are bound by oaths please protect me
And help me to accomplish all the attainments.
Eradicate all untimely death, sicknesses,
Harm from spirits, and hindrances.
Eliminate bad dreams,
Ill omens, and bad actions.

May there be happiness in the world, may the years be
    good,
May crops increase, and may Dharma flourish.
May all goodness and happiness come about,
And may all wishes be accomplished.

By the force of this bountiful giving,
May I become a Buddha for the sake of living beings;
And through my generosity may I liberate
All those not liberated by previous Buddhas.

Dedication

Thus, through my virtues from correctly performing
    the offerings, praises, and recitations
Of the generation stage of Glorious Heruka,
May I complete all the stages
Of the common and uncommon paths.

For the sake of all living beings,
May I become Heruka;
And then lead every living being
To Heruka's supreme state.

And if I do not attain this supreme state in this life,
At my deathtime may I be met by the venerable Father
    and Mother and their retinue,
With clouds of breathtaking offerings, heavenly music,
And many excellent, auspicious signs.

Then, at the end of the clear light of death,
May I be led to Pure Dakini Land,
The abode of the Knowledge Holders who practise the
    supreme path;
And there may I swiftly complete this profound path.

May the most profound practice and instruction of Heruka,
Practised by millions of powerful Yogis, greatly increase;
And may it remain for a very long time without
    degenerating,
As the main gateway for those seeking liberation.

May the Heroes, Dakinis, and their retinues
Abiding in the twenty-four supreme places of this world,
Who possess unobstructed power for accomplishing this
    method,
Never waver from always assisting practitioners.

Auspicious prayers

May there be the auspiciousness of a great treasury
    of blessings
Arising from the excellent deeds of all the root and
    lineage Gurus,
Who have accomplished the supreme attainment of
    Buddha Heruka
By relying upon the excellent, secret path of the King
    of Tantras.

May there be the auspiciousness of the great excellent
    deeds of the Three Jewels –
The holy Buddha Jewel, the pervading nature Heruka;
The ultimate, great, secret Dharma Jewel, the scriptures
    and realizations of Heruka Tantra;
And the supreme Sangha Jewel, the assemblies of
    Heruka's retinue Deities.

Through all the great good fortune there is
In the precious, celestial mansions as extensive as the
    three thousand worlds,
Adorned with ornaments like the rays of the sun and
    the moon,
May all worlds and their beings have happiness,
    goodness, glory, and prosperity.

Colophon: This sadhana was compiled from traditional sources
by Venerable Geshe Kelsang Gyatso.

Heruka Retreat Preliminary Jewel

RETREAT PRELIMINARIES FOR
HERUKA BODY MANDALA

Introduction

On the morning of the day that your retreat begins, you should clean your meditation room and the area around it. In front of a shrine containing statues or pictures of Buddha Shakyamuni, Je Tsongkhapa, Heruka, your Spiritual Guide, and Dharmapala Dorje Shugdän, set out tormas, outer offerings, and tsog offerings.

You should set out three tormas, which can either be made in the traditional way according to the illustration on page 488, or can consist simply of any clean, fresh food such as honey or cakes. The central torma is for the Deities of the great bliss wheel – Heruka Father and Mother and the four Yoginis; the torma to its left is for the supramundane retinues of Heruka; and the torma to its right is for the mundane retinues of Heruka.

In front of the tormas, set out three rows of offerings. The first row, nearest the shrine, is for the supramundane in-front-generated Deities, and the second row is for the mundane Dakas and Dakinis. Both these rows start from the left side of the shrine, your right, and include AHRGHAM, PADĀM, PUPE, DHUPE, DIWE, GĀNDHE, and NEWIDE. Nothing is set out for the SHAPTA offering. The third row, which is for the self-generated Deities, starts from the right side of the shrine and includes AHRGHAM, PADĀM, ĀNTZAMANAM, PUPE, DHUPE, DIWE, GĀNDHE, and NEWIDE. On a small table in front of your meditation seat, arrange your inner offering, vajra, bell, damaru, mala, and sadhana.

In the afternoon, before supper, you should engage in the actual preliminary practices. First sit on your meditation seat and practise the *Heart Jewel* sadhana with Lamrim meditation, especially the meditation on bodhichitta, to pacify obstacles, receive blessings, and generate a pure motivation. Then practise *Heruka Retreat Preliminary Jewel*.

Heruka Retreat Preliminary Jewel

Recite the following while concentrating on its meaning:

Going for refuge

I and all sentient beings, until we achieve enlightenment,
Go for refuge to Buddha, Dharma, and Sangha.   (3x)

Generating bodhichitta

Through the virtues I collect by giving and other
     perfections,
May I become a Buddha for the benefit of all.   (3x)

Instantaneous self-generation

In an instant I become Heruka, with a blue-coloured
body, one face, and two hands, holding vajra and bell,
and embracing Vajravarahi. I stand with my right leg
outstretched.

Meditate briefly on divine pride.

Blessing the inner offering

OM KHANDAROHI HUM HUM PHAT
OM SÖBHAWA SHUDDHA SARWA DHARMA SÖBHAWA
     SHUDDHO HAM
Everything becomes emptiness.

From the state of emptiness, from YAM comes wind, from
RAM comes fire, from AH a grate of three human heads.
Upon this from AH appears a broad and expansive skullcup.
Inside, from OM, KHAM, AM, TRAM, HUM come the five

Khandarohi

nectars; from LAM, MAM, PAM, TAM, BAM come the five meats, each marked by these letters. The wind blows, the fire blazes, and the substances inside the skullcup melt. Above them from HUM there arises a white, upside-down khatanga, which falls into the skullcup and melts whereby the substances take on the colour of mercury. Above them three rows of vowels and consonants, standing one above the other, transform into OM AH HUM. From these, light rays draw the nectar of exalted wisdom from the hearts of all the Tathagatas, Heroes, and Yoginis of the ten directions. When this is added the contents increase and become vast.
OM AH HUM   (3x)

With strong concentration, contemplate that the nectar in front of you possesses three qualities: it is a medicine nectar that prevents all diseases, it is a life nectar that destroys death, and it is a wisdom nectar that eradicates all delusions. Now taste the nectar and meditate briefly on bliss and emptiness.

Blessing the meditation room, the implements, and oneself

Holding the inner offering container in your right hand, with your left ring finger sprinkle inner offering three times over your room, your seat, your implements, and your body, while reciting:

OM AH HUM

Contemplate that everything is blessed and purified.

Averting obstacles

Imagine that wrathful red Khandarohi Goddesses emanate from your heart and drive away all obstructing spirits and other hindrances in each of the ten directions. While imagining this, play the damaru and bell, and recite many times:

OM KHANDAROHI HUM HUM PHAT

Think that until your retreat is finished all obstructing spirits and other hindrances have been banished to a great distance.

Meditation on the protection circle

Visualize the protection circle. Below is the vajra ground, around is the vajra fence, and above is the vajra tent and canopy. All are blue in colour and made of indestructible vajras. Outside there is a mass of five-coloured flames: red, white, yellow, green, and blue, which are the nature of the five exalted wisdoms. The flames all swirl counter-clockwise. Imagine this very strongly and then recite:

OM SUMBHANI SUMBHA HUM HUM PHAT
OM GRIHANA GRIHANA HUM HUM PHAT
OM GRIHANA PAYA GRIHANA PAYA HUM HUM PHAT
OM ANAYA HO BHAGAWÄN BYÄ RADZA HUM HUM PHAT

Generate a firm conviction that the protection circle actually exists and is completely effective in protecting you from harm and hindrances.

Establishing the retreat boundaries

Now recollect your retreat boundaries of body, speech, and mind, and firmly resolve not to transgress them until your retreat is completed. Meditate on this determination for a while.

Blessing the meditation seat

Hold the bell in your left hand at the level of your navel. Your hand should be palm upwards and the opening of the bell should face your navel. Hold the vajra in your right hand and place the palm of your right hand on your right knee so that the tips of your fingers touch your meditation seat. Contemplate strongly that your meditation seat is the nature of vajra wisdom, indestructible and immovable. Then recite seven times:

OM AH: VAJRA AHSANA HUM SÖHA

Blessing the mala

With the divine pride of being Heruka, hold your right hand palm upwards at the level of your heart and contemplate that it is the nature of bliss. Place the mala in your right hand and enclose it with your left hand, which is the nature of emptiness. Then, remembering that the nature of the mala is emptiness, recite three or seven times:

OM PÄMA NIRTE SHÖRI HUM HUM PHAT

Now blow on the mala between your hands. With strong concentration contemplate that your mala is now the nature of vajra speech, inseparable from great bliss and emptiness.

Blessing the vajra and bell

Hold the vajra in your right hand at the level of your heart and the bell in your left hand. Contemplate that the vajra is method and the bell is wisdom, and then recite:

The vajra is method and the bell is wisdom. Both together are the nature of ultimate bodhichitta.

OM VAJRA AH HUM

Then play the bell while reciting:

OM VAJRA GHANTA HUM

Dedication prayers

For the sake of all living beings,
May I become Heruka;
And then lead every living being
To Heruka's supreme state.

And if I do not attain this supreme state in this life,
At my deathtime may I be met by the venerable Father
    and Mother, and their retinue,
With clouds of breathtaking offerings, heavenly music,
And many excellent auspicious signs.

Then, at the end of the clear light of death,
May I be led to Pure Dakini Land,
The abode of the Knowledge Holders who practise the
supreme path;
And there may I swiftly complete this profound path.

May the most profound practice and instruction of Heruka,
Practised by millions of powerful Yogis greatly increase;
And may it remain for a very long time without
degenerating,
As the main gateway for those seeking liberation.

May the Heroes, Dakinis, and their retinues
Abiding in the twenty-four supreme places of this world,
Who possess unobstructed power for accomplishing this
method,
Never waver from always assisting practitioners.

*Now take a short rest, and after dusk begin the first full
session of your retreat.*

Colophon: This sadhana was compiled from traditional sources
by Venerable Geshe Kelsang Gyatso.

Heruka Body Mandala
Burning Offering

———

Introduction

The purpose of this ritual practice is to fulfil the commitments of close retreat, and to purify the negativities, downfalls, and mistakes made during the retreat.

First you should find a place where it is suitable to perform a burning offering. If this place has never previously been used for this ritual practice, seek permission from the local guardians by offering them a torma; and imagine that they are happy with your activities. Then to purify the ground touch it with your right hand while holding a vajra, and recite:

OM HANA HANA KRODHA HUM PHAT

The wrathful Deities destroy all obstacles, and the blessings
of the body, speech, and mind of all Buddhas purify all
faults of the site.

This, combined with reciting the essence mantra of Heruka one hundred times, is the conventional purification. For the ultimate purification, contemplate while reciting:

All phenomena such as the ground become emptiness,
completely purified of inherent existence.

On ground that is naturally white, or that has been coloured white, begin by determining the very centre; and from that point draw lines in each of the cardinal and intermediate directions. Take a piece of thread half a cubit in length (approx 20cm), hold one end at the centre, and describe a circle. Add four finger-widths and describe another circle, and then add another four finger-widths and describe a third circle. The second circle is called 'Murän' and the third circle is called 'Kakyer'.

Now on each of the four cardinal lines mark a point two finger-widths beyond the outer circle. From these, measure off the distance to each of the four intermediate lines and join these lines to form a square. In the centre of the hearth, draw an eight-petalled lotus, and at the centre of the lotus draw a vajra that is eight finger-widths long and one finger-width wide. Within Murän, draw a circle of fire, and within Kakyer draw a rosary of vajras. At each of the four outer corners of the hearth, draw a half moon marked by a vajra. The hearth is illustrated on page 490. When you have finished preparing the hearth, erect a circle of small pieces of clean firewood around Murän.

To your right, you should set up a suitable table covered with a white cloth. On this, set out two sets of outer offerings consisting of AHRGHAM, PADÄM, ÄNTZAMANAM, PROKYANAM, PUPE, DHUPE, ALOKE, GÄNDHE, and NEWIDE. In front of these, set out two rows of the twelve burning substances that are to be offered to the mundane and supramundane Fire Deities, from milkwood to the special pacifying substance. To the right or left of the outer offerings, set out the tormas – one for the Fire Deity, and two tambula tormas for the mundane and supramundane Fire Deities. You can either make traditional tormas or simply use cakes. You should also set out two white cloths (such as silken scarves) to represent sets of garments, a small bundle of kusha grass, and a wind flag to fan the fire. You should set out the molten butter, ladle, and funnel next to the hearth and close to hand.

On a small table to your left, arrange the vase, inner offering, vajra, bell, damaru, and so forth (see illustration on page 492). In this way, assemble all the necessary ritual articles.

Heruka Body Mandala
Burning Offering

The actual ritual has three parts:

1 *The preliminaries*
2 *The actual practice*
3 *The concluding practices*

THE PRELIMINARIES

Before engaging in the burning offering, you should practise the self-generation up to and including the torma offering. During the self-generation, after the mantra recitation, focus your mind on the action vase and accomplish the cleansing water by reciting the Khandarohi mantra several times.

Blessing the vajra and bell

The vajra is method and the bell is wisdom. Both together are the nature of ultimate bodhichitta.

While maintaining this thought, hold the vajra between the thumb and ring finger of your right hand at the level of your heart and recite:

OM SARWA TATHAGATA SIDDHI VAJRA SAMAYA TIKTA EKA TÖN DHARAYAMI VAJRA SATTÖ HI HI HI HI HI HUM HUM HUM PHAT SÖHA

Now hold the bell between the thumb and ring finger of your left hand at your left hip and recite:

OM VAJRA GHANTA HUM

Contemplate:

I delight Vajrasattva and the assembly of holy beings.

Hold up the vajra while reciting:

HUM
It is excellent to hold the vajra,
The Dharma activity of perfect liberation
That frees all living beings from confusion;
Therefore, with delight I hold the vajra.
HUM HUM HUM HO HO HO

Hold the vajra at your right hip and play the bell by moving the clapper from the centre through the eight directions while reciting:

OM VAJRA DHARMA RANITA, PARANITA, SAMPARANITA, SARWA BUDDHA KHYETRA PATZALINI PENJA PARAMITA NADA SÖBHAWA BENZA SATTÖ HRIDAYA, SANTO KHANI HUM HUM HUM HO HO HO SÖHA

From now until the burning offering is completed do not let either the vajra or the bell leave your hands.

Cleansing the hearth, the offerings, and oneself

Holding the kusha grass from the action vase in your right hand, dip the tips into the cleansing water of the vase and, beginning on your left side and circling to the right, sprinkle the hearth, all the offering substances, the ladle, the funnel, and yourself three times while reciting the action mantra:

OM KHANDAROHI HUM HUM PHAT

Now sprinkle inner offering three times in the same way.

Blessing the substances to be offered to mundane Fire Deity

OM KHANDAROHI HUM HUM PHAT
OM SÖBHAWA SHUDDHA SARWA DHARMA SÖBHAWA
  SHUDDHO HAM
Everything becomes emptiness.

From the state of emptiness, from KAMs come broad and expansive skullcups, inside which from HUMs come water for drinking, water for the feet, water for the mouth, water for sprinkling, flowers, incense, lights, perfume, food, and music. By nature emptiness, they have the aspect of the individual offering substances, and function as objects of enjoyment of the six senses to bestow special, uncontaminated bliss.

OM AHRGHAM AH HUM
OM PADÄM AH HUM
OM ÄNTZAMANAM AH HUM
OM PROKYANAM AH HUM
OM VAJRA PUPE AH HUM
OM VAJRA DHUPE AH HUM
OM VAJRA DIWE AH HUM
OM VAJRA GÄNDHE AH HUM
OM VAJRA NEWIDE AH HUM
OM VAJRA SHAPTA AH HUM

Now hold both hands in the mudra for cleansing the substances by pressing together two vajra fists with the two middle fingers raised and touching each other at the tips. Recite:

OM SÖHA

contemplate that all those substances are purified.

OM AH SÖHA

contemplate that the milkwood is purified.

OM SHRI SÖHA

contemplate that the molten butter is purified.

OM DZIM SÖHA

contemplate that the grains are purified.

OM KURU KURU SÖHA

contemplate:

The remaining substances are purified of all impurities, and they become the nature of the five inner nectars.

Lighting the fire

Set light to the torch while reciting three times:

OM AH HUM

Set light to the firewood on the hearth:

OM KHANDAROHI HUM HUM PHAT

Now purify the fire by sprinkling it three times with cleansing water and three times with inner offering while reciting:

OM KHANDAROHI HUM HUM PHAT

Fan the fire with the wind flag while reciting:

OM DZÖ LA DZÖ LA HUM

HUM

Pour seven ladles of molten butter on the fire so that it blazes while reciting the essence mantra of the Father:

OM SHRI VAJRA HE HE RU RU KAM HUM HUM PHAT DAKINI DZALA SHAMBARAM SÖHA

Preparing the kusha grass seat

Holding the bundle of kusha grass in both hands at the level of your heart, recite seven times:

OM VAJRA SATTÖ AH

OM
This kusha grass is clean and virtuous,
The essence of all that grows in the earth.

It pleases the divine Brahmins,
And brings delight to all Three Jewels.
Please pacify all my obstacles,
And make everything auspicious.

While reciting:

OM VAJRA SATTÖ AH

pass some of the kusha grass to the assistant, who, starting from the left side of the hearth, places four pairs around Kakyer with the tips pointing in a clockwise direction. Then you should arrange the remaining kusha grass in the shape of a diagonal cross and place it in the centre of the hearth.

Now, holding vajra and bell, and with your palms pressed together, recite:

O Blessed One Vajrasattva, please pacify all obstacles and make everything auspicious.

THE ACTUAL PRACTICE

This has three parts:

1 *Initial offering to mundane Fire Deity*
2 *Offerings to the supramundane Fire Deities*
3 *Final offering to mundane Fire Deity*

INITIAL OFFERING TO MUNDANE FIRE DEITY

This has three parts:

1 *Generating the hearth and Fire Deity, and absorbing the wisdom being*
2 *Making offerings and praises, and proclaiming the commitment*
3 *Offering the burning substances and once again making offerings*

Fire Deity

GENERATING THE HEARTH AND FIRE DEITY, AND ABSORBING THE WISDOM BEING

Generating the hearth and Fire Deity

To purify the hearth, sprinkle cleansing water and recite:

OM KHANDAROHI HUM HUM PHAT
OM SÖBHAWA SHUDDHA SARWA DHARMA SÖBHAWA
SHUDDHO HAM
Everything becomes emptiness.

From the state of emptiness comes a white HUM which melts and transforms into an exalted wisdom hearth. It is white in colour, circular in shape, and complete with Murän and Kakyer. Within Kakyer there is a rosary of vajras. At each of the four corners there is a half moon marked by a vajra. Everything is clear and unobstructed.

Within the hearth, from RAM there arises a blazing fire triangle, in the centre of which there is a lotus of various colours and a moon seat. Upon this from RAM comes a white lotus marked by a RAM. This completely transforms into Fire Deity, who is white in colour and has a very peaceful aspect. He has one face and four hands. His right hands hold a crystal mala and a white lotus, and his left hands hold a long-necked vase and a trident. He wears white silk garments and is adorned with jewelled ornaments. At his heart there is a fire triangle marked by a RAM.

Inviting and absorbing the wisdom being

Light rays radiate from the seed-letter at the heart of the commitment being and manifest as the wrathful Deity Dö Gyal, who invites from the south-east Fire Deity, similar to the visualization, surrounded by a retinue of Rishis.

Hold your right hand in the mudra of fearlessness and move the thumb while reciting:

OM
O Great Being come here, come here please,
Supreme Brahmin, divine Rishi.
Please come to this place
To enjoy the food from the blazing ladle.
VAJRA DHARA AHNGYA PAYATI SÖHA

Please remain on the seat of kusha grass within Kakyer,
the boundary of the fire on the hearth.

Drive away the obstructing spirits who are following the
wisdom being by sprinkling cleansing water and reciting:

OM KHANDAROHI HUM HUM PHAT

DZA HUM BAM HO
The wisdom being becomes non-dual with the commitment
being.

MAKING OFFERINGS AND PRAISES, AND
PROCLAIMING THE COMMITMENT

Offering the four waters

OM AH HRIH PRAVARA SÄKARAM PROKYANAM PARTITZA
  HUM SÖHA
OM AH HRIH PRAVARA SÄKARAM ÄNTZAMANAM
  PARTITZA HUM SÖHA
OM AH HRIH PRAVARA SÄKARAM AHRGHAM PARTITZA
  HUM SÖHA
OM AH HRIH PRAVARA SÄKARAM PADÄM PARTITZA HUM
  SÖHA

Offering the remaining outer offerings

OM AGNIYE AHDIBÄ AHDIBÄ AMBISHA AMBISHA MAHA SHRIYE
  HAMBÄ KABÄ BAHA NAYE VAJRA PUPE AH HUM SÖHA
VAJRA DHUPE AH HUM SÖHA
VAJRA ALOKE AH HUM SÖHA
VAJRA GÄNDHE AH HUM SÖHA

VAJRA NEWIDE AH HUM SÖHA
VAJRA SHAPTA AH HUM SÖHA

Inner offering

OM AGNIYE AHDIBÄ AHDIBÄ AMBISHA AMBISHA MAHA
SHRIYE HAMBÄ KABÄ BAHA NAYE OM AH HUM

Praise

Play the bell while reciting the following verses:

Lord of the world, Son of Brahma, powerful Protector,
King of Fire Deities, empowered by Takki,
Who consume all delusions with your supreme wisdom,
To you, O Protector Fire Deity, I prostrate.

If you wish to make extensive praises, continue with:

O Son of Brahma, Protector of the world,
King of Fire Deities, supreme Rishi,
You manifest this form out of compassion
To fully protect all living beings.

In the aspect of a Rishi accomplished in knowledge
    mantras,
With the light of wisdom consuming delusions,
And a blazing brilliance like the fire of the aeon,
You are endowed with clairvoyance and miracle powers.

Out of skilful means you ride an emanation vehicle.
Holding a mala you recite knowledge mantras.
You hold a vase of essential nectar
And bring coolness to all with the nectar of Dharma.

You are free from faults and have perfected purity.
Though you abide in the world you have passed beyond
    sorrow;
Though you have attained peace you have great
    compassion;
Therefore I make praises and prostrations to you.

Proclaiming the commitment

Recite three times:

OM VAJRA AHNALA MAHA BHUTA DZÖLA DZÖLAYA, SARWA
BHÄMI KURU, SARWA DUTRAM HUM PHAT, TIRSHA DZA
HUM BAM HO: SAMAYA TÖN SAMAYA HO

OFFERING THE BURNING SUBSTANCES AND
ONCE AGAIN MAKING OFFERINGS

Contemplate:

The tongue of Fire Deity is in the aspect of a white vajra
marked by a letter RAM, and the mouth of the funnel is
marked by a letter HUM radiating rays of light.

Initial offering of molten butter

*Holding the funnel over the fire with your left hand, and
holding the ladle with your right, scoop up seven ladles of
molten butter and pour them into the funnel while reciting:*

OM AGNIYE AHDIBÄ AHDIBÄ AMBISHA AMBISHA MAHA
SHRIYE HAMBÄ KABÄ BAHA NAYE SÖHA

While playing the bell, recite the following:

For all of us disciples, our benefactors, and others, may
all obstacles to attaining liberation and omniscience, all
transgressions of the three vows, all natural non-virtues,
all inauspiciousness, all unclear concentration, all incorrect
recitation of mantras, and all faults of excess and omission
in the rituals be purified SHÄNTING KURUYE SÖHA.

*Now offer each burning substance three or seven times while
reciting the mantras, and play the bell while reciting the
prayers. Imagine that the Deity promises to perform his deeds.*

*You should keep a small amount of each substance for the
final offering.*

Offering the milkwood

The milkwood becomes nectar, the nature of the Bodhi Tree.
OM AGNIYE AHDIBÄ AHDIBÄ AMBISHA AMBISHA MAHA
  SHRIYE HAMBÄ KABÄ BAHA NAYE
OM BODHI PIKYAYE
For all of us disciples, our benefactors, and others, may
all obstacles to attaining liberation and omniscience, all
transgressions of the three vows, all natural non-virtues,
all inauspiciousness, all unclear concentration, all incorrect
recitation of mantras, all faults of excess and omission in
the rituals, and especially all obstacles to increased vitality
be purified SHÄNTING KURUYE SÖHA.

Offering the molten butter

OM AGNIYE AHDIBÄ AHDIBÄ AMBISHA AMBISHA MAHA
  SHRIYE HAMBÄ KABÄ BAHA NAYE
OM AGNIYE
For all of us disciples, our benefactors, and others, may
all obstacles to attaining liberation and omniscience, all
transgressions of the three vows, all natural non-virtues,
all inauspiciousness, all unclear concentration, all incorrect
recitation of mantras, all faults of excess and omission in
the rituals, and especially all obstacles to increased wealth
be purified SHÄNTING KURUYE SÖHA.

Offering the sesame seeds

OM AGNIYE AHDIBÄ AHDIBÄ AMBISHA AMBISHA MAHA
  SHRIYE HAMBÄ KABÄ BAHA NAYE
OM SARWA PAPAM DAHANA VAJRA YE
For all of us disciples, our benefactors, and others, may
all obstacles to attaining liberation and omniscience, all
transgressions of the three vows, all natural non-virtues,
all inauspiciousness, all unclear concentration, all incorrect
recitation of mantras, all faults of excess and omission in
the rituals, and especially all negativities be purified
SHÄNTING KURUYE SÖHA.

Offering the couch grass

OM AGNIYE AHDIBÄ AHDIBÄ AMBISHA AMBISHA MAHA
  SHRIYE HAMBÄ KABÄ BAHA NAYE
OM VAJRA AHYUKE
For all of us disciples, our benefactors, and others, may
all obstacles to attaining liberation and omniscience, all
transgressions of the three vows, all natural non-virtues,
all inauspiciousness, all unclear concentration, all incorrect
recitation of mantras, all faults of excess and omission in
the rituals, and especially all obstacles to increased life
span be purified SHÄNTING KURUYE SÖHA.

Offering the rice

OM AGNIYE AHDIBÄ AHDIBÄ AMBISHA AMBISHA MAHA
  SHRIYE HAMBÄ KABÄ BAHA NAYE
OM VAJRA PUTRAYE
For all of us disciples, our benefactors, and others, may
all obstacles to attaining liberation and omniscience, all
transgressions of the three vows, all natural non-virtues,
all inauspiciousness, all unclear concentration, all incorrect
recitation of mantras, all faults of excess and omission in
the rituals, and especially all obstacles to increased merit
be purified SHÄNTING KURUYE SÖHA.

Offering the crumbled cake mixed with yoghurt

OM AGNIYE AHDIBÄ AHDIBÄ AMBISHA AMBISHA MAHA
  SHRIYE HAMBÄ KABÄ BAHA NAYE
OM SARWA SAMPA DE
For all of us disciples, our benefactors, and others, may
all obstacles to attaining liberation and omniscience, all
transgressions of the three vows, all natural non-virtues,
all inauspiciousness, all unclear concentration, all incorrect
recitation of mantras, all faults of excess and omission in
the rituals, and especially all obstacles to supreme bliss
be purified SHÄNTING KURUYE SÖHA.

Offering the kusha grass

OM AGNIYE AHDIBÄ AHDIBÄ AMBISHA AMBISHA MAHA
  SHRIYE HAMBÄ KABÄ BAHA NAYE
OM AHTRATI HATA VAJRAYE
For all of us disciples, our benefactors, and others, may
all obstacles to attaining liberation and omniscience, all
transgressions of the three vows, all natural non-virtues,
all inauspiciousness, all unclear concentration, all incorrect
recitation of mantras, all faults of excess and omission in
the rituals, and especially all obstacles to supreme purity
be purified SHÄNTING KURUYE SÖHA.

Offering the white mustard seeds

OM AGNIYE AHDIBÄ AHDIBÄ AMBISHA AMBISHA MAHA
  SHRIYE HAMBÄ KABÄ BAHA NAYE
OM SARWA AHRTA SIDDHA YE
For all of us disciples, our benefactors, and others, may
all obstacles to attaining liberation and omniscience, all
transgressions of the three vows, all natural non-virtues,
all inauspiciousness, all unclear concentration, all incorrect
recitation of mantras, all faults of excess and omission in
the rituals, and especially all obstacles created by spirits
be purified SHÄNTING KURUYE SÖHA.

Offering the barley with husks

OM AGNIYE AHDIBÄ AHDIBÄ AMBISHA AMBISHA MAHA
  SHRIYE HAMBÄ KABÄ BAHA NAYE
OM VAJRA BINZAYE
For all of us disciples, our benefactors, and others, may
all obstacles to attaining liberation and omniscience, all
transgressions of the three vows, all natural non-virtues,
all inauspiciousness, all unclear concentration, all incorrect
recitation of mantras, all faults of excess and omission in
the rituals, and especially all obstacles to wealth and
abundant harvests be purified SHÄNTING KURUYE SÖHA.

Offering the barley without husks

OM AGNIYE AHDIBÄ AHDIBÄ AMBISHA AMBISHA MAHA
    SHRIYE HAMBÄ KABÄ BAHA NAYE
OM MAHA BEGAYE
For all of us disciples, our benefactors, and others, may
all obstacles to attaining liberation and omniscience, all
transgressions of the three vows, all natural non-virtues,
all inauspiciousness, all unclear concentration, all incorrect
recitation of mantras, all faults of excess and omission in
the rituals, and especially all obstacles to excellent quick
mental powers be purified SHÄNTING KURUYE SÖHA.

Offering the peas

OM AGNIYE AHDIBÄ AHDIBÄ AMBISHA AMBISHA MAHA
    SHRIYE HAMBÄ KABÄ BAHA NAYE
OM MAHA BALAYE
For all of us disciples, our benefactors, and others, may
all obstacles to attaining liberation and omniscience, all
transgressions of the three vows, all natural non-virtues,
all inauspiciousness, all unclear concentration, all incorrect
recitation of mantras, all faults of excess and omission in
the rituals, and especially all obstacles to increased
strength be purified SHÄNTING KURUYE SÖHA.

Offering the wheat

OM AGNIYE AHDIBÄ AHDIBÄ AMBISHA AMBISHA MAHA
    SHRIYE HAMBÄ KABÄ BAHA NAYE
OM VAJRA GHAMA RI
For all of us disciples, our benefactors, and others, may
all obstacles to attaining liberation and omniscience, all
transgressions of the three vows, all natural non-virtues,
all inauspiciousness, all unclear concentration, all incorrect
recitation of mantras, all faults of excess and omission in
the rituals, and especially all sickness be purified
SHÄNTING KURUYE SÖHA.

Offering the special pacifying substance

OM AGNIYE AHDIBÄ AHDIBÄ AMBISHA AMBISHA MAHA
SHRIYE HAMBÄ KABÄ BAHA NAYE
For all of us disciples, our benefactors, and others, may
all obstacles to attaining liberation and omniscience, all
transgressions of the three vows, all natural non-virtues,
all inauspiciousness, all unclear concentration, all incorrect
recitation of mantras, all faults of excess and omission in
the rituals, and especially all obstacles to accomplishing
supreme attainments be purified SHÄNTING KURUYE SÖHA.

Offering the four waters

OM AH HRIH PRAVARA SÄKARAM PROKYANAM PARTITZA
HUM SÖHA
OM AH HRIH PRAVARA SÄKARAM ÄNTZAMANAM
PARTITZA HUM SÖHA
OM AH HRIH PRAVARA SÄKARAM AHRGHAM PARTITZA
HUM SÖHA
OM AH HRIH PRAVARA SÄKARAM PADÄM PARTITZA HUM
SÖHA

OFFERINGS TO THE SUPRAMUNDANE FIRE DEITIES

This has three parts:

1 *Generating the celestial mansion and the seats
   at the heart of Fire Deity*
2 *Generating the Deities at their places*
3 *The stages of making offerings to the Deities*

GENERATING THE CELESTIAL MANSION AND
THE SEATS AT THE HEART OF FIRE DEITY

In the centre of a blazing fire mandala at the heart of Fire
Deity, from DHRUM comes a celestial mansion, which is
square with four doorways. The jewelled walls have five
layers coloured white, yellow, red, green, and blue from

the outside in. Around the top of the wall is a red jewelled
moulding studded with square, triangular, and other-
shaped jewels. Upon this are four layers of golden bands.
Upon these, and extending beyond, are rafters whose ends
form the shape of sea-monsters, with full and half-length
strings of pearls hanging from their mouths. Overhanging
these are sharpu, special jewelled decorations, suspended
from the eaves. Above these is a parapet in the shape of
half lotus petals. It is adorned with eight victory banners
and eight other banners, all set in golden vases, and
parasols on top of the four outer corners.

Around the outer foot of the wall runs a red ledge for the
objects of desire. Upon this stand goddesses of various
colours and postures making offerings. At the outer
corners of the doorways and hallways, as well as at the
four outer and four inner corners of the mansion, stand
half moons, upon which rest red jewels adorned at the
top by vajras.

At the front of each entrance, upon square pedestals,
four pillars set in vases support a square, eleven-tiered
archway. Above each archway is a Dharma Wheel flanked
right and left by a male and a female deer. To the right
and left of each archway, set in golden vases, are wish-
granting trees bearing the seven precious possessions of a
king. In the space around are Siddhas, and emerging from
clouds are offering gods and goddesses holding garlands
of flowers, making everything exquisitely beautiful.

Beyond this is the protection circle of a fence of vajras of
various sizes, and so forth. Surrounding the protection circle
are five-coloured vajra fires blazing like the fire of the aeon.
They swirl counter-clockwise, covering all directions – above,
below, and all around. Beyond these are the eight great
charnel grounds. In each charnel ground there is a tree,
at the foot of which there sits a directional guardian. At
the top of the tree there is a regional guardian with the
upper half of his body emerging from the branches. There

is a lake, in which there lives a naga, and above each lake
there is a cloud. There is a mountain, on top of which
there is a white stupa, and there is a wisdom fire.

Throughout the charnel grounds wild birds and animals
such as ravens, owls, vultures, wolves, jackals, and snakes
wander around; and spirits such as givers of harm, zombies,
and cannibals utter the sound 'Kili Kili'. There are also
Yogis and Yoginis such as those who have accomplished
attainments, and Knowledge Holders keeping their
commitments purely. They are all single-pointedly
practising Heruka's path. They are naked, with freely
hanging hair, and are adorned with five mudras. They
hold hand-drums, skullcups, and khatangas, and their
crowns are adorned with skulls. All the beings abiding
in the charnel grounds instil the place with a sense of
wonder.

Inside the celestial mansion eight pillars support vajra
beams adorning the ceiling. The roof is surmounted at its
crest by a precious jewel and a vajra. Within the celestial
mansion, at the four doors and the four corners, are eight
corpse seats. Within this circle is the white body wheel,
with eight spokes and a rosary of wheels at its rim. Within
this is the red speech wheel, with eight spokes and a rosary
of lotuses at its rim. Within this is the blue heart wheel,
with eight spokes and a rosary of vajras at its rim. At its
centre is the great bliss wheel, an eight-petalled lotus of
various colours, with a rosary of curved knives at its rim.

Thus visualize clearly the celestial mansion and the seats.

GENERATING THE DEITIES AT THEIR PLACES

On the central sun seat appear HUM BAM; on the lotus
petals of the four cardinal directions of the great bliss
wheel RIM RIM LIM LIM; on the eight spokes of the heart
wheel KAM KHAM GAM GHAM NGAM TSAM TSHAM DZAM;
on the eight spokes of the speech wheel DZHAM NYAM

TrAM THrAM DrAM DHrAM NAM TAM; on the eight spokes
of the body wheel THAM DAM DHAM NAM PAM PHAM BAM
BHAM; and at the four doors and the four corners YAM
RAM LAM WAM SHAM KAM SAM HAM.

These completely transform, and on the central sun seat
arises Glorious Heruka, with a dark-blue body and four
faces. The principal face is dark blue, the left face green,
the back face red, and the right face yellow. Each face has
three eyes and a rosary of five-pronged vajras on its
forehead. His right leg is outstretched and treads on the
head of black Bhairawa, who has four hands. The first
two hands are pressed together, the second right hand
holds a damaru, and the second left a sword. His bent left
leg treads on the breast of red Kalarati, who has four
hands. The first two hands are pressed together, and the
other two hold a skullcup and a khatanga. Both the beings
beneath his feet have one face and three eyes, and are
adorned with five mudras.

He has twelve arms. The first two embrace Vajravarahi,
with his right hand holding a five-pronged vajra and his
left hand a bell. The next two hands hold a bloody, white
elephant skin stretched across his back; the right hand
holds the left foreleg, and the left the left hind leg. Both
these hands are in the threatening mudra with the tips of
the outstretched fingers at the level of his eyebrows. His
third right hand holds a damaru, the fourth an axe, the
fifth a curved knife, and the sixth an upright three-pointed
spear. His third left hand holds a khatanga marked with a
vajra, the fourth a skullcup brimming with blood, the fifth
a vajra noose, and the sixth a four-faced head of Brahma.

His hair is tied up in a topknot marked with a crossed vajra.
Each head is adorned with a crown of five skulls strung
together top and bottom with a rosary of black vajras. On
the left side of his crown is a half moon, slightly tilted. His
facial expressions change, and his four sets of four fangs
are bared and terrifying. He displays nine moods: three

physical moods of majesty, heroism, and menace; three verbal moods of laughter, wrath, and ferocity; and three mental moods of compassion, attentiveness, and serenity. He wears a lower garment of a tiger skin, and a long necklace of fifty human heads strung together with human entrails. Adorned with six mudras, his entire body is smeared with ashes of human bone.

Embracing the Blessed One is the Blessed Mother Vajravarahi, who has a red-coloured body, one face, two hands, and three eyes. She is naked with freely hanging hair and wears a lower garment made from fragments of skull. Her left hand, embracing the Father's neck, holds a skullcup brimming with the blood of the four maras. Her right hand in the threatening mudra brandishes a curved knife, opposing the malignant forces of the ten directions. Her body shines with a brilliance like that of the fire of the aeon. Her two legs are clasped around the Father's thighs. She is the nature of blissful great compassion. Adorned with five mudras, she wears a crown of five human skulls and a necklace of fifty human skulls.

On the eastern petal of the lotus is dark-blue Dakini, on the northern petal green Lama, on the western petal red Khandarohi, and on the southern petal yellow Rupini. They each have one face with three eyes and bared fangs, and are naked with freely hanging hair. They each have two hands, the right holding a curved knife and the left a skullcup, with a khatanga held in the crook of their left elbow. They stand with their right leg outstretched and are adorned with five mudras. They wear a crown of five human skulls and a long necklace of fifty human skulls. On the four intermediate petals, such as Fire, are skullcups brimming with five nectars.

In the heart wheel at the eastern spoke, Puliramalaya, are Khandakapala and Partzandi; at the northern spoke, Dzalandhara, are Mahakankala and Tzändriakiya; at the western spoke, Odiyana, are Kankala and Parbhawatiya;

at the southern spoke, Arbuta, are Vikatadamshtri and Mahanasa; at the fire spoke, Godawari, are Suraberi and Biramatiya; at the free-from-truth spoke, Rameshöri, are Amitabha and Karwariya; at the wind spoke, Dewikoti, are Vajraprabha and Lamkeshöriya; and at the powerful spoke, Malawa, are Vajradeha and Drumatzaya.

In the speech wheel at the eastern spoke, Kamarupa, are Ankuraka and Airawatiya; at the northern spoke, Ote, are Vajrajatila and Mahabhairawi; at the western spoke, Trishakune are Mahavira and Bayubega; at the southern spoke, Kosala, are Vajrahumkara and Surabhakiya; at the fire spoke, Kalinga, are Subhadra and Shamadewi; at the free-from-truth spoke, Lampaka, are Vajrabhadra and Suwatre; at the wind spoke, Kancha, are Mahabhairawa and Hayakarna; and at the powerful spoke, Himalaya, are Virupaksha and Khaganana.

In the body wheel at the eastern spoke, Pretapuri, are Mahabala and Tzatrabega; at the northern spoke, Grihadewata, are Ratnavajra and Khandarohi; at the western spoke, Shauraktra, are Hayagriva and Shaundini; at the southern spoke, Suwanadvipa, are Akashagarbha and Tzatrawarmini; at the fire spoke, Nagara, are Shri Heruka and Subira; at the free-from-truth spoke, Sindhura, are Pämanarteshvara and Mahabala; at the wind spoke, Maru, are Vairochana and Tzatrawartini; and at the powerful spoke, Kuluta, are Vajrasattva and Mahabire.

All twenty-four Heroes such as Khandakapala have one face, two hands, and three eyes; and their heads are adorned with a crown of five human skulls. They hold a vajra and bell, and embrace their consort. Their hair is tied up in a topknot, adorned with a vajra and a crescent moon. They have a rosary of vajras on their forehead and are adorned with six mudras. Wearing a long necklace of fifty human heads and a lower garment of a tiger skin, they stand with their right leg outstretched.

All twenty-four Heroines such as Partzandi have one face, two hands, and three eyes, which are red and blaze like fire. Their right hand raised in a threatening mudra holds a curved knife, and their left hand embracing the Father's neck holds a skullcup filled with the blood of the four maras. Their two legs are clasped around the Father's thighs. Wearing a lower garment made from fragments of skull, a crown of five human skulls, and a necklace of fifty human skulls, they have freely hanging hair and are adorned with five mudras.

Around the Deities of the body wheel on corpse seats are: in the east dark-blue Kakase; in the north green Ulukase; in the west red Shönase; in the south yellow Shukarase; on the fire corpse seat Yamadhati, who is blue on the right and yellow on the left; on the free-from-truth corpse seat Yamaduti, who is yellow on the right and red on the left; on the wind corpse seat Yamadangtrini, who is red on the right and green on the left; and on the powerful corpse seat Yamamatani, who is green on the right and blue on the left.

These Heroines have one face with three eyes and bared fangs, and are naked with freely hanging hair. They have two hands, the right holding a curved knife and the left a skullcup, and grip a khatanga with the crook of their left elbow. They are adorned with five mudras and stand with their right leg outstretched. They wear a crown of five human skulls and a long necklace of fifty human skulls.

A mass of white light radiates from the bodies of all the Deities.

Putting on the armour

From white OM HA at the heart of the Principal appears white Vajrasattva with three faces – white, red, and black – and six arms. His three right hands hold a vajra, a damaru, and a head; and his three left hands hold a bell, a skullcup, and a khatanga. He embraces Varahi.

From yellow NAMA HI at his head appears yellow Vairochana with one face and four arms. His two right hands hold a wheel and a damaru, and his two left hands hold a bell and a skullcup, together with a khatanga. He embraces Yamani.

From red SÖHA HU at his crown appears red Pämanarteshvara with one face and four arms. His two right hands hold a lotus and a damaru, and his two left hands hold a bell and a skullcup, together with a khatanga. He embraces Mohani.

From black BOKE HE at his two shoulders appears black Heruka with one face and four arms. His two right hands hold a vajra and a damaru, and his two left hands hold a bell and a skullcup, together with a khatanga. He embraces Sachalani.

From orange HUM HUM HO at his two eyes appears orange Vajrasurya with one face and four arms. His two right hands hold a jewel and a damaru, and his two left hands hold a bell and a skullcup, together with a khatanga. He embraces Samtrasani.

From green PHAT HAM at his forehead, by nature the physical power of all his limbs, appears green Paramashawa with one face and four arms. His two right hands hold a sword and a damaru, and his two left hands hold a bell and a skullcup, together with a khatanga. He embraces Chandika.

Vajrasattva stands on a moon mandala and has an aura of moonlight. The other five stand on sun mandalas and have auras of sunlight. All six Heroes have one face and three eyes, and are adorned with six mudras. Wearing a crown of five human skulls, a long necklace of fifty human heads, and a lower garment of a tiger skin, they stand with their right leg outstretched.

From red OM BAM at the navel of the Principal Lady appears red Vajravarahi with three faces – red, blue, and green – and six arms. Her three right hands hold a curved knife, a Brahma's head, and an iron hook; and her three left hands hold a skullcup, a khatanga, and a noose. She embraces Vajrasattva.

From blue HAM YOM at her heart appears blue Yamani embracing Vairochana; from white HRIM MOM at her throat white Mohani embracing Pämanarteshvara; from yellow HRIM HRIM at her head yellow Sachalani embracing Heruka; from green HUM HUM at her crown green Samtrasani embracing Vajrasurya; and from smoke-coloured PHAT PHAT at her forehead, by nature the physical power of all her limbs, smoke-coloured Chandika embracing Paramashawa.

Mohani stands on a moon mandala and has an aura of moonlight. The other five stand on sun mandalas and have auras of sunlight. All six Heroines have one face and three eyes, and are adorned with five mudras. They have four arms; their two right hands hold a damaru and a curved knife, and their two left hands hold a bell and a skullcup, together with a khatanga. Wearing a crown of five human skulls and a long necklace of fifty human skulls, they are naked with freely hanging hair and stand with their right leg outstretched.

Inviting and absorbing the wisdom beings

PHAIM
The wisdom beings, the supported and supporting mandala, are invited together with the empowering Deities.

OM SHRI HERUKA AHRGHAM, PADÄM, PUPE, DHUPE, DIWE, GÄNDHE, NEWIDE, SHAPTA PARTITZA HUM SÖHA

VAJRA ANKUSHA DZA
VAJRA PASHA HUM
VAJRA POTA BAM
VAJRA GHANTA HO

The wisdom beings each become non-dual with their respective commitment being.

Granting empowerment and adorning the crown

O, all you Tathagatas, please grant the empowerment.

Requested in this way, the eight Goddesses of the doorways drive away hindrances, the Heroes recite auspicious verses, the Heroines sing vajra songs, and the Rupavajras and so forth make offerings. The Principal mentally resolves to grant the empowerment and the four Mothers together with Varahi, holding jewelled vases filled with the five nectars, confer the empowerment through the crown of their heads.

'Just as all the Tathagatas granted ablution
At the moment of [Buddha's] birth,
Likewise do we now grant ablution
With the pure water of the gods.

OM SARWA TATHAGATA ABHIKEKATA SAMAYA SHRIYE HUM'

Saying this, they grant the empowerment with a stream of nectar through the crown. All the Deities become the nature of great bliss. The excess water remaining on the crown completely transforms, and the Principal is crowned with Vajrasattva, Varahi with Akshobya, the Four Mothers with Ratnasambhava, the Deities of the heart wheel with Akshobya, the Deities of the speech wheel with Amitabha, the Deities of the body wheel with Vairochana, and the Deities of the commitment wheel with Amoghasiddhi.

THE STAGES OF MAKING OFFERINGS TO THE DEITIES

Blessing the offering substances

OM KHANDAROHI HUM HUM PHAT
OM SÖBHAWA SHUDDHA SARWA DHARMA SÖBHAWA
   SHUDDHO HAM
Everything becomes emptiness.

From the state of emptiness, from KAMs come broad and expansive skullcups, inside which from HUMs come water for drinking, water for the feet, water for the mouth, water for sprinkling, flowers, incense, lights, perfume, food, and music. By nature emptiness, they have the aspect of the individual offering substances, and function as objects of enjoyment of the six senses to bestow special, uncontaminated bliss.

OM AHRGHAM AH HUM
OM PADÄM AH HUM
OM ÄNTZAMANAM AH HUM
OM PROKYANAM AH HUM
OM VAJRA PUPE AH HUM
OM VAJRA DHUPE AH HUM
OM VAJRA DIWE AH HUM
OM VAJRA GÄNDHE AH HUM
OM VAJRA NEWIDE AH HUM
OM VAJRA SHAPTA AH HUM

Outer offerings

OM AH HRIH PRAVARA SÄKARAM PROKYANAM PARTITZA
    HUM SÖHA
OM AH HRIH PRAVARA SÄKARAM ÄNTZAMANAM
    PARTITZA HUM SÖHA
OM AH HRIH PRAVARA SÄKARAM AHRGHAM PARTITZA
    HUM SÖHA
OM AH HRIH PRAVARA SÄKARAM PADÄM PARTITZA HUM
    SÖHA
OM VAJRA PUPE AH HUM SÖHA
OM VAJRA DHUPE AH HUM SÖHA
OM VAJRA DIWE AH HUM SÖHA
OM VAJRA GÄNDHE AH HUM SÖHA
OM VAJRA NEWIDE AH HUM SÖHA
OM VAJRA SHAPTA AH HUM SÖHA

Offering the sixteen knowledge goddesses

OM VAJRA WINI HUM HUM PHAT
OM VAJRA WAMSHE HUM HUM PHAT

OM VAJRA MITAMGI HUM HUM PHAT
OM VAJRA MURANDZE HUM HUM PHAT

OM VAJRA HASÄ HUM HUM PHAT
OM VAJRA LASÄ HUM HUM PHAT
OM VAJRA GIRTI HUM HUM PHAT
OM VAJRA NIRTÄ HUM HUM PHAT

OM VAJRA PUPE HUM HUM PHAT
OM VAJRA DHUPE HUM HUM PHAT
OM VAJRA DIWE HUM HUM PHAT
OM VAJRA GÄNDHE HUM HUM PHAT

OM RUPA BENZ HUM HUM PHAT
OM RASA BENZ HUM HUM PHAT
OM PARSHE BENZ HUM HUM PHAT
OM DHARMA DHATU BENZ HUM HUM PHAT

Inner offering

OM SHRI VAJRA HE HE RU RU KAM HUM HUM PHAT DAKINI
　　DZALA SHAMBARAM SÖHA OM AH HUM

OM VAJRA BEROTZANIYE HUM HUM PHAT SÖHA OM AH HUM

OM RIM RIM LIM LIM, KAM KHAM GAM GHAM NGAM,
TSAM TSHAM DZAM DZHAM NYAM, TrAM THrAM DrAM
DHrAM NAM, TAM THAM DAM DHAM NAM, PAM PHAM
BAM BHAM, YAM RAM LAM WAM, SHAM KAM SAM HAM
HUM HUM PHAT OM AH HUM

Eight lines of praise to the Father

OM I prostrate to the Blessed One, Lord of the Heroes
　　HUM HUM PHAT
OM To you with a brilliance equal to the fire of the great
　　aeon HUM HUM PHAT
OM To you with an inexhaustible topknot HUM HUM PHAT
OM To you with a fearsome face and bared fangs HUM
　　HUM PHAT
OM To you whose thousand arms blaze with light HUM
　　HUM PHAT

OM To you who hold an axe, an uplifted noose, a spear,
and a khatanga HUM HUM PHAT
OM To you who wear a tiger-skin garment HUM HUM PHAT
OM I bow to you whose great smoke-coloured body
dispels obstructions HUM HUM PHAT

Eight lines of praise to the Mother

OM I prostrate to Vajravarahi, the Blessed Mother HUM
HUM PHAT
OM To the Superior and powerful Knowledge Lady
unconquered by the three realms HUM HUM PHAT
OM To you who destroy all fears of evil spirits with your
great vajra HUM HUM PHAT
OM To you with controlling eyes who remain as the vajra
seat unconquered by others HUM HUM PHAT
OM To you whose wrathful fierce form desiccates Brahma
HUM HUM PHAT
OM To you who terrify and dry up demons, conquering
those in other directions HUM HUM PHAT
OM To you who conquer all those who make us dull,
rigid, and confused HUM HUM PHAT
OM I bow to Vajravarahi, the Great Mother, the Dakini
consort who fulfils all desires HUM HUM PHAT

Offering the burning substances

Now contemplate:

The tongues of the Deities are in the aspect of white vajras,
the nature of light, marked by a letter HUM.

Initial offering of molten butter

OM SHRI VAJRA HE HE RU RU KAM HUM HUM PHAT DAKINI
DZALA SHAMBARAM SÖHA
For all of us disciples, our benefactors, and others, may
all obstacles to attaining liberation and omniscience, all
transgressions of the three vows, all natural non-virtues,
all inauspiciousness, all unclear concentration, all incorrect

recitation of mantras, all faults of excess and omission in
the rituals be purified SHÄNTING KURUYE SÖHA.

*Each of the twelve substances should be offered first to the
Principal Deity Father and Mother, and then to the Deities
of the retinue.*

*When making many offerings of each of the twelve sub-
stances, such as the milkwood, to the Principal Deity Father
and Mother, for the first offering you should recite the
Deities' mantras, the substance mantra, and the prayer of
request; for the second and subsequent offerings you should
recite only the Deities' mantras; and for the last offering you
should once again recite all three: the Deities' mantras, the
substance mantra, and the prayer of request.*

*When making the offerings to the retinue Deities, you
should make each offering twice.*

*The milkwood and the molten butter are the principal
offering substances. Since each time one of these is offered
together with a mantra it is counted as one burning offering,
you should try to offer many of these.*

*In this way, you should finish offering the burning sub-
stances.*

Offering the milkwood to the Principal Deity Father and Mother

The milkwood becomes nectar, the nature of the Bodhi Tree.
OM SHRI VAJRA HE HE RU RU KAM HUM HUM PHAT DAKINI
    DZALA SHAMBARAM SÖHA
OM VAJRA BEROTZANIYE HUM HUM PHAT SÖHA
OM BODHI PIKYAYE
For all of us disciples, our benefactors, and others, may
all obstacles to attaining liberation and omniscience, all
transgressions of the three vows, all natural non-virtues,
all inauspiciousness, all unclear concentration, all incorrect
recitation of mantras, all faults of excess and omission in
the rituals, and especially all obstacles to increased vitality
be purified SHÄNTING KURUYE SÖHA.

Offering the milkwood to the retinues (2x)

OM DAKINIYE HUM HUM PHAT
OM LAME HUM HUM PHAT
OM KHANDAROHI HUM HUM PHAT
OM RUPINIYE HUM HUM PHAT

OM KARA KARA HUM HUM PHAT, OM PARTZANDI HUM
HUM PHAT, OM KURU KURU HUM HUM PHAT, OM
TZÄNDRIAKIYE HUM HUM PHAT, OM BÄNDHA BÄNDHA
HUM HUM PHAT, OM PARBHAWATIYE HUM HUM PHAT, OM
TrASAYA TrASAYA HUM HUM PHAT, OM MAHANASE HUM
HUM PHAT, OM KYOMBHAYA KYOMBHAYA HUM HUM
PHAT, OM BIRAMATIYE HUM HUM PHAT, OM HROM HROM
HUM HUM PHAT, OM KARWARIYE HUM HUM PHAT, OM
HRAH HRAH HUM HUM PHAT, OM LAMKESHÖRIYE HUM
HUM PHAT, OM PHAIM PHAIM HUM HUM PHAT, OM
DRUMATZAYE HUM HUM PHAT

OM PHAT PHAT HUM HUM PHAT, OM AIRAWATIYE HUM
HUM PHAT, OM DAHA DAHA HUM HUM PHAT, OM
MAHABHAIRAWI HUM HUM PHAT, OM PATSA PATSA HUM
HUM PHAT, OM BAYUBEGE HUM HUM PHAT, OM BHAKYA
BHAKYA BASA RUDHI ÄNTRA MALA WALAMBINE HUM
HUM PHAT, OM SURABHAKIYE HUM HUM PHAT, OM
GRIHANA GRIHANA SAPTA PATALA GATA BHUDZAMGAM
SARWAMPA TARDZAYA TARDZAYA HUM HUM PHAT, OM
SHAMADEWI HUM HUM PHAT, OM AKANDYA AKANDYA
HUM HUM PHAT, OM SUWATRE HUM HUM PHAT, OM HRIM
HRIM HUM HUM PHAT, OM HAYAKARNE HUM HUM PHAT,
OM GYÖN GYÖN HUM HUM PHAT, OM KHAGANANE HUM
HUM PHAT

OM KYAMA KYAMA HUM HUM PHAT, OM TZATRABEGE
HUM HUM PHAT, OM HAM HAM HUM HUM PHAT, OM
KHANDAROHI HUM HUM PHAT, OM HIM HIM HUM HUM
PHAT, OM SHAUNDINI HUM HUM PHAT, OM HUM HUM
HUM HUM PHAT, OM TZATRAWARMINI HUM HUM PHAT,
OM KILI KILI HUM HUM PHAT, OM SUBIRE HUM HUM PHAT,
OM SILI SILI HUM HUM PHAT, OM MAHABALE HUM HUM

PHAT, OM HILI HILI HUM HUM PHAT, OM TZATRAWARTINI
HUM HUM PHAT, OM DHILI DHILI HUM HUM PHAT, OM
MAHABIRE HUM HUM PHAT

OM KAKASE HUM HUM PHAT, OM ULUKASE HUM HUM
PHAT, OM SHÖNASE HUM HUM PHAT, OM SHUKARASE
HUM HUM PHAT, OM YAMADHATI HUM HUM PHAT, OM
YAMADUTI HUM HUM PHAT, OM YAMADANGTRINI HUM
HUM PHAT, OM YAMAMATANI HUM HUM PHAT

OM BODHI PIKYAYE
For all of us disciples, our benefactors, and others, may
all obstacles to attaining liberation and omniscience, all
transgressions of the three vows, all natural non-virtues,
all inauspiciousness, all unclear concentration, all incorrect
recitation of mantras, all faults of excess and omission in
the rituals, and especially all obstacles to increased vitality
be purified SHÄNTING KURUYE SÖHA.

Offering the molten butter to the Principal Deity Father and Mother

OM SHRI VAJRA HE HE RU RU KAM HUM HUM PHAT DAKINI
    DZALA SHAMBARAM SÖHA
OM VAJRA BEROTZANIYE HUM HUM PHAT SÖHA
OM AGNIYE
For all of us disciples, our benefactors, and others, may
all obstacles to attaining liberation and omniscience, all
transgressions of the three vows, all natural non-virtues,
all inauspiciousness, all unclear concentration, all incorrect
recitation of mantras, all faults of excess and omission in
the rituals, and especially all obstacles to increased wealth
be purified SHÄNTING KURUYE SÖHA.

Offering the molten butter to the retinues (2x)

OM DAKINIYE HUM HUM PHAT
OM LAME HUM HUM PHAT
OM KHANDAROHI HUM HUM PHAT
OM RUPINIYE HUM HUM PHAT

OM KARA KARA HUM HUM PHAT, OM PARTZANDI HUM
HUM PHAT, OM KURU KURU HUM HUM PHAT, OM
TZÄNDRIAKIYE HUM HUM PHAT, OM BÄNDHA BÄNDHA
HUM HUM PHAT, OM PARBHAWATIYE HUM HUM PHAT, OM
TrASAYA TrASAYA HUM HUM PHAT, OM MAHANASE HUM
HUM PHAT, OM KYOMBHAYA KYOMBHAYA HUM HUM
PHAT, OM BIRAMATIYE HUM HUM PHAT, OM HROM HROM
HUM HUM PHAT, OM KARWARIYE HUM HUM PHAT, OM
HRAH HRAH HUM HUM PHAT, OM LAMKESHÖRIYE HUM
HUM PHAT, OM PHAIM PHAIM HUM HUM PHAT, OM
DRUMATZAYE HUM HUM PHAT

OM PHAT PHAT HUM HUM PHAT, OM AIRAWATIYE HUM
HUM PHAT, OM DAHA DAHA HUM HUM PHAT, OM
MAHABHAIRAWI HUM HUM PHAT, OM PATSA PATSA HUM
HUM PHAT, OM BAYUBEGE HUM HUM PHAT, OM BHAKYA
BHAKYA BASA RUDHI ÄNTRA MALA WALAMBINE HUM
HUM PHAT, OM SURABHAKIYE HUM HUM PHAT, OM
GRIHANA GRIHANA SAPTA PATALA GATA BHUDZAMGAM
SARWAMPA TARDZAYA TARDZAYA HUM HUM PHAT, OM
SHAMADEWI HUM HUM PHAT, OM AKANDYA AKANDYA
HUM HUM PHAT, OM SUWATRE HUM HUM PHAT, OM HRIM
HRIM HUM HUM PHAT, OM HAYAKARNE HUM HUM PHAT,
OM GYÖN GYÖN HUM HUM PHAT, OM KHAGANANE HUM
HUM PHAT

OM KYAMA KYAMA HUM HUM PHAT, OM TZATRABEGE
HUM HUM PHAT, OM HAM HAM HUM HUM PHAT, OM
KHANDAROHI HUM HUM PHAT, OM HIM HIM HUM HUM
PHAT, OM SHAUNDINI HUM HUM PHAT, OM HUM HUM
HUM HUM PHAT, OM TZATRAWARMINI HUM HUM PHAT,
OM KILI KILI HUM HUM PHAT, OM SUBIRE HUM HUM PHAT,
OM SILI SILI HUM HUM PHAT, OM MAHABALE HUM HUM
PHAT, OM HILI HILI HUM HUM PHAT, OM TZATRAWARTINI
HUM HUM PHAT, OM DHILI DHILI HUM HUM PHAT, OM
MAHABIRE HUM HUM PHAT

OM KAKASE HUM HUM PHAT, OM ULUKASE HUM HUM
PHAT, OM SHÖNASE HUM HUM PHAT, OM SHUKARASE

HUM HUM PHAT, OM YAMADHATI HUM HUM PHAT, OM
YAMADUTI HUM HUM PHAT, OM YAMADANGTRINI HUM
HUM PHAT, OM YAMAMATANI HUM HUM PHAT

OM AGNIYE
For all of us disciples, our benefactors, and others, may
all obstacles to attaining liberation and omniscience, all
transgressions of the three vows, all natural non-virtues,
all inauspiciousness, all unclear concentration, all incorrect
recitation of mantras, all faults of excess and omission in
the rituals, and especially all obstacles to increased wealth
be purified SHÄNTING KURUYE SÖHA.

Offering the sesame seeds to the Principal Deity Father and Mother

OM SHRI VAJRA HE HE RU RU KAM HUM HUM PHAT DAKINI
    DZALA SHAMBARAM SÖHA
OM VAJRA BEROTZANIYE HUM HUM PHAT SÖHA
OM SARWA PAPAM DAHANA VAJRA YE
For all of us disciples, our benefactors, and others, may
all obstacles to attaining liberation and omniscience, all
transgressions of the three vows, all natural non-virtues,
all inauspiciousness, all unclear concentration, all incorrect
recitation of mantras, all faults of excess and omission in
the rituals, and especially all negativities be purified
SHÄNTING KURUYE SÖHA.

Offering the sesame seeds to the retinues (2x)

OM DAKINIYE HUM HUM PHAT
OM LAME HUM HUM PHAT
OM KHANDAROHI HUM HUM PHAT
OM RUPINIYE HUM HUM PHAT

OM KARA KARA HUM HUM PHAT, OM PARTZANDI HUM
HUM PHAT, OM KURU KURU HUM HUM PHAT, OM
TZÄNDRIAKIYE HUM HUM PHAT, OM BÄNDHA BÄNDHA
HUM HUM PHAT, OM PARBHAWATIYE HUM HUM PHAT, OM
TrASAYA TrASAYA HUM HUM PHAT, OM MAHANASE HUM

HUM PHAT, OM KYOMBHAYA KYOMBHAYA HUM HUM
PHAT, OM BIRAMATIYE HUM HUM PHAT, OM HROM HROM
HUM HUM PHAT, OM KARWARIYE HUM HUM PHAT, OM
HRAH HRAH HUM HUM PHAT, OM LAMKESHÖRIYE HUM
HUM PHAT, OM PHAIM PHAIM HUM HUM PHAT, OM
DRUMATZAYE HUM HUM PHAT

OM PHAT PHAT HUM HUM PHAT, OM AIRAWATIYE HUM
HUM PHAT, OM DAHA DAHA HUM HUM PHAT, OM
MAHABHAIRAWI HUM HUM PHAT, OM PATSA PATSA HUM
HUM PHAT, OM BAYUBEGE HUM HUM PHAT, OM BHAKYA
BHAKYA BASA RUDHI ÄNTRA MALA WALAMBINE HUM
HUM PHAT, OM SURABHAKIYE HUM HUM PHAT, OM
GRIHANA GRIHANA SAPTA PATALA GATA BHUDZAMGAM
SARWAMPA TARDZAYA TARDZAYA HUM HUM PHAT, OM
SHAMADEWI HUM HUM PHAT, OM AKANDYA AKANDYA
HUM HUM PHAT, OM SUWATRE HUM HUM PHAT, OM HRIM
HRIM HUM HUM PHAT, OM HAYAKARNE HUM HUM PHAT,
OM GYÖN GYÖN HUM HUM PHAT, OM KHAGANANE HUM
HUM PHAT

OM KYAMA KYAMA HUM HUM PHAT, OM TZATRABEGE
HUM HUM PHAT, OM HAM HAM HUM HUM PHAT, OM
KHANDAROHI HUM HUM PHAT, OM HIM HIM HUM HUM
PHAT, OM SHAUNDINI HUM HUM PHAT, OM HUM HUM
HUM HUM PHAT, OM TZATRAWARMINI HUM HUM PHAT,
OM KILI KILI HUM HUM PHAT, OM SUBIRE HUM HUM PHAT,
OM SILI SILI HUM HUM PHAT, OM MAHABALE HUM HUM
PHAT, OM HILI HILI HUM HUM PHAT, OM TZATRAWARTINI
HUM HUM PHAT, OM DHILI DHILI HUM HUM PHAT, OM
MAHABIRE HUM HUM PHAT

OM KAKASE HUM HUM PHAT, OM ULUKASE HUM HUM
PHAT, OM SHÖNASE HUM HUM PHAT, OM SHUKARASE
HUM HUM PHAT, OM YAMADHATI HUM HUM PHAT, OM
YAMADUTI HUM HUM PHAT, OM YAMADANGTRINI HUM
HUM PHAT, OM YAMAMATANI HUM HUM PHAT

OM SARWA PAPAM DAHANA VAJRA YE
For all of us disciples, our benefactors, and others, may
all obstacles to attaining liberation and omniscience, all
transgressions of the three vows, all natural non-virtues,
all inauspiciousness, all unclear concentration, all incorrect
recitation of mantras, all faults of excess and omission in
the rituals, and especially all negativities be purified
SHÄNTING KURUYE SÖHA.

Offering the couch grass to the Principal Deity Father and Mother

OM SHRI VAJRA HE HE RU RU KAM HUM HUM PHAT DAKINI
    DZALA SHAMBARAM SÖHA
OM VAJRA BEROTZANIYE HUM HUM PHAT SÖHA
OM VAJRA AHYUKE
For all of us disciples, our benefactors, and others, may
all obstacles to attaining liberation and omniscience, all
transgressions of the three vows, all natural non-virtues,
all inauspiciousness, all unclear concentration, all incorrect
recitation of mantras, all faults of excess and omission in
the rituals, and especially all obstacles to increased life
span be purified SHÄNTING KURUYE SÖHA.

Offering the couch grass to the retinues (2x)

OM DAKINIYE HUM HUM PHAT
OM LAME HUM HUM PHAT
OM KHANDAROHI HUM HUM PHAT
OM RUPINIYE HUM HUM PHAT

OM KARA KARA HUM HUM PHAT, OM PARTZANDI HUM
HUM PHAT, OM KURU KURU HUM HUM PHAT, OM
TZÄNDRIAKIYE HUM HUM PHAT, OM BÄNDHA BÄNDHA
HUM HUM PHAT, OM PARBHAWATIYE HUM HUM PHAT, OM
TrASAYA TrASAYA HUM HUM PHAT, OM MAHANASE HUM
HUM PHAT, OM KYOMBHAYA KYOMBHAYA HUM HUM
PHAT, OM BIRAMATIYE HUM HUM PHAT, OM HROM HROM
HUM HUM PHAT, OM KARWARIYE HUM HUM PHAT, OM

HRAH HRAH HUM HUM PHAT, OM LAMKESHÖRIYE HUM
HUM PHAT, OM PHAIM PHAIM HUM HUM PHAT, OM
DRUMATZAYE HUM HUM PHAT

OM PHAT PHAT HUM HUM PHAT, OM AIRAWATIYE HUM
HUM PHAT, OM DAHA DAHA HUM HUM PHAT, OM
MAHABHAIRAWI HUM HUM PHAT, OM PATSA PATSA HUM
HUM PHAT, OM BAYUBEGE HUM HUM PHAT, OM BHAKYA
BHAKYA BASA RUDHI ÄNTRA MALA WALAMBINE HUM
HUM PHAT, OM SURABHAKIYE HUM HUM PHAT, OM
GRIHANA GRIHANA SAPTA PATALA GATA BHUDZAMGAM
SARWAMPA TARDZAYA TARDZAYA HUM HUM PHAT, OM
SHAMADEWI HUM HUM PHAT, OM AKANDYA AKANDYA
HUM HUM PHAT, OM SUWATRE HUM HUM PHAT, OM HRIM
HRIM HUM HUM PHAT, OM HAYAKARNE HUM HUM PHAT,
OM GYÖN GYÖN HUM HUM PHAT, OM KHAGANANE HUM
HUM PHAT

OM KYAMA KYAMA HUM HUM PHAT, OM TZATRABEGE
HUM HUM PHAT, OM HAM HAM HUM HUM PHAT, OM
KHANDAROHI HUM HUM PHAT, OM HIM HIM HUM HUM
PHAT, OM SHAUNDINI HUM HUM PHAT, OM HUM HUM
HUM HUM PHAT, OM TZATRAWARMINI HUM HUM PHAT,
OM KILI KILI HUM HUM PHAT, OM SUBIRE HUM HUM PHAT,
OM SILI SILI HUM HUM PHAT, OM MAHABALE HUM HUM
PHAT, OM HILI HILI HUM HUM PHAT, OM TZATRAWARTINI
HUM HUM PHAT, OM DHILI DHILI HUM HUM PHAT, OM
MAHABIRE HUM HUM PHAT

OM KAKASE HUM HUM PHAT, OM ULUKASE HUM HUM
PHAT, OM SHÖNASE HUM HUM PHAT, OM SHUKARASE
HUM HUM PHAT, OM YAMADHATI HUM HUM PHAT, OM
YAMADUTI HUM HUM PHAT, OM YAMADANGTRINI HUM
HUM PHAT, OM YAMAMATANI HUM HUM PHAT

OM VAJRA AHYUKE
For all of us disciples, our benefactors, and others, may
all obstacles to attaining liberation and omniscience, all
transgressions of the three vows, all natural non-virtues,
all inauspiciousness, all unclear concentration, all incorrect

recitation of mantras, all faults of excess and omission in the rituals, and especially all obstacles to increased life span be purified SHÄNTING KURUYE SÖHA.

Offering the rice to the Principal Deity Father and Mother

OM SHRI VAJRA HE HE RU RU KAM HUM HUM PHAT DAKINI
DZALA SHAMBARAM SÖHA
OM VAJRA BEROTZANIYE HUM HUM PHAT SÖHA
OM VAJRA PUTRAYE
For all of us disciples, our benefactors, and others, may all obstacles to attaining liberation and omniscience, all transgressions of the three vows, all natural non-virtues, all inauspiciousness, all unclear concentration, all incorrect recitation of mantras, all faults of excess and omission in the rituals, and especially all obstacles to increased merit be purified SHÄNTING KURUYE SÖHA.

Offering the rice to the retinues (2x)

OM DAKINIYE HUM HUM PHAT
OM LAME HUM HUM PHAT
OM KHANDAROHI HUM HUM PHAT
OM RUPINIYE HUM HUM PHAT

OM KARA KARA HUM HUM PHAT, OM PARTZANDI HUM
HUM PHAT, OM KURU KURU HUM HUM PHAT, OM
TZÄNDRIAKIYE HUM HUM PHAT, OM BÄNDHA BÄNDHA
HUM HUM PHAT, OM PARBHAWATIYE HUM HUM PHAT, OM
TrASAYA TrASAYA HUM HUM PHAT, OM MAHANASE HUM
HUM PHAT, OM KYOMBHAYA KYOMBHAYA HUM HUM
PHAT, OM BIRAMATIYE HUM HUM PHAT, OM HROM HROM
HUM HUM PHAT, OM KARWARIYE HUM HUM PHAT, OM
HRAH HRAH HUM HUM PHAT, OM LAMKESHÖRIYE HUM
HUM PHAT, OM PHAIM PHAIM HUM HUM PHAT, OM
DRUMATZAYE HUM HUM PHAT

OM PHAT PHAT HUM HUM PHAT, OM AIRAWATIYE HUM
HUM PHAT, OM DAHA DAHA HUM HUM PHAT, OM
MAHABHAIRAWI HUM HUM PHAT, OM PATSA PATSA HUM

HUM PHAT, OM BAYUBEGE HUM HUM PHAT, OM BHAKYA
BHAKYA BASA RUDHI ÄNTRA MALA WALAMBINE HUM
HUM PHAT, OM SURABHAKIYE HUM HUM PHAT, OM
GRIHANA GRIHANA SAPTA PATALA GATA BHUDZAMGAM
SARWAMPA TARDZAYA TARDZAYA HUM HUM PHAT, OM
SHAMADEWI HUM HUM PHAT, OM AKANDYA AKANDYA
HUM HUM PHAT, OM SUWATRE HUM HUM PHAT, OM HRIM
HRIM HUM HUM PHAT, OM HAYAKARNE HUM HUM PHAT,
OM GYÖN GYÖN HUM HUM PHAT, OM KHAGANANE HUM
HUM PHAT

OM KYAMA KYAMA HUM HUM PHAT, OM TZATRABEGE
HUM HUM PHAT, OM HAM HAM HUM HUM PHAT, OM
KHANDAROHI HUM HUM PHAT, OM HIM HIM HUM HUM
PHAT, OM SHAUNDINI HUM HUM PHAT, OM HUM HUM
HUM HUM PHAT, OM TZATRAWARMINI HUM HUM PHAT,
OM KILI KILI HUM HUM PHAT, OM SUBIRE HUM HUM PHAT,
OM SILI SILI HUM HUM PHAT, OM MAHABALE HUM HUM
PHAT, OM HILI HILI HUM HUM PHAT, OM TZATRAWARTINI
HUM HUM PHAT, OM DHILI DHILI HUM HUM PHAT, OM
MAHABIRE HUM HUM PHAT

OM KAKASE HUM HUM PHAT, OM ULUKASE HUM HUM
PHAT, OM SHÖNASE HUM HUM PHAT, OM SHUKARASE
HUM HUM PHAT, OM YAMADHATI HUM HUM PHAT, OM
YAMADUTI HUM HUM PHAT, OM YAMADANGTRINI HUM
HUM PHAT, OM YAMAMATANI HUM HUM PHAT

OM VAJRA PUTRAYE
For all of us disciples, our benefactors, and others, may
all obstacles to attaining liberation and omniscience, all
transgressions of the three vows, all natural non-virtues,
all inauspiciousness, all unclear concentration, all incorrect
recitation of mantras, all faults of excess and omission in
the rituals, and especially all obstacles to increased merit
be purified SHÄNTING KURUYE SÖHA.

Offering the crumbled cake mixed with yoghurt to the Principal Deity Father and Mother

OM SHRI VAJRA HE HE RU RU KAM HUM HUM PHAT DAKINI
DZALA SHAMBARAM SÖHA
OM VAJRA BEROTZANIYE HUM HUM PHAT SÖHA
OM SARWA SAMPA DE
For all of us disciples, our benefactors, and others, may
all obstacles to attaining liberation and omniscience, all
transgressions of the three vows, all natural non-virtues,
all inauspiciousness, all unclear concentration, all incorrect
recitation of mantras, all faults of excess and omission in
the rituals, and especially all obstacles to supreme bliss
be purified SHÄNTING KURUYE SÖHA.

Offering the crumbled cake mixed with yoghurt to the retinues (2x)

OM DAKINIYE HUM HUM PHAT
OM LAME HUM HUM PHAT
OM KHANDAROHI HUM HUM PHAT
OM RUPINIYE HUM HUM PHAT

OM KARA KARA HUM HUM PHAT, OM PARTZANDI HUM
HUM PHAT, OM KURU KURU HUM HUM PHAT, OM
TZÄNDRIAKIYE HUM HUM PHAT, OM BÄNDHA BÄNDHA
HUM HUM PHAT, OM PARBHAWATIYE HUM HUM PHAT, OM
TrASAYA TrASAYA HUM HUM PHAT, OM MAHANASE HUM
HUM PHAT, OM KYOMBHAYA KYOMBHAYA HUM HUM
PHAT, OM BIRAMATIYE HUM HUM PHAT, OM HROM HROM
HUM HUM PHAT, OM KARWARIYE HUM HUM PHAT, OM
HRAH HRAH HUM HUM PHAT, OM LAMKESHÖRIYE HUM
HUM PHAT, OM PHAIM PHAIM HUM HUM PHAT, OM
DRUMATZAYE HUM HUM PHAT

OM PHAT PHAT HUM HUM PHAT, OM AIRAWATIYE HUM
HUM PHAT, OM DAHA DAHA HUM HUM PHAT, OM
MAHABHAIRAWI HUM HUM PHAT, OM PATSA PATSA HUM
HUM PHAT, OM BAYUBEGE HUM HUM PHAT, OM BHAKYA
BHAKYA BASA RUDHI ÄNTRA MALA WALAMBINE HUM

HUM PHAT, OM SURABHAKIYE HUM HUM PHAT, OM
GRIHANA GRIHANA SAPTA PATALA GATA BHUDZAMGAM
SARWAMPA TARDZAYA TARDZAYA HUM HUM PHAT, OM
SHAMADEWI HUM HUM PHAT, OM AKANDYA AKANDYA
HUM HUM PHAT, OM SUWATRE HUM HUM PHAT, OM HRIM
HRIM HUM HUM PHAT, OM HAYAKARNE HUM HUM PHAT,
OM GYÖN GYÖN HUM HUM PHAT, OM KHAGANANE HUM
HUM PHAT

OM KYAMA KYAMA HUM HUM PHAT, OM TZATRABEGE
HUM HUM PHAT, OM HAM HAM HUM HUM PHAT, OM
KHANDAROHI HUM HUM PHAT, OM HIM HIM HUM HUM
PHAT, OM SHAUNDINI HUM HUM PHAT, OM HUM HUM
HUM HUM PHAT, OM TZATRAWARMINI HUM HUM PHAT,
OM KILI KILI HUM HUM PHAT, OM SUBIRE HUM HUM PHAT,
OM SILI SILI HUM HUM PHAT, OM MAHABALE HUM HUM
PHAT, OM HILI HILI HUM HUM PHAT, OM TZATRAWARTINI
HUM HUM PHAT, OM DHILI DHILI HUM HUM PHAT, OM
MAHABIRE HUM HUM PHAT

OM KAKASE HUM HUM PHAT, OM ULUKASE HUM HUM
PHAT, OM SHÖNASE HUM HUM PHAT, OM SHUKARASE
HUM HUM PHAT, OM YAMADHATI HUM HUM PHAT, OM
YAMADUTI HUM HUM PHAT, OM YAMADANGTRINI HUM
HUM PHAT, OM YAMAMATANI HUM HUM PHAT

OM SARWA SAMPA DE
For all of us disciples, our benefactors, and others, may
all obstacles to attaining liberation and omniscience, all
transgressions of the three vows, all natural non-virtues,
all inauspiciousness, all unclear concentration, all incorrect
recitation of mantras, all faults of excess and omission in
the rituals, and especially all obstacles to supreme bliss
be purified SHÄNTING KURUYE SÖHA.

Offering the kusha grass to the Principal Deity Father and Mother

OM SHRI VAJRA HE HE RU RU KAM HUM HUM PHAT DAKINI
DZALA SHAMBARAM SÖHA
OM VAJRA BEROTZANIYE HUM HUM PHAT SÖHA
OM AHTRATI HATA VAJRA YE
For all of us disciples, our benefactors, and others, may
all obstacles to attaining liberation and omniscience, all
transgressions of the three vows, all natural non-virtues,
all inauspiciousness, all unclear concentration, all incorrect
recitation of mantras, all faults of excess and omission in
the rituals, and especially all obstacles to supreme purity
be purified SHÄNTING KURUYE SÖHA.

Offering the kusha grass to the retinues (2x)

OM DAKINIYE HUM HUM PHAT
OM LAME HUM HUM PHAT
OM KHANDAROHI HUM HUM PHAT
OM RUPINIYE HUM HUM PHAT

OM KARA KARA HUM HUM PHAT, OM PARTZANDI HUM
HUM PHAT, OM KURU KURU HUM HUM PHAT, OM
TZÄNDRIAKIYE HUM HUM PHAT, OM BÄNDHA BÄNDHA
HUM HUM PHAT, OM PARBHAWATIYE HUM HUM PHAT, OM
TrASAYA TrASAYA HUM HUM PHAT, OM MAHANASE HUM
HUM PHAT, OM KYOMBHAYA KYOMBHAYA HUM HUM
PHAT, OM BIRAMATIYE HUM HUM PHAT, OM HROM HROM
HUM HUM PHAT, OM KARWARIYE HUM HUM PHAT, OM
HRAH HRAH HUM HUM PHAT, OM LAMKESHÖRIYE HUM
HUM PHAT, OM PHAIM PHAIM HUM HUM PHAT, OM
DRUMATZAYE HUM HUM PHAT

OM PHAT PHAT HUM HUM PHAT, OM AIRAWATIYE HUM
HUM PHAT, OM DAHA DAHA HUM HUM PHAT, OM
MAHABHAIRAWI HUM HUM PHAT, OM PATSA PATSA HUM
HUM PHAT, OM BAYUBEGE HUM HUM PHAT, OM BHAKYA
BHAKYA BASA RUDHI ÄNTRA MALA WALAMBINE HUM
HUM PHAT, OM SURABHAKIYE HUM HUM PHAT, OM

GRIHANA GRIHANA SAPTA PATALA GATA BHUDZAMGAM
SARWAMPA TARDZAYA TARDZAYA HUM HUM PHAT, OM
SHAMADEWI HUM HUM PHAT, OM AKANDYA AKANDYA
HUM HUM PHAT, OM SUWATRE HUM HUM PHAT, OM HRIM
HRIM HUM HUM PHAT, OM HAYAKARNE HUM HUM PHAT,
OM GYÖN GYÖN HUM HUM PHAT, OM KHAGANANE HUM
HUM PHAT

OM KYAMA KYAMA HUM HUM PHAT, OM TZATRABEGE
HUM HUM PHAT, OM HAM HAM HUM HUM PHAT, OM
KHANDAROHI HUM HUM PHAT, OM HIM HIM HUM HUM
PHAT, OM SHAUNDINI HUM HUM PHAT, OM HUM HUM
HUM HUM PHAT, OM TZATRAWARMINI HUM HUM PHAT,
OM KILI KILI HUM HUM PHAT, OM SUBIRE HUM HUM PHAT,
OM SILI SILI HUM HUM PHAT, OM MAHABALE HUM HUM
PHAT, OM HILI HILI HUM HUM PHAT, OM TZATRAWARTINI
HUM HUM PHAT, OM DHILI DHILI HUM HUM PHAT, OM
MAHABIRE HUM HUM PHAT

OM KAKASE HUM HUM PHAT, OM ULUKASE HUM HUM
PHAT, OM SHÖNASE HUM HUM PHAT, OM SHUKARASE
HUM HUM PHAT, OM YAMADHATI HUM HUM PHAT, OM
YAMADUTI HUM HUM PHAT, OM YAMADANGTRINI HUM
HUM PHAT, OM YAMAMATANI HUM HUM PHAT

OM AHTRATI HATA VAJRA YE
For all of us disciples, our benefactors, and others, may
all obstacles to attaining liberation and omniscience, all
transgressions of the three vows, all natural non-virtues,
all inauspiciousness, all unclear concentration, all incorrect
recitation of mantras, all faults of excess and omission in
the rituals, and especially all obstacles to supreme purity
be purified SHÄNTING KURUYE SÖHA.

Offering the white mustard seeds to the Principal Deity Father and Mother

OM SHRI VAJRA HE HE RU RU KAM HUM HUM PHAT
    DAKINI DZALA SHAMBARAM SÖHA
OM VAJRA BEROTZANIYE HUM HUM PHAT SÖHA

OM SARWA AHRTA SIDDHA YE
For all of us disciples, our benefactors, and others, may
all obstacles to attaining liberation and omniscience, all
transgressions of the three vows, all natural non-virtues,
all inauspiciousness, all unclear concentration, all incorrect
recitation of mantras, all faults of excess and omission in
the rituals, and especially all obstacles created by spirits
be purified SHÄNTING KURUYE SÖHA.

Offering the white mustard seeds to the retinues (2x)

OM DAKINIYE HUM HUM PHAT
OM LAME HUM HUM PHAT
OM KHANDAROHI HUM HUM PHAT
OM RUPINIYE HUM HUM PHAT

OM KARA KARA HUM HUM PHAT, OM PARTZANDI HUM
HUM PHAT, OM KURU KURU HUM HUM PHAT, OM
TZÄNDRIAKIYE HUM HUM PHAT, OM BÄNDHA BÄNDHA
HUM HUM PHAT, OM PARBHAWATIYE HUM HUM PHAT, OM
TrASAYA TrASAYA HUM HUM PHAT, OM MAHANASE HUM
HUM PHAT, OM KYOMBHAYA KYOMBHAYA HUM HUM
PHAT, OM BIRAMATIYE HUM HUM PHAT, OM HROM HROM
HUM HUM PHAT, OM KARWARIYE HUM HUM PHAT, OM
HRAH HRAH HUM HUM PHAT, OM LAMKESHÖRIYE HUM
HUM PHAT, OM PHAIM PHAIM HUM HUM PHAT, OM
DRUMATZAYE HUM HUM PHAT

OM PHAT PHAT HUM HUM PHAT, OM AIRAWATIYE HUM
HUM PHAT, OM DAHA DAHA HUM HUM PHAT, OM
MAHABHAIRAWI HUM HUM PHAT, OM PATSA PATSA HUM
HUM PHAT, OM BAYUBEGE HUM HUM PHAT, OM BHAKYA
BHAKYA BASA RUDHI ÄNTRA MALA WALAMBINE HUM
HUM PHAT, OM SURABHAKIYE HUM HUM PHAT, OM
GRIHANA GRIHANA SAPTA PATALA GATA BHUDZAMGAM
SARWAMPA TARDZAYA TARDZAYA HUM HUM PHAT, OM
SHAMADEWI HUM HUM PHAT, OM AKANDYA AKANDYA
HUM HUM PHAT, OM SUWATRE HUM HUM PHAT, OM HRIM
HRIM HUM HUM PHAT, OM HAYAKARNE HUM HUM PHAT,

OM GYÖN GYÖN HUM HUM PHAT, OM KHAGANANE HUM HUM PHAT

OM KYAMA KYAMA HUM HUM PHAT, OM TZATRABEGE HUM HUM PHAT, OM HAM HAM HUM HUM PHAT, OM KHANDAROHI HUM HUM PHAT, OM HIM HIM HUM HUM PHAT, OM SHAUNDINI HUM HUM PHAT, OM HUM HUM HUM HUM PHAT, OM TZATRAWARMINI HUM HUM PHAT, OM KILI KILI HUM HUM PHAT, OM SUBIRE HUM HUM PHAT, OM SILI SILI HUM HUM PHAT, OM MAHABALE HUM HUM PHAT, OM HILI HILI HUM HUM PHAT, OM TZATRAWARTINI HUM HUM PHAT, OM DHILI DHILI HUM HUM PHAT, OM MAHABIRE HUM HUM PHAT

OM KAKASE HUM HUM PHAT, OM ULUKASE HUM HUM PHAT, OM SHÖNASE HUM HUM PHAT, OM SHUKARASE HUM HUM PHAT, OM YAMADHATI HUM HUM PHAT, OM YAMADUTI HUM HUM PHAT, OM YAMADANGTRINI HUM HUM PHAT, OM YAMAMATANI HUM HUM PHAT

OM SARWA AHRTA SIDDHA YE
For all of us disciples, our benefactors, and others, may all obstacles to attaining liberation and omniscience, all transgressions of the three vows, all natural non-virtues, all inauspiciousness, all unclear concentration, all incorrect recitation of mantras, all faults of excess and omission in the rituals, and especially all obstacles created by spirits be purified SHÄNTING KURUYE SÖHA.

Offering the barley with husks to the Principal Deity Father and Mother

OM SHRI VAJRA HE HE RU RU KAM HUM HUM PHAT DAKINI DZALA SHAMBARAM SÖHA
OM VAJRA BEROTZANIYE HUM HUM PHAT SÖHA
OM VAJRA BINZAYE
For all of us disciples, our benefactors, and others, may all obstacles to attaining liberation and omniscience, all transgressions of the three vows, all natural non-virtues, all inauspiciousness, all unclear concentration, all incorrect

403

recitation of mantras, all faults of excess and omission in the rituals, and especially all obstacles to wealth and abundant harvests be purified SHÄNTING KURUYE SÖHA.

Offering the barley with husks to the retinues (2x)

OM DAKINIYE HUM HUM PHAT
OM LAME HUM HUM PHAT
OM KHANDAROHI HUM HUM PHAT
OM RUPINIYE HUM HUM PHAT

OM KARA KARA HUM HUM PHAT, OM PARTZANDI HUM HUM PHAT, OM KURU KURU HUM HUM PHAT, OM TZÄNDRIAKIYE HUM HUM PHAT, OM BÄNDHA BÄNDHA HUM HUM PHAT, OM PARBHAWATIYE HUM HUM PHAT, OM TrASAYA TrASAYA HUM HUM PHAT, OM MAHANASE HUM HUM PHAT, OM KYOMBHAYA KYOMBHAYA HUM HUM PHAT, OM BIRAMATIYE HUM HUM PHAT, OM HROM HROM HUM HUM PHAT, OM KARWARIYE HUM HUM PHAT, OM HRAH HRAH HUM HUM PHAT, OM LAMKESHÖRIYE HUM HUM PHAT, OM PHAIM PHAIM HUM HUM PHAT, OM DRUMATZAYE HUM HUM PHAT

OM PHAT PHAT HUM HUM PHAT, OM AIRAWATIYE HUM HUM PHAT, OM DAHA DAHA HUM HUM PHAT, OM MAHABHAIRAWI HUM HUM PHAT, OM PATSA PATSA HUM HUM PHAT, OM BAYUBEGE HUM HUM PHAT, OM BHAKYA BHAKYA BASA RUDHI ÄNTRA MALA WALAMBINE HUM HUM PHAT, OM SURABHAKIYE HUM HUM PHAT, OM GRIHANA GRIHANA SAPTA PATALA GATA BHUDZAMGAM SARWAMPA TARDZAYA TARDZAYA HUM HUM PHAT, OM SHAMADEWI HUM HUM PHAT, OM AKANDYA AKANDYA HUM HUM PHAT, OM SUWATRE HUM HUM PHAT, OM HRIM HRIM HUM HUM PHAT, OM HAYAKARNE HUM HUM PHAT, OM GYÖN GYÖN HUM HUM PHAT, OM KHAGANANE HUM HUM PHAT

OM KYAMA KYAMA HUM HUM PHAT, OM TZATRABEGE HUM HUM PHAT, OM HAM HAM HUM HUM PHAT, OM KHANDAROHI HUM HUM PHAT, OM HIM HIM HUM HUM

PHAT, OM SHAUNDINI HUM HUM PHAT, OM HUM HUM
HUM HUM PHAT, OM TZATRAWARMINI HUM HUM PHAT,
OM KILI KILI HUM HUM PHAT, OM SUBIRE HUM HUM PHAT,
OM SILI SILI HUM HUM PHAT, OM MAHABALE HUM HUM
PHAT, OM HILI HILI HUM HUM PHAT, OM TZATRAWARTINI
HUM HUM PHAT, OM DHILI DHILI HUM HUM PHAT, OM
MAHABIRE HUM HUM PHAT

OM KAKASE HUM HUM PHAT, OM ULUKASE HUM HUM
PHAT, OM SHÖNASE HUM HUM PHAT, OM SHUKARASE
HUM HUM PHAT, OM YAMADHATI HUM HUM PHAT, OM
YAMADUTI HUM HUM PHAT, OM YAMADANGTRINI HUM
HUM PHAT, OM YAMAMATANI HUM HUM PHAT

OM VAJRA BINZAYE
For all of us disciples, our benefactors, and others, may
all obstacles to attaining liberation and omniscience, all
transgressions of the three vows, all natural non-virtues,
all inauspiciousness, all unclear concentration, all incorrect
recitation of mantras, all faults of excess and omission in
the rituals, and especially all obstacles to wealth and
abundant harvests be purified SHÄNTING KURUYE SÖHA.

Offering the barley without husks to the Principal Deity Father and Mother

OM SHRI VAJRA HE HE RU RU KAM HUM HUM PHAT DAKINI
    DZALA SHAMBARAM SÖHA
OM VAJRA BEROTZANIYE HUM HUM PHAT SÖHA
OM MAHA BEGAYE
For all of us disciples, our benefactors, and others, may
all obstacles to attaining liberation and omniscience, all
transgressions of the three vows, all natural non-virtues,
all inauspiciousness, all unclear concentration, all incorrect
recitation of mantras, all faults of excess and omission in
the rituals, and especially all obstacles to excellent quick
mental powers be purified SHÄNTING KURUYE SÖHA.

Offering the barley without husks to the retinues (2x)

OM DAKINIYE HUM HUM PHAT
OM LAME HUM HUM PHAT
OM KHANDAROHI HUM HUM PHAT
OM RUPINIYE HUM HUM PHAT

OM KARA KARA HUM HUM PHAT, OM PARTZANDI HUM
HUM PHAT, OM KURU KURU HUM HUM PHAT, OM
TZÄNDRIAKIYE HUM HUM PHAT, OM BÄNDHA BÄNDHA
HUM HUM PHAT, OM PARBHAWATIYE HUM HUM PHAT, OM
TrASAYA TrASAYA HUM HUM PHAT, OM MAHANASE HUM
HUM PHAT, OM KYOMBHAYA KYOMBHAYA HUM HUM
PHAT, OM BIRAMATIYE HUM HUM PHAT, OM HROM HROM
HUM HUM PHAT, OM KARWARIYE HUM HUM PHAT, OM
HRAH HRAH HUM HUM PHAT, OM LAMKESHÖRIYE HUM
HUM PHAT, OM PHAIM PHAIM HUM HUM PHAT, OM
DRUMATZAYE HUM HUM PHAT

OM PHAT PHAT HUM HUM PHAT, OM AIRAWATIYE HUM
HUM PHAT, OM DAHA DAHA HUM HUM PHAT, OM
MAHABHAIRAWI HUM HUM PHAT, OM PATSA PATSA HUM
HUM PHAT, OM BAYUBEGE HUM HUM PHAT, OM BHAKYA
BHAKYA BASA RUDHI ÄNTRA MALA WALAMBINE HUM
HUM PHAT, OM SURABHAKIYE HUM HUM PHAT, OM
GRIHANA GRIHANA SAPTA PATALA GATA BHUDZAMGAM
SARWAMPA TARDZAYA TARDZAYA HUM HUM PHAT, OM
SHAMADEWI HUM HUM PHAT, OM AKANDYA AKANDYA
HUM HUM PHAT, OM SUWATRE HUM HUM PHAT, OM HRIM
HRIM HUM HUM PHAT, OM HAYAKARNE HUM HUM PHAT,
OM GYÖN GYÖN HUM HUM PHAT, OM KHAGANANE HUM
HUM PHAT

OM KYAMA KYAMA HUM HUM PHAT, OM TZATRABEGE
HUM HUM PHAT, OM HAM HAM HUM HUM PHAT, OM
KHANDAROHI HUM HUM PHAT, OM HIM HIM HUM HUM
PHAT, OM SHAUNDINI HUM HUM PHAT, OM HUM HUM
HUM HUM PHAT, OM TZATRAWARMINI HUM HUM PHAT,
OM KILI KILI HUM HUM PHAT, OM SUBIRE HUM HUM PHAT,
OM SILI SILI HUM HUM PHAT, OM MAHABALE HUM HUM

PHAT, OM HILI HILI HUM HUM PHAT, OM TZATRAWARTINI
HUM HUM PHAT, OM DHILI DHILI HUM HUM PHAT, OM
MAHABIRE HUM HUM PHAT

OM KAKASE HUM HUM PHAT, OM ULUKASE HUM HUM
PHAT, OM SHÖNASE HUM HUM PHAT, OM SHUKARASE
HUM HUM PHAT, OM YAMADHATI HUM HUM PHAT, OM
YAMADUTI HUM HUM PHAT, OM YAMADANGTRINI HUM
HUM PHAT, OM YAMAMATANI HUM HUM PHAT

OM MAHA BEGAYE
For all of us disciples, our benefactors, and others, may
all obstacles to attaining liberation and omniscience, all
transgressions of the three vows, all natural non-virtues,
all inauspiciousness, all unclear concentration, all incorrect
recitation of mantras, all faults of excess and omission in
the rituals, and especially all obstacles to excellent quick
mental powers be purified SHÄNTING KURUYE SÖHA.

Offering the peas to the Principal Deity Father and Mother

OM SHRI VAJRA HE HE RU RU KAM HUM HUM PHAT DAKINI
     DZALA SHAMBARAM SÖHA
OM VAJRA BEROTZANIYE HUM HUM PHAT SÖHA
OM MAHA BALAYE
For all of us disciples, our benefactors, and others, may
all obstacles to attaining liberation and omniscience, all
transgressions of the three vows, all natural non-virtues,
all inauspiciousness, all unclear concentration, all incorrect
recitation of mantras, all faults of excess and omission in
the rituals, and especially all obstacles to increased
strength be purified SHÄNTING KURUYE SÖHA.

Offering the peas to the retinues (2x)

OM DAKINIYE HUM HUM PHAT
OM LAME HUM HUM PHAT
OM KHANDAROHI HUM HUM PHAT
OM RUPINIYE HUM HUM PHAT

OM KARA KARA HUM HUM PHAT, OM PARTZANDI HUM
HUM PHAT, OM KURU KURU HUM HUM PHAT, OM
TZÄNDRIAKIYE HUM HUM PHAT, OM BÄNDHA BÄNDHA
HUM HUM PHAT, OM PARBHAWATIYE HUM HUM PHAT, OM
TrASAYA TrASAYA HUM HUM PHAT, OM MAHANASE HUM
HUM PHAT, OM KYOMBHAYA KYOMBHAYA HUM HUM
PHAT, OM BIRAMATIYE HUM HUM PHAT, OM HROM HROM
HUM HUM PHAT, OM KARWARIYE HUM HUM PHAT, OM
HRAH HRAH HUM HUM PHAT, OM LAMKESHÖRIYE HUM
HUM PHAT, OM PHAIM PHAIM HUM HUM PHAT, OM
DRUMATZAYE HUM HUM PHAT

OM PHAT PHAT HUM HUM PHAT, OM AIRAWATIYE HUM
HUM PHAT, OM DAHA DAHA HUM HUM PHAT, OM
MAHABHAIRAWI HUM HUM PHAT, OM PATSA PATSA HUM
HUM PHAT, OM BAYUBEGE HUM HUM PHAT, OM BHAKYA
BHAKYA BASA RUDHI ÄNTRA MALA WALAMBINE HUM
HUM PHAT, OM SURABHAKIYE HUM HUM PHAT, OM
GRIHANA GRIHANA SAPTA PATALA GATA BHUDZAMGAM
SARWAMPA TARDZAYA TARDZAYA HUM HUM PHAT, OM
SHAMADEWI HUM HUM PHAT, OM AKANDYA AKANDYA
HUM HUM PHAT, OM SUWATRE HUM HUM PHAT, OM HRIM
HRIM HUM HUM PHAT, OM HAYAKARNE HUM HUM PHAT,
OM GYÖN GYÖN HUM HUM PHAT, OM KHAGANANE HUM
HUM PHAT

OM KYAMA KYAMA HUM HUM PHAT, OM TZATRABEGE
HUM HUM PHAT, OM HAM HAM HUM HUM PHAT, OM
KHANDAROHI HUM HUM PHAT, OM HIM HIM HUM HUM
PHAT, OM SHAUNDINI HUM HUM PHAT, OM HUM HUM
HUM HUM PHAT, OM TZATRAWARMINI HUM HUM PHAT,
OM KILI KILI HUM HUM PHAT, OM SUBIRE HUM HUM PHAT,
OM SILI SILI HUM HUM PHAT, OM MAHABALE HUM HUM
PHAT, OM HILI HILI HUM HUM PHAT, OM TZATRAWARTINI
HUM HUM PHAT, OM DHILI DHILI HUM HUM PHAT, OM
MAHABIRE HUM HUM PHAT

OM KAKASE HUM HUM PHAT, OM ULUKASE HUM HUM
PHAT, OM SHÖNASE HUM HUM PHAT, OM SHUKARASE
HUM HUM PHAT, OM YAMADHATI HUM HUM PHAT, OM

YAMADUTI HUM HUM PHAT, OM YAMADANGTRINI HUM
HUM PHAT, OM YAMAMATANI HUM HUM PHAT

OM MAHA BALAYE
For all of us disciples, our benefactors, and others, may
all obstacles to attaining liberation and omniscience, all
transgressions of the three vows, all natural non-virtues,
all inauspiciousness, all unclear concentration, all incorrect
recitation of mantras, all faults of excess and omission in
the rituals, and especially all obstacles to increased
strength be purified SHÄNTING KURUYE SÖHA.

Offering the wheat to the Principal Deity Father and Mother

OM SHRI VAJRA HE HE RU RU KAM HUM HUM PHAT DAKINI
    DZALA SHAMBARAM SÖHA
OM VAJRA BEROTZANIYE HUM HUM PHAT SÖHA
OM VAJRA GHAMA RI
For all of us disciples, our benefactors, and others, may
all obstacles to attaining liberation and omniscience, all
transgressions of the three vows, all natural non-virtues,
all inauspiciousness, all unclear concentration, all incorrect
recitation of mantras, all faults of excess and omission in
the rituals, and especially all sickness be purified
SHÄNTING KURUYE SÖHA.

Offering the wheat to the retinues (2x)

OM DAKINIYE HUM HUM PHAT
OM LAME HUM HUM PHAT
OM KHANDAROHI HUM HUM PHAT
OM RUPINIYE HUM HUM PHAT

OM KARA KARA HUM HUM PHAT, OM PARTZANDI HUM
HUM PHAT, OM KURU KURU HUM HUM PHAT, OM
TZÄNDRIAKIYE HUM HUM PHAT, OM BÄNDHA BÄNDHA
HUM HUM PHAT, OM PARBHAWATIYE HUM HUM PHAT, OM
TrASAYA TrASAYA HUM HUM PHAT, OM MAHANASE HUM
HUM PHAT, OM KYOMBHAYA KYOMBHAYA HUM HUM

PHAT, OM BIRAMATIYE HUM HUM PHAT, OM HROM HROM
HUM HUM PHAT, OM KARWARIYE HUM HUM PHAT, OM
HRAH HRAH HUM HUM PHAT, OM LAMKESHÖRIYE HUM
HUM PHAT, OM PHAIM PHAIM HUM HUM PHAT, OM
DRUMATZAYE HUM HUM PHAT

OM PHAT PHAT HUM HUM PHAT, OM AIRAWATIYE HUM
HUM PHAT, OM DAHA DAHA HUM HUM PHAT, OM
MAHABHAIRAWI HUM HUM PHAT, OM PATSA PATSA HUM
HUM PHAT, OM BAYUBEGE HUM HUM PHAT, OM BHAKYA
BHAKYA BASA RUDHI ÄNTRA MALA WALAMBINE HUM
HUM PHAT, OM SURABHAKIYE HUM HUM PHAT, OM
GRIHANA GRIHANA SAPTA PATALA GATA BHUDZAMGAM
SARWAMPA TARDZAYA TARDZAYA HUM HUM PHAT, OM
SHAMADEWI HUM HUM PHAT, OM AKANDYA AKANDYA
HUM HUM PHAT, OM SUWATRE HUM HUM PHAT, OM HRIM
HRIM HUM HUM PHAT, OM HAYAKARNE HUM HUM PHAT,
OM GYÖN GYÖN HUM HUM PHAT, OM KHAGANANE HUM
HUM PHAT

OM KYAMA KYAMA HUM HUM PHAT, OM TZATRABEGE
HUM HUM PHAT, OM HAM HAM HUM HUM PHAT, OM
KHANDAROHI HUM HUM PHAT, OM HIM HIM HUM HUM
PHAT, OM SHAUNDINI HUM HUM PHAT, OM HUM HUM
HUM HUM PHAT, OM TZATRAWARMINI HUM HUM PHAT,
OM KILI KILI HUM HUM PHAT, OM SUBIRE HUM HUM PHAT,
OM SILI SILI HUM HUM PHAT, OM MAHABALE HUM HUM
PHAT, OM HILI HILI HUM HUM PHAT, OM TZATRAWARTINI
HUM HUM PHAT, OM DHILI DHILI HUM HUM PHAT, OM
MAHABIRE HUM HUM PHAT

OM KAKASE HUM HUM PHAT, OM ULUKASE HUM HUM
PHAT, OM SHÖNASE HUM HUM PHAT, OM SHUKARASE
HUM HUM PHAT, OM YAMADHATI HUM HUM PHAT, OM
YAMADUTI HUM HUM PHAT, OM YAMADANGTRINI HUM
HUM PHAT, OM YAMAMATANI HUM HUM PHAT

OM VAJRA GHAMA RI
For all of us disciples, our benefactors, and others, may
all obstacles to attaining liberation and omniscience, all

transgressions of the three vows, all natural non-virtues, all inauspiciousness, all unclear concentration, all incorrect recitation of mantras, all faults of excess and omission in the rituals, and especially all sickness be purified SHÄNTING KURUYE SÖHA.

Offering the special pacifying substance to the Principal Deity Father and Mother

Since there is no separate mantra for the special pacifying substance, it should be offered with the Deities' mantras:

OM SHRI VAJRA HE HE RU RU KAM HUM HUM PHAT DAKINI DZALA SHAMBARAM SÖHA

OM VAJRA BEROTZANIYE HUM HUM PHAT SÖHA

For all of us disciples, our benefactors, and others, may all obstacles to attaining liberation and omniscience, all transgressions of the three vows, all natural non-virtues, all inauspiciousness, all unclear concentration, all incorrect recitation of mantras, all faults of excess and omission in the rituals, and especially all obstacles to accomplishing supreme attainments be purified SHÄNTING KURUYE SÖHA.

Offering the special pacifying substance to the retinues

(2x)

OM DAKINIYE HUM HUM PHAT
OM LAME HUM HUM PHAT
OM KHANDAROHI HUM HUM PHAT
OM RUPINIYE HUM HUM PHAT

OM KARA KARA HUM HUM PHAT, OM PARTZANDI HUM HUM PHAT, OM KURU KURU HUM HUM PHAT, OM TZÄNDRIAKIYE HUM HUM PHAT, OM BÄNDHA BÄNDHA HUM HUM PHAT, OM PARBHAWATIYE HUM HUM PHAT, OM TrASAYA TrASAYA HUM HUM PHAT, OM MAHANASE HUM HUM PHAT, OM KYOMBHAYA KYOMBHAYA HUM HUM PHAT, OM BIRAMATIYE HUM HUM PHAT, OM HROM HROM HUM HUM PHAT, OM KARWARIYE HUM HUM PHAT, OM HRAH HRAH HUM HUM PHAT, OM LAMKESHÖRIYE HUM

HUM PHAT, OM PHAIM PHAIM HUM HUM PHAT, OM
DRUMATZAYE HUM HUM PHAT

OM PHAT PHAT HUM HUM PHAT, OM AIRAWATIYE HUM
HUM PHAT, OM DAHA DAHA HUM HUM PHAT, OM
MAHABHAIRAWI HUM HUM PHAT, OM PATSA PATSA HUM
HUM PHAT, OM BAYUBEGE HUM HUM PHAT, OM BHAKYA
BHAKYA BASA RUDHI ÄNTRA MALA WALAMBINE HUM
HUM PHAT, OM SURABHAKIYE HUM HUM PHAT, OM
GRIHANA GRIHANA SAPTA PATALA GATA BHUDZAMGAM
SARWAMPA TARDZAYA TARDZAYA HUM HUM PHAT, OM
SHAMADEWI HUM HUM PHAT, OM AKANDYA AKANDYA
HUM HUM PHAT, OM SUWATRE HUM HUM PHAT, OM HRIM
HRIM HUM HUM PHAT, OM HAYAKARNE HUM HUM PHAT,
OM GYÖN GYÖN HUM HUM PHAT, OM KHAGANANE HUM
HUM PHAT

OM KYAMA KYAMA HUM HUM PHAT, OM TZATRABEGE
HUM HUM PHAT, OM HAM HAM HUM HUM PHAT, OM
KHANDAROHI HUM HUM PHAT, OM HIM HIM HUM HUM
PHAT, OM SHAUNDINI HUM HUM PHAT, OM HUM HUM
HUM HUM PHAT, OM TZATRAWARMINI HUM HUM PHAT,
OM KILI KILI HUM HUM PHAT, OM SUBIRE HUM HUM PHAT,
OM SILI SILI HUM HUM PHAT, OM MAHABALE HUM HUM
PHAT, OM HILI HILI HUM HUM PHAT, OM TZATRAWARTINI
HUM HUM PHAT, OM DHILI DHILI HUM HUM PHAT, OM
MAHABIRE HUM HUM PHAT

OM KAKASE HUM HUM PHAT, OM ULUKASE HUM HUM
PHAT, OM SHÖNASE HUM HUM PHAT, OM SHUKARASE
HUM HUM PHAT, OM YAMADHATI HUM HUM PHAT, OM
YAMADUTI HUM HUM PHAT, OM YAMADANGTRINI HUM
HUM PHAT, OM YAMAMATANI HUM HUM PHAT

For all of us disciples, our benefactors, and others, may
all obstacles to attaining liberation and omniscience, all
transgressions of the three vows, all natural non-virtues,
all inauspiciousness, all unclear concentration, all impure
recitation of mantras, all faults of excess and omission in
the rituals, and especially all obstacles to accomplishing
supreme attainments be purified SHÄNTING KURUYE SÖHA.

Ablution

Now contemplate:

From the Deities' hearts emanate Buddhas holding aloft white vases brimming with white nectar. Those whom we wish to benefit are sitting on moon mandalas. They receive ablution, whereby all their sickness, spirits, negativities, obstructions, and so forth are purified; and their bodies become as clear as crystal.

Offer three or seven ladles of butter while reciting:

OM HRIH HA HA HUM HUM PHAT

Offering the garments

Imagine offering new garments to the Fire Deity while reciting:

OM VAJRA WASA SÄ SÖHA

Offering the tambula torma

Offer the tambula to the Fire Deity while reciting:

OM VAJRA TAMBULAYE SÖHA

Outer offerings

OM VAJRA PUPE AH HUM SÖHA
OM VAJRA DHUPE AH HUM SÖHA
OM VAJRA DIWE AH HUM SÖHA
OM VAJRA GÄNDHE AH HUM SÖHA
OM VAJRA NEWIDE AH HUM SÖHA
OM VAJRA SHAPTA AH HUM SÖHA

OM VAJRA WINI HUM HUM PHAT
OM VAJRA WAMSHE HUM HUM PHAT
OM VAJRA MITAMGI HUM HUM PHAT
OM VAJRA MURANDZE HUM HUM PHAT

OM VAJRA HASÄ HUM HUM PHAT
OM VAJRA LASÄ HUM HUM PHAT
OM VAJRA GIRTI HUM HUM PHAT
OM VAJRA NIRTÄ HUM HUM PHAT

OM VAJRA PUPE HUM HUM PHAT
OM VAJRA DHUPE HUM HUM PHAT
OM VAJRA DIWE HUM HUM PHAT
OM VAJRA GÄNDHE HUM HUM PHAT

OM RUPA BENZ HUM HUM PHAT
OM RASA BENZ HUM HUM PHAT
OM PARSHE BENZ HUM HUM PHAT
OM DHARMA DHATU BENZ HUM HUM PHAT

Inner offering

OM SHRI VAJRA HE HE RU RU KAM HUM HUM PHAT DAKINI
  DZALA SHAMBARAM SÖHA OM AH HUM

OM VAJRA BEROTZANIYE HUM HUM PHAT SÖHA OM AH HUM

OM RIM RIM LIM LIM, KAM KHAM GAM GHAM NGAM,
TSAM TSHAM DZAM DZHAM NYAM, TrAM THrAM DrAM
DHrAM NAM, TAM THAM DAM DHAM NAM, PAM PHAM
BAM BHAM, YAM RAM LAM WAM, SHAM KAM SAM HAM
HUM HUM PHAT OM AH HUM

Eight lines of praise to the Father

OM I prostrate to the Blessed One, Lord of the Heroes
  HUM HUM PHAT
OM To you with a brilliance equal to the fire of the great
  aeon HUM HUM PHAT
OM To you with an inexhaustible topknot HUM HUM PHAT
OM To you with a fearsome face and bared fangs HUM
  HUM PHAT
OM To you whose thousand arms blaze with light HUM
  HUM PHAT
OM To you who hold an axe, an uplifted noose, a spear,
  and a khatanga HUM HUM PHAT
OM To you who wear a tiger-skin garment HUM HUM PHAT
OM I bow to you whose great smoke-coloured body
  dispels obstructions HUM HUM PHAT

Eight lines of praise to the Mother

OM I prostrate to Vajravarahi, the Blessed Mother HUM
HUM PHAT

OM To the Superior and powerful Knowledge Lady
unconquered by the three realms HUM HUM PHAT

OM To you who destroy all fears of evil spirits with your
great vajra HUM HUM PHAT

OM To you with controlling eyes who remain as the vajra
seat unconquered by others HUM HUM PHAT

OM To you whose wrathful fierce form desiccates Brahma
HUM HUM PHAT

OM To you who terrify and dry up demons, conquering
those in other directions HUM HUM PHAT

OM To you who conquer all those who make us dull,
rigid, and confused HUM HUM PHAT

OM I bow to Vajravarahi, the Great Mother, the Dakini
consort who fulfils all desires HUM HUM PHAT

Prostration

OM PARNA MAMI SARWA TATHAGATÄN

Now offer drinking water:

OM AH HRIH PRAVARA SÄKARAM AHRGHAM PARTITZA
HUM SÖHA

Requesting forbearance

*To purify any faults of excess or omission, such as lacking
any of the ritual articles, press your palms together at your
heart while holding a flower and recite:*

Whatever I have done out of confusion,
Even the slightest faulty action,
O Protector, because you are the refuge of all beings,
It is fitting for you to be patient with these.

Whatever mistakes I have made
Through not finding, not understanding,
Or not having the ability,
Please, O Protector, be patient with all of these.

Requesting fulfilment of wishes

O Blessed Ones, the assembly of Deities of Glorious Chakrasambara, for all of us disciples, our benefactors, and others, please completely pacify all adverse circumstances and unfavourable conditions, and our negativities, obstructions, sickness, spirits, obstacles, and so forth accumulated during beginningless lives in samsara. Please increase our life span, merit, glory, wealth, good qualities of scripture and realization, and so forth. Most especially, please bless us to generate within our mental continuum every single stage of the common and uncommon paths and quickly to attain the state of the union of Heruka.

You can make either this general request or specific requests for wishes to be fulfilled.

Now recite several times:

OM VAJRA SATTÖ AH

Purifying any mistakes made during this practice with the hundred-letter mantra of Heruka

OM VAJRA HERUKA SAMAYA, MANU PALAYA, HERUKA TENO PATITA, DRIDHO ME BHAWA, SUTO KAYO ME BHAWA, SUPO KAYO ME BHAWA, ANURAKTO ME BHAWA, SARWA SIDDHI ME PRAYATZA, SARWA KARMA SUTZA ME, TZITAM SHRIYAM KURU HUM, HA HA HA HA HO BHAGAWÄN, VAJRA HERUKA MA ME MUNTSA, HERUKA BHAWA, MAHA SAMAYA SATTÖ AH HUM PHAT

Departure of the supramundane Fire Deities

OM
You who fulfil the welfare of all living beings
And bestow attainments as they are needed,
Please return to the Land of the Buddhas
And return here again in the future.

OM AH: OM SHRI VAJRA HE HE RU RU KAM HUM HUM PHAT
DAKINI DZALA SHAMBARAM SÖHA HUM MU

Imagine:

The wisdom beings return to their natural abodes and the commitment beings dissolve into me.

FINAL OFFERING TO MUNDANE FIRE DEITY

Now make offerings to mundane Fire Deity on the hearth:

OM AGNIYE AHDIBÄ AHDIBÄ AMBISHA AMBISHA MAHA
SHRIYE HAMBÄ KABÄ BAHA NAYE VAJRA PUPE PARTITZA
HUM SÖHA
VAJRA DHUPE PARTITZA HUM SÖHA
VAJRA DIWE PARTITZA HUM SÖHA
VAJRA GÄNDHE PARTITZA HUM SÖHA
VAJRA NEWIDE PARTITZA HUM SÖHA
VAJRA SHAPTA PARTITZA HUM SÖHA

and the inner offering:

OM AGNIYE AHDIBÄ AHDIBÄ AMBISHA AMBISHA MAHA
SHRIYE HAMBÄ KABÄ BAHA NAYA OM AH HUM

Now offer water for sprinkling and water for the mouth:

OM AH HRIH PRAVARA SÄKARAM PROKYANAM PARTITZA
HUM SÖHA
OM AH HRIH PRAVARA SÄKARAM ÄNTZAMANAM PARTITZA
HUM SÖHA

Offering the tambula torma

OM VAJRA TAMBULAYE SÖHA

Offering the garments

OM VAJRA WASA SÄ SÖHA

Offering the burning substances

Now offer the remaining burning substances to mundane Fire Deity:

Offering the milkwood

The milkwood becomes nectar, the nature of the Bodhi Tree.
OM AGNIYE AHDIBÄ AHDIBÄ AMBISHA AMBISHA MAHA
SHRIYE HAMBÄ KABÄ BAHA NAYE
OM BODHI PIKYAYE
For all of us disciples, our benefactors, and others, may
all obstacles to attaining liberation and omniscience, all
transgressions of the three vows, all natural non-virtues,
all inauspiciousness, all unclear concentration, all incorrect
recitation of mantras, all faults of excess and omission in
the rituals, and especially all obstacles to increased vitality
be purified SHÄNTING KURUYE SÖHA.

Offering the molten butter

OM AGNIYE AHDIBÄ AHDIBÄ AMBISHA AMBISHA MAHA
SHRIYE HAMBÄ KABÄ BAHA NAYE
OM AGNIYE
For all of us disciples, our benefactors, and others, may
all obstacles to attaining liberation and omniscience, all
transgressions of the three vows, all natural non-virtues,
all inauspiciousness, all unclear concentration, all incorrect
recitation of mantras, all faults of excess and omission in
the rituals, and especially all obstacles to increased wealth
be purified SHÄNTING KURUYE SÖHA.

Offering the sesame seeds

OM AGNIYE AHDIBÄ AHDIBÄ AMBISHA AMBISHA MAHA
SHRIYE HAMBÄ KABÄ BAHA NAYE
OM SARWA PAPAM DAHANA VAJRAYE
For all of us disciples, our benefactors, and others, may
all obstacles to attaining liberation and omniscience, all
transgressions of the three vows, all natural non-virtues,
all inauspiciousness, all unclear concentration, all incorrect
recitation of mantras, all faults of excess and omission in
the rituals, and especially all negativities be purified
SHÄNTING KURUYE SÖHA.

Offering the couch grass

OM AGNIYE AHDIBÄ AHDIBÄ AMBISHA AMBISHA MAHA
  SHRIYE HAMBÄ KABÄ BAHA NAYE
OM VAJRA AHYUKE
For all of us disciples, our benefactors, and others, may
all obstacles to attaining liberation and omniscience, all
transgressions of the three vows, all natural non-virtues,
all inauspiciousness, all unclear concentration, all incorrect
recitation of mantras, all faults of excess and omission in
the rituals, and especially all obstacles to increased life
span be purified SHÄNTING KURUYE SÖHA.

Offering the rice

OM AGNIYE AHDIBÄ AHDIBÄ AMBISHA AMBISHA MAHA
  SHRIYE HAMBÄ KABÄ BAHA NAYE
OM VAJRA PUTRAYE
For all of us disciples, our benefactors, and others, may
all obstacles to attaining liberation and omniscience, all
transgressions of the three vows, all natural non-virtues,
all inauspiciousness, all unclear concentration, all incorrect
recitation of mantras, all faults of excess and omission in
the rituals, and especially all obstacles to increased merit
be purified SHÄNTING KURUYE SÖHA.

Offering the crumbled cake mixed with yoghurt

OM AGNIYE AHDIBÄ AHDIBÄ AMBISHA AMBISHA MAHA
  SHRIYE HAMBÄ KABÄ BAHA NAYE
OM SARWA SAMPA DE
For all of us disciples, our benefactors, and others, may
all obstacles to attaining liberation and omniscience, all
transgressions of the three vows, all natural non-virtues,
all inauspiciousness, all unclear concentration, all incorrect
recitation of mantras, all faults of excess and omission in
the rituals, and especially all obstacles to supreme bliss
be purified SHÄNTING KURUYE SÖHA.

Offering the kusha grass

OM AGNIYE AHDIBÄ AHDIBÄ AMBISHA AMBISHA MAHA
  SHRIYE HAMBÄ KABÄ BAHA NAYE
OM AHTRATI HATA VAJRA YE
For all of us disciples, our benefactors, and others, may
all obstacles to attaining liberation and omniscience, all
transgressions of the three vows, all natural non-virtues,
all inauspiciousness, all unclear concentration, all incorrect
recitation of mantras, all faults of excess and omission in
the rituals, and especially all obstacles to supreme purity
be purified SHÄNTING KURUYE SÖHA.

Offering the white mustard seeds

OM AGNIYE AHDIBÄ AHDIBÄ AMBISHA AMBISHA MAHA
  SHRIYE HAMBÄ KABÄ BAHA NAYE
OM SARWA AHRTA SIDDHA YE
For all of us disciples, our benefactors, and others, may
all obstacles to attaining liberation and omniscience, all
transgressions of the three vows, all natural non-virtues,
all inauspiciousness, all unclear concentration, all incorrect
recitation of mantras, all faults of excess and omission in
the rituals, and especially all obstacles created by spirits
be purified SHÄNTING KURUYE SÖHA.

Offering the barley with husks

OM AGNIYE AHDIBÄ AHDIBÄ AMBISHA AMBISHA MAHA
  SHRIYE HAMBÄ KABÄ BAHA NAYE
OM VAJRA BINZAYE
For all of us disciples, our benefactors, and others, may
all obstacles to attaining liberation and omniscience, all
transgressions of the three vows, all natural non-virtues,
all inauspiciousness, all unclear concentration, all incorrect
recitation of mantras, all faults of excess and omission in
the rituals, and especially all obstacles to wealth and
abundant harvests be purified SHÄNTING KURUYE SÖHA.

Offering the barley without husks

OM AGNIYE AHDIBÄ AHDIBÄ AMBISHA AMBISHA MAHA
SHRIYE HAMBÄ KABÄ BAHA NAYE
OM MAHA BEGAYE
For all of us disciples, our benefactors, and others, may
all obstacles to attaining liberation and omniscience, all
transgressions of the three vows, all natural non-virtues,
all inauspiciousness, all unclear concentration, all incorrect
recitation of mantras, all faults of excess and omission in
the rituals, and especially all obstacles to excellent quick
mental powers be purified SHÄNTING KURUYE SÖHA.

Offering the peas

OM AGNIYE AHDIBÄ AHDIBÄ AMBISHA AMBISHA MAHA
SHRIYE HAMBÄ KABÄ BAHA NAYE
OM MAHA BALAYE
For all of us disciples, our benefactors, and others, may
all obstacles to attaining liberation and omniscience, all
transgressions of the three vows, all natural non-virtues,
all inauspiciousness, all unclear concentration, all incorrect
recitation of mantras, all faults of excess and omission in
the rituals, and especially all obstacles to increased
strength be purified SHÄNTING KURUYE SÖHA.

Offering the wheat

OM AGNIYE AHDIBÄ AHDIBÄ AMBISHA AMBISHA MAHA
SHRIYE HAMBÄ KABÄ BAHA NAYE
OM VAJRA GHAMA RI
For all of us disciples, our benefactors, and others, may
all obstacles to attaining liberation and omniscience, all
transgressions of the three vows, all natural non-virtues,
all inauspiciousness, all unclear concentration, all incorrect
recitation of mantras, all faults of excess and omission in
the rituals, and especially all sickness be purified
SHÄNTING KURUYE SÖHA.

Offering the special pacifying substance

OM AGNIYE AHDIBÄ AHDIBÄ AMBISHA AMBISHA MAHA
   SHRIYE HAMBÄ KABÄ BAHA NAYE
For all of us disciples, our benefactors, and others, may
all obstacles to attaining liberation and omniscience, all
transgressions of the three vows, all natural non-virtues,
all inauspiciousness, all unclear concentration, all incorrect
recitation of mantras, all faults of excess and omission in
the rituals, and especially all obstacles to accomplishing
supreme attainments be purified SHÄNTING KURUYE SÖHA.

Praise

While playing the bell recite:

Lord of the world, Son of Brahma, powerful Protector,
King of Fire Deities, empowered by Takki,
Who consume all delusions with your supreme wisdom,
To you, O Protector Fire Deity, I prostrate.

If you wish to make extensive praises, continue with:

O Son of Brahma, Protector of the world,
King of Fire Deities, supreme Rishi,
You manifest this form out of compassion
To fully protect all living beings.

In the aspect of a Rishi accomplished in knowledge
   mantras,
With the light of wisdom consuming delusions,
And a blazing brilliance like the fire of the aeon,
You are endowed with clairvoyance and miracle powers.

Out of skilful means you ride an emanation vehicle.
Holding a mala you recite knowledge mantras.
You hold a vase of essential nectar
And bring coolness to all with the nectar of Dharma.

You are free from faults and have perfected purity.
Though you abide in the world you have passed beyond
   sorrow;

422

Though you have attained peace you have great
compassion;
Therefore I make praises and prostrations to you.

Now offer water for the mouth and water for sprinkling:

OM AH HRIH PRAVARA SÄKARAM ÄNTZAMANAM PARTITZA
HUM SÖHA
OM AH HRIH PRAVARA SÄKARAM PROKYANAM PARTITZA
HUM SÖHA

Offer flowers, incense, lights, perfume, food, and music:

OM AGNIYE AHDIBÄ AHDIBÄ AMBISHA AMBISHA MAHA
SHRIYE HAMBÄ KABÄ BAHA NAYE VAJRA PUPE PARTITZA
HUM SÖHA
VAJRA DHUPE PARTITZA HUM SÖHA
VAJRA DIWE PARTITZA HUM SÖHA
VAJRA GÄNDHE PARTITZA HUM SÖHA
VAJRA NEWIDE PARTITZA HUM SÖHA
VAJRA SHAPTA PARTITZA HUM SÖHA

Blessing the torma

OM KHANDAROHI HUM HUM PHAT
OM SÖBHAWA SHUDDHA SARWA DHARMA SÖBHAWA
SHUDDHO HAM
Everything becomes emptiness.

From the state of emptiness, from YAM comes wind, from
RAM comes fire, from AH a grate of three human heads.
Upon this from AH appears a broad and expansive skullcup.
Inside from OM, KHAM, AM, TRAM, HUM come the five
nectars; from LAM, MAM, PAM, TAM, BAM come the five
meats, each marked by these letters. The wind blows, the
fire blazes, and the substances inside the skullcup melt.
Above them from HUM there arises a white, upside-down
khatanga, which falls into the skullcup and melts whereby
the substances take on the colour of mercury. Above them
three rows of vowels and consonants, standing one above
the other, transform into OM AH HUM. From these, light

rays draw the nectar of exalted wisdom from the hearts of all the Tathagatas, Heroes, and Yoginis of the ten directions. When this is added the contents increase and become vast. OM AH HUM   (3x)

Offering the torma

Offer the torma by reciting three times:

OM AGNIYE AHDIBÄ AHDIBÄ AMBISHA AMBISHA MAHA SHRIYE HAMBÄ KABÄ BAHA NAYE AHKAROMUKAM SARWA DHARMANÄN ADENUWATEN NADÖ DA OM AH HUM PHAT SÖHA

Once again offer the close offerings and music as before:

OM AGNIYE AHDIBÄ AHDIBÄ AMBISHA AMBISHA MAHA
  SHRIYE HAMBÄ KABÄ BAHA NAYE VAJRA PUPE PARTITZA
  HUM SÖHA
VAJRA DHUPE PARTITZA HUM SÖHA
VAJRA DIWE PARTITZA HUM SÖHA
VAJRA GÄNDHE PARTITZA HUM SÖHA
VAJRA NEWIDE PARTITZA HUM SÖHA
VAJRA SHAPTA PARTITZA HUM SÖHA

Requesting assistance

Play the bell while reciting:

O Deity, who eat what is burned in the fire,
King of Rishis and Lord of the spirits,
Together with the hosts of Fire Deities from the south-east,
To you I make offerings, praises, and prostrations.

May I and other practitioners
Have good health, long life, power,
Glory, fame, fortune,
And extensive enjoyments.
Please grant me the attainments
Of pacifying, increasing, controlling, and wrathful actions.
You who are bound by oaths please protect me
And help me to accomplish all the attainments.

Eradicate all untimely death, sicknesses,
Harm from spirits, and hindrances.
Eliminate bad dreams,
Ill omens, and bad actions.

May there be happiness in the world, may the years
    be good,
May crops increase, and may Dharma flourish.
May all goodness and happiness come about,
And may all wishes be accomplished.

Now offer water for drinking:

OM AH HRIH PRAVARAM SÄKARAM AHRGHAM PARTITZA
HUM SÖHA

Requesting forbearance

Whatever I have done out of confusion,
Even the slightest faulty action,
O Protector because you are the refuge of all beings
It is fitting for you to be patient with these.

OM VAJRA SATTÖ AH

Departure of mundane Fire Deity

O Eater of burning offerings,
Who accomplish one's own and others' purposes,
Please depart and return at the appropriate time
To help me accomplish all the attainments.

Contemplate:

OM MU
The wisdom being, Fire Deity, returns to his natural abode,
and the commitment being assumes the aspect of a blazing
fire.

THE CONCLUDING PRACTICES

Dissolution and generating the action Deities

The charnel grounds and protection circle dissolve into the celestial mansion. The celestial mansion dissolves into the Deities of the commitment wheel. They dissolve into the Deities of the body wheel. They dissolve into the Deities of the speech wheel. They dissolve into the Deities of the heart wheel. They dissolve into the four Yoginis of the great bliss wheel. They dissolve into me, the Principal Deity Father and Mother, the nature of the white and red indestructible drop. I, the Principal Deity Father and Mother, also melt into light and dissolve into the letter HUM at my heart, in nature the emptiness of the Dharmakaya.

The letter HUM completely transforms and I arise as the Blessed One Heruka, with a blue-coloured body, one face, and two hands. I hold a vajra and bell, and stand with my right leg outstretched. I embrace red Vajravarahi, who has one face and two hands holding a curved knife and a skullcup.

Meditating on the first of the five stages of completion stage, the stage of blessing the self

Inside my central channel, in the centre of the Dharma Wheel at my heart, is a drop the size of a small pea. Its upper half is white and its lower half is red, and it radiates five-coloured rays of light. At its centre is a tiny letter HUM, white with a shade of red, the nature of Heruka. The minute three-curved nada of the HUM, as fine as the tip of a hair, is red at the top and reddish-white at the bottom. The nature of great bliss, it is extremely bright, radiates red light, and drips nectar. My mind mixes inseparably with the nada.

Adorning our body with the armour Deities

At my heart on a moon mandala appears white OM HA, the nature of Vajrasattva; at my head on a sun, yellow

NAMA HI, the nature of Vairochana; at my crown on a sun, red SÖHA HU, the nature of Pämanarteshvara; at my two shoulders on a sun, black BOKE HE, the nature of Glorious Heruka; at my two eyes on a sun, orange HUM HUM HO, the nature of Vajrasurya; at my forehead on a sun, green PHAT HAM, the nature of Paramashawa.

At the Principal Mother's navel on a sun mandala appears red OM BAM, the nature of Vajravarahi; at her heart on a sun, blue HAM YOM, the nature of Yamani; at her throat on a moon, white HRIM MOM, the nature of Mohani; at her head on a sun, yellow HRIM HRIM, the nature of Sachalani; at her crown on a sun, green HUM HUM, the nature of Samtrasani; at her forehead on a sun, smoke-coloured PHAT PHAT, the nature of Chandika.

The mantra emanating from the four faces

OM SUMBHANI SUMBHA HUM HUM PHAT
OM GRIHANA GRIHANA HUM HUM PHAT
OM GRIHANA PAYA GRIHANA PAYA HUM HUM PHAT
OM ANAYA HO BHAGAWÄN BYÄ RADZA HUM HUM PHAT

Dedication

Now recite the extensive dedication prayers and auspicious prayers from the self-generation sadhana (pp 276-82).

Colophon: This sadhana was translated under the compassionate guidance of Venerable Geshe Kelsang Gyatso.

Union of No More Learning

HERUKA BODY MANDALA
SELF-INITIATION SADHANA

Introduction

By engaging in this practice of self-initiation, those who have completed a close retreat of actions of Heruka body mandala can maintain their Tantric vows and commitments and the blessings of the four empowerments of the body mandala that they received from their Spiritual Guide.

In front of a shrine containing a statue or picture of Heruka, you should set out three tormas. These can either be made in the traditional way according to the illustration on page 488, or can consist simply of any clean, fresh food such as honey or cakes. The central torma is for the Deities of the great bliss wheel – Heruka Father and Mother and the four Yoginis; the torma to its left is for the supramundane retinues of Heruka; and the torma to its right is for the mundane retinues of Heruka.

In front of the tormas, set out five rows of offerings. The first row, nearest the shrine, is for the accomplished mandala. This row starts from the left side of the shrine, your right, and includes AHRGHAM, PADÄM, ÄNTZAMANAM, PROKYA-NAM, PUPE, DHUPE, DIWE, GÄNDHE, and NEWIDE. The second row is for the supramundane and mundane guests, the third is for the Deities of the vase, and the fourth is for the empowering Deities. These three rows also start from the left side of the shrine, and include AHRGHAM, PADÄM, PUPE, DHUPE, DIWE, GÄNDHE, and NEWIDE. The fifth row, which is for the self-generated Deities, starts from the right side of the shrine and includes AHRGHAM, PADÄM, ÄNTZAMANAM, PUPE, DHUPE, DIWE, GÄNDHE, and NEWIDE.

The tsog offering can be set out at any suitable place in front of the shrine, and can consist of clean, fresh foods such as cakes, biscuits, honey, and fruit. You can also offer a tsog offering torma made in the traditional way according to the illustration on page 489. If you possess them, you can also set out the empowering ritual objects: the vajra, bell, crown, khatanga, damaru, kapala, Brahmin thread, and secret substances for the secret empowerment.

On a small table in front of your meditation seat, arrange from left to right your inner offering, vajra, bell, damaru, and mala; and a small conch shell, a miniature vajra with a long mantra thread of five colours wound around it, and two vases containing saffron water – the victory vase adorned with a vajra, and the action vase adorned with a curved knife (see illustration on page 493).

Having made these preparations, you should begin the actual practice with a pure motivation and a happy mind. If you are unable to prepare the shrine and the offerings as described here, simply imagine that they are actually present in front of you, and practise the sadhana with strong faith.

Union of No More Learning

THE ACTUAL PRACTICE

This has six parts:

1 *Accomplishing the mandala*
2 *Accomplishing the vases*
3 *Offerings to the mandala*
4 *Entering the mandala*
5 *Receiving the empowerments*
6 *Conclusion*

ACCOMPLISHING THE MANDALA

This is performed in accordance with the section in the self-generation sadhana, from the preliminary practices up to and including purifying any mistakes made during mantra recitation with the hundred-letter mantra of Heruka (pp 235-67).

ACCOMPLISHING THE VASES

Generating the vases and the Deities within

OM KHANDAROHI HUM HUM PHAT
OM SÖBHAWA SHUDDHA SARWA DHARMA SÖBHAWA
   SHUDDHO HAM
Everything becomes emptiness.

From the state of emptiness from PAMs come lotuses of various colours and from AHs come moons. Upon these from BAMs come white jewelled vases possessing all the essential features such as large bellies, long necks, and down-turned lips.

OM DAB DE DAB DE MAHA DAB DE SÖHA

The water in the vases and the divine river Ganges become inseparable. Inside the victory vase on the centre of an eight-petalled lotus stand the vowels and consonants, which are by nature the signs and indications of a fully enlightened being. These completely transform, and there arises a moon mandala, white with a shade of red. Reflected in it are the forms of the vowels and consonants. In the centre is a letter HUM, white with a shade of red. From this, five-coloured light rays radiate, and on the tip of each light ray is an assembly of Deities of the five wheels of Heruka. They lead all migrators to the state of the Deities of the five wheels, and invite all at once the Heroes, Yoginis, and so forth, who have existed since beginningless time, from the Pure Lands of the ten directions where they abide. They engage in the union of embrace, and melt and dissolve into the nada of the letter HUM whereby the letter HUM becomes the nature of spontaneous joy.

OM AH HUM OM SARWA BIRA YOGINI KAYA WAKA CHITTA
    VAJRA SÖBHAWA ÄMAKO HAM
OM VAJRA SHUDDHA SARWA DHARMA VAJRA SHUDDHO
    HAM

The moon, vowels, consonants, and HUM completely transform, and the sixty-two Deities and their places arise fully and all at once.

Thus, inside the victory vase in the outer circle, in the cardinal and intermediate directions, are the corpse seats. Inside this is the white body wheel, inside this is the red speech wheel, inside this is the blue heart wheel, and in the very centre is the great bliss wheel – a lotus of various colours with a sun mandala at its centre. Upon this stand Heruka Father and Mother. On the lotus petal in the east stands black Dakini, in the north green Lama, in the west red Khandarohi, and in the south yellow Rupini. On the four lotus petals in the intermediate directions, the southeast and so forth, are skullcups filled with five nectars. On the eight spokes of the heart wheel are the Heroes and Heroines of the heart family, on the eight spokes of the speech wheel are the Heroes and Heroines of the speech family, and on the eight spokes of the body wheel are the Heroes and Heroines of the body family. Outside these in the cardinal and intermediate directions are the eight Heroines of the doorways.

At the place where the vajra adorns the victory vase is a lotus and sun seat. Upon this from HUM and BAM come a vajra and a curved knife marked by a HUM and a BAM, from which arise Glorious Heruka Father and Mother.

Inside the action vase, and at the place where it is adorned by the curved knife, is a lotus and sun seat. Upon these sun seats from BAM comes a curved knife marked by a BAM. These both completely transform and Khandarohi arises in both places.

PHAIM
The assembly of wisdom beings, and the wisdom beings of the Deities of the adorned places, are invited together with the empowering Deities.

OM AHRGHAM PARTITZA HUM SÖHA

VAJRA ANKUSHA DZA
VAJRA PASHA HUM
VAJRA POTA BAM
VAJRA GHÄNTA HO

The wisdom beings become inseparable from their respective commitment beings.

The empowering Deities grant the empowerment and the crown of each is adorned by their respective Lord of the lineage.

Blessing the offerings

OM KHANDAROHI HUM HUM PHAT
OM SÖBHAWA SHUDDHA SARWA DHARMA SÖBHAWA
   SHUDDHO HAM
Everything becomes emptiness.

From the state of emptiness, from KAMs come broad and
expansive skullcups, inside which from HUMs come water
for drinking, water for the feet, flowers, incense, lights,
perfume, food, and music. By nature emptiness, they
have the aspect of the individual offering substances,
and function as objects of enjoyment of the six senses
to bestow special, uncontaminated bliss.

OM AHRGHAM AH HUM
OM PADÄM AH HUM
OM VAJRA PUPE AH HUM
OM VAJRA DHUPE AH HUM
OM VAJRA DIWE AH HUM
OM VAJRA GÄNDHE AH HUM
OM VAJRA NEWIDE AH HUM
OM VAJRA SHAPTA AH HUM

Making the offerings

Outer offerings

OM AHRGHAM PARTITZA HUM SÖHA
OM PADÄM PARTITZA HUM SÖHA
OM VAJRA PUPE AH HUM SÖHA
OM VAJRA DHUPE AH HUM SÖHA
OM VAJRA DIWE AH HUM SÖHA
OM VAJRA GÄNDHE AH HUM SÖHA
OM VAJRA NEWIDE AH HUM SÖHA
OM VAJRA SHAPTA AH HUM SÖHA

OM AH VAJRA ADARSHE HUM
OM AH VAJRA WINI HUM
OM AH VAJRA GÄNDHE HUM
OM AH VAJRA RASE HUM

OM AH VAJRA PARSHE HUM
OM AH VAJRA DHARME HUM

Inner offering

OM HUM BAM RIM RIM LIM LIM, KAM KHAM GAM GHAM
NGAM, TSAM TSHAM DZAM DZHAM NYAM, TrAM THrAM
DrAM DHrAM NAM, TAM THAM DAM DHAM NAM, PAM
PHAM BAM BHAM, YAM RAM LAM WAM, SHAM KAM SAM
HAM HUM HUM PHAT OM AH HUM

OM KHANDAROHI HUM HUM PHAT OM AH HUM

Secret and thatness offerings

Father and Mother enter into the union of embrace.
The Deities of the vases absorb in the concentration of
inseparable spontaneous bliss and thatness, and delight
in the thatness offering.

Mantra offering

OM HUM BAM RIM RIM LIM LIM, KAM KHAM GAM GHAM
NGAM, TSAM TSHAM DZAM DZHAM NYAM, TrAM THrAM
DrAM DHrAM NAM, TAM THAM DAM DHAM NAM, PAM
PHAM BAM BHAM, YAM RAM LAM WAM, SHAM KAM SAM
HAM HUM HUM PHAT

Eight lines of praise to the Father

OM NAMO BHAGAWATE WIRE SHAYA HUM HUM PHAT
OM MAHA KÄLWA AHGNI SAMNI BHAYA HUM HUM PHAT
OM DZATA MUGUTRA KORTAYA HUM HUM PHAT
OM DHAMKHATRA KARA LOTRA BHIKANA MUKAYA HUM
    HUM PHAT
OM SAHARA BHUNDZA BHASURAYA HUM HUM PHAT
OM PARASHUWA SHODHÄDA SHULA KHATAMGA DHARINE
    HUM HUM PHAT
OM BHÄGADZINAM WARA DHARAYA HUM HUM PHAT
OM MAHA DHUMBA ÄNDHAKARA WAWUKAYA HUM HUM
    PHAT

Eight lines of praise to the Mother

OM NAMO BHAGAWATI VAJRA VARAHI BAM HUM HUM
PHAT

OM NAMO ARYA APARADZITE TRE LOKYA MATI BIYE SHÖRI
HUM HUM PHAT

OM NAMA SARWA BUTA BHAYA WAHI MAHA VAJRE HUM
HUM PHAT

OM NAMO VAJRA SANI ADZITE APARADZITE WASHAM
KARANITRA HUM HUM PHAT

OM NAMO BHRAMANI SHOKANI ROKANI KROTE KARALENI
HUM HUM PHAT

OM NAMA DRASANI MARANI PRABHE DANI PARADZAYE
HUM HUM PHAT

OM NAMO BIDZAYE DZAMBHANI TAMBHANI MOHANI
HUM HUM PHAT

OM NAMO VAJRA VARAHI MAHA YOGINI KAME SHÖRI
KHAGE HUM HUM PHAT

Blessing the water in the vases

Light rays radiate from the mantra rosary at the heart of
the Principal Deity of the vase and draw back the wisdom
nectars of all the Buddhas and Bodhisattvas of the ten
directions, which dissolve into the water in the vases.

HUM

*Hold the mantra thread, with the miniature vajra at one
end placed on the victory vase, and recite the mantras:*

The essence mantra of the Father

OM SHRI VAJRA HE HE RU RU KAM HUM HUM PHAT DAKINI
DZALA SHAMBARAM SÖHA   (108x)

The close essence mantra of the Father

OM HRIH HA HA HUM HUM PHAT   (21x)

The essence mantra of the Mother

OM VAJRA BEROTZANIYE HUM HUM PHAT SÖHA   (108x)

The close essence mantra of the Mother

OM SARWA BUDDHA DAKINIYE VAJRA WARNANIYE HUM
HUM PHAT SÖHA   (21x)

The condensed essence mantra of the sixty retinue Deities

OM RIM RIM LIM LIM, KAM KHAM GAM GHAM NGAM,
TSAM TSHAM DZAM DZHAM NYAM, TrAM THrAM DrAM
DHrAM NAM, TAM THAM DAM DHAM NAM, PAM PHAM
BAM BHAM, YAM RAM LAM WAM, SHAM KAM SAM HAM
HUM HUM PHAT   (21x)

Place the mantra thread on the action vase and recite:

OM KHANDAROHI HUM HUM PHAT   (108x)

*Place the mantra thread on both vases and recite several
times:*

OM SARWA TATHAGATA ABHIKEKATA SAMAYA SHRIYE HUM

Focusing on the water in the conch, recite:

OM VAJRA AMRITA UDAKA HUM

OM AH HUM   (7x)

Contemplate:

Every atom of the water in the conch becomes wisdom
nectar, the nature of vajra atoms.

OM HRIH HA HA HUM HUM PHAT

Offer the water to the two vases:

HUM   (7x)

Offer flowers to each vase:

OM KHANDAROHI HUM HUM PHAT

OM SARWA TATHAGATA PUPE PARTITZA SÖHA
OM SARWA TATHAGATA DHUPE PARTITZA SÖHA
OM SARWA TATHAGATA DIWE PARTITZA SÖHA
OM SARWA TATHAGATA GÄNDHE PARTITZA SÖHA
OM SARWA TATHAGATA NEWIDE PARTITZA SÖHA
OM SARWA TATHAGATA SHAPTA PARTITZA SÖHA

Sprinkle the environment with cleansing water:

OM KHANDAROHI HUM HUM PHAT

Until I have completed the activities of accomplishing the mandala, please pacify all obstacles.

Through the fire of great bliss, the Deities within the vases melt and become of one taste with the water of the vases, which is the nature of bodhichitta. The Deities of the adorned places also melt and each appears in the aspect of their respective hand implement.

OFFERINGS TO THE MANDALA

Like a candle flame dividing in two, I, the Principal, manifest a second form just outside the eastern doorway of the mandala to perform the actions of the offerings.

Blessing the outer offerings

OM KHANDAROHI HUM HUM PHAT
OM SÖBHAWA SHUDDHA SARWA DHARMA SÖBHAWA
SHUDDHO HAM
Everything becomes emptiness.

From the state of emptiness, from KAMs come broad and expansive skullcups, inside which from HUMs come water for drinking, water for the feet, water for the mouth, water for sprinkling, flowers, incense, lights, perfume, food, and music. By nature emptiness, they have the aspect of the individual offering substances, and function as objects of enjoyment of the six senses to bestow special, uncontaminated bliss.

OM AHRGHAM AH HUM
OM PADÄM AH HUM
OM ÄNTZAMANAM AH HUM
OM PROKYANAM AH HUM
OM VAJRA PUPE AH HUM
OM VAJRA DHUPE AH HUM
OM VAJRA DIWE AH HUM
OM VAJRA GÄNDHE AH HUM
OM VAJRA NEWIDE AH HUM
OM VAJRA SHAPTA AH HUM

OM RUPA AH HUM
OM SHAPTA AH HUM
OM GÄNDHE AH HUM
OM RASA AH HUM
OM PARSHE AH HUM

Offering goddesses emanate from my heart and perform the offerings.

Outer offerings

OM AHRGHAM PARTITZA HUM SÖHA
OM PADÄM PARTITZA HUM SÖHA
OM ÄNTZAMANAM PARTITZA HUM SÖHA
OM PROKYANAM PARTITZA HUM SÖHA
OM VAJRA PUPE AH HUM SÖHA
OM VAJRA DHUPE AH HUM SÖHA
OM VAJRA DIWE AH HUM SÖHA
OM VAJRA GÄNDHE AH HUM SÖHA
OM VAJRA NEWIDE AH HUM SÖHA
OM VAJRA SHAPTA AH HUM SÖHA

OM VAJRA WINI HUM HUM PHAT
OM VAJRA WAMSHE HUM HUM PHAT
OM VAJRA MITAMGI HUM HUM PHAT
OM VAJRA MURANDZE HUM HUM PHAT

OM VAJRA HASÄ HUM HUM PHAT
OM VAJRA LASÄ HUM HUM PHAT
OM VAJRA GIRTI HUM HUM PHAT
OM VAJRA NIRTÄ HUM HUM PHAT

OM VAJRA PUPE HUM HUM PHAT
OM VAJRA DHUPE HUM HUM PHAT
OM VAJRA DIWE HUM HUM PHAT
OM VAJRA GÄNDHE HUM HUM PHAT

OM RUPA BENZ HUM HUM PHAT
OM RASA BENZ HUM HUM PHAT
OM PARSHE BENZ HUM HUM PHAT
OM DHARMA DHATU BENZ HUM HUM PHAT

OM SHRI HERUKA SAPARIWARA MAHA SAPTA RATNA
PARTITZA HUM SÖHA

Inner offering

OM HUM BAM RIM RIM LIM LIM, KAM KHAM GAM GHAM
NGAM, TSAM TSHAM DZAM DZHAM NYAM, TrAM THrAM
DrAM DHrAM NAM, TAM THAM DAM DHAM NAM, PAM
PHAM BAM BHAM, YAM RAM LAM WAM, SHAM KAM SAM
HAM HUM HUM PHAT OM AH HUM

Secret offering

The Father enters into union with the Mother. The
bodhichitta melts, and as it descends from the crown
to the throat he experiences joy, as it descends from
the throat to the heart he experiences supreme joy, as
it descends from the heart to the navel he experiences
extraordinary joy, and as it descends from the navel to the
tip of the jewel he generates spontaneous exalted wisdom,
and all the Deities experience great bliss.

Thatness offering

The Deities of the mandala absorb in the concentration of
inseparable spontaneous bliss and thatness, and delight in
the thatness offering.

Eight lines of praise to the Father

OM I prostrate to the Blessed One, Lord of the Heroes
  HUM HUM PHAT
OM To you with a brilliance equal to the fire of the great
  aeon HUM HUM PHAT
OM To you with an inexhaustible topknot HUM HUM PHAT
OM To you with a fearsome face and bared fangs HUM
  HUM PHAT
OM To you whose thousand arms blaze with light HUM
  HUM PHAT
OM To you who hold an axe, an uplifted noose, a spear,
  and a khatanga HUM HUM PHAT
OM To you who wear a tiger-skin garment HUM HUM PHAT
OM I bow to you whose great smoke-coloured body
  dispels obstructions HUM HUM PHAT

Eight lines of praise to the Mother

OM I prostrate to Vajravarahi, the Blessed Mother HUM
  HUM PHAT
OM To the Superior and powerful Knowledge Lady
  unconquered by the three realms HUM HUM PHAT
OM To you who destroy all fears of evil spirits with your
  great vajra HUM HUM PHAT
OM To you with controlling eyes who remain as the vajra
  seat unconquered by others HUM HUM PHAT
OM To you whose wrathful fierce form desiccates Brahma
  HUM HUM PHAT
OM To you who terrify and dry up demons, conquering
  those in other directions HUM HUM PHAT
OM To you who conquer all those who make us dull,
  rigid, and confused HUM HUM PHAT
OM I bow to Vajravarahi, the Great Mother, the Dakini
  consort who fulfils all desires HUM HUM PHAT

ENTERING THE MANDALA

Blessing the offerings to the empowering Deities

OM KHANDAROHI HUM HUM PHAT
OM SÖBHAWA SHUDDHA SARWA DHARMA SÖBHAWA
  SHUDDHO HAM
Everything becomes emptiness.

From the state of emptiness from KAMs come broad and
expansive skullcups, inside which from HUMs come water
for drinking, water for the feet, flowers, incense, lights,
perfume, food, and music. By nature emptiness, they
have the aspect of the individual offering substances,
and function as objects of enjoyment of the six senses
to bestow special, uncontaminated bliss.

OM AHRGHAM AH HUM
OM PADÄM AH HUM
OM VAJRA PUPE AH HUM
OM VAJRA DHUPE AH HUM
OM VAJRA DIWE AH HUM
OM VAJRA GÄNDHE AH HUM
OM VAJRA NEWIDE AH HUM
OM VAJRA SHAPTA AH HUM

*First offer a mandala and then recite the following request
three times:*

O Great Joyful Teacher
Please listen to what I now say.
I am seeking a special method
For attaining great enlightenment.
Please grant me the commitments;
Please grant me the vows;
Please grant me refuge
In Buddha, Dharma, and Sangha;
And please guide me to the supreme city of great
  liberation.

Putting on the eye ribbon

OM CHAKYU BANDHA WARAMANAYE HUM

Receiving the flower garland

AH KAM BIRA HUM

Blessing the three doors

Now sprinkle cleansing water while reciting:

OM KHANDAROHI HUM HUM PHAT

I have the clarity of Heruka. My three places – the crown, throat, and heart – are marked by OM, AH, and HUM.

Imagine Guru Heruka asks the questions, and you reply:

'Dear one, who are you and what do you seek?'
I am a Fortunate One seeking great bliss.

'Dear one, why do you seek great bliss?'
To fulfil the commitment of supreme Buddhahood.

Taking the Bodhisattva vows

I go for refuge to the Three Jewels
And confess individually all negative actions.
I rejoice in the virtues of all beings
And promise to accomplish a Buddha's enlightenment.

(3x)

Generating the mind of all yogas

At my heart is a moon, upon which stands a white vajra. They are the nature of my conventional and ultimate bodhichitta.

OM SARWA YOGA TSITA UPATAYAMI

To stabilize the two bodhichittas, recite:

OM SURA TE SAMAYA TÖN HO: SIDDHI VAJRA YATA SUKAM

Pledging secrecy

Guru Heruka gives you the following advice:

'Today you will receive the blessings of all the Tathagatas. You should not mention this supreme secret of the mandala of all the Tathagatas to those who have not entered the mandala or to those who have no faith.'

Imagine that you enter the mandala and arrive in front of the Principal of the mandala, while reciting:

HUM DZA HUM

Imagine that you are circumambulating the Principal counter-clockwise three times while reciting:

MAHA RATA SUTRITHA SUTOKO SUSUGO VAJRA SATTÖ ADHI SIDDHA MI

Make three prostrations while reciting:

OM NAMATE HUM
NAMAMI HUM
NAMO NAMA HUM SÖHA

Taking Tantric vows

Recite three times:

All Buddhas and Bodhisattvas
Please listen to what I now say.
From this time forth
Until I reach the essence of enlightenment,
I, whose name is Akshobya,
Shall generate the sacred, unsurpassed mind of
    enlightenment,
Just as all the Conquerors of the three times
Have assured themselves of enlightenment in this way.

I shall maintain all the general and specific vows and
    commitments of the five Buddha families.
I shall deliver those not delivered,
Liberate those not liberated,

Give breath to those unable to breath,
And lead all beings to a state beyond sorrow.

Taking the uncommon vows of Mother Tantra

Recite three times:

O Glorious Heruka and all the Heroes,
And all you countless Bodhisattvas,
The Nangdzä Yoginis and so forth,
Please listen to what I now say.

From this time forth
Until I abide in non-duality
I shall maintain perfectly
The twenty-two pure practices of non-duality.

Generating the basis for absorbing the wisdom beings

OM SÖBHAWA SHUDDHA SARWA DHARMA SÖBHAWA
  SHUDDHO HAM
Everything becomes emptiness.

From the state of emptiness I arise as Heruka, blue in
colour, with four faces and twelve arms, together with my
consort. At my heart my indestructible drop becomes the
Principal Father and Mother. The heart channel petals in
the four directions become the four heart Yoginis, and the
heart channel petals in the four intermediate directions
become skullcups filled with nectars. From the channels
and drops of my twenty-four places arise the twenty-four
Heroes and twenty-four Heroines, and from the channels
of the eight doors of the senses arise the eight Heroines of
the doorways.

The places of the principal Deity's body are marked by
OM HA, NAMA HI, SÖHA HU, BOKE HE, HUM HUM HO, and
PHAT HAM.

The places of the consort's body are marked by OM BAM,
HAM YOM, HRIM MOM, HRIM HRIM, HUM HUM, and PHAT
PHAT.

Request to absorb the wisdom beings

Please grant me the blessings
Of all the Heroes and Heroines,
And cause Glorious Heruka
To descend into me.

Dissolving the wisdom beings

Light rays radiate from the HUM at the heart of the
principal Deity of the mandala, who is inseparable from
my Guru. These invite all the Buddhas and Bodhisattvas
together with all the Heroes and Heroines, in the aspect
of the Deities of Chakrasambara. Like rain falling, they
descend and enter into my body through every hair pore.
They dissolve into me and I become inseparable from
Heruka Father and Mother.

While playing the bell and damaru, recite:

OM HRIH HA HA HUM HUM PHAT

OM TIKTRA MAHA KRODHA AH BE SHAYA HUM

To stabilize the blessings, recite:

TIKTRA VAJRA

Now offer the flower to the Principal of the mandala:

OM PRATITZA VAJRA HO

Now touch the flower to your crown:

OM PRATI GRIHANA TÖN IMAM SATTÖ MAHABALA

*Imagine that you purify your eyes and attain vajra eyes.
Encourage yourself by reciting:*

'Today, O Glorious Heruka,
You have sought to open your eyes;
And by opening them you have attained
Unsurpassed vajra eyes that can see everything.'

OM VAJRA NETRA APAHARA PATRA LAM HRIH

Remove the eye ribbon.

HE VAJRA PASHÄ

Thus you are exhorted to look. Think:

I see clearly the entire supported and supporting mandala.

Meditate on this imagined mandala.

RECEIVING THE EMPOWERMENTS

The vase empowerment of the vajra disciple

First offer a mandala and then make the following request three times:

Please grant me the empowerment,
The Dharma Truth that has inconceivable meaning.

Blessing the empowering ritual objects

Sprinkle water from the action vase and recite:

OM KHANDAROHI HUM HUM PHAT
OM SÖBHAWA SHUDDHA SARWA DHARMA SÖBHAWA
   SHUDDHO HAM
Everything becomes emptiness.

From the state of emptiness come the empowering ritual
objects – the water of the vase, the crown, the vajra, and
the bell – which instantaneously transform into Akshobya,
Ratnasambhava, Amitabha, and Amoghasiddhi Father
and Mother respectively.

From the HUM at the heart of the Principal inseparable
from my Guru, light rays radiate and invite the wisdom
beings together with the empowering Deities.

PHAIM
DZA HUM BAM HO
They become non-dual.

The empowering Deities grant empowerment to the Deities of the empowering ritual objects, and their crowns are adorned by Vajrasattva.

Offerings to the Deities of the empowering ritual objects

OM AHRGHAM PARTITZA HUM SÖHA
OM PADÄM PARTITZA HUM SÖHA
OM VAJRA PUPE AH HUM SÖHA
OM VAJRA DHUPE AH HUM SÖHA
OM VAJRA DIWE AH HUM SÖHA
OM VAJRA GÄNDHE AH HUM SÖHA
OM VAJRA NEWIDE AH HUM SÖHA
OM VAJRA SHAPTA AH HUM SÖHA

Transforming the Deities into the empowering ritual objects

Father and Mother enter into union and melt into the nature of great bliss from which arise the empowering ritual objects – the water of the vase, the crown, the vajra, and the bell.

Receiving the water empowerment of Akshobya

Light rays radiate from the HUM at the heart of the principal Deity of the mandala, who is inseparable from my Guru, and invite the empowering Deities – the Blessed One Chakrasambara together with his retinue.

OM AHRGHAM PARTITZA HUM SÖHA
OM PADÄM PARTITZA HUM SÖHA
OM VAJRA PUPE PARTITZA HUM SÖHA
OM VAJRA DHUPE PARTITZA HUM SÖHA
OM VAJRA DIWE PARTITZA HUM SÖHA
OM VAJRA GÄNDHE PARTITZA HUM SÖHA
OM VAJRA NEWIDE PARTITZA HUM SÖHA
OM VAJRA SHAPTA PARTITZA HUM SÖHA

In order to protect migrators
Buddha received the empowerment.

Just like this, O Vajra Holder,
Please grant me the empowerment.

Requested in this way, the eight Goddesses of the doorways
drive away hindrances, the Heroes recite auspicious verses,
the Heroines sing vajra songs, and the Rupavajras and so
forth make offerings. The Principal and the mandala
Deities resolve to grant the empowerment, and the four
Mothers together with Varahi, holding jewelled vases
filled with five nectars, confer the empowerment through
the crown of my head.

The auspiciousness that arises from the Dharmadhatu
Is the blazing body of Glorious Heruka, king of the fearless.

By the truth of the vajra enjoying the lotus of the wisdom
    Varahi,
May there be the auspiciousness of abiding in great bliss.

'By granting you empowerment
I will give you the great vajra
That comes from the three secrets of all the Buddhas
And is an object of prostration in the three realms.'

OM TSATRA BIRA TAM ABHIKINTZA MI

*Now taste some water from the victory vase and touch some
on your crown.*

Saying this, they grant the water empowerment of
Akshobya. I am empowered to purify the aggregate of
consciousness and transform it into the wisdom of the
Dharmadhatu.

Receiving the crown empowerment of Ratnasambhava

'By granting you empowerment
I will give you the great vajra
That comes from the three secrets of all the Buddhas
And is an object of prostration in the three realms.'

OM SARWA BUDDHA DAKINIYE VAJRA WARNANIYE HUM
    HUM PHAT SÖHA

OM RIM RIM LIM LIM, KAM KHAM GAM GHAM NGAM,
TSAM TSHAM DZAM DZHAM NYAM, TrAM THrAM DrAM
DHrAM NAM, TAM THAM DAM DHAM NAM, PAM PHAM
BAM BHAM, YAM RAM LAM WAM, SHAM KAM SAM HAM
HUM HUM PHAT

Now touch the crown to your head.

Saying this, they grant the crown empowerment of
Ratnasambhava. I am empowered to purify the aggregate
of feeling and transform it into the wisdom of equality.

Receiving the vajra empowerment of Amitabha

'By granting you empowerment
I will give you the great vajra
That comes from the three secrets of all the Buddhas
And is an object of prostration in the three realms.'

Just as all the Buddhas
Attained enlightenment by holding the vajra,
Today Glorious Heruka and the assembly of Heroes
Grant you the empowerment.

Now touch the vajra to your heart.

Saying this, they grant the vajra empowerment of
Amitabha. I am empowered to purify the aggregate
of discrimination and transform it into the wisdom of
individual realization.

Receiving the bell empowerment of Amoghasiddhi

'By granting you empowerment
I will give you the great vajra
That comes from the three secrets of all the Buddhas
And is an object of prostration in the three realms.'

It is taught that all Yoginis
Follow the sound of the bell.
You should always hold it
And attain the supreme enlightenment of the Conquerors.

Now place the bell in your left hand.

Saying this, they grant the bell empowerment of Amoghasiddhi. I am empowered to purify the aggregate of compositional factors and transform it into the wisdom of accomplishing activities.

Receiving the name empowerment of Vairochana

'By granting you empowerment
I will give you the great vajra
That comes from the three secrets of all the Buddhas
And is an object of prostration in the three realms.'

OM VAJRA SATTÖ TAM ABHIKINTZA MI
VAJRA NAMA ABHIKEKATA

Now ring the bell while reciting:

O Glorious One you are called Tathagata Vajra Akshobya
[or whatever is your secret name].

Saying this, they grant the name empowerment of Vairochana. I am empowered to purify the aggregate of form and transform it into the mirror-like wisdom.

Thus I have received the empowerment of the five Buddha families. The stains of the five delusions and five aggregates are purified; and I am empowered to attain the state of the five Buddha families.

Receiving the mantra empowerment

A rosary of the essence mantra arises from the heart of the Principal of the mandala inseparable from my Guru. Leaving through his mouth, it enters my mouth, and encircles counter-clockwise the letter HUM at my heart. Light rays radiate from the HUM and mantra rosary, purifying all defilements.

OM SHRI VAJRA HE HE RU RU KAM HUM HUM PHAT DAKINI
    DZALA SHAMBARAM SÖHA   (3x)

Receiving the empowerment of the common practice – the practice of the vajra, great bliss

I become Vajrasattva, white in colour, together with my consort.
From HUM comes a vajra, the nature of great bliss.

Now place the vajra in your right hand and recite:

To always keep in mind the practice of great bliss
I will never be separate from the vajra.

OM SARWA TATHAGATA SIDDHI VAJRA SAMAYA TIKTRA
EKATAM DARA YAMI OM HA HA HA HA HI

Receiving the empowerment of the uncommon practice – the practice of the yoga of Heruka's body, speech, and mind

I become Heruka with a blue-coloured body, four faces, and twelve arms, together with my consort.

OM SHRI VAJRA HE HE RU RU KAM HUM HUM PHAT DAKINI
DZALA SHAMBARAM SÖHA   (3x)

OM VAJRA BEROTZANIYE HUM HUM PHAT   (3x)

The khatanga symbolizes Heruka's body,
The damaru symbolizes Heruka's speech,
The skullcup symbolizes Heruka's mind of inseparable
    bliss and emptiness,
And the Brahmin thread indicates that all these are the
    nature of the great bliss of non-conceptual wisdom;
Realizing this, I will never be separate from them.

Heruka Father and Mother, the size of only a thumb,
remain at my heart.

Receiving the empowerment of prediction

I become the supreme Deity, the Guru Conqueror
Shakyamuni.

Encourage yourself by reciting:

'Soon you will become a Tathagata called Glorious Heruka.
SHRI HERUKA DAKINI NAMA SARWA TATHAGATA SIDDHI
SAMAYA TAM BUBU WASA
You will be victorious over all the hosts of maras
And abide in the supreme city of enlightenment.'

Receiving the vase empowerment of the Vajra Master

*First offer a mandala and then make the following request
three times:*

O Great Hero,
Please grant me here and now
The irreversible empowerment
That leads migrators to signlessness.

Generating ourself as the supreme Spiritual Master, Vajradhara

Sprinkle water from the action vase over yourself and recite:

OM KHANDAROHI HUM HUM PHAT
OM SÖBHAWA SHUDDHA SARWA DHARMA SÖBHAWA
SHUDDHO HAM
Everything becomes emptiness.

From the state of emptiness, on a lion throne, lotus, and
sun, from HUM comes a vajra marked by a HUM. From this
I arise as Vajradhara with a blue-coloured body, one face,
and two hands, holding vajra and bell, and embracing Vajra
Nyem Ma, who has a blue-coloured body and holds a
curved knife and a skullcup. At my crown is a letter OM, at
my throat a letter AH, and at my heart a letter HUM. Light
rays radiate from the HUM at the heart of the Principal
inseparable from the Guru and invite the wisdom beings.

PHAIM
DZA HUM BAM HO
We become non-dual.

Above are parasols, to the right are victory banners, to the left are other banners, and all around are clouds of offerings.

Taking the three commitments

Sprinkle the vajra and bell with water from the action vase:

OM KHANDAROHI HUM HUM PHAT
OM SÖBHAWA SHUDDHA SARWA DHARMA SÖBHAWA
    SHUDDHO HAM
Everything becomes emptiness.

From the state of emptiness, from HUM comes a vajra, the nature of Vajrasattva, and from AH a bell, the nature of Vajra Nyem Ma.

The mind commitment of the vajra

Hold the vajra.

OM MAHA VAJRA HUM

The exalted wisdom of great bliss inseparable from
    emptiness is the secret vajra.
To remember this I will always keep a vajra.

The speech commitment of the bell

Play the bell.

OM VAJRA GHANTA HUM

The sound of the bell reveals the lack of inherent existence
    of all phenomena.
To remember this I will always keep a bell.

The mudra commitment of the body

Generating my body as the Deity's body is the
    unchangeable mudra commitment.
By uniting this with the wisdom mudra I will accomplish
    all attainments.

The actual Vajra Master empowerment

I, Vajradhara, embrace my consort and generate inseparable bliss and emptiness, the nature of the Vajra Master empowerment.

'Just as all the Tathagatas granted ablution
At the moment of [Buddha's] birth,
Likewise do we now grant ablution
With the pure water of the gods.

OM SARWA TATHAGATA ABHIKEKATA SAMAYA SHRIYE HUM
OM TSATRA BIRA TAM ABHIKINTZA MI'

Saying this, the empowering Deities grant the empowerment. My whole body is filled with nectar and I generate great bliss. All stains are purified, and the excess water remaining on my crown transforms into the crown ornament, the nature of the five Buddha families.

The empowering Deities dissolve through the crown of my head.

OM SUPRATIKTRA VAJRA YE SÖHA

I become the King of the Dharma of the three worlds.

Offerings to the self generation

OM AHRGHAM PARTITZA HUM SÖHA
OM PADÄM PARTITZA HUM SÖHA
OM VAJRA PUPE AH HUM SÖHA
OM VAJRA DHUPE AH HUM SÖHA
OM VAJRA DIWE AH HUM SÖHA
OM VAJRA GÄNDHE AH HUM SÖHA
OM VAJRA NEWIDE AH HUM SÖHA
OM VAJRA SHAPTA AH HUM SÖHA

The three practices for daily life given by Vajradhara

Contemplate while reciting:

'You should enjoy the five objects of desire with the experience of inseparable bliss and emptiness.

You should make offerings to yourself, regarding yourself
as Heruka, the embodiment of all the Heroes and
Yoginis.
You should benefit living beings with the knowledge that
the world and its inhabitants are like an illusion.'

Thus I have received the vase empowerment in the body
mandala of Guru Heruka. All faults of my body are
purified, I am empowered to meditate on the profound
generation stage of the body mandala, and I shall have the
good fortune to attain the resultant Emanation Body.

Receiving the secret empowerment

*First offer a mandala and then make the following request
three times:*

O Great Being, the Principal,
Please help me to become just like you,
And please protect me
From drowning in the swamp of samsara.

I become Amitabha, red in colour, holding a lotus and a
bell. Through the sound of the joy of Guru Deity Father
and Mother, the Principal of the mandala, embracing, all
the Heroes and Heroines are invited. They enter through
the mouths of the Father and Mother, and, due to the fire
of great bliss, melt into red and white bodhichittas at the
heart.

Receiving the secret substance, the red and white
bodhichitta of Guru Heruka Father and Mother

'This is the supreme commitment
Of the Heroes and Heroines.
Discerning the taste with the five elements
You should experience that bliss.'

*Thus you are exhorted. Now taste the secret substance
regarding it as red and white bodhichitta, the nature of
all the Heroes and Heroines.*

Oh, what great bliss!

In dependence upon tasting the bodhichitta, bliss and emptiness are united inseparably. This is the secret empowerment.

Heruka Father and Mother emanate from the heart of Guru Father and Mother and dissolve into my throat.

Thus I have received the secret empowerment in the mandala of conventional bodhichitta – the white and red drop of Guru Heruka Father and Mother. All faults of my speech are purified, I am empowered to meditate on the completion stage of illusory body, and I shall have the good fortune to attain the resultant Enjoyment Body.

Receiving the wisdom-mudra empowerment.

First offer a mandala and then make the following request three times:

O Great Being, the Principal,
Please help me to become just like you,
And please protect me
From drowning in the swamp of samsara.

Now imagine that an emanation of Vajravarahi appears in front of you, and Guru Heruka says:

'Dear one, I give you
This Goddess, a great consort.'

Thus he introduces her. Now Vajravarahi asks you:

'Dear one, having respect for me,
Would you like to experience the five nectars, the five omniscient wisdoms?'

You reply:

O Goddess, why should I not be delighted
With all the commitments you have explained?

Vajravarahi is delighted and says:

'How wonderful, in dependence upon my lotus
You can attain Buddhahood in this life.
PÄMA BHANJA HO'

*Now sprinkle yourself and the knowledge goddess with
water from the action vase:*

OM KHANDAROHI HUM HUM PHAT
OM SÖBHAWA SHUDDHA SARWA DHARMA SÖBHAWA
   SHUDDHO HAM
Everything becomes emptiness.

From the state of emptiness, upon a lotus and sun, from
HUM comes a vajra marked by a HUM. From this I arise
as the Blessed One Glorious Heruka, with four faces and
twelve arms.

From BAM comes a curved knife marked by a BAM, and
from this arises the knowledge goddess, the Blessed One
Vajravarahi, holding a curved knife and a skullcup. We
enter into embrace.

Thinking that in dependence upon this method I will
generate uncontaminated bliss, I engage in union. As
the bodhichitta descends from my crown to my throat I
experience joy; as it descends from my throat to my heart
I experience supreme joy; as it descends from my heart to
my navel I experience extraordinary joy; and as it descends
from my navel to the tip of my jewel I experience
spontaneous joy inseparable from emptiness, the nature
of the wisdom-mudra empowerment.

*When we arise from the meditation on great bliss and
emptiness, we make the following determination:*

From now until I reach
The essence of enlightenment,
I will work solely for the benefit
Of dream-like sentient beings.

Thus I have received the wisdom-mudra empowerment in the bhaga mandala. All faults of my mind are purified, I am empowered to meditate on the completion stage of the clear light of the Mahamudra, and I shall have the good fortune to attain the resultant Truth Body.

Receiving the word empowerment

First offer a mandala and then make the following request three times:

Through your kindness I have received
The three principal empowerments.
Now through your kindness please grant me
The precious fourth empowerment.

Imagine that Guru Heruka says:

'When you received the third empowerment, you imagined your body as the Deity body and your mind as inseparable bliss and emptiness. By continuing to improve this imagined Deity body and mind, eventually you will attain the actual resultant Deity body arising from your indestructible wind in the aspect of Father and Mother embracing, and your mind will become the inseparable union of spontaneous bliss and emptiness. This is the Union of No More Learning.'

Through hearing these words I develop a joyful feeling. This is the word empowerment.

'Ultimate truth is naturally beautiful,
It is utterly unlike physical form.
Without this mudra there is no other method for
    attaining Buddhahood.
Dear one, enjoy the contact of this mudra
For there is no higher contact.'

Thus I have received the precious word empowerment in the mandala of the ultimate mind of enlightenment. All faults of my body, speech, and mind are purified, I am empowered to meditate on the completion stage of inconceivability, and I shall have the good fortune to attain the resultant union of Vajradhara.

Now offer a thanking mandala.

Blessing the outer offerings

OM KHANDAROHI HUM HUM PHAT
OM SÖBHAWA SHUDDHA SARWA DHARMA SÖBHAWA
   SHUDDHO HAM
Everything becomes emptiness.

From the state of emptiness, from KAMs come broad and expansive skullcups, inside which from HUMs come water for drinking, water for the feet, flowers, incense, lights, perfume, food, and music. By nature emptiness, they have the aspect of the individual offering substances, and function as objects of enjoyment of the six senses to bestow special, uncontaminated bliss.

OM AHRGHAM AH HUM
OM PADÄM AH HUM
OM VAJRA PUPE AH HUM
OM VAJRA DHUPE AH HUM
OM VAJRA DIWE AH HUM
OM VAJRA GÄNDHE AH HUM
OM VAJRA NEWIDE AH HUM
OM VAJRA SHAPTA AH HUM

Blessing the tormas

OM KHANDAROHI HUM HUM PHAT
OM SÖBHAWA SHUDDHA SARWA DHARMA SÖBHAWA
   SHUDDHO HAM
Everything becomes emptiness.

From the state of emptiness, from YAM comes wind, from RAM comes fire, from AH a grate of three human heads. Upon this from AH appears a broad and expansive skullcup. Inside from OM, KHAM, AM, TRAM, HUM come the five nectars; from LAM, MAM, PAM, TAM, BAM come the five meats, each marked by these letters. The wind blows, the fire blazes, and the substances inside the skullcup melt. Above them from HUM there arises a white, upside-down khatanga, which falls into the skullcup and melts whereby the substances take on the colour of mercury. Above them three rows of vowels and consonants, standing one above the other, transform into OM AH HUM. From these, light rays draw the nectar of exalted wisdom from the hearts of all the Tathagatas, Heroes, and Yoginis of the ten directions. When this is added the contents increase and become vast. OM AH HUM   (3x)

Offering the torma to the supramundane Deities

From a white HUM in the tongue of all the mandala Deities, there arises a white, three-pronged vajra, through which they partake of the nectar of the torma by drawing it through straws of vajra light the thickness of only a grain of barley.

Offering the torma to the Deities of the great bliss wheel

OM VAJRA AH RA LI HO: DZA HUM BAM HO: VAJRA DAKINI
    SAMAYA TÖN TRISHAYA HO   (3x)

Offering the torma to the Deities of the heart wheel, speech wheel, and body wheel

OM KARA KARA, KURU KURU, BÄNDHA BÄNDHA, TrASAYA
TrASAYA, KYOMBHAYA KYOMBHAYA, HROM HROM, HRAH
HRAH, PHAIM PHAIM, PHAT PHAT, DAHA DAHA, PATSA
PATSA, BHAKYA BHAKYA BASA RUDHI ÄNTRA MALA
WALAMBINE, GRIHANA GRIHANA SAPTA PATALA GATA
BHUDZAMGAM SARWAMPA TARDZAYA TARDZAYA,
AKANDYA AKANDYA, HRIM HRIM, GYÖN GYÖN, KYAMA
KYAMA, HAM HAM, HIM HIM, HUM HUM, KILI KILI, SILI
SILI, HILI HILI, DHILI DHILI, HUM HUM PHAT

Offering the torma to the Deities of the commitment wheel

OM VAJRA AH RA LI HO: DZA HUM BAM HO: VAJRA DAKINI
SAMAYA TÖN TRISHAYA HO   (2x)

Outer offerings

OM AHRGHAM PARTITZA SÖHA
OM PADÄM PARTITZA SÖHA
OM VAJRA PUPE AH HUM SÖHA
OM VAJRA DHUPE AH HUM SÖHA
OM VAJRA DIWE AH HUM SÖHA
OM VAJRA GÄNDHE AH HUM SÖHA
OM VAJRA NEWIDE AH HUM SÖHA
OM VAJRA SHAPTA AH HUM SÖHA

OM AH VAJRA ADARSHE HUM
OM AH VAJRA WINI HUM
OM AH VAJRA GÄNDHE HUM
OM AH VAJRA RASE HUM
OM AH VAJRA PARSHE HUM
OM AH VAJRA DHARME HUM

Inner offering

OM HUM BAM RIM RIM LIM LIM, KAM KHAM GAM GHAM
NGAM, TSAM TSHAM DZAM DZHAM NYAM, TrAM THrAM
DrAM DHrAM NAM, TAM THAM DAM DHAM NAM, PAM
PHAM BAM BHAM, YAM RAM LAM WAM, SHAM KAM SAM
HAM HUM HUM PHAT OM AH HUM

Secret and thatness offerings

Through Father and Mother uniting in embrace, all the
principal and retinue Deities enjoy a special experience
of great bliss and emptiness.

Eight lines of praise to the Father

OM I prostrate to the Blessed One, Lord of the Heroes
HUM HUM PHAT

OM To you with a brilliance equal to the fire of the great
    aeon HUM HUM PHAT
OM To you with an inexhaustible topknot HUM HUM PHAT
OM To you with a fearsome face and bared fangs HUM
    HUM PHAT
OM To you whose thousand arms blaze with light HUM
    HUM PHAT
OM To you who hold an axe, an uplifted noose, a spear,
    and a khatanga HUM HUM PHAT
OM To you who wear a tiger-skin garment HUM HUM PHAT
OM I bow to you whose great smoke-coloured body
    dispels obstructions HUM HUM PHAT

Eight lines of praise to the Mother

OM I prostrate to Vajravarahi, the Blessed Mother HUM
    HUM PHAT
OM To the Superior and powerful Knowledge Lady
    unconquered by the three realms HUM HUM PHAT
OM To you who destroy all fears of evil spirits with your
    great vajra HUM HUM PHAT
OM To you with controlling eyes who remain as the vajra
    seat unconquered by others HUM HUM PHAT
OM To you whose wrathful fierce form desiccates Brahma
    HUM HUM PHAT
OM To you who terrify and dry up demons, conquering
    those in other directions HUM HUM PHAT
OM To you who conquer all those who make us dull,
    rigid, and confused HUM HUM PHAT
OM I bow to Vajravarahi, the Great Mother, the Dakini
    consort who fulfils all desires HUM HUM PHAT

Requesting the fulfilment of wishes

You who have destroyed equally attachment to samsara
    and solitary peace, as well as all conceptualizations,
Who see all things that exist throughout space;
O Protector endowed with strong compassion, may I be
    blessed by the waters of your compassion,
And may the Dakinis take me into their loving care.

Offering the torma to the mundane Deities

The directional guardians, regional guardians, nagas, and so forth, who reside in the eight great charnel grounds, instantly enter into the clear light, and arise in the form of the Deities of Heruka in the aspect of Father and Mother. From a white HUM in the tongue of each guest, there arises a white, three-pronged vajra, through which they partake of the essence of the torma by drawing it through straws of light the thickness of only a grain of barley.

OM KHA KHA, KHAHI KHAHI, SARWA YAKYA RAKYASA, BHUTA, TRETA, PISHATSA, UNATA, APAMARA, VAJRA DAKA, DAKI NÄDAYA, IMAM BALING GRIHANTU, SAMAYA RAKYANTU, MAMA SARWA SIDDHI METRA YATZANTU, YATIPAM, YATETAM, BHUDZATA, PIWATA, DZITRATA, MATI TRAMATA, MAMA SARWA KATAYA, SÄDSUKHAM BISHUDHAYE, SAHAYEKA BHAWÄNTU, HUM HUM PHAT PHAT SÖHA   (2x)

With the first recitation offer the torma to the guests in the cardinal directions, and with the second to the guests in the intermediate directions.

Outer offerings

OM AHRGHAM PARTITZA SÖHA
OM PADÄM PARTITZA SÖHA
OM VAJRA PUPE AH HUM SÖHA
OM VAJRA DHUPE AH HUM SÖHA
OM VAJRA DIWE AH HUM SÖHA
OM VAJRA GÄNDHE AH HUM SÖHA
OM VAJRA NEWIDE AH HUM SÖHA
OM VAJRA SHAPTA AH HUM SÖHA

Inner offering

To the mouths of the directional guardians, regional guardians, nagas, and so forth, OM AH HUM

Requests

You the entire gathering of gods,
The entire gathering of nagas,
The entire gathering of givers of harm,
The entire gathering of cannibals,
The entire gathering of evil spirits,
The entire gathering of hungry ghosts,
The entire gathering of flesh-eaters,
The entire gathering of crazy-makers,
The entire gathering of forgetful-makers,
The entire gathering of dakas,
The entire gathering of female spirits,
All of you without exception
Please come here and listen to me.
O Glorious attendants, swift as thought,
Who have taken oaths and heart commitments
To guard the doctrine and benefit living beings,
Who subdue the malevolent and destroy the dark forces
With terrifying forms and inexhaustible wrath,
Who grant results to yogic actions,
And who have inconceivable powers and blessings,
To you eight types of guest I prostrate.

I request all of you together with your consorts, children,
    and servants
To grant me the fortune of all the attainments.
May I and other practitioners
Have good health, long life, power,
Glory, fame, fortune,
And extensive enjoyments.
Please grant me the attainments
Of pacifying, increasing, controlling, and wrathful actions.
O Guardians, always assist me.
Eradicate all untimely death, sicknesses,
Harm from spirits, and hindrances.
Eliminate bad dreams,
Ill omens, and bad actions.

May there be happiness in the world, may the years be
  good,
May crops increase, and may Dharma flourish.
May all goodness and happiness come about,
And may all wishes be accomplished.

*At this point you should make the tsog offering from the
self-generation sadhana (pp 283-92).*

*Purify any mistakes made during this ritual practice by
reciting:*

OM VAJRA HERUKA SAMAYA, MANU PALAYA, HERUKA
TENO PATITA, DRIDHO ME BHAWA, SUTO KAYO ME BHAWA,
SUPO KAYO ME BHAWA, ANURAKTO ME BHAWA, SARWA
SIDDHI ME PRAYATZA, SARWA KARMA SUTZA ME, TZITAM
SHRIYAM KURU HUM, HA HA HA HA HO BHAGAWÄN,
VAJRA HERUKA MA ME MUNTSA, HERUKA BHAWA, MAHA
SAMAYA SATTÖ AH HUM PHAT

I dissolve into Guru Heruka, the principal of the mandala,
and we become non-dual.

CONCLUSION

Dissolution and generating the action Deities

The charnel grounds and protection circle dissolve into the
celestial mansion. The celestial mansion dissolves into the
Deities of the commitment wheel. They dissolve into the
Deities of the body wheel. They dissolve into the Deities
of the speech wheel. They dissolve into the Deities of the
heart wheel. They dissolve into the four Yoginis of the
great bliss wheel. They dissolve into me, the Principal
Deity Father and Mother, the nature of the white and red
indestructible drop. I, the Principal Deity Father and Mother,
also melt into light and dissolve into the letter HUM at my
heart, in nature the emptiness of the Dharmakaya.

From the state of emptiness, our world arises as Heruka's Pure Land, Keajra. I and all sentient beings arise as the Blessed One Heruka, with a blue-coloured body, one face, and two arms embracing Vajravarahi.

Meditating on the first of the five stages of completion stage, the stage of blessing the self

Inside my central channel, in the centre of the Dharma Wheel at my heart, is a drop the size of a small pea. Its upper half is white and its lower half is red, and it radiates five-coloured rays of light. At its centre is a tiny letter HUM, white with a shade of red, the nature of Heruka. The minute three-curved nada of the HUM, as fine as the tip of a hair, is red at the top and reddish-white at the bottom. The nature of great bliss, it is extremely bright, radiates red light, and drips nectar. My mind mixes inseparably with the nada.

Adorning our body with the armour Deities

At my heart on a moon mandala appears white OM HA, the nature of Vajrasattva; at my head on a sun, yellow NAMA HI, the nature of Vairochana; at my crown on a sun, red SÖHA HU, the nature of Pämanarteshvara; at my two shoulders on a sun, black BOKE HE, the nature of Glorious Heruka; at my two eyes on a sun, orange HUM HUM HO, the nature of Vajrasurya; and at my forehead on a sun, green PHAT HAM, the nature of Paramashawa.

At the Principal Mother's navel on a sun mandala appears red OM BAM, the nature of Vajravarahi; at her heart on a sun, blue HAM YOM, the nature of Yamani; at her throat on a moon, white HRIM MOM, the nature of Mohani; at her head on a sun, yellow HRIM HRIM, the nature of Sachalani; at her crown on a sun, green HUM HUM, the nature of Samtrasani; and at her forehead on a sun, smoke-coloured PHAT PHAT, the nature of Chandika.

The mantra emanating from the four faces

OM SUMBHANI SUMBHA HUM HUM PHAT
OM GRIHANA GRIHANA HUM HUM PHAT
OM GRIHANA PAYA GRIHANA PAYA HUM HUM PHAT
OM ANAYA HO BHAGAWÄN BYÄ RADZA HUM HUM PHAT

Dedication

*Now recite either the extensive or the brief dedication
followed by the auspicious prayers from the self-generation
sadhana (pp 276-82).*

Colophon: This sadhana was compiled from traditional sources by Venerable Geshe Kelsang Gyatso. The verse to Geshe Kelsang Gyatso in *Requesting the lineage Gurus* was composed at the request of Geshe Kelsang's faithful disciples by the glorious Dharma Protector, Düldzin Dorje Shugdän. We requested permission from Geshe Kelsang to include this verse in the sadhana to express our heartfelt gratitude for his kindness; and for the use, in group or individual practice, of practitioners who have received initiation from him.

Appendix III
Diagrams and Illustrations

CONTENTS

Deity Charts

Inner place	Outer place	Hero (Bodhisattva)	Heroine
Hairline	Puliramalaya	Khandakapala (*Samantabhadra*)	Partzandi
Crown	Dzalandhara	Mahakankala (*Manjushri*)	Tzändriakiya
Right ear	Odiyana	Kankala (*Avalokiteshvara*)	Parbhawatiya
Back of neck	Arbuta	Vikatadamshtri (*Ksitigarbha*)	Mahanasa
Left ear	Godawari	Suraberi (*Vajrapani*)	Biramatiya
Point between eyebrows	Rameshöri	Amitabha (*Maitreya*)	Karwariya
Two eyes	Dewikoti	Vajraprabha (*Akashagarbha*)	Lamkeshöriya
Two shoulders	Malawa	Vajradeha (*Akashakosha – Space Treasure*)	Drumatzaya

The Deities of the heart wheel

Inner place	Outer place	Hero (Bodhisattva)	Heroine
Two armpits	Kamarupa	Ankuraka (*Sarvanivaranaviskambini*)	Airawatiya
Two breasts	Ote	Vajrajatila (*Gadze Dhupe – Elephant Incense*)	Mahabhairawi
Navel	Trishakune	Mahavira (*Lodrö Mitsepa – Inexhaustible Wisdom*)	Bayubega
Tip of nose	Kosala	Vajrahumkara (*Yeshe Tog – Highest Exalted Wisdom*)	Surabhakiya
Mouth	Kalinga	Subhadra (*Monpa Kunjom – Dispelling all Darkness*)	Shamadewi
Throat	Lampaka	Vajrabhadra (*Powa Tseg – Accomplishing Confidence*)	Suwatre
Heart	Kancha	Mahabhairawa (*Ngensong Kunden – Liberating all Lower Realms*)	Hayakarna
Two testicles	Himalaya	Virupaksha (*Drawa Chenkyö – Web of Light*)	Khaganana

The Deities of the speech wheel

Inner place	Outer place	Hero (Bodhisattva)	Heroine (Bodhisattva)
Tip of sex organ	Pretapuri	Mahabala (*Daö Shönnu – Youthful Moonlight*)	Tzatrabega (*Gyenpung – Shoulder Ornament*)
Anus	Grihadewata	Ratnavajra (*Dorje Ö – Vajra Light*)	Khandarohi (*Sordang – Individual Liberator*)
Two thighs	Shauraktra	Hayagriva (*Nyimi Ökyi Nyingpo – Essence of Sunlight*)	Shaundini (*Macha Chenmo – Great Powerful One*)
Two calves	Suwanadvipa	Akashagarbha (*Dorje Öser – Vajra Light Rays*)	Tzatrawarmini (*Logyonma – One Wearing Leaves*)
Eight fingers and eight toes	Nagara	Shri Heruka (*Tuchen Tog – Powerful Attainment*)	Subira (*Dorje Lukugyü – Continuous Circle of Vajras*)
Tops of feet	Sindhura	Pämanarteshvara (*Norsang – Excellent Wealth*)	Mahabala (*Chirdog Chenmo – Great Pacifier*)
Two thumbs and two big toes	Maru	Vairochana (*Sangden – Excellent Carer*)	Tzatrawartini (*Tsugtor Kharmo – White Ushnisha*)
Two knees	Kuluta	Vajrasattva (*Lodrö Gyatso – Ocean of Wisdom*)	Mahabire (*Dorje Jigma – Wrathful Vajra*)

The Deities of the body wheel

Doorway	Heroine	Bodhisattva	Consort
Root of tongue	Kakase	Kaouri	Aparajita
Navel	Ulukase	Tzowri	Amritakundalini
Sex organ	Shönase	Bukase	Hayagriva
Anus	Shukarase	Petali	Yamantaka
Point between eyebrows	Yamadhati	Kamari	Niladanda
Two ears	Yamaduti	Shawati	Takkiraja
Two eyes	Yamadangtrini	Dzandali	Achala
Two nostrils	Yamamatani	Tombini	Mahabala

The Deities of the commitment wheel

Seed-letters

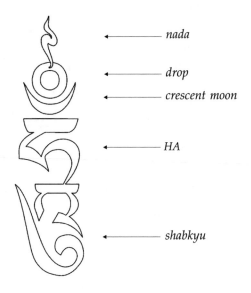

The letter HUM

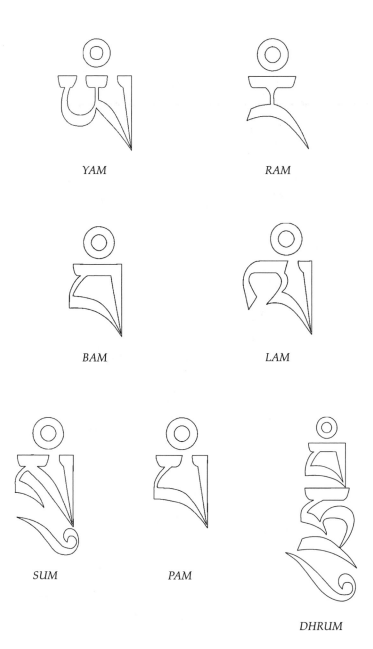

YAM

RAM

BAM

LAM

SUM

PAM

DHRUM

481

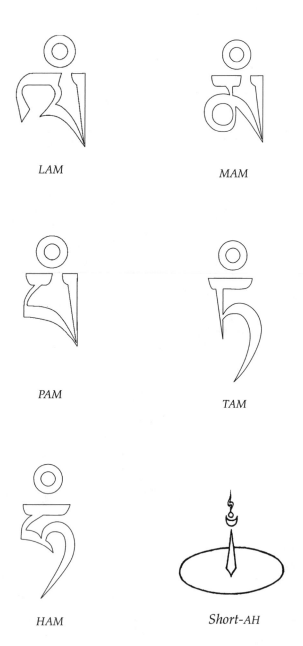

LAM

MAM

PAM

TAM

HAM

Short-AH

OM HA

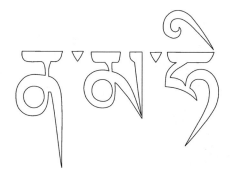

NA MA HI

SÖHA HU

BOKE HE

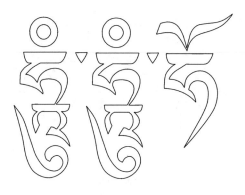

HUM HUM HO

PHAT HAM

OM BAM

HAM YOM

HRIM MOM

HRIM HRIM

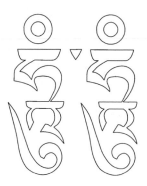

HUM HUM

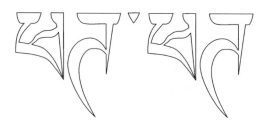

PHAT PHAT

Ritual Objects

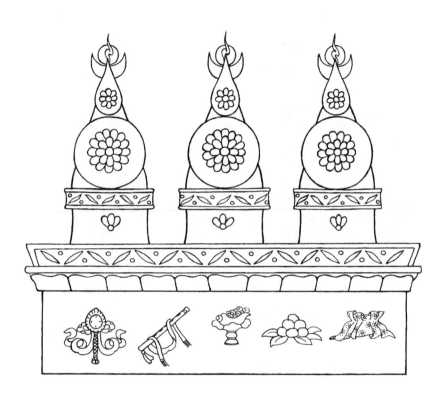

Offering tormas for the assembly of Heruka

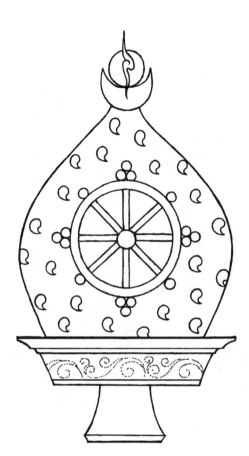

*Traditional tsog
offering torma*

Tambula torma

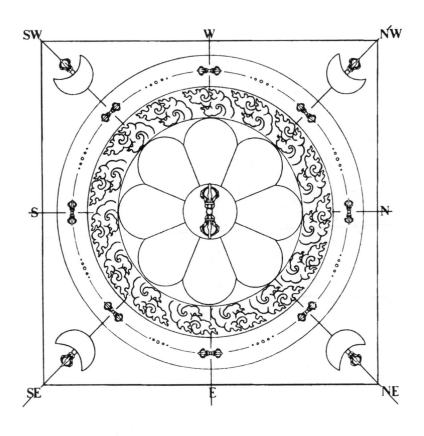

Fire puja mandala

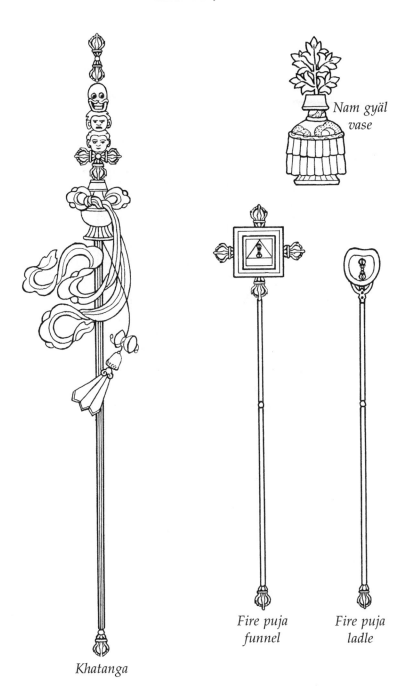

Nam gyäl
vase

Khatanga

Fire puja
funnel

Fire puja
ladle

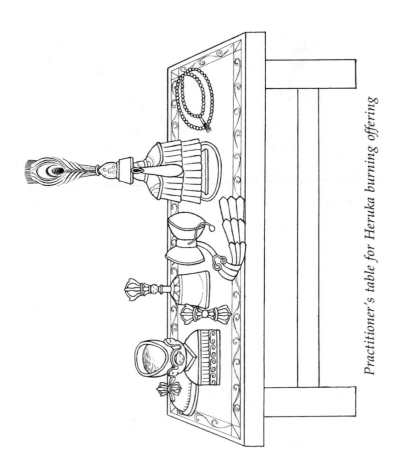

Practitioner's table for Heruka burning offering

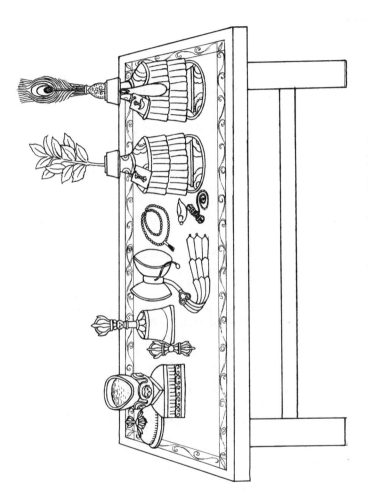

Practitioner's table for Heruka self-initiation

Glossary

Analytical meditation The mental process of investigating a virtuous object – analyzing its nature, function, characteristics, and other aspects. See *The New Meditation Handbook*.

Atisha (AD 982-1054) A famous Indian Buddhist scholar and meditation master. He was Abbot of the great Buddhist monastery of Vikramashila at a time when Mahayana Buddhism was flourishing in India. He was later invited to Tibet and his arrival there led to the re-establishment of Buddhism in Tibet. He is the author of the first text on the stages of the path, *Lamp for the Path*. His tradition later became known as the 'Kadampa Tradition'. See *Joyful Path of Good Fortune*.

Attachment A deluded mental factor that observes a contaminated object, regards it as a cause of happiness, and wishes for it. See *Joyful Path of Good Fortune* and *Understanding the Mind*.

Basis of imputation All phenomena are imputed upon their parts; therefore, any of the individual parts, or the entire collection of the parts, of any phenomenon is its basis of imputation. A phenomenon is imputed by mind in dependence upon its basis of imputation appearing to that mind. See *Heart of Wisdom*.

Beginningless time According to the Buddhist world view, there is no beginning to mind, and so no beginning to time. Therefore, all sentient beings have taken countless previous rebirths.

Behar A type of malevolent spirit. See *Heart Jewel*.

Bhaga Sanskrit word for the female sex organ.

Blessing 'Jin gyi lab pa' in Tibetan. The transformation of our mind from a negative state to a positive state, from an unhappy state to a happy state, or from a state of weakness to a state of strength, through the inspiration of holy beings such as our Spiritual Guide, Buddhas, and Bodhisattvas.

Bodhisattva A person who has generated spontaneous bodhichitta but who has not yet become a Buddha. From the moment a practitioner generates a non-artificial, or spontaneous, bodhichitta, he or she becomes a Bodhisattva and enters the first Mahayana path, the path of accumulation. An ordinary Bodhisattva is one who has not realized emptiness directly, and a Superior Bodhisattva is one who has attained a direct realization of emptiness. See *Joyful Path of Good Fortune* and *Meaningful to Behold.*

Brahma A worldly god, who resides in the first form realm. See *Ocean of Nectar.*

Brahmin's thread The Tibetan term for Brahmin's thread is 'tsang pi kupa', where 'tsang pa' means 'purity' and 'kupa' means 'thread'. Thus, a Brahmin's thread is a ritual thread symbolizing non-conceptual omniscient wisdom that is complete purity.

Buddha family There are five main Buddha families: the families of Vairochana, Ratnasambhava, Amitabha, Amoghasiddhi, and Akshobya. They are the five purified aggregates – the aggregates of form, feeling, discrimination, compositional factors, and consciousness, respectively; and the five exalted wisdoms – the exalted mirror-like wisdom, the exalted wisdom of equality, the exalted wisdom of individual realization, the exalted wisdom of accomplishing activities, and the exalted wisdom of the Dharmadhatu, respectively. See *Great Treasury of Merit.*

Buddha nature The root mind of a sentient being, and its ultimate nature. Buddha nature, Buddha seed, and Buddha lineage are synonyms. All sentient beings have Buddha nature and therefore the potential to attain Buddhahood.

Buddha's bodies A Buddha has four bodies – the Wisdom Truth Body, the Nature Body, the Enjoyment Body, and the Emanation Body. The first is Buddha's omniscient mind. The second is the emptiness, or ultimate nature, of his or her mind. The third is his or her subtle Form Body. The fourth, of which each Buddha manifests a countless number, are gross Form Bodies that are visible to ordinary beings. The Wisdom Truth Body and the Nature Body are both included within the Truth Body, and the Enjoyment Body and the Emanation Body are both included within the Form Body. See *Joyful Path of Good Fortune* and *Ocean of Nectar.*

Central channel The principal channel at the very centre of the body, along which the channel wheels are located. See *Clear Light of Bliss.*

Chakra See *Channel wheel.*

495

Channels Subtle inner passageways of the body through which flow subtle drops moved by inner winds. See *Clear Light of Bliss*.

Channel wheel 'Chakra' in Sanskrit. A focal centre where secondary channels branch out from the central channel. Meditating on these points can cause the inner winds to enter the central channel. See *Clear Light of Bliss*.

Clear light A manifest very subtle mind that perceives an appearance like clear, empty space. See *Clear Light of Bliss*.

Close retreat A retreat during which we strive to draw close to a particular Deity. This can be understood in two ways: drawing close in the sense of developing a special relationship with a friend, and drawing close in the sense of becoming more and more like the Deity. An action close retreat is a close retreat in which we collect a certain number of mantras and conclude with a fire puja.

Collection of merit A virtuous action motivated by bodhichitta that is a main cause of attaining the Form Body of a Buddha. Examples are: making offerings and prostrations to holy beings with bodhichitta motivation, and the practice of the perfections of giving, moral discipline, and patience.

Collection of wisdom A virtuous mental action motivated by bodhichitta that is a main cause of attaining the Truth Body of a Buddha. Examples are: listening to, contemplating, and meditating on emptiness with bodhichitta motivation.

Commitments Promises and pledges taken when engaging in certain spiritual practices.

Compassion A virtuous mind that wishes others to be free from suffering. See also *Great compassion*. See *Eight Steps to Happiness* and *Universal Compassion*.

Concentration A mental factor that makes its primary mind remain on its object single-pointedly. See *Joyful Path of Good Fortune*.

Conceptual mind A thought that apprehends its object through a generic, or mental, image. See *Understanding the Mind*.

Confession Purification of negative karma by means of the four opponent powers – the power of reliance, the power of regret, the power of the opponent force, and the power of promise.

Contaminated aggregate Any of the aggregates of form, feeling, discrimination, compositional factors, and consciousness of a samsaric being. See *Heart of Wisdom*.

Conventional truth Any phenomenon other than emptiness. Conventional truths are true with respect to the minds of ordinary beings, but in reality they are false. See *Heart of Wisdom*, *Meaningful to Behold*, and *Ocean of Nectar*.

Dakini Land The Pure Land of Heruka and Vajrayogini. In Sanskrit it is called 'Keajra' and in Tibetan 'Dagpa Khachö'. See *Guide to Dakini Land*.

Dakinis/Dakas Dakinis are female Tantric Buddhas and those women who have attained the realization of meaning clear light. Dakas are the male equivalent. See *Guide to Dakini Land*.

Damaru A small hand-drum used in Tantric rituals. Playing the damaru symbolizes the gathering of the outer Dakinis into our body, and the manifestation of the inner Dakini (the mind of clear light) within our mind through the blazing of inner fire. It is also used as a music offering to the Buddhas.

Dedication Dedication is by nature a virtuous mental factor; it is the virtuous intention that functions both to prevent accumulated virtue from degenerating and to cause its increase. See *Joyful Path of Good Fortune*.

Degenerate times A period when spiritual activity degenerates.

Deity 'Yidam' in Sanskrit. A Tantric enlightened being.

Deity body Divine body. When a practitioner attains an illusory body, he or she attains an actual divine body, or Deity body, but not a Deity's body. A Deity's body is necessarily a body of a Tantric enlightened being. See also *Divine body*. See *Tantric Grounds and Paths*.

Delusion A mental factor that arises from inappropriate attention and functions to make the mind unpeaceful and uncontrolled. There are three main delusions: ignorance, desirous attachment, and anger. From these arise all the other delusions, such as jealousy, pride, and deluded doubt. See *Understanding the Mind*.

Demon See *Mara/Demon*.

Dependent-related links Dependent-related ignorance, compositional actions, consciousness, name and form, six sources, contact, feeling, craving, grasping, existence, birth, and ageing and death. These twelve links are causes and effects that keep ordinary beings bound within samsara. See *Joyful Path of Good Fortune* and *Heart of Wisdom*.

Desire realm The environment of hell beings, hungry spirits, animals, human beings, demi-gods, and the gods who enjoy the five objects of desire.

Dharma Buddha's teachings and the inner realizations that are attained in dependence upon practising them. 'Dharma' means 'protection'. By practising Buddha's teachings, we protect ourself from suffering and problems.

Dharmadhatu The ultimate truth of phenomena.

Dharmakaya Sanskrit word for the Truth Body of a Buddha.

Dharma Protector A manifestation of a Buddha or Bodhisattva, whose main function is to eliminate obstacles and gather all necessary conditions for pure Dharma practitioners. Also called 'Dharmapala'. See *Heart Jewel*.

Dharma Wheel A collection of Buddha's teachings. Sometimes 'Dharma Wheel' is used to refer to the heart channel wheel because this is the place where we visualize the Dharmakaya, which is the source of the Dharma Wheel. See also *Wheel of Dharma*.

Divine body A subtle body arising from the mounted wind of ultimate example clear light or meaning clear light. See also *Deity body*. See *Tantric Grounds and Paths*.

Dorje Shugdän A Dharma Protector who is an emanation of the Wisdom Buddha Manjushri. See *Heart Jewel*.

Drops There are two types of drop in the body: white drops and red drops. These are the pure essence of sperm and blood. When the drops melt and flow through the inner channels, they give rise to an experience of bliss. See *Clear Light of Bliss*.

Dualistic appearance The appearance to mind of an object together with the inherent existence of that object. See *Heart of Wisdom*.

Eight signs of dissolution Internal signs that the inner winds are dissolving within the central channel. For a detailed description of each sign, see *Clear Light of Bliss*.

Element The nature of any phenomenon. All phenomena hold their own natures, which are all included within the eighteen elements. See also *Four elements*. See *Heart of Wisdom*.

Emanation Animate or inanimate form manifested by Buddhas or high Bodhisattvas to benefit others.

Empowerment A special potential power to attain any of the four Buddha bodies that is received by a Tantric practitioner from his or her Guru, or from other holy beings, by means of Tantric ritual. It is the gateway to the Vajrayana. See *Tantric Grounds and Paths*.

Emptiness Lack of inherent existence, the ultimate nature of phenomena. See *Heart of Wisdom* and *Ocean of Nectar*.

Energy winds See *Inner winds*.

Example clear light A mind of clear light that realizes emptiness by means of a generic image. See *Clear Light of Bliss*.

Faith A naturally virtuous mind that functions mainly to oppose the perception of faults in its observed object. There are three types of faith: believing faith, admiring faith, and wishing faith. See *Transform Your Life*.

Field of Merit The Three Jewels. Just as external seeds grow in a field of soil, so the virtuous internal seeds produced by virtuous actions grow in dependence upon Buddha Jewel, Dharma Jewel, and Sangha Jewel. Also known as 'Field for Accumulating Merit'.

Fire Deity The Deity to whom we make the burning offering, for example in the practice of Heruka. A Fire Deity can be either mundane or supramundane. Mundane Fire Deities are not real mundane beings but appear in the aspect of mundane beings.

Five exalted wisdoms Buddha's omniscient wisdom has five parts: (1) the exalted mirror-like wisdom, which perceives all phenomena simultaneously as a mirror reflects objects; (2) the exalted wisdom of equality, which realizes that all phenomena are equal in emptiness; (3) the exalted wisdom of individual realization, which realizes all individual phenomena directly; (4) the exalted wisdom of accomplishing activities, whose function is to accomplish all the activities of a Buddha; and (5) the exalted wisdom of the Dharmadhatu, which realizes the Dharmadhatu, the ultimate nature of all phenomena.

Five stages of completion stage In general, this refers to isolated speech, isolated mind, illusory body, clear light, and union. Sometimes it is used to refer to the five stages of blessing the self and so forth. See *Tantric Grounds and Paths*.

Form Body The Enjoyment Body and the Emanation Body of a Buddha. See also *Buddha's bodies*.

Form realm The environment of the gods who possess form.

Four classes of Tantra Buddha taught four classes of Tantra: Action (Skt. Kriya) Tantra, Performance (Skt. Charya) Tantra, Yoga Tantra, and Highest Yoga (Skt. Anuttarayoga) Tantra. Each of the four classes of Tantra contains its own special techniques for transforming sensual bliss. See *Tantric Grounds and Paths*.

Four elements Earth, water, fire, and wind. All matter can be said to be composed of a combination of these elements. There are four inner elements (those that are conjoined with the continuum of a person), and four outer elements (those that are not conjoined with the continuum of a person). These four elements are not the same as the earth of a field, the water of a river, and so forth. Rather, the elements of earth, water, fire, and wind in broad terms are the properties of solidity, liquidity, heat, and movement respectively. All matter can be said to be composed of a combination of these elements.

Four joys Four stages of bliss that are generated in the generation and completion stages of Highest Yoga Tantra. See *Clear Light of Bliss*.

Four maras See *Mara/Demon*.

Four ways of gathering disciples The four ways of gathering disciples practised by Bodhisattvas are: (1) pleasing others by giving them material things or whatever they need; (2) teaching Dharma to lead others to liberation; (3) helping others in their Dharma practice by giving them encouragement; and (4) showing others a good example by always practising what we teach.

Generic image The appearing object of a conceptual mind. A generic image, or mental image, of an object is like a reflection of that object. Conceptual minds know their object through the appearance of a generic image of that object, not by seeing the object directly. See *Understanding the Mind*.

God 'Deva' in Sanskrit. A being of the god realm, the highest of the six realms of samsara. There are many different types of god. Some are desire realm gods, while others are form or formless realm gods. See *Joyful Path of Good Fortune*.

Goddesses of the doorways The four Goddesses of the doorways are Kakase, literally 'crow-faced one'; Ulukase, 'owl-faced one'; Shönase, 'dog-faced one'; and Shukarase, 'pig-faced one'. Although they have human-shaped heads and ears, their names reflect the appearances of their faces, which are like a crow, like an owl, and so on, rather as if they are wearing masks.

Great compassion A mind wishing to protect all sentient beings from suffering. See *Universal Compassion* and *Ocean of Nectar*.

Guhyasamaja A Highest Yoga Tantra Deity. See *Great Treasury of Merit*.

Hell realm The lowest of the six realms of samsara. See *Joyful Path of Good Fortune*.

Hero/Heroine A Hero is a male Tantric Deity generally embodying method. A Heroine is a female Tantric Deity generally embodying wisdom. See *Guide to Dakini Land*.

Highest Yoga Tantra A Tantric instruction that includes the method for transforming sexual bliss into the spiritual path. See *Tantric Grounds and Paths*.

Hinayana Sanskrit word for 'Lesser Vehicle'. The Hinayana goal is to attain merely one's own liberation from suffering by completely abandoning delusions. See *Joyful Path of Good Fortune*.

Hungry spirit A being of the hungry spirit realm, the second lowest of the six realms of samsara. Also known as 'Hungry ghost'. See *Joyful Path of Good Fortune*.

Ignorance A mental factor that is confused about the ultimate nature of phenomena. See also *Self-grasping*. See *Understanding the Mind*.

Illusory body The subtle divine body that is principally developed from the indestructible wind. When a practitioner of Highest Yoga Tantra rises from the meditation of the isolated mind of ultimate example clear light, he or she attains a body that is not the same as his or her ordinary physical body. This new body is the illusory body. It has the same appearance as the body of the personal Deity of generation stage except that it is white in colour, and it can be perceived only by those who have already attained an illusory body. See *Clear Light of Bliss* and *Tantric Grounds and Paths*.

Imputation, mere According to the Madhyamika-Prasangika school, all phenomena are merely imputed by conception in dependence upon their basis of imputation. Therefore, they are mere imputation and do not exist from their own side in the least. See *Heart of Wisdom*.

Indestructible drop The most subtle drop, which is located at the heart. It is formed from the essence of the white and red drops received from our parents at conception, and encloses the very subtle mind and its mounted wind. These red and white drops do not separate until the time of death, when they open and allow the very subtle mind and its mounted wind to depart to the next life. See *Clear Light of Bliss*.

Inherent existence An imagined mode of existence whereby phenomena are held to exist from their own side, independent of other phenomena. In reality, all phenomena lack or are empty of inherent existence because they depend upon their parts. See *Heart of Wisdom*.

Inner fire 'Tummo' in Tibetan. An inner heat located at the centre of the navel channel wheel. See *Clear Light of Bliss*.

Inner winds Special subtle winds related to the mind that flow through the channels of our body. Our body and mind cannot function without these winds. See *Clear Light of Bliss*.

Intermediate state 'Bardo' in Tibetan. The state between death and rebirth. It begins the moment the consciousness leaves the body, and ceases the moment the consciousness enters the body of the next life. See *Joyful Path of Good Fortune* and *Clear Light of Bliss*.

Ishvara A god who abides in the Land of Controlling Emanations, the highest state of existence within the desire realm. Ishvara has limited, contaminated miracle powers that make him more powerful than other beings in the desire realm. If we entrust ourself to Ishvara we may receive some temporary benefit in this life, such as an increase in wealth or possessions, but wrathful Ishvara is the enemy of those who seek liberation and he interferes with their spiritual progress. He is therefore said to be a type of Devaputra mara.

Je Tsongkhapa (AD 1357-1419) An emanation of the Wisdom Buddha Manjushri, whose appearance in fourteenth-century Tibet as a monk, and the holder of the lineage of pure view and pure deeds, was prophesied by Buddha. He spread a very pure Buddhadharma throughout Tibet, showing how to combine the practices of Sutra and Tantra, and how to practise pure Dharma during degenerate times. His tradition later became known as the 'Gelug', or 'Ganden Tradition'. See *Heart Jewel* and *Great Treasury of Merit*.

Kadampa A Tibetan word in which 'Ka' means 'word' and refers to all Buddha's teachings, 'dam' refers to Atisha's special Lamrim instructions known as the 'stages of the path to enlightenment', and 'pa' refers to a follower of Kadampa Buddhism who integrates all the teachings of Buddha that they know into their Lamrim practice. See also *Kadampa Buddhism* and *Kadampa Tradition*.

Kadampa Buddhism A Mahayana Buddhist school founded by the great Indian Buddhist Master Atisha (AD 982-1054). See also *Kadampa*, *Kadampa Tradition*, and *New Kadampa Tradition*.

Kadampa Tradition The pure tradition of Buddhism established by Atisha. Followers of this tradition up to the time of Je Tsongkhapa are known as 'Old Kadampas', and those after the time of Je Tsongkhapa are known as 'New Kadampas'. See also *Kadampa*, *Kadampa Buddhism*, and *New Kadampa Tradition*.

Karma Sanskrit word meaning 'action'. Through the force of intention, we perform actions with our body, speech, and mind, and all of these actions produce effects. The effect of virtuous actions is happiness and the effect of negative actions is suffering. See *Joyful Path of Good Fortune*.

Khädrubje (AD 1385-1438) One of the principal disciples of Je Tsongkhapa, who did much to promote the tradition of Je Tsongkhapa after he passed away. See *Great Treasury of Merit*.

Khatanga A ritual object symbolizing the sixty-two Deities of Heruka.

Lamrim A Tibetan term, literally meaning 'stages of the path'. A special arrangement of all Buddha's teachings that is easy to understand and put into practice. It reveals all the stages of the path to enlightenment. For a full commentary, see *Joyful Path of Good Fortune*.

Lineage A line of instruction that has been passed down from Spiritual Guide to disciple, with each Spiritual Guide in the line having gained personal experience of the instruction before passing it on to others.

Lojong A Tibetan term, literally meaning 'training the mind'. A special lineage of instructions that came from Buddha Shakyamuni through Manjushri and Shantideva to Atisha and the Kadampa Geshes, which emphasizes the generation of bodhichitta through the practices of equalizing and exchanging self with others combined with taking and giving. See *Universal Compassion* and *Eight Steps to Happiness*.

Mahasiddha Sanskrit word for 'greatly accomplished one', which is used to refer to Yogis or Yoginis with high attainments.

Mahayana Sanskrit word for 'Great Vehicle', the spiritual path to great enlightenment. The Mahayana goal is to attain Buddhahood for the benefit of all sentient beings by completely abandoning delusions and their imprints. See *Joyful Path of Good Fortune*.

Mandala Usually the celestial mansion in which a Tantric Deity abides, or the environment or Deities of a Buddha's Pure Land. Sometimes it is used to refer to the essence of an element, for example 'wind mandala'.

Manjushri The embodiment of the wisdom of all the Buddhas. See *Great Treasury of Merit* and *Heart Jewel*.

Mantra A Sanskrit word, literally meaning 'mind protection'. Mantra protects the mind from ordinary appearances and conceptions. There are four types of mantra: mantras that are mind, mantras that are inner wind, mantras that are sound, and mantras that are form. In general, there are three types of mantra recitation: verbal recitation, mental recitation, and vajra recitation. See *Tantric Grounds and Paths*.

Mara/Demon 'Mara' is Sanskrit for 'demon', and refers to anything that obstructs the attainment of liberation or enlightenment. There are four principal types of mara: the mara of the delusions, the mara of contaminated aggregates, the mara of uncontrolled death, and the Devaputra maras. Of these, only the last are actual sentient beings. The principal Devaputra mara is wrathful Ishvara, the highest of the desire realm gods, who inhabits Land of Controlling Emanations. Buddha is called a 'Conqueror' because he or she has conquered all four types of mara. See *Heart of Wisdom*.

Meaning clear light A mind of clear light that realizes emptiness directly without a generic image. Synonymous with inner Dakini Land. See *Clear Light of Bliss*.

Mental awareness All minds are included within the five sense awarenesses and mental awareness. Mental awareness is an awareness that is developed in dependence upon its uncommon dominant condition, a mental power. There are two types: conceptual mental awareness and non-conceptual mental awareness. Conceptual mental awareness and conceptual mind are synonyms. See *Understanding the Mind*.

Merit The good fortune created by virtuous actions. It is the potential power to increase our good qualities and produce happiness.

Migrator A being within samsara who migrates from one uncontrolled rebirth to another.

Mind That which is clarity and cognizes. Mind is clarity because it always lacks form and because it possesses the actual power to perceive objects. Mind cognizes because its function is to know or perceive objects. See *Clear Light of Bliss* and *Understanding the Mind*.

Mindfulness A mental factor that functions not to forget the object realized by the primary mind. See *Understanding the Mind*.

Mount Meru According to Buddhist cosmology, a divine mountain that stands at the centre of the universe. See *Great Treasury of Merit*.

Mudra Generally, the Sanskrit word for 'seal', as in 'Mahamudra', the 'great seal'. More specifically, 'mudra' is used to refer to a consort, as in 'action mudra' or 'wisdom mudra'; and to hand gestures used in Tantric rituals.

Nada A three-curved line that appears above certain seed-letters.

Naga A non-human being not normally visible to human beings. Their upper half is said to be human, their lower half serpent. Nagas usually live in the oceans of the world but they sometimes inhabit land in the region of rocks and trees. They are very powerful, some being benevolent and some malevolent. Many diseases, known as 'naga diseases', are caused by nagas and can only be cured through performing certain naga rituals.

New Kadampa Tradition The union of Kadampa Buddhist Centres, an international association of study and meditation centres that follow the pure tradition of Mahayana Buddhism derived from the Buddhist meditator and scholar Je Tsongkhapa, introduced into the West by the Buddhist teacher Venerable Geshe Kelsang Gyatso.

Non-virtuous actions Paths that lead to the lower realms. Non-virtuous actions are countless, but most of them are included within the ten: killing, stealing, sexual misconduct, lying, divisive speech, hurtful speech, idle gossip, covetousness, malice, and holding wrong views. See *Joyful Path of Good Fortune*.

Obstructions to liberation Obstructions that prevent the attainment of liberation. All delusions, such as ignorance, attachment, and anger, together with their seeds, are obstructions to liberation. Also called 'delusion-obstructions'.

Obstructions to omniscience The imprints of delusions, which prevent simultaneous and direct realization of all phenomena. Only Buddhas have overcome these obstructions.

Oral transmission The granting of blessings through verbal instruction. Receiving these blessings is essential for gaining authentic realizations.

Ordinary being Anyone who has not realized emptiness directly.

Perfection of wisdom Any wisdom maintained by bodhichitta motivation. See *Heart of Wisdom*.

Phabongkhapa, Je (AD 1878-1941) A great Tibetan Lama who was an emanation of Heruka. Phabongkha Rinpoche was the holder of many lineages of Sutra and Secret Mantra. He was the root Guru of Yongdzin Trijang Dorjechang (Trijang Rinpoche).

Phenomena source A phenomenon that appears only to mental awareness. It is also the name given to Vajrayogini's mandala, which is shaped like a double tetrahedron. See *Guide to Dakini Land*.

Placement meditation Single-pointed concentration on a virtuous object. See *The New Meditation Handbook*.

Preliminary guide Altogether there are nine preliminary guides, so called because by engaging in them we are guided to the actual spiritual paths of Tantra. The four main ones are: (1) the guide of going for refuge and generating bodhichitta, (2) the guide of meditation and recitation of Vajrasattva, (3) the guide of Guru yoga, and (4) the guide of making mandala offerings. See *Guide to Dakini Land*.

Profound path The profound path includes all the wisdom practices that lead to a direct realization of emptiness and ultimately to the Truth Body of a Buddha. See *Joyful Path of Good Fortune*.

Pure Land A pure environment in which there are no true sufferings. There are many Pure Lands. For example, Tushita is the Pure Land of Buddha Maitreya; Sukhavati is the Pure Land of Buddha Amitabha; and Dakini Land, or Keajra, is the Pure Land of Buddha Vajrayogini and Buddha Heruka.

Renunciation The wish to be released from samsara. See *Joyful Path of Good Fortune*.

Root Guru The principal Spiritual Guide from whom we have received the empowerments, instructions, and oral transmissions of our main practice. See *Great Treasury of Merit* and *Joyful Path of Good Fortune*.

Root mind The very subtle mind located at the centre of the heart channel wheel. It is known as the 'root mind' because all other minds arise from it and dissolve back into it.

Samsara This can be understood in two ways – as uninterrupted rebirth without freedom or control, or as the aggregates of a being who has taken such a rebirth. Samsara is characterized by suffering and dissatisfaction. There are six realms of samsara. Listed in ascending order according to the type of karma that causes rebirth in them, they are the realms of the hell beings, hungry spirits, animals, human beings, demi-gods, and gods. The first three are lower realms or unhappy migrations, and the second three are higher realms or happy migrations. Although from the point of view of the karma that causes rebirth there, the god realm is the highest realm in samsara, the human realm is said to be the most fortunate realm because it provides the best conditions for attaining liberation and enlightenment. See *Joyful Path of Good Fortune.*

Sanskrit vowels and consonants The source of the three letters OM AH HUM, and of all mantras in general, is the sixteen Sanskrit vowels and the thirty-four Sanskrit consonants. The sixteen vowels are: A, AA, I, II, U, UU, RI, RII, LI, LII, E, AI, O, AU, AM, AH. The thirty-four consonants are: KA, KHA, GA, GHA, NGA, CHA, CHHA, JA, JHA, NYA, DA, THA, TA, DHA, NA, DrA, THrA, TrA, DHrA, NA, BA, PHA, PA, BHA, MA, YA, RA, LA, WA, SHA, KA, SA, HA, KYA.

Secret Mantra Synonymous with Tantra. Secret Mantra teachings are distinguished from Sutra teachings in that they reveal methods for training the mind by bringing the future result, or Buddhahood, into the present path. Secret Mantra is the supreme path to full enlightenment. The term 'Mantra' indicates that it is Buddha's special instruction for protecting our mind from ordinary appearances and conceptions. Practitioners of Secret Mantra overcome ordinary appearances and conceptions by visualizing their body, environment, enjoyments, and deeds as those of a Buddha. The term 'Secret' indicates that the practices are to be done in private, and that they can be practised only by those who have received a Tantric empowerment. See *Tantric Grounds and Paths.*

Seed-letter The sacred letter from which a Deity is generated. Each Deity has a particular seed-letter. For example, the seed-letter of Manjushri is DHI, of Tara is TAM, of Vajrayogini is BAM, and of Heruka is HUM. To accomplish Tantric realizations, we need to recognize that Deities and their seed-letters are the same nature.

Self-grasping A conceptual mind that holds any phenomenon to be inherently existent. The mind of self-grasping gives rise to all other delusions, such as anger and attachment. It is the root cause of all suffering and dissatisfaction. See *Heart of Wisdom* and *Ocean of Nectar.*

Sentient being 'Sem chän' in Tibetan. Any being who possesses a mind that is contaminated by delusions or their imprints. Both 'sentient being' and 'living being' are terms used to distinguish beings whose minds are contaminated by either of these two obstructions from Buddhas, whose minds are completely free from these obstructions.

Six perfections The perfections of giving, moral discipline, patience, effort, mental stabilization, and wisdom. They are called 'perfections' because they are motivated by bodhichitta. See *Meaningful to Behold.*

Spontaneous great bliss A special bliss that is produced by the drops melting inside the central channel. It is attained by gaining control over the inner winds. See *Clear Light of Bliss*.

Stages of the path See *Lamrim*.

Subsequent attainment The period between meditation sessions.

Superior being 'Arya' in Sanskrit. A being who has a direct realization of emptiness.

Sutra The teachings of Buddha that are open to everyone to practise without the need for empowerment. These include Buddha's teachings of the three turnings of the Wheel of Dharma.

Tantra See *Secret Mantra*.

Ten directions The four cardinal directions, the four intermediate directions, and the directions above and below.

Ten perfections The six perfections as well as the perfections of skilful means, prayer, force, and exalted awareness. See *Ocean of Nectar*.

Training the mind See *Lojong*.

Tranquil abiding A concentration that possesses the special bliss of physical and mental suppleness that is attained in dependence upon completing the nine mental abidings. See *Joyful Path of Good Fortune* and *Meaningful to Behold*.

Transference of consciousness 'Powa' in Tibetan. A practice for transferring the consciousness to a Pure Land at the time of death. See *Living Meaningfully, Dying Joyfully* and *Great Treasury of Merit*.

Trijang Dorjechang (AD 1901-1981) A special Tibetan Lama of the twentieth century who was an emanation of Buddha Shakyamuni, Heruka, Atisha, Amitabha, and Je Tsongkhapa. Also known as 'Trijang Rinpoche' and 'Losang Yeshe'.

Truth Body The Nature Body and the Wisdom Truth Body of a Buddha. See also *Buddha's bodies*.

Tsog offering An offering made by an assembly of Heroes and Heroines. See *Guide to Dakini Land*.

Tummo See *Inner fire*.

Ultimate nature All phenomena have two natures – a conventional nature and an ultimate nature. In the case of a table, for example, the table itself, and its shape, colour, and so forth are all the conventional nature of the table. The ultimate nature of the table is the table's lack of inherent existence. The conventional nature of a phenomenon is a conventional truth, and its ultimate nature is an ultimate truth. See *Heart of Wisdom* and *Ocean of Nectar*.

Uncontaminated bliss A realization of bliss conjoined with a wisdom directly realizing emptiness.

Vajra Generally, the Sanskrit word 'vajra' means indestructible like a diamond and powerful like a thunderbolt. In the context of Secret Mantra, it can mean the indivisibility of method and wisdom, omniscient great wisdom, or spontaneous great bliss. It is also the name given to a metal ritual object. See *Tantric Grounds and Paths*.

Vajra and bell A ritual sceptre symbolizing great bliss and a ritual hand-bell symbolizing emptiness. See *Tantric Grounds and Paths*.

Vajra body Generally, the channels, drops, and inner winds. More specifically, the pure illusory body. The body of a Buddha is known as the 'resultant vajra body'. See *Clear Light of Bliss*.

Vajradhara The founder of Vajrayana, or Tantra. He is the same mental continuum as Buddha Shakyamuni but displays a different aspect. Buddha Shakyamuni appears in the aspect of an Emanation Body, and Conqueror Vajradhara appears in the aspect of an Enjoyment Body. See *Great Treasury of Merit*.

Vajra Master A fully qualified Tantric Spiritual Guide. See *Great Treasury of Merit*.

Vajra posture A perfect posture for meditation, in which the legs are crossed in the full vajra posture, with the left foot placed sole upwards on the right thigh and the right foot sole upwards on the left thigh. The right hand is placed on top of the left hand with both palms facing upwards, and the two thumbs are raised and touching at the level of the navel. The back is straight and the shoulders are level. The mouth is gently closed, the head is inclined very slightly forwards, and the eyes are neither wide open nor tightly closed but either slightly open or gently closed.

Vajrasattva Buddha Vajrasattva is the aggregate of consciousness of all the Buddhas, appearing in the aspect of a white-coloured Deity specifically in order to purify sentient beings' negativity. He is the same nature as Buddha Vajradhara, differing only in aspect. The practice of meditation and recitation of Vajrasattva is a very powerful method for purifying our impure mind and actions. See *Guide to Dakini Land*.

Vajrayana The Secret Mantra vehicle. See also *Secret Mantra*.

Valid cognizer/mind A cognizer that is non-deceptive with respect to its engaged object. There are two types: inferential valid cognizers and direct valid cognizers. See *Heart of Wisdom* and *Understanding the Mind*.

Vast path The vast path includes all the method practices from the initial cultivation of compassion through to the final attainment of the Form Body of a Buddha. See *Joyful Path of Good Fortune*.

Vinaya Sutras Sutras in which Buddha principally explains the practice of moral discipline, and in particular the Pratimoksha moral discipline.

Wheel of Dharma Buddha gave his teachings in three main phases, which are known as 'the three turnings of the Wheel of Dharma'. During the first Wheel he taught the four noble truths, during the second he taught the *Perfection of Wisdom Sutras* and revealed the Madhyamika-Prasangika view, and during the third he taught the Chittamatra view. These teachings were given according to the inclinations and dispositions of his disciples. Buddha's final view is that of the second Wheel. Dharma is compared to the precious wheel, one of the possessions of a legendary chakravatin king. This wheel could transport the king across great distances in a very short time, and it is said that wherever the precious wheel travelled the king reigned. In a similar way, when Buddha revealed the path to enlightenment he was said to have 'turned the Wheel of Dharma' because, wherever these teachings are present, deluded minds are brought under control. See also *Dharma Wheel*.

Yidam See *Deity*.

Yoga A term used for various spiritual practices that entail maintaining a special view, such as Guru yoga and the yogas of sleeping, rising, and experiencing nectar. 'Yoga' also refers to 'union', such as the union of tranquil abiding and superior seeing. See *Guide to Dakini Land*.

Yogi/Yogini Sanskrit words usually referring to a male or a female meditator who has attained the union of tranquil abiding and superior seeing.

Bibliography

Geshe Kelsang Gyatso is a highly respected meditation master and scholar of the Mahayana Buddhist tradition founded by Je Tsong-khapa. Since arriving in the West in 1977, Geshe Kelsang has worked tirelessly to establish pure Buddhadharma throughout the world. Over this period he has given extensive teachings on the major scriptures of the Mahayana. These teachings are currently being published and provide a comprehensive presentation of the essential Sutra and Tantra practices of Mahayana Buddhism.

Books

The following books by Geshe Kelsang are all published by Tharpa Publications.

The Bodhisattva Vow. A practical guide to helping others. (2nd. edn., 1995)

Clear Light of Bliss. Tantric meditation manual. (2nd. edn., 1992)

Eight Steps to Happiness. The Buddhist way of loving kindness. (2000)

Essence of Vajrayana. The Highest Yoga Tantra practice of Heruka body mandala. (1997)

Great Treasury of Merit. The practice of relying upon a Spiritual Guide. (1992)

Guide to Dakini Land. The Highest Yoga Tantra practice of Buddha Vajrayogini. (2nd. edn., 1996)

Guide to the Bodhisattva's Way of Life. How to enjoy a life of great meaning and altruism. (A translation of Shantideva's famous verse masterpiece.) (2002)

Heart Jewel. The essential practices of Kadampa Buddhism. (2nd. edn., 1997)

Heart of Wisdom. An explanation of the *Heart Sutra*. (4th. edn., 2001)

Introduction to Buddhism. An explanation of the Buddhist way of life. (2nd. edn., 2001)

Joyful Path of Good Fortune. The complete Buddhist path to enlightenment. (2nd. edn., 1995)

Living Meaningfully, Dying Joyfully. The profound practice of transference of consciousness. (1999)

511

Meaningful to Behold. The Bodhisattva's way of life. (4th. edn., 1994)
The New Meditation Handbook. Meditations to make our life happy
and meaningful. (2003)
Ocean of Nectar. The true nature of all things. (1995)
Tantric Grounds and Paths. How to enter, progress on, and complete
the Vajrayana path. (1994)
Transform Your Life. A blissful journey. (2001)
Understanding the Mind. The nature and power of the mind.
(2nd. edn., 1997)
Universal Compassion. Inspiring solutions for difficult times.
(4th. edn., 2002)

Sadhanas

Geshe Kelsang has also supervised the translation of a collection of
essential sadhanas, or prayer booklets.

Assembly of Good Fortune. The tsog offering for Heruka body
mandala.
Avalokiteshvara Sadhana. Prayers and requests to the Buddha of
Compassion.
The Bodhisattva's Confession of Moral Downfalls. The purification
practice of the *Mahayana Sutra of the Three Superior Heaps*.
Condensed Essence of Vajrayana. Condensed Heruka body mandala
self-generation sadhana.
Dakini Yoga. Six-session Guru yoga combined with self-generation
as Vajrayogini.
Drop of Essential Nectar. A special fasting and purification practice
in conjunction with Eleven-faced Avalokiteshvara.
Essence of Good Fortune. Prayers for the six preparatory practices for
meditation on the stages of the path to enlightenment.
Essence of Vajrayana. Heruka body mandala self-generation sadhana
according to the system of Mahasiddha Ghantapa.
Feast of Great Bliss. Vajrayogini self-initiation sadhana.
Great Compassionate Mother. The sadhana of Arya Tara.
Great Liberation of the Mother. Preliminary prayers for Mahamudra
meditation in conjunction with Vajrayogini practice.
The Great Mother. A method to overcome hindrances and obstacles
by reciting the *Essence of Wisdom Sutra* (the *Heart Sutra*).
Heartfelt Prayers. Funeral service for cremations and burials.
Heart Jewel. The Guru yoga of Je Tsongkhapa combined with the
condensed sadhana of his Dharma Protector.
The Hundreds of Deities of the Joyful Land. The Guru yoga of Je
Tsongkhapa.
The Kadampa Way of Life. The essential practice of Kadam Lamrim.

Liberation from Sorrow. Praises and requests to the Twenty-one Taras.

Mahayana Refuge Ceremony and Bodhisattva Vow Ceremony.

Medicine Buddha Sadhana. The method for making requests to the Assembly of Seven Medicine Buddhas.

Meditation and Recitation of Solitary Vajrasattva.

Melodious Drum Victorious in all Directions. The extensive fulfilling and restoring ritual of the Dharma Protector, the great king Dorje Shugdän, in conjunction with Mahakala, Kalarupa, Kalindewi, and other Dharma Protectors.

Offering to the Spiritual Guide (Lama Chöpa). A special Guru yoga practice of Je Tsongkhapa's tradition.

Pathway to the Pure Land. Training in powa – the transference of consciousness.

Prayers for Meditation. Brief preparatory prayers for meditation.

A Pure Life. The practice of taking and keeping the eight Mahayana precepts.

The Quick Path. A condensed practice of Heruka Five Deities according to Master Ghantapa's tradition.

Quick Path to Great Bliss. Vajrayogini self-generation sadhana.

Treasury of Blessings. The condensed meaning of Vajrayana Mahamudra and prayers of request to the lineage Gurus.

Treasury of Wisdom. The sadhana of Venerable Manjushri.

Vajra Hero Yoga. A brief essential practice of Heruka body mandala self-generation, and condensed six-session yoga.

The Vows and Commitments of Kadampa Buddhism.

Wishfulfilling Jewel. The Guru yoga of Je Tsongkhapa combined with the sadhana of his Dharma Protector.

The Yoga of Buddha Amitayus. A special method for increasing lifespan, wisdom, and merit.

The Yoga of White Tara, Buddha of Long Life.

To order any of our publications, or to receive a catalogue, please contact:

Tharpa Publications
Conishead Priory
Ulverston
Cumbria LA12 9QQ
England

Tel: 01229-588599
Fax: 01229-483919

E-mail: tharpa@tharpa.com
Website: www.tharpa.com

Tharpa Publications
47 Sweeney Road
P.O. Box 430
Glen Spey, NY 12737, USA

Tel: 845-856-5102 or
888-741-3475 (toll free)
Fax: 845-856-2110

Email: sales@tharpa-us.com
Website: www.tharpa.com

- NKT -

Study Programmes of
Kadampa Buddhism

Kadampa Buddhism is a Mahayana Buddhist school founded by the great Indian Buddhist Master Atisha (AD 982-1054). His followers are known as 'Kadampas'. 'Ka' means 'word' and refers to Buddha's teachings, and 'dam' refers to Atisha's special Lamrim instructions known as 'the stages of the path to enlightenment'. By integrating their knowledge of all Buddha's teachings into their practice of Lamrim, and by integrating this into their everyday lives, Kadampa Buddhists are encouraged to use Buddha's teachings as practical methods for transforming daily activities into the path to enlightenment. The great Kadampa Teachers are famous not only for being great scholars, but also for being spiritual practitioners of immense purity and sincerity.

The lineage of these teachings, both their oral transmission and blessings, was then passed from Teacher to disciple, spreading throughout much of Asia, and now to many countries throughout the Western world. Buddha's teachings, which are known as 'Dharma', are likened to a wheel that moves from country to country in accordance with changing conditions and people's karmic inclinations. The external forms of presenting Buddhism may change as it meets with different cultures and societies, but its essential authenticity is ensured through the continuation of an unbroken lineage of realized practitioners.

Kadampa Buddhism was first introduced into the West in 1977 by the renowned Buddhist Master, Venerable Geshe Kelsang Gyatso. Since that time, he has worked tirelessly to spread Kadampa Buddhism throughout the world by giving extensive teachings, writing many profound texts on Kadampa Buddhism, and founding the New Kadampa Tradition (NKT), which now has over five hundred Kadampa Buddhist Centres worldwide. Each Centre offers study programmes on Buddhist psychology, philosophy, and meditation instruction, as well as retreats for all levels of practitioner. The emphasis is on integrating Buddha's teachings into daily life to solve our human problems and to spread lasting peace and happiness throughout the world.

The Kadampa Buddhism of the NKT is an entirely independent Buddhist tradition and has no political affiliations. It is an association of Buddhist Centres and practitioners that derive their inspiration and guidance from the example of the ancient Kadampa Buddhist Masters and their teachings, as presented by Geshe Kelsang.

There are three reasons why we need to study and practise the teachings of Buddha: to develop our wisdom, to cultivate a good heart, and to maintain a peaceful state of mind. If we do not strive to develop our wisdom, we will always remain ignorant of ultimate truth – the true nature of reality. Although we wish for happiness, our ignorance leads us to engage in non-virtuous actions, which are the main cause of all our suffering. If we do not cultivate a good heart, our selfish motivation destroys harmony and good relationships with others. We have no peace, and no chance to gain pure happiness. Without inner peace, outer peace is impossible. If we do not maintain a peaceful state of mind, we are not happy even if we have ideal conditions. On the other hand, when our mind is peaceful, we are happy, even if our external conditions are unpleasant. Therefore, the development of these qualities is of utmost importance for our daily happiness.

Geshe Kelsang Gyatso, or 'Geshe-la' as he is affectionately called by his students, has designed three special spiritual programmes for the systematic study and practice of Kadampa Buddhism that are especially suited to the modern world – the General Programme (GP), the Foundation Programme (FP), and the Teacher Training Programme (TTP).

GENERAL PROGRAMME

The General Programme provides a basic introduction to Buddhist view, meditation, and practice that is suitable for beginners. It also includes advanced teachings and practice from both Sutra and Tantra.

FOUNDATION PROGRAMME

The Foundation Programme provides an opportunity to deepen our understanding and experience of Buddhism through a systematic study of five texts:

1 *Joyful Path of Good Fortune* – a commentary to Atisha's Lamrim instructions, the stages of the path to enlightenment.
2 *Universal Compassion* – a commentary to Bodhisattva Chekhawa's *Training the Mind in Seven Points.*
3 *Heart of Wisdom* – a commentary to the *Heart Sutra.*
4 *Meaningful to Behold* – a commentary to Venerable Shantideva's *Guide to the Bodhisattva's Way of Life.*
5 *Understanding the Mind* – a detailed explanation of the mind, based on the works of the Buddhist scholars Dharmakirti and Dignaga.

515

The benefits of studying and practising these texts are as follows:

(1) *Joyful Path of Good Fortune* – we gain the ability to put all Buddha's teachings of both Sutra and Tantra into practice. We can easily make progress on, and complete, the stages of the path to the supreme happiness of enlightenment. From a practical point of view, Lamrim is the main body of Buddha's teachings, and the other teachings are like its limbs.

(2) *Universal Compassion* – we gain the ability to integrate Buddha's teachings into our daily life and solve all our human problems.

(3) *Heart of Wisdom* – we gain a realization of the ultimate nature of reality. By gaining this realization, we can eliminate the ignorance of self-grasping, which is the root of all our suffering.

(4) *Meaningful to Behold* – we transform our daily activities into the Bodhisattva's way of life, thereby making every moment of our human life meaningful.

(5) *Understanding the Mind* – we understand the relationship between our mind and its external objects. If we understand that objects depend upon the subjective mind, we can change the way objects appear to us by changing our own mind. Gradually, we will gain the ability to control our mind and in this way solve all our problems.

TEACHER TRAINING PROGRAMME

The Teacher Training Programme is designed for people who wish to train as authentic Dharma Teachers. In addition to completing the study of twelve texts of Sutra and Tantra, which include the five texts mentioned above, the student is required to observe certain commitments with regard to behaviour and way of life, and to complete a number of meditation retreats.

All Kadampa Buddhist Centres are open to the public. Every year we celebrate Festivals in the USA and Europe, including two in England, where people gather from around the world to receive special teachings and empowerments and to enjoy a spiritual vacation. Please feel free to visit us at any time! For further information, please contact:

UK NKT Office
Conishead Priory
Ulverston
Cumbria LA12 9QQ
England
Tel/Fax: 01229-588533

Email: kadampa@dircon.co.uk
Website: www.kadampa.org

US NKT Office
Kadampa Meditation Center
47 Sweeney Road, P.O. Box 447
Glen Spey, NY 12737, USA

Tel: 845-856-9000
Fax: 845-856-2110

Email: info@kadampacenter.org
Website: www.kadampacenter.org

Index

The letter 'g' indicates an entry in the glossary.